JILL D. SNIDER

Lucean Arthur Headen
The Making of a Black Inventor
and Entrepreneur

The University of North Carolina Press *Chapel Hill*

© 2020 Jill D. Snider
All rights reserved
Set in Arno Pro by Westchester Publishing Services
Manufactured in the United States of America

The University of North Carolina Press has been a member of the
Green Press Initiative since 2003.

Cataloging-in-Publication data for this title is available at the Library of Congress,
https://lccn.loc.gov/2019054570

ISBN 978-1-4696-5435-5 (cloth: alk. paper)
ISBN 978-1-4696-5436-1 (ebook)

Jacket illustrations: Passport photo of Lucean Arthur Headen courtesy of the National Archives; *Old Biplane* and *Front View of a Model T* © iStock.

In memory of my mother
Hazel P. G. Snider (1922–2006)
whose warm spirit I still miss

and in gratitude to many, but especially
Vickie, Kent, Mary, and Mary Jo

Contents

Note on Method xi

Abbreviations in the Text xiii

Introduction 1

CHAPTER ONE
A Dream Begins 5

CHAPTER TWO
A Dream Is Deferred 25

CHAPTER THREE
A Dream Seeks a Path 37

CHAPTER FOUR
A Dream Takes Flight 48

CHAPTER FIVE
A Dream Finds Allies 60

CHAPTER SIX
A Dream Becomes a Company 76

CHAPTER SEVEN
Dreams Collide 95

CHAPTER EIGHT
A Dream Begins Anew 110

CHAPTER NINE
A Dream Crosses the Pond 129

Epilogue 161

Acknowledgments 173

Notes 177

Bibliography 263

Index 297

Illustrations

Tyson & Jones Buggy Company, 1897 9

Dayton Academy, 1897 16

Lucean Headen, Mineola, Long Island, in Curtiss-type biplane 51

Lucean Headen, passport photo, 1915 64

Lucean Headen, passport photo, 1917 72

Headen Motor Company, brochure, 1922 84

James Lillie Street, ca. 1915–1920 89

Tena Drye Headen Meares, ca. 1929 127

Lucean Headen, British national ID card, 1931 131

Headen vaporizing manifold, side view, 1931 133

Headen's propeller deicing design from GB 506,444 142

Headen in Home Guard uniform, ca. 1940 149

Gladys Hollamby, ca. 1945 151

Nannie Kathleen Headen Jones, 1946 159

Note on Method

The story of Lucean Headen—inventor, entrepreneur, and early sportsman—has been a challenge to tell. He preserved no diaries, business records, or mementos. Scattered correspondence, exchanged with Secretary of the Navy Josephus Daniels in 1917, *Chicago Defender* editor Robert Abbott in the 1930s, and U.S. Embassy officials in England in the 1950s, offers critical insights into his thoughts, but the extant letters total fewer than twenty. Headen's laconic nature also meant these communications were often brief and businesslike.

Other sources do exist. A brochure Headen created for the Headen Motor Company, which he established in Chicago in December 1921, has survived. We also have statements he made to reporters and before commercial and other groups in the United States and in England, where he emigrated in 1931. These are augmented by U.S. and British patent records and a handful of family photographs and British identification papers kept by his son. Combined with comments that Headen's actions and inventions elicited in newspapers and trade publications, they make it possible to trace his career on both sides of the Atlantic. They also provide important glimpses into his personal affairs.

Still, creating a biography from this small number of records demanded that I improvise, as Headen himself frequently had to do. The approach on which I landed was inspired by the work of others, and informed by a new cache of sources that promises to open for study lives once considered lost to history. This book owes its existence to one historian in particular. In 1983, Juliet E. K. Walker wrote the biography *Free Frank*. The book chronicled the life of her great-great-grandfather Frank McWorter, a slave who purchased his family's freedom and founded an all-black town in Illinois after the Civil War. Walker wrote her book with only a small box of materials directly related to McWorter. Without the firsthand accounts needed to reproduce his detailed view of the world, she recreated the world around him, drawing heavily on scholarly publications on slave life and the American frontier to fill in the missing pieces. I have followed Walker's lead, turning to the historical literature that has blossomed since the 1980s to establish the context in which Headen lived.

I have supplemented scholarly information with an exciting wealth of newly accessible materials. Not yet in the historian's toolbox when Walker wrote *Free Frank*, the Internet and the scanning, digitization, and search technologies created by electronics and software engineers have opened to view an amazing lode of sources previously too labor intensive to mine. Just clicks away lie tax, land, and estate documents; genealogical records; city and business directories; small-town newspapers filled with local news and gossip columns; school catalogs; the organs of trade, religious, and fraternal groups; railroad and highway maps; government publications; company newsletters; and rare pamphlets that would have taken decades to access through traditional means. In addition, international patent databases now shed light on the inventive process across numerous borders, and electronic finding aids, which detail the contents of archives around the world, quickly point toward a trove of not-yet-digitized manuscripts.

Electronic resources, added to the archival records that have long served as the historian's larder, made it possible to map in detail Headen's social networks. They illuminated his school, church, work, and political connections, as well as those of his family, friends, business partners, and financiers. And they enabled me to track his financial ups and downs and to note where and how he traveled, as well as with whom he visited while on his journeys. I have gleaned from them observations of Headen made by individuals ranging from fellow dining car waiters on the Erie Railroad early in his career, to white newsmen in southern Georgia, to English distributors of his products. Rebuilding Headen's environment using a bevy of "micro" sources, and viewing the details they provided through the bird's-eye view of historical works, allowed me to build a larger scaffolding on which to hang the small number of personal sources I did have for Headen. The result, I think, is a far fuller picture of the man.

I do not claim that this method has yielded a complete portrait. All biography struggles to accomplish that goal, and with so few direct sources, it is too tall an order here. However, this approach made it possible to document a remarkable life, and to probe not only Headen's motives and experiences but his place within the world of invention, business, and sport. It also provided a means to explore what his actions meant to others.

My principal hope is that this book has in some way met the challenge Rayvon Fouché laid before historians in 2003. Fouché asked that we move beyond treating black innovators as one-dimensional heroic figures whose accomplishments fill "black inventor lists," and instead explore their lives more intimately. If this biography has done that alone, I will consider it a success.

Abbreviations in the Text

AAAA (aka Four As)	Afro-American Automobile Association
AAERO	African American Education and Research Organization
A&M	Greensboro Agricultural & Mechanical College (today North Carolina A&T State University)
A&T	North Carolina Agricultural & Technical State University
AEC	Associated Equipment Company Ltd.
AMEZ	African Methodist Episcopal Zion
BIR	Board of Invention and Research
CI&W Railroad	Cincinnati, Indianapolis & Western Railroad
DER	Director of Experiments and Research
DSO	Distinguished Service Order
IBPOEW	Improved Benevolent and Protective Order of Elks of the World
JT&KW Railway	Jacksonville, Tampa, and Key West Railway
NAACP	National Association for the Advancement of Colored People
NACA	National Advisory Committee for Aeronautics
NCAA	National Colored Automobile Association
NCCU	North Carolina Central University
PCUS	Presbyterian Church in the United States (aka Presbyterian Church South)
PCUSA	Presbyterian Church in the United States of America (aka Presbyterian Church North)
PTA	Parent Teacher Association
RAC	Royal Automobile Club
R&D	Research and Development

RAE	Royal Aircraft Establishment
RAF	Royal Air Force
SAL	Seaboard Air Line Railway
SUNY	State University of New York
TD	Territorial Decoration
TVO	Tractor Vaporizing Oil
YMCA	Young Men's Christian Association
YWCA	Young Women's Christian Association

Lucean Arthur Headen

Introduction

Lucean Arthur Headen was fascinated by wheels. If something moved, he wanted to move with it. Born in rural North Carolina in 1879, he eventually lived in six states and two countries, relocating whenever needed to chase his dream of becoming an inventor. Determined, talented, and resilient, he contested Jim Crow's strictures and overcame the financial and logistical obstacles every experimenter faces to create innovative engine designs and develop recognized anti-icing methods for aircraft. A man of eclectic interests, Headen deemed no problem too large, or too small, to warrant his attention. In the First World War, the U.S. and British navies investigated a mirror-based optical cloaking device he crafted for ships. In the 1920s he manufactured his own "Headen Pace Setter" and "Headen Six" cars, and in the 1930s introduced a converter kit that gave motorists the ability to burn cheap crude oil in engines designed for gasoline. Among the inveterate tinkerer's humbler creations were an airtight cover for the carts that cities used to haul away coal ashes, raingear for cyclists, and a replaceable tip for plowshares.

Equally capable as an entrepreneur, Headen counted himself among the thin ranks of inventors who supported themselves through their ideas. When he died in 1957, at the age of seventy-eight, he had spent almost four decades at the head of companies in the United States and England that manufactured first his cars and later a series of products based on his patents. Many of the latter, including his converter kit, an oil-burning carburetor for tractors, and his plowshare tip, found markets across Europe and the British Commonwealth.

Headen also became a public advocate for transportation technologies. One of the first black Americans to fly, he took to the air in a Curtiss-type biplane in November 1911 at Mineola, Long Island, and the following year traveled as an exhibition pilot in the South and Midwest. A decade later, in 1924, he founded the Afro-American Automobile Association, the first black auto racing organization with a national reach. Organizing dirt-track competitions under its auspices, he popularized the sleek "Headen Special," a racer in which the speedster churned up dust and mud from Chicago to New York to Savannah. Headen's exploits in the air and on the track, and the extended travels he undertook to promote his inventions and his cars, made him a familiar figure in the black press, and the views he expressed helped galvanize African Americans' interest in the airplane and the automobile.

On first glance, Headen fits the classic mold of the self-made man. Raised in the small town of Carthage, North Carolina, he showed unflagging resolve in the face of admonitions to a "colored boy" not to set his sights too high. He was eager to advance what he described in 1917 as "my mechanical ingenuity," and over his long career he displayed an uncommon willingness to take monetary and emotional risks to stay true to his aims. Possessed of the aptitude, self-confidence, and singularity of mind to overcome great challenges, he defied anyone to derail him from the track on which he set himself.

Headen's abilities and determination, however, only partially account for his success. The myth of the self-made man, with its exclusive focus on personal qualities, often obscures the multiple contingencies at work in grabbing the brass ring. The full story was more complex. Headen first learned to love wheels watching his grandfather, a wheelwright, practice his craft. From the skilled artisan he gained an understanding that making a wheel demanded not only exceptional ability and focus, but quality materials, the right tools, and effective collaborators. The hub and spokes had to be of the strongest woods. The inner rim, which held the spokes in place, required a precision lathe to form. And without an artful blacksmith to forge the perfect metal outer rim and heat it to the correct temperature before dousing it with cold water and hammering it into place, a wheel could be ruined. Headen, like his grandfather, needed resources and supporting players to bring potential to fruition.

To understand Headen, we may thus profit by viewing his life as a wheel, built by many hands. The family, church, and school that defined his early years provided the hub. Radiating from it were the examples of his grandfather and an inventive great-uncle who sparked his dreams; a pastor who imparted strategic knowledge; teachers (among them his aunts) who helped hone his intellect and gave encouragement and emotional support; and a father and uncles who modeled enterprise and political courage. Tena Elizabeth Drye, whom Headen married in 1903, would provide the inner circle of support her talented but not yet socially sophisticated husband needed, standing by him through years of disappointment and "near misses," and developing community relationships key to his advancement. She allowed Headen to hold onto his ambitions until he matured as an inventor and businessman. Finally, in his later life, American and British business partners became the financial smiths that allowed Headen to put his ideas to work.

This biography—the story of a man and of his community—traces Headen's journey from the Reconstruction and Jim Crow South through a series of migrations across the country, and finally to England. It chronicles too the legacy of the former slave artisans in Carthage, who worked with allies, black and white, north and south, to build the institutions that gave Headen his start. The networks they created within the Republican Party and Presbyterian Church flourished in North Carolina, and were transported across the country by their children and grandchildren, as they fled the political turmoil that engulfed the state at the turn of the century.

As Headen left the South on his own quest, he turned repeatedly to these networks to further his aspirations. He marketed his early inventions with assistance from northern contacts of his childhood pastor, the Reverend Henry Wood. Wood taught him the nuts and bolts of institution building, and it was Wood's "coalition economics" approach that became the model on which Headen based both his Headen Motor Company and the Afro-American Automobile Association. Headen also regularly relied on social connections, including school, religious, professional, and fraternal ties forged by his uncles Henry and Guy Tyson, his wife Tena, his older sister Nannie, her husband Will Jones, his half-brother James L. Street, and James's wife Idella Armwood Street. These individuals linked him to a steady pool of investors, provided him community standing before he could claim success on his own, and most important, helped him pick himself up and start again when his efforts came up short.

Headen's debt to his family and to his minister was great, and their support was critical, forming a bridge over increasingly turbulent waters. He embarked on his career just as legal segregation took shape. The landscape of invention also was changing. The independent inventor touted as a national hero in Headen's childhood was by the late 1910s beginning to cede ground to the "industrial scientist." A new generation of inventors abandoned backyard sheds and personal workshops to enroll in universities and technical institutes, eager to learn what was needed to enter the corporate research and development (R&D) laboratories springing up across the country.

In this environment, experimenters like Headen found it increasingly difficult to raise capital, and to compete with skilled, well-equipped teams. Although industry leaders continued (even as late as the 1950s) to integrate some self-financed inventors into the R&D realm, purchasing their patents and hiring them as consultants, this did little to mitigate Headen's dilemma. With few personal funds, he needed initial investment to develop his ideas and capture the interest of larger investors. And his brown skin meant he was barred from the institutions that offered advanced training.[1]

To find a way past the obstacles before him, Headen forged coalitions that included not only family members and friends but a spectrum of allies. Those to whom he turned to illuminate for us some of the avenues that still remained for inventors and investors on the periphery of America's rising research establishment. Backing came from an emergent black business and professional class quick to seize the freedom of driving, and to use the automobile to preserve and expand the social networks that their parents and grandparents had built. Headen also discovered supporters who might surprise us today. Along his path's many twists and turns, he shared the road with some unlikely fellow travelers, among them a white Chicago gangster, a white inventor from Georgia, a black beautician of the same state, and investors—black and white, north and south, American and British—who provided both encouragement and funds.

Developing his talents and ideas through hard work and the support of diverse partners, Headen would continually discover what his grandfather already knew. Every wheel has many makers.

CHAPTER ONE

A Dream Begins

"NEGRO AVIATOR GETS MEDAL," the *New York Age* proudly announced in January 1912. Only eight years after the Wright Brothers steered their boxlike *Flyer* over the sands of Kitty Hawk, Lucean Headen became one of the first African Americans to master the air. A Long Island aeronautical society, the *Age* reported, had marked the event by awarding him a gold medallion. Delighted readers of the black weekly could admire a photo of the dashing, mustachioed Headen seated at the controls of a large biplane atop the paper's front page. "It is impossible to keep the Negro down," an editorial exulted the following week, exclaiming that Headen had "looked all to the high and cool in his airship" and had shown that the race's adventurers were matching their white brothers in all that required "right thinking and high doing." Black editors across the country joined the chorus, reprinting the original article, often multiple times.

While praising Headen's bravery, journalists also highlighted another facet of the newly minted airman—he reportedly had an application pending for a patent. Headen had devised an anticrash mechanism that, according to the *Age*'s reporter, stopped airplanes from "tilting when falling." In a muddled understanding of Headen's "equalizer," the writer described a forty-pound ball connected to an electrical source. In the event a wing began to tip, he stated, the pilot pressed a button on the steering wheel to "put the ball in play." The weight of the ball, as it shifted to counterbalance the inclination of the wing, theoretically could stabilize a plane.[1]

The paper captured the thrill of having a black hero among the ranks of America's early aviators. Its emphasis on the equalizer, though, bore the stamp of Headen's hand. Eager to promote his invention, he told a St. Louis newspaper later that year that he had learned to fly to demonstrate its utility. Although he would pilot airplanes and race automobiles for several years, pursuits others would have exploited for the celebrity they brought, Headen consistently turned public attention to his ideas and designs. It was mechanical ingenuity, not derring-do, for which he wished recognition. He would spend a lifetime promoting his mechanical creations.[2]

To understand how Headen came to so value the products of his mind and hand, we need look no farther than the central North Carolina town where he spent the first two decades of his life. In Carthage, the seat of Moore County in the pine-knotted Sandhills region of the state, he discovered the value of craftsmanship and practical innovation and found encouragement for his goals. Here he marveled at steam-powered engines and the first locomotive that sent shivers down his spine. And here, with his family as an example, he learned to navigate the social networks, black and white, that would help him launch his career.

When Headen was born on the farm owned by his grandparents, Adam Guy Tyson Sr. and Ann Person Tyson, on August 26, 1879, few would have considered Carthage a likely incubator for a successful inventor. The small village could not yet boast of a railroad, and it had no machine works, no bustling manufactories. In 1880 it had only 366 residents, and even Carthage Township, which encompassed farms and hamlets that stretched for miles, counted only 2,336 inhabitants. Although the county seat perked up with visitors during court weeks, for most of the year Carthage was a quiet spot tucked among orchards, vineyards, and fields of cotton and tobacco, and its principal signs of industry were small turpentine distilleries and scattered lumber mills that sat at the end of rough sand-clay roads cut into the pine forests. The town's sole exception, the Tyson & Jones Buggy Company, employed only twenty-seven workers, and they carried out most of their tasks using water power and hand tools. Co-owner William T. Jones even declared in 1884 that "if a man had selected Carthage eighteen years ago as a place to establish a pretentious manufactory he would have been a fool."[3]

Even fewer would have deemed Carthage a likely place to nurture the inventive dreams of a black boy. In the volatile years after the Civil War, Moore County smoldered with emotion. Although armed conflict had ceased, defeated Confederates still spoiled for a fight. Freed men and women, intent on gaining full citizenship, squared off against them in the political arena. The Democratic Party took up the cause of those who opposed black equality. Lincoln's temporarily ascendant Republican coalition embraced the newly emancipated.

Between 1865 and 1877, in the period of civic reform known as Reconstruction, Republican-led amendments to the U.S. Constitution made Lucean's parents, Jerry M. and Laura A. Tyson Headen, citizens. They granted Jerry access to the ballot box and declared him equal before the law. Enforcing these changes, however, necessitated U.S. troops at the courthouse to protect those trying to vote and federal marshals to pursue outlaws who vandalized black churches, torched the barns of black and white Republicans, and administered whippings or worse to those they perceived as challenging, through personal relationships or politics, the tenets of white supremacy.

Headen's parents came of age in the midst of this turmoil. They were in their early teens in 1869 when news spread of the shooting of Daniel Blue and the brutal murder of his pregnant wife and children, burned to death in their home in nearby Blue's Crossing (now Aberdeen) after Blue testified in a trial against several Ku Klux Klansmen. Jerry Headen spent his youth in Jonesboro, a Klan stronghold a few miles northeast of Carthage, where a spate of vicious beatings, arsons, and rapes were perpetrated in 1870 and 1871. An orphan, he had no mother or father to assuage the fears such acts must have engendered in a boy of fifteen.[4]

What happened to Jerry Headen's parents is unknown, but surviving records suggest a tragic story. Born enslaved in 1855, Jerry was likely a native of adjacent Chatham County, where the 1860 census recorded twelve white Headen households, five of which together owned more than 125 slaves. In August 1870, when census taker Thomas Ritter made his rounds of Moore County, he counted only three Headens: Jerry, age 15, living with a servant named Mariah Street in Jonesboro; Allis, age 12, residing with Matilda Cheek in close-by Prosperity; and Delia, 11, staying with a white couple in Jonesboro. Their unique name and the sequence of their ages suggest that they were the remnants of a family separated, either by sale during slavery or by their parents' deaths. Raised apart and with little chance for an education, the children made the best of their situation. The girls went to work as household servants and Jerry as a hand in a sawmill.[5]

By the time Jerry and Laura married in the mid-1870s and had their first child, Nannie Kathleen, the couple had lost many of their new rights, in practical if not in legal terms. The year 1877, when Nannie was born, marked the formal end of Reconstruction's reforms. In the election of 1876, the first in which Jerry could vote, Moore County's Democrats had resolved to regain control, and they resorted to extreme measures. White employers and landowners threatened to fire workers and cut off vital credit to farmers who did not support their candidates. When these tactics failed, many appeared at the polls brandishing pistols and shotguns. Such intimidation ensured that former Confederate leaders, including Carthage's Capt. James D. McIver, would represent Moore in the state legislature and the U.S. Congress, and it solidified conservative Democrats' dominance over the county. This scenario was replicated across North Carolina and other southern states in 1876. After that year's U.S. presidential race ended in a tie, Democrats asserted their resulting power to force a deal. They agreed to cede the election to the Republican candidate if the federal government would remove its troops from the South. Republican acceptance of the offer left those freed by the war, including Lucean's family, vulnerable once again.[6]

Fortunately for Lucean, other forces were at work within Moore County that would help make his unlikely dream possible. Soon after his birth, the county began to grow. New towns sprang up, including Parkwood near Carthage, where the Taylor Manufacturing Company of Maryland opened a steam-operated millstone company. Northern speculators invested in gold and gem mines in the northwestern part of Moore, and tourists began to frequent the new health and golf resorts of Southern Pines and Pinehurst in the county's lower regions. Jerry Headen and other sawmill laborers worked double time to produce the lumber needed for hotels, shops and restaurants, hunting lodges, horse and livery stables, clubhouses, and summer homes.[7]

Carthage was eager to join the boom. In August 1888, as Lucean turned nine, the newly laid tracks of the Carthage Railroad, a spur from the Raleigh & Augusta Air Line, connected the county seat directly to the East Coast's growing railway traffic. Train service brought with it a new telegraph installed at the depot on Main Street and a brightening economic outlook. Two weeks after the first passengers arrived from Cameron, ten miles away, the *Carthage Blade* observed with satisfaction, "Since our railroad has been in operation, we note a considerable increase in the business of our merchants." The locomotive also benefitted local growers and manufacturers. As Lucean and other children shifted from foot to foot at the station, breathlessly awaiting the whistle of the Saturday morning train, they dodged wagons squeaking beneath the weight of bales of cotton, stacks of lumber and wooden shingles, and aromatic barrels of tar and turpentine destined for loading onto freight cars. Perhaps the only person happier at this scene than Lucean was William T. Jones, who no longer had to use horses to haul strings of newly built buggies to market.[8]

As a boy Lucean watched with excitement as Jones and his business partner, Thomas B. Tyson, transformed Carthage from a sleepy government seat into a company town filled, the *Blade* noted, with "life and bustle." After the trains arrived, Tyson & Jones set out to double their capacity, and on each trip into town Lucean could inspect new additions. Next to an already impressive steam-powered machine shop, described as "a more imposing structure than the court house," soon rose a two-story paint shop, expanded blacksmiths' quarters, a water tower to supply the growing array of steam boilers, and a towering three-story brick building that housed a trim shop, offices, and storage facilities. With state-of-the-art machinery, improved facilities, and freight cars at the ready, business boomed, and Lucean and others in Carthage could take pride in an entity that soon became "the largest and best equipped plant in the South." They could also brag of their growing town. In the blocks around the factory, Thomas Tyson, along with his son and grandson, constructed a lumber

This 1897 photo of Tyson & Jones Buggy Company captures the scale and energy of the firm. A smoke plume escapes from the blacksmith's quarters, where Headen's great-uncle Joseph Tyson worked for more than forty years before opening his own shop. Courtesy of the North Carolina Department of Natural and Cultural Resources.

mill, a steam-driven cotton gin, a saddle- and harness-making shop, a general store, and houses to rent to workers. Others followed suit, opening new shops along the square and its side streets, and laying plans for a new hotel.[9]

Lucean found endless fascination in his visits to town, and especially to Tyson & Jones. There he took in the hiss and heat of steam emanating from red-hot boilers, the crackle of flames and smoke roiling from the smiths' forges, the whirr of belts and pulleys and clank of machinery, odors of sawdust and paint, and the sparkle of bright red and green phaetons, cabriolets, landaus, and victorias. He knew the place well, not only because it was the biggest show around but because his grandfather was a prized employee. Adam Tyson was one of a small elite of wheelwrights and one of only seventeen African Americans known to have worked for the company in its seventy-three-year history. Watching his grandfather, Lucean learned the secret of wheels, axles, springs, and gears, and one can imagine him peppering the elder man with questions on the workings of the plant's lathes, presses, drills, and jointing machines.[10]

Cognizant of his grandfather's knowledge and his status as a craftsman, Lucean likely also sensed the unusual social position Adam Tyson occupied. Adam's presence at Tyson & Jones stemmed from his relationship to Thomas B. Tyson. During slavery, Adam had belonged to the Tyson family, and strong evidence suggests that he may have been part of it. Adam's mother, Jenny Tyson, was a favorite servant in the home of Thomas Tyson's father (planter John

Tyson), and she had nursed Thomas and his sister Elizabeth when they were children. In 1851, when John Tyson fell gravely ill, he revealed a concern for Adam's fate not uncommon among men who fathered children with their slaves. Tyson went to great pains to ensure Adam stayed with the family. From his sickbed, he initiated a deed of gift to give Adam to Thomas. Fearing it might not be legally recorded before he died, he added a codicil to his will specifying that Thomas inherit Adam. "My will and intention is that my beloved son Thomas B. Tyson is to have my Negroe man Adam," he wrote, emphasizing, "I have already intended so to convey him by deed of Gift and this my will is hereby expressed in the event he may not be so fully conveyed." Tyson expressed no such sentiment for his remaining slaves. Although his will specified that he wished one woman, Rose, to become the property of his wife, he took no particular measures to guarantee the transfer, and he instructed Thomas as executor to hire out or sell the others, as would "best promote the interests of the heirs." The subsequent sale included Adam's younger brother Joseph, purchased by Thomas Tyson's close friend Alexander Kelly.[11]

Although any possibility of blood relationship would have been denied publicly, the status Lucean's grandfather enjoyed saved him from work in the fields. He served as overseer on the Tyson plantation, and when Thomas Tyson purchased a small wagon-making concern in 1850, he learned the art of wheelmaking from its former owner Isaac Seawell, a man noted for "fine craftsmanship." At what became Tyson & Kelly six years later, when Alexander Kelly joined Tyson and the two turned the one-man shop into a buggy factory, Adam worked alongside his brother Joseph and another young blacksmith named Edinboro. The trio formed a critical part of the initial eight-man workforce. Adam worked for the company that would in 1873 become Tyson & Jones for thirty-nine years, successfully adapting in the 1880s when the work moved from hand to machine production. He hung up his leather apron only in November 1895, when at the age of sixty-seven he crushed the fingers of his left hand in a painful accident while operating a jointing machine.[12]

From his grandfather's experience, Lucean learned how mastering a craft could command respect. Two weeks after Adam's accident, Tyson & Jones earned a gold medal for its buggies at the Cotton States and International Exposition in Atlanta. Adam's brother Joseph and friend Kade Kelly were in attendance at the fair when the medal was awarded. Adam, because of his injury, could not accompany them, and the *Carthage Blade* consoled him, bemoaning the "most distressing accident" and informing him that "the whole town sympathizes with him." When writing about black residents, the *Blade* generally printed "darky" and "pickaninny" stories, crime news, and vicious political attacks. Lucean's grandfather, on the other hand, and other local black artisans, including brick mason Kade Kelly and talented cabinetmaker Duncan J. McRae (also an in-demand barber), garnered praise as "clever" and "respected." Townspeople regularly read of events in their lives in social columns usually restricted to the comings and goings of prominent whites.[13]

Lucean also saw firsthand the material benefits of a trade. While most black families and many white ones struggled to survive, his grandfather and grandmother owned land. Their 150-acre farm just southwest of town, where they raised their nine children, was valued at $800 in 1870. Six years later Adam Tyson purchased an additional 140 acres from Thomas Tyson, allowing him to supplement his livestock and crops with apple and peach orchards and a vineyard. By 1880, the farm's operations were bustling and the couple had taken on a hired hand and a live-in housekeeper. Four years later they had amassed enough capital for Adam to try his hand at business, becoming a partner in a Carthage grocery and dry goods store with a relative, James A. Tyson.[14]

Sometime between Lucean's second and third year, his grandparents' farm became his permanent home. In June 1880, he and Nannie were living with their parents in Jonesboro, but Laura Headen died not long afterward. While no date for her death has survived, it is unlikely she lived past 1881 or 1882. Jerry Headen's will indicates that Nannie and Lucean, born two years apart, were his and Laura's only children. Had Laura lived longer, it would be expected that another child would have soon followed. Jerry Headen did not remarry until 1901, and although he remained a principal influence in his children's lives, Adam and Ann became their primary caretakers.[15]

Life in the Tyson home, where Lucean and Nannie were surrounded by a host of aunts and uncles, was loving. It was also demanding, with particular stress placed on education. The Tysons had insisted all their children attend school. Only months before Lucean's birth, his uncles John and Henry had graduated from the State Colored Normal School in Fayetteville (formerly the Howard School and now Fayetteville State University). Henry was valedictorian, and both men won accolades for their temperance work. Lucean's uncle William graduated from the same institution in 1882, and his aunt Lucy attended it until 1881, when she transferred to Scotia Seminary in Concord. Adam Jr. (called Guy) completed studies at Greensboro's Bennett Seminary. Lucean's mother and her sister Elizabeth could also, according to the census, read and write, but no class record has been found for them or for a younger sibling, Alice.[16]

The youngest Tyson, Lucean, did not survive past childhood. Dying between 1870 and 1880, he may have been the victim of a diphtheria outbreak in

1875 that, according to one local doctor, "almost wiped out" children under the age of ten in Moore County. The painful memory of his death may be what led those on the farm to call the newest member of the household by his middle name, Arthur, rather than Lucean. Throughout his life Lucean would be known as Arthur to family and friends.[17]

As grandparents, Adam and Ann Tyson also demanded of their new charges piety and self-reliance, virtues they themselves modeled. As a slave, Adam had attended Carthage Presbyterian Church, whose steeple overlooked the Tyson & Jones Buggy Company, and he remained on the church's rolls after the war. Ann joined the church in 1874. When it became clear over time, however, that Carthage Presbyterian would not relent in forcing blacks to occupy a segregated gallery and would refuse to open the pulpit and lay positions to them, the Tysons and other black communicants, along with equally disaffected members from Union Presbyterian east of town, established an independent church. The new congregation officially organized Carthage Church in 1876 and built a rough-hewn, dirt-floored meeting house on land donated by Thomas Tyson in nearby Sassafras Springs. This humble structure was likely where Lucean was christened.[18]

Active in the affairs of the church, Lucean's aunts and uncles provided examples of Christian zeal and social commitment. His uncle John, after returning from school to live on the farm, helped form a local chapter of the Independent Order of Good Templars. He led the group with George B. Kelly, the son of Adam Tyson's coworker Edinboro. While the Templars encouraged sobriety, they also dedicated themselves to education, and the public lectures and debates they sponsored opened opportunities for Carthage's black residents to practice oratorical and dialectic skills. His uncle William, along with several Carthage Church members, pursued his vision through politics. Before entering Lincoln University in Chester, Pennsylvania, he joined elder Duncan McRae as an organizer for the Republican Executive Committee of Moore County. Through the Grand Old Party, the men built alliances with like-minded blacks and whites, hoping to loosen the strengthening grip of white Democrats on government.[19]

Lucean received his own introduction to the Christian faith at John Hall Chapel, the successor to Carthage Church. The congregation erected John Hall Chapel in 1884, when Lucean was five, on land near his grandparents' farm. When it was dedicated on October 19, 1884, John Hall was one of the finest places of worship, black or white, in the county. As Lucean and Nannie dangled their feet in its pews on dedication day, no doubt they understood that they were part of something special. Visitors from as far as forty miles away, eager to see the impressive tongue-and-groove clapboard structure, complete with bell tower and an upstairs gallery, began arriving the morning before "from all directions, in all sorts of conveyances." The proceedings that Sunday left a lasting impression. "Such a service, as well as such a house of worship, is quite beyond anything of the kind ever witnessed here," the church's minister wrote with pride. Enthusiasm would only increase. John Hall more than doubled its membership between 1884 and 1891, by which time it had 216 communicants. Its Sunday school also blossomed, soon counting 200 scholars, many of whom hailed from far outside Carthage.[20]

John Hall Chapel would help shape Lucean as a boy, and the influence of the two people at its heart—the Reverend Henry Davis Wood and his wife, Anna "Annie" M. Riter Wood—could long be seen in his life. In 1883, the Woods convinced the Board of Missions for Freedmen of the Presbyterian Church North, the entity under whose auspices Carthage Church and later John Hall Chapel organized, to support a parochial school in Carthage. By the time Lucean was old enough to attend, classes were conducted for five months each year in the church building. There he received instruction not only from the Woods but from his uncle Henry's new wife, Jane.[21]

Each day Lucean and his fellow students studied reading, writing, basic arithmetic, and especially the rules of community. Instead of striving to achieve an elite status, the Woods focused on meeting the needs of as many as possible. Scattered public schools had opened in Moore County for black students by the mid-1880s, but most ran for only two months, had scant funding, and did not accept pupils over twenty-one. John Hall opened its doors to everyone at no charge. As Lucean recited his ABCs and began to decipher words, he did so next to pupils of all denominations and ages. One of the adults seated next to him may have been his father, who in 1880 could not write, but who by 1900 had achieved full literacy.[22]

Access to more advanced schooling was assured when the Woods founded the Dayton Industrial and Normal School in 1889. At Dayton, Lucean received the best education available to black students in Moore County. That first October, as he pushed open the doors of the "handsome" three-story structure located next to the church, he was one of 115 eager scholars. The school broadened Lucean's horizons, bringing new teachers into his life and introducing him to new subjects. By the time he was thirteen, he would have the benefit not only of the knowledge of Henry and Annie Wood but of two new faculty members. One was Marie Walker Tyson, who had recently wed his uncle Guy, and the other a part-time music teacher, Susan Nichols McRae, wife of Duncan McRae. In 1892, Lucean spent from mid-September through mid-March in the classroom, a remarkable amount of time away from farm or other work for children of the time.[23]

At Dayton, Lucean and his classmates imbibed what one historian has described as the Board of Missions for Freedmen's "universal training program," which balanced academic, vocational, and religious instruction. As Henry Wood put it, the goal of his work was to build character through "a symmetrical culture of the faculties of head hand and heart." The three components of this "symmetrical culture" were fully integrated into Lucean's daily routine. He honed his reading skills using the Bible, the *Westminster Lesson Leaf*, from which he learned the catechism and the meaning of Bible stories, and the *Africo-American Presbyterian*, a newspaper Henry Wood helped incorporate the same year he opened Dayton Academy. As he advanced through the grades, Lucean took on a more challenging curriculum that included theological, historical, and biographical works repurposed from John Hall's Sunday school, among them A. A. Hodge's *Outlines of Theology*, Ezra Hall Gillett's *History of the Presbyterian Church*, Richard Baxter's devotional *The Saints' Everlasting Rest*, and *The Life of Robert Murray McCheyne*, which recounted the inspirational story of a Scottish cleric.[24]

Just as it combined head and heart in developing reading skills, Dayton Academy linked head and hand in its mathematical instruction. Besides memorizing units of measure and completing equations on a slate, Lucean figured angles and ruled and cut lumber to repair rotted floorboards and window casings, while Nannie applied her measurement and spatial skills to refit donated clothing for needy students. Classes in writing also emphasized the hand as Marie Tyson, much admired for her penmanship, required her students to practice the art. The graceful style of both Lucean's and Nannie's handwriting would reflect her influence.[25]

No evidence has survived of the other subjects Lucean studied at Dayton, but the school's offerings would have included more than the obligatory instruction in history, geography, and English grammar, especially after Dayton was designated an academy in 1894, allowing it to expand its academic offerings. The trades Lucean learned are also unknown. If like other Presbyterian industrial schools, Dayton would have provided instruction in some combination of bricklaying, carpentry, mechanical drawing, and shoemaking. Bricklaying and woodworking are particularly good possibilities since Kade Kelly and Duncan McRae were John Hall elders. More important than the specific skills Lucean developed, however, was Dayton's cultivation of an appreciation for practical applications and solutions. In a time of limited resources, ingenuity was a must.[26]

Dayton Academy also became an emotional refuge for Lucean in his teenage years. Even as he thrilled at the vibrant town growing around him, he and his family faced an unrelenting series of misfortunes. The adversity began in 1890, when a dispute over the purchase of land for a cemetery ripped through John Hall's congregation, disrupting church life and straining personal relationships. By 1892, half of John Hall's members, including trustee Edinboro Kelly and original founder Nathan Brown, had returned to Sassafras Springs to start a new church. Headen would feel the absence of friends who had recited Bible verses next to him in Sunday school and chased him through the churchyard in games of tag.[27]

Amidst this upset, Lucean's beloved grandmother Ann died in January 1892, when he was twelve. Two years later, in June 1894, death again visited when Lucean's uncle John fell victim to an acute strain of tuberculosis. On the heels of John's demise came the loss of schoolmate William Worthy in July, and Lucean's great-grandmother Jenny in August. Following these blows, that fall Nannie entered Scotia Seminary in Concord, seventy-five miles away, depriving Lucean of the one person who had always been a constant in his life.[28]

The first year that Nannie was away brought new sorrows. In the spring of 1895, the Tyson home burned with all the family's belongings, leaving Lucean, his grandfather, his uncle Guy, a pregnant Marie, and the couple's two-year-old daughter Edith searching for a place to stay. Having no insurance, his grandfather lost the full $2,500 value of his home, an enormous sum for the time. To make matters worse, later that month the pond connected to the farm's gristmill flooded (for the second time that year), angering neighbors, and in November, in a final cruel twist of fate, Adam Tyson suffered the deforming injury to his hand at Tyson & Jones.[29]

Missing companions, surrounded by death, bereft of his sister, uprooted from home, and watching those he loved in distress, Lucean needed support, and Dayton Academy lent it. Annie Wood, a woman with a soft spot for motherless children (she herself had been one), Susie McRae, and his aunt Marie offered solace. And school events, such as a Fourth of July picnic in 1894, which featured the all-black Sanford Brass Band, foot and sack races, baseball games, and the opportunity to socialize with local girls, supplied welcome levity.[30]

Fortunately for Lucean, he also had another place to take his mind off his troubles—his great-uncle Joseph's blacksmith shop. Occupying the corner of Ray and Saunders Streets a block off the town square, this hub of creativity "fascinated every child in town," explained one resident who grew up in the thrall of its wonders. Everybody for counties around knew about the silver-handled steel razor Joe Tyson had hand-forged in 1884, which according to the

16 *Chapter One*

The Dayton Academy in 1897, with teachers and students posing for a school portrait. The man on the balcony is likely the Reverend Henry Wood, and the two women at the center of the photo may be Mrs. Annie Wood and Marie Walker Tyson. Courtesy of the North Carolina Department of Natural and Cultural Resources.

Carthage Blade was so sharp, "never have we seen a job to excel it." Joseph Tyson would provide razors to at least three U.S. presidents—Grover Cleveland, William McKinley, and Theodore Roosevelt—and his work was displayed at the North Carolina State Fair in Raleigh.[31]

Tyson, however, was more than a talented smith. Praised by the *Moore County News* as "one of the most gifted persons at making many things the Carthage area has ever seen," he was also an inventor. As Lucean spent time in his great-uncle's company, he saw hooked to the walls a myriad of tools the master artisan had designed for local turpentine distillers and farmers. Tyson's low-hanging fruit pruner, the *Moore Gazette* assured orchard owners in 1881, was a "valuable implement" that anyone would find "worth the price charged for it." By the 1890s, Tyson was selling his creations to buyers as far south as Louisiana and as far north as New England.[32]

Watching Joe Tyson shape metal to the specifications of his imagination, Lucean learned how to think beyond the observable. And as he daydreamed of his future, becoming an inventor presented itself as a logical choice. His grandfather and his great-uncle had earned admiration through craftsmanship and creativity, despite the persistence of racial animosity in Carthage. He could see the material fruits of their labors and take pride in the display of their accomplishments at the North Carolina State Fair and the Cotton States Exposition. What then, he must have asked himself, was there to prevent him from joining the ranks of America's mechanical innovators, whose star was so clearly on the rise?

By the time Lucean began the transition from boy to man, the United States was speeding headlong into the industrial age, and men of science had become national and international heroes. In Carthage, the *Blade* anticipated a brilliant technological future. In 1888, it called Thomas Edison's phonograph a "Marvelous Machine" filled with possibilities, and in 1897, it chortled that Nikola Tesla's experiments with wireless communication (quoting Shakespeare) would "make the whole earth kin." Those with more down-to-earth expectations, such as local resident Eugene Macon Cole, were content simply to become part of the patent process. In 1890, Cole received U.S. Patent 439,773 for a wheeled seed planter.[33]

Local enthusiasm for invention received a decided boost in the summer of 1890 when Thomas Edison himself boarded a train to North Carolina in search of gold. Having designed an electromagnetic "extractor" to separate gold and platinum trapped in quartz, Edison hoped to identify suitable sites to employ it. His quest brought him to explore several mines in Carter's Mills, ten miles north of Carthage. The excitement sparked by his visit could not have escaped a boy like Lucean. As early as March, anticipation of Edison's arrival began to build across the county, and landowners scrambled to test potential sites on their own properties in hopes of striking gold and selling the rights to Edison or other northern investors. In early March, W. G. Carter of Carter's Mills announced he had discovered new deposits south of the Deep River, and in April Adam Tyson's neighbor (and clerk of superior court) Alexander H. McNeill identified manganese on land he held nearby. While not as valuable as gold, the element was much sought after for its use in industrial processes.[34]

The *Blade* followed Edison's itinerary closely, reporting prematurely that the inventor was to arrive in nearby Sanford on May 8. When he did not come, it noted the next week that he "is looked for almost any day." It is unknown whether Lucean caught a glimpse of "the Wizard of Menlo Park" when he finally did arrive in Moore County in June, but it is hard to imagine he would have missed the opportunity. Several of the mining outfits in Carter's Mills, including the Grampers, Bell, and Brown mines, had their offices in Carthage, where they conducted business with Edison during his two-week stay. Newspapers also reported that Edison had taken an option on 1,000 acres south of the Deep River, and he would have needed to register his claim at the courthouse.[35]

Then eleven-year-old Lucean revered figures like Edison and yearned to emulate them. This desire only grew once he encountered, at the age of sixteen, the technology that would transform his life—the automobile. As soon as motorized vehicles made their appearance, he told the *Albany Herald* of Georgia some three decades later, he became enamored of them, and he thereafter undertook an "exhaustive study of the automotive industry." The initial spark for his fervor was likely an 1895 article published in the *Blade*, which described a road race from Paris to Bordeaux. Staged between steam, electric, and gasoline vehicles, the dramatic competition captured imaginations across the nation, including in North Carolina.[36]

To capitalize on the rising public curiosity, a traveling company known as the "Combined John Robinson and Franklin Brothers Circus" in 1896 arranged to purchase a motor car. That fall it uncrated "the wonderful horseless carriage" for display at its show in Durham, a tantalizing forty miles from Carthage. Each year afterward, it sponsored speed tests in a more advanced gasoline-powered car, to the delight of gawking crowds at the North Carolina State Fair in Raleigh. As frequent visitors to the fair, Lucean's family may well have taken him to see the gleaming machine lead the opening parade and sputter around the fairgrounds track. The automobile, and later any technology that promised speed and mobility, became the permanent fodder for Lucean's inventive dreams.[37]

Invention, besides its ready appeal for a boy raised around machines, may also have served an important emotional purpose for Lucean. William Polite, a black inventor in Wilmington, North Carolina, who in 1917 patented an antiaircraft gun, explained that as a youngster he had "a burning desire to be recognized by the universe as a man of importance and because of this desire I decided to become an inventor." In Carthage, where black men were often addressed as "boy," and where a craftsman like Adam Tyson, despite his status, was often called "Uncle Adam," the patenting process gave Lucean, like William Polite, a color-blind avenue to adulthood and respect. Patent applications did not ask one's race. It is not surprising, then, that as he scanned advertisements run by patent agents in the *Carthage Blade*, the *Jonesboro Leader*, and the *Africo-American Presbyterian*, he would begin scheming how to earn one of his own.[38]

To achieve that goal, Lucean needed a place to gain practical knowledge. He would find it in 1893, when his father and his uncle Guy founded Headen & Tyson Saw and Shingle Mill south of town. The business sprang up in the wake of a forest fire outside Carthage that had left thousands of partially burned trees in need of salvage. Bolstered by Jerry Headen's many years' experience lumbering, Guy Tyson's salesmanship, and a fortuitous extension of the Carthage Railroad that passed nearby, the new company quickly prospered. It would not be long before, as one newspaper noted, it was doing "an excellent business" in Moore and neighboring Cumberland County. The sawmill gave Lucean not only a model for personal enterprise and risk-taking, but also his first direct experience with steam-powered machinery. He could marvel at the mechanical wonders at the buggy company when visiting his grandfather, but in such a busy workplace he could only be an observer. At his father's side, he discovered firsthand how a boiler, piston, fly wheel, and belt drive worked and how these components, operating in concert, turned the saws. He could also learn how to run, monitor, oil, clean, and repair each piece of the machinery.[39]

Lucean may not have been the only family member building new skills at Headen & Tyson. Before marrying Lucean's mother Laura, Jerry Headen had fathered a son in Jonesboro. Born November 13, 1875, James Lillie Street was raised by his mother, Lillie Ann Street, and he took her family name. We know little about the relationship Lucean and James had as children, but the two would collaborate later in life, and they shared a love of machines. After leaving Moore County in the late 1890s, James worked for the Jacksonville, Tampa and Key West Railway, where he inspected and repaired wheels, axles, brakes, and couplings and ensured loads were properly secured. Because these duties required mechanical expertise that would have been difficult to obtain elsewhere, it is conceivable Lucean and James worked side by side at their father's mill. If so, James may have added an older brother's example to stoke the fires of Lucean's ambitions.[40]

Lucean could fully appreciate the sawmill's contribution to his goals. He was likely less aware of the utility of what he was learning at school, at church, and at home. It would be in these places, however, that he gained much of the knowledge critical to addressing the thornier side of invention. Many a talented mechanic has watched original ideas fail from a lack of insight into the complexity of the inventive process. Ingenuity is the wellspring of an inventor's career. But success requires tenacity, the ability to gain support for an idea and work with others to develop it, the savvy to navigate the legal labyrinth governing patents, and the capacity to convince others to help manufacture and distribute a product. In short, it requires an understanding of networks—governmental, technical, financial, professional, and political—and their internal workings, as well as the shrewdness to bend them to one's goals. No amount of technical brilliance can substitute for social acumen.

Three men who loomed large in Lucean's life, Rev. Henry Wood and his uncles Guy and Henry Tyson, helped him develop those critical skills. While Wood and the Tyson brothers built their careers, Lucean absorbed strategies and practical lessons that he would later employ. Henry Wood's example was central. The minister, who arrived in Carthage the year Lucean was born, was likely the person most responsible for Lucean's future wanderlust. Wood's life had been a testament to the possibilities of mobility. Born free in Trenton, New Jersey, he had lived in Albany and Brooklyn, New York; Newport, Rhode Island; and Chester, Pennsylvania, where he earned a master's degree from Lincoln University Theological Seminary in 1878. He had also traveled widely as a military man, fighting in South Carolina during the Civil War as a soldier with the famed 54th Massachusetts Infantry, and later touring England, France, and Spain as a captain's steward in the U.S. Navy. Living only a few doors from the Tyson farm, the peregrinating reverend had ample opportunity to regale Lucean with tales of the world beyond the Carolina Sandhills.[41]

Wood also gave Lucean his first lessons in coalition building and persistence. From childhood Lucean watched the energetic organizer find allies in far-flung and often unlikely places. In 1884, Wood persuaded one-time Klan member Alexander H. McNeill to donate the land needed for John Hall Chapel. Gaining such support was no mean feat for a northern black soldier whose regiment had captured South Carolina's Fort Wagner in 1863 (an event immortalized in the 1989 movie *Glory*). With land secured, Wood solicited the bulk of the construction funds from women, white and black, of his home church (First Presbyterian of Trenton), wrangled a $300 loan from the interracial Yadkin Presbytery, and asked the Board of Missions for Freedmen to pay part of his salary during the period. He then turned his attention to winning over white community figures, inviting county officials and prominent Carthaginians to church services. In September 1885, as six-year-old Lucean stole glances into the gallery (where in a social reversal the white visitors now sat), he could see squeezed into the seats above him district solicitor James D. McIver, county superintendent of instruction William J. Stuart, register of deeds Thomas Ritter, and a number of local attorneys and merchants, accompanied by their wives.[42]

Wood also overcame skepticism within the black community, some of whom, especially Methodists, were wary of a northern Presbyterian. When an elderly woman attending John Hall's dedication day openly challenged Wood on Presbyterians' discouragement of shouting during services, the diplomatic minister responded that the church approved of shouting as long as it was "followed by a Christian life." Thus reassured, the woman arose and "shouted to her heart's content." Flexible on doctrine, Wood fostered ties with congregations such as St. Augustine African Methodist Episcopal Zion (AMEZ) Church, which stood less than a quarter of a mile away. His encouragement of church members to focus on commonalities bridged the denominational divide, and by the 1890s Lucean, Nannie, and the other children of

John Hall were regularly attending picnics and church programs with Methodist friends.[43]

As a youngster, Lucean also observed Henry Wood unite disparate parties to construct Dayton Academy. The project demanded the cooperation of black residents across Moore County, local white business leaders, northern church women, representatives of the Board of Missions for Freedmen, and northern industrialists hoping to invest in the South. Wood spoke directly to the motives of each. To black parents, he promised a better education for their children than the ill-funded public schools could offer. To women such as Margaret Dayton, who headed the fundraising effort at Trenton's First Presbyterian, he offered a legacy, giving the school her name. To white businessmen such as Alexander McNeill, who sold the land for the schoolhouse at a greatly reduced price and donated the timber, Wood pledged to help achieve the aim of economic development. McNeill, like Thomas Tyson and William Jones, was eager to become part of the "New South," and he understood that an educated workforce was required to attract outside capital. Education funded by the northern church suited the needs of white leaders perfectly, because it allowed them to offer northern industrialists trained black workers without upsetting white taxpayers, who were actively opposed to spending tax funds on black schools.[44]

Lucean learned as well from Wood that furthering a coalition sometimes required adopting a conciliatory approach, even when it was personally painful. In an 1896 letter to the *Carthage Vindicator*, written during a time when his church was under attack for its members' political activism, Wood reminded those in Carthage that his work to build Dayton Academy had brought an investment of thousands of dollars, contributing "not a little to the material progress of this community." He was careful, however, to flatter the town's white citizens, claiming that as someone who had "travelled as extensively in this and other countries as any one in the county," he had "yet to see the place, or the people, that compares with Carthage in its opportunities for the colored man." He struck a similar tone in letters to northern white supporters, praising their generosity. Unable to speak his mind freely, Wood maintained a cooperative profile, declaring himself "not a politician."[45]

Simple conciliation, however, was not Wood's full lesson. In the more promising venue of the Yadkin Presbytery, he showed Lucean another side. As Yadkin's stated clerk and the head of several key committees, Wood openly battled racism within the church. Under his leadership the presbytery regularly petitioned the church's General Assembly to remove freedmen's issues from the pro-southern Board of Missions for Freedmen, to apply the same rules to black and white candidates for the ministry, and to block reunification of the northern and southern halves of the Presbyterian Church, if such unity required segregation. Wood had also taken an important step toward ensuring a wider black voice when he had worked with ministers from the Yadkin and Catawba Presbyteries to incorporate the *Africo-American Presbyterian*, a newspaper that had been publishing in Wilmington since 1879. Observing his pastor's actions, Lucean gained insight into how to elicit support in unpromising circumstances, turn the motives of others to one's own use, and to take what actions one could to preserve a dream, even when it encountered overwhelming resistance.[46]

Guy and Henry Tyson, who embraced political activism, gave Lucean insight into a set of alternative strategies. In the 1890s, Guy, along with Dayton Academy student Charles Foushee and others in Carthage, took up where Lucean's uncle William had left off, becoming leaders in Moore County's resurgent Republican Party. Guy rose quickly to prominence. He was chosen in 1894 as a representative to the State Republican Convention and was nominated as a candidate for register of deeds. Two years later, his political stock rose after he helped persuade black voters to join an alliance between Republicans and other groups who had become disenchanted with Democratic policies. In the election of 1896, Populist farmers, Prohibitionists, and some wage workers joined Republicans in a "Fusionist" coalition that flourished not only in Carthage but across North Carolina. The Fusionists mounted the first fundamental challenge to Democratic power since Reconstruction, returning a Republican to the governor's mansion for the first time in twenty years. They also captured Moore County's congressional district, secured a state senate seat, and elected Fusionists and their Republican allies to the key positions of sheriff, register of deeds, treasurer, and surveyor.[47]

Having helped tip the scales, Guy Tyson was awarded a postmaster's position, becoming head of the post office for Flynn, a small community near his sawmill, in 1899. As Guy presided at contentious political conventions and manned the polls in hotly contested political fights, he modeled courage for Lucean. An equally important, though less obvious, bequest involved his knowledge of bureaucratic procedures and chains of command. Observing his uncle complete county and federal paperwork, interpret postal regulations, organize mail deliveries, and leverage contacts, Lucean got his first glimpse into the intricacies of government, preparing him for the rigorous process he would later face when applying for and protecting his patents.[48]

Living in Washington, D.C., Henry Tyson had less contact with his nephew than his brother Guy, but he influenced him nonetheless. Henry was an imposing figure who dedicated his life to education and politics. After delivering the valedictorian's speech at the State Colored Normal School in Fayetteville in May 1879, he had joined its faculty, later becoming assistant to its principal, future novelist Charles Chesnutt. He and Chesnutt married sisters. When Henry moved to Washington in 1883, he sat for the civil service exam, and after passing it, traded his teacher's desk for that of a clerk in the Sixth Auditor's Office of the Internal Revenue Service. He did not, however, abandon his commitment to service. One of a cadre of black federal workers and professionals dubbed the "Tarheel bunch," he quickly gained political prominence as he joined distinguished black Republicans such as Frederick Douglass and Robert and Mary Church Terrell to work for racial change. It would be Henry who delivered Joseph Tyson's razors directly to the Oval Office.[49]

Henry also exercised considerable influence in his home state. Often returning to North Carolina during Lucean's teenage years, he increased his presence after becoming private secretary to Congressman Henry P. Cheatham, and gaining an appointment to the board of trustees for the recently founded Greensboro Agricultural & Mechanical College, today's North Carolina Agricultural & Technical (A&T) State University. Cheatham represented North Carolina's coastal Second Congressional District (known as the "Black Second" because of its heavy concentration of African American voters) between 1889 and 1893, and Henry accompanied him to the eastern part of the state when Cheatham campaigned for reelection in 1892. Lucean's grandmother Ann was suffering ill health during that trip, and when Henry took a detour from the campaign trail to visit her, he brought Cheatham with him. The visit likely made thirteen-year-old Lucean the envy of his classmates as they watched his uncle introduce Cheatham to a racially mixed crowd of 500 at the Moore County Courthouse and heard the hearty cheers given the congressman's speech. The event demythologized the national politician for Lucean, and introduced him to the notion that even those of high status were approachable.[50]

Henry Tyson also encouraged Lucean's love of technology. Tyson had embraced mechanical progress early, enthusing in Carthage's *Moore Index* in 1879 over the first Colored Industrial Fair held in Raleigh. Five years later, he marveled that the "iron horse sweeps with such wonderful rapidity from the Atlantic to the Pacific," and that Americans could through the telegraph and the telephone "communicate with the world with lightning speed." By the 1890s, Tyson had also forged direct connections with black inventors in Washington. A leader in the influential Bethel Literary and Historical Association, he mingled there with what historian Rayvon Fouché has called a "loose and small community of African American inventors" who belonged to the organization. Among them were Robert Pelham, who patented an adding machine device for the U.S. Bureau of the Census, Shelby Davidson, Henry's coworker at the Treasury Department, who took out patents on similar devices used there, and Henry E. Baker, the U.S. Patent Office's only black patent examiner. Besides attending political and civic functions with these men, Tyson socialized with them on vacations at the Maryland shore. Thus he was in a position to offer Lucean the ear of individuals with experience and knowledge of the patent process.[51]

By the time Lucean completed his last years at Dayton Academy, he was in many ways well equipped to begin the upward struggle of an inventor. Heir to a strong craft tradition, son of a successful businessman, and protégé of men and women of learning, influence, and broad experience, he had gained technical skills and social knowledge far beyond what many Americans could claim. He could also trust that his mechanical passions would be embraced. As he struggled to find his own footing, however, he would need to draw on every lesson he had learned, and to lean on what shoulders he could, because the terrain of his path forward was about to change dramatically.

CHAPTER TWO

A Dream Is Deferred

In May 1902, Lucean stood behind a lectern at Albion Academy, an advanced preparatory school in Franklinton, North Carolina, and delivered an address called "Memory's Message." He was twenty-two years old. The text of his speech, which won second place in the junior class's debating contest, has been lost, but its title was prophetic. It implied that the past informed the present and should be borne in mind. It was a sentiment that had immediate meaning for Lucean. The years between his graduation from Dayton Academy and his arrival on Albion's campus had fundamentally reshaped his expectations. Marked by painful realities, they had brought him to the school's door with hopes of reviving the promise that had filled his childhood.[1]

How Lucean found himself at Albion is a story of ambition interrupted. In 1898, having exhausted what he could learn at Dayton Academy and at his father's sawmill, he had aspired to train, like Adam and Joseph Tyson, as a craftsman and inventor. But as he set out to pursue his goals, political winds shifted. Following the Fusion victory of 1896, white Democrats struck back, launching a brutal campaign to reassert white supremacy in North Carolina. Assailing African Americans as immoral, unintelligent, and dangerous, they renewed attacks on black bodies and property, and revived an old postwar bugaboo of black men as brutes and rapists. Caught in their net, Lucean and his family suffered devastating losses.

Lucean's experience between 1896 and 1901 was that of many talented men and women who absorbed the wrath of white "Redemptionists." Forced to divert youthful energies from their goals in order to survive an increasingly bewildering array of assaults, they were put back on their heels. Lucean's first great shock came in 1898, three months after he turned nineteen. That November, news reached Carthage of an antiblack riot in Wilmington, North Carolina, where his family had many friends. The violence, which left twenty-five black citizens dead, had long been brewing. Seeking to undo Republican and Fusionist gains made in the city, Democrats had begun to beat the drum of "Negro Domination" in the lead-up to scheduled state elections. Just before the balloting, paramilitary groups known as the Red Shirts and the Rough Riders marched through Wilmington's black neighborhoods to discourage turnout. On Election Day, they brandished guns and knives, threatening to kill any black man who dared to exercise his legal right. After the election, a mob burned the offices of the local black newspaper, and put the torch to black homes and businesses, sparking two days of confrontation. In a final dramatic move, Democrats then staged an illegal takeover of the municipal government, pushing from office all elected black officials, and any white officials who opposed the move, under threat of death.[2]

Lucean was surrounded by justifications of the white offensive in Democratic papers such as the *Carthage Blade*, *Fayetteville Observer*, and Raleigh *News & Observer*. More personal accounts came from sources closer to home. In early December, AMEZ bishop James Walker Hood spoke in Carthage on the "sadness, sorrow, and gloom" the riot had brought to "many hearts." Not long afterward, Guy Tyson gained particulars from Congressman George H. White, the representative for Wilmington's district, when the two men attended the Presbyterian Church North's General Assembly together. Lucean's sister Nannie, too, undoubtedly heard details from her many Scotia classmates who hailed from the beleaguered city.[3]

With no memory of the Civil War or Reconstruction, Lucean had never witnessed the full vehemence of white supremacy. Thus, although he felt the gravity of the new threat Wilmington represented, he seems to have struggled to accept its full implications. Not involved in politics, he likely hoped that his abilities, like those of his grandfather and his great-uncle Joseph, would insulate him, and he chose to remain in Carthage. As the vise of discrimination tightened, however, events pressed on him more directly. He received his first formal introduction to Jim Crow in January 1899, when the North Carolina Assembly enacted a law that compelled black passengers to ride separately on trains passing through the state. His beloved aunts and uncles, and his respected teachers, including Susie McRae, who regularly took the train to see her sister Tena Nichols in Raleigh, would now suffer the indignities of the hot, cramped, cinder-strewn "colored" car behind the engine.[4]

Only a year later, Lucean witnessed white brutality at its worst. In the spring of 1900, George Ritter, a newlywed described by the county coroner as "simple and unoffensive," was murdered in Carthage. A white farmer whose barn had burned suspected Ritter as the incendiary, and he and a local merchant kidnapped Ritter from his home in the middle of the night. They beat and shot him and hanged his "shockingly mutilated" body from a tree. Both men then abruptly moved to neighboring Richmond County. At an indictment hearing almost a year later, they denied any wrongdoing and, despite substantial evidence against them, were never convicted. Ritter's murder and the failure to bring his killers to justice gave stark new clarity to Jerry Headen's stories about the violence that had marked his youth. It also put Lucean and his community on notice.[5]

The shock of Ritter's killing was reinforced four months later when Democrats converged on Carthage in a menacing rally. Staged to promote an amendment to the state constitution to limit black suffrage, the gathering featured gubernatorial candidate Charles Aycock and noted Franklin County orator Frank Spruill. The two men steamed into town aboard the Carthage Railroad on July 17 and, after being greeted at the depot by local civic leaders and a large contingent of Red Shirts, marched with them in a parade through the courthouse square. Animating the procession was a white-uniformed band playing atop a rolling platform drawn by six mules. Behind trailed a line of buggies, wagons, and floats, many carrying white women hoisting signs that pleaded "Protect Us" and demanded "White Supremacy." At the rear clopped a column of men on horseback waving red, white, and blue banners asserting "White Rule for Tarheels." A reported 2,500 spectators (a number far exceeding the town's entire white population) cheered and hurrahed as the marchers snaked their way past the courthouse, Carthage Presbyterian, Tyson & Jones Buggy Company, and Joe Tyson's and Duncan McRae's blacksmith and barber shops. After a "long detour through the resident portion of the town," the cavalcade halted for speeches at the home of superior court judge James D. McIver. The mood of the event, led by Carthage's white elite, contrasted sharply with the cooperative spirit Lucean had witnessed sixteen years earlier as he peered into John Hall Chapel's gallery to see McIver, then district solicitor, seated in support of his minister.[6]

When the suffrage amendment passed by popular vote the following month, it hit Lucean especially hard. August was the very month he reached majority and became eligible to register. He could only watch in anger as the amendment's new literacy requirement closed the ballot box to his grandfather, who although he never learned to read or write, had long been on the voter rolls of West Carthage Precinct. More galling, a "grandfather clause" opened the polls to any man, regardless of literacy, if his lineal ancestor could vote in or before 1867. Since blacks did not gain the right to the ballot until 1868, this excluded Adam Tyson while preserving suffrage rights for his illiterate white neighbors.[7]

By the end of 1900, the danger in which Lucean's family now lived became abundantly clear. On the night of December 13, Headen & Tyson Saw and Shingle Mill burned. No local newspaper describing the event has survived, and notices of it picked up by other papers fail to state what sparked the blaze. Given the political atmosphere and Guy Tyson's position of prominence in the Republican Party, however, those in Carthage's black community could not help but wonder at the suspicious timing of the fire. Only months after flames engulfed the mill, Tyson was stripped of his postmaster's position. His experience was shared across the state as Democrats instigated a purge of black post office employees, three years later gloating that "the last of the negro officials of any consequence in North Carolina" had finally been removed.[8]

The destruction of Headen & Tyson saddled Headen's father and uncle with a loss of $6,500. It also prompted Jerry Headen to leave Carthage. Determined not to be defeated, he relocated to Aberdeen, where the following year he married schoolteacher Nettie B. Jackson and began to reestablish himself as a lumberman and peach grower. The couple welcomed a daughter, Louise, in 1906. Guy Tyson, after struggling to find work, secured a position as a sales agent for the black-operated (though white-owned) Ashley & Bailey silk mill in Fayetteville. The commissions he earned and Marie's meager pay from Dayton Academy enabled the couple to survive, but they found it difficult to feed their growing family, which besides Edith now also included daughter Guyrene and sons Wilbur and Roland.[9]

For Lucean, his father's and uncles' experiences rendered Henry Wood's claim that Carthage had no rival in "opportunities for the colored man" hollow. How hollow became evident as he encountered the limits placed on his own possibilities. White craftsmen across the state had for decades clamored for a ban on "negro mechanics." Resenting the use of slave labor to undercut their wages in the antebellum years, after the war they sought a white monopoly. Those responsible for the bloody coup in Wilmington, keenly aware of the need for white artisanal support, had actively stoked such tensions. Now in command of votes important to Democrats, white craftsmen prevailed, and Democratic leaders, including those in Carthage, once loyal to the skilled black workers they had often earlier held as property, capitulated to political pressure.[10]

The result for Lucean was that Tyson & Jones, the workplace of his grandfather for almost four decades, would hire few new black workers after 1900, and when it did, it severely limited their opportunities. In Lucean's youth, when he peered into the company's blacksmith shops, he saw no fewer than six black men manning the forges. By 1910, only two, Edinboro Kelly and Calvin Peace, remained. Likewise, in 1910 the firm had only two black trim painters, Sandy A. Jackson, who had begun work at Tyson & Jones in the early 1890s, and A. Thomas Person, who seems to have been the only new hire with any expertise. The remaining workers that year were janitor Thomas Buckner, who had mopped the office's floors since the 1880s, Morris Tyson, who began crating buggies in the trim shop around the same time, and three new employees, all unskilled. These included fireman Will Robertson, whose job was to shovel coal into the boiler fireboxes, and general laborers King Goins and Tom Clegg. Clearly, no special place would be reserved for Lucean as there had been for Adam Tyson.[11]

In fact, as he searched for work, Lucean could find no job save that of railroad porter. The census for 1900, which recorded his occupation as "Porter-RR," does not tell us the line for which he worked. He may have served on the Carthage Railroad, although he is more likely to have been hired by the larger Raleigh & Augusta Air Line. The Carthage spur was shortened in 1899 to only an eighteen-and-a-half-mile stretch of track between Cameron and Hallison, and the train made only one full trip each day, with one additional ten-mile run between Cameron and Carthage. The Raleigh & Augusta, on the other hand, had recently been incorporated into the larger Seaboard Air Line Railway (the SAL), which handled traffic through its main lines on routes from New York to Tampa to New Orleans. In 1900, the SAL was undergoing expansion and hired a full force of conductors, porters, and waiters for its passenger and dining cars.[12]

The porter's tasks were mundane—carrying bags, sweeping cars, cleaning coal ash from windowsills and soot from oil lamps, polishing shoes, and attending to other needs of riders. Still, Lucean could find compensation in the wave of excitement created by the raw power of the steam engine and the joy of discovery. He was not alone in appreciating the job's travel benefit. One Atlantic Coast Line porter conjectured in 1892 that more men joined the train service "for the opportunity of shifting from place to place and seeing with the naked eye the different portions of this country . . . than for any other purpose." Lucean and his coworkers also enjoyed the admiration of others. Few black men in Carthage, or anywhere in the South, held jobs that allowed them to wear uniforms and clean shoes, thus the "railroad man" was a highly respected figure within black communities. As Charles Douglass, a theater owner in Macon, Georgia, later recalled, as a teenager he had been "deeply impressed" at the sight of the well-dressed attendants who descended from the train when it stopped near the sawmill where he worked, and he had marveled at their "smug and satisfied air." It was their example, he claimed, that had stirred his own ambitions.[13]

In late October 1900, just weeks before his father lost his mill, Lucean left his first employer to join the Pullman Company, becoming a porter on the sleeper cars that Pullman rented to railroads such as the SAL to accommodate wealthy passengers traveling overnight. His work for Pullman brought higher wages and increased prestige within the trainman's world but also new stresses.

The company required porters to prepare cars for trips, a task requiring a considerable amount of work for no pay. Arriving at odd hours to make up sleeping berths, load food and newspapers onboard, and double-check passenger lists, Pullman workers often grumbled at the unreasonable demand. More intimate and prolonged contact with passengers also tested Lucean's patience. As a limited-distance porter, he had worked standard shifts, allowing him time at the end of each day to escape the demeaning treatment often meted out by intoxicated, hostile, or simply patronizing passengers. He now had to maintain a subservient facade for twenty-four hours or more, on call around the clock to satisfy the whims of those who insisted on dubbing him, as all porters, "George," regardless of their names.[14]

Thus, although his Pullman position was a coveted one in his community, for Lucean it was small consolation for the dream he had been forced to abandon. He would persevere on the sleeper cars for only a few months before his lack of enthusiasm caught up with him. At the beginning of March, the Pullman Company discharged him for "unsatisfactory service." His firing brought Lucean to a crossroads. Not ready to reconcile himself to a life of deferential obedience, he nonetheless had to face mounting evidence that his family's unique position in Carthage, which might have provided him other possibilities, was forever gone. Alexander H. McNeill, who had supported John Hall Chapel and Dayton Academy, was growing old and infirm, and Thomas B. Tyson's death in 1893 had robbed Adam Tyson and his family of their most important white ally. (Susie McRae, too, lost much with Thomas Tyson's death. He was her father.)[15]

The sons and grandsons of such men, including George W. McNeill, Lucien P. Tyson, and Thomas B. Tyson II, were at the controls of Moore County's Democratic machinery, and their outlook, fired in the kiln of political competition, bore little resemblance to that of their paternalistic forebears. The younger elite's attitude, illustrated in the changing employment policies of Tyson & Jones, surfaced as well in a dispute simmering between George McNeill and Lucean's grandfather. Alexander McNeill, out of respect for his elderly neighbor, had tolerated the fact that the earthen dam at Adam Tyson's mill pond often flooded, damaging his crops. Despite the ongoing problem, he continued to take his corn to be ground there. George McNeill, replacing his father as manager of the family land, informed Tyson that if he continued to rebuild the dam, he would sue him.[16]

With courtesies once extended to black craftsmen withering, businesses such as his father's proving targets, and political attacks intensifying, Lucean realized in the spring of 1901 that he needed to make a new plan for his life.

Not surprisingly, that plan involved education. Two years earlier, Nannie had made a similar assessment. After graduating from Scotia Seminary in 1897, she had taught at Dayton Academy. In 1899, however, she left to enter a teaching program at Shaw University in Raleigh. Advanced training would bolster her long-term chances of remaining employed and of possibly finding a better position. Lucean took out his own insurance policy against an uncertain future by enrolling in Albion Academy in October 1901.[17]

Albion would give Lucean much more than a degree. The school helped him rebuild his confidence. At once new and familiar, Albion was an extension of the supportive networks of his childhood. Like Dayton Academy, it ascribed to the principles of "head hand and heart," and it maintained a religious character, requiring that students take classes in "The Bible" and the "Evidences of Christianity," and that they study the catechism daily. Established by the Presbyterian Church North, it had been renamed the Franklinton Colored State Normal and Industrial School after it became part of the North Carolina state educational system, but Lucean and his classmates seldom called it that, preferring to honor its history. Rev. John Savage, Albion's president, was a Lincoln University classmate and friend of Henry Wood, and Wood had formerly served as vice president of the school's board of trustees.[18]

Albion's faculty, capable and well trained, encouraged Lucean to harness his energies and focus his attention while the political maelstrom swirled around him. At his teachers' urging, he tackled unfamiliar subjects and gathered the courage to master public speaking. In the classroom with Charles Tucker, holder of a doctorate from Lincoln University, and Louis Neal and Benjamin Person, both graduates of Shaw University, he studied geography, history, philosophy, English literature, Latin, and Greek. More important, he applied himself to higher algebra and plane geometry and discovered the rudiments of the scientific method through lectures and laboratory studies in chemistry, astronomy, and geology. Excelling at his studies, Lucean scored well enough in the spring of 1902 to be among four students honored for their scholarship.[19]

Besides academic rigor, Lucean found at Albion an appreciation for innovation and "know-how." His instructors assigned essays on "The Ingenuity of Man" and "The Progress of Civilization," and Henry Fuller, head of the school's mechanical department, emphasized practical engineering. Guided by Fuller, who had been a master carpenter for more than three decades, Lucean and his male classmates constructed a campus dormitory, sorely needed since the current accommodations had "three students in one bed, and three beds in nearly all the rooms." Helping erect "the barracks," a two-story frame structure that housed sixty-five, Lucean learned how to convert blueprints into physical reality and honed his ability to solve the problems resulting from a tight construction budget.[20]

Lucean also participated in a project Fuller spearheaded in 1902 to install a "hydraulic ram" system to supply the school with water. Weary of hauling heavy pails from a natural spring, a task particularly onerous in winter, Lucean and his classmates readily heeded their teacher's call. Catching the spring water as it cascaded downhill, they routed it into a manual pump fitted with two valves. The entry valve, forced open by the momentum of the water rushing in, closed when the pump filled to capacity. The exit valve, located on the top of the pump, then popped open under the pressure of the trapped water, sending the water spurting upward into a tank. From there it was piped via gravity into the school buildings. The pupils at Albion thus became the first residents of Franklin County to enjoy indoor plumbing. Their handiwork was still in use as late as 1916.[21]

In Albion's print and blacksmith shops, a curious Lucean learned the workings of a mechanical press and gained a greater knowledge of metallurgy. Already having absorbed much from watching his great-uncle Joseph at the forge, at Albion he could test metals for himself and feel how they behaved under heat. His experience would serve him well as he later designed motors for automobiles. With large-scale machine tools scarce, early engine components often had to be smithed by hand.[22]

Lucean also found peers at Albion with whom to share the frustrations of escalating Jim Crow policies, which increasingly punctuated their daily lives with new indignities. After the 1900 suffrage amendment passed, legislators appointed a solidly Democratic State Elections Board and empowered it to select county election officials. This guaranteed only Democrats would serve as registrars. As Lucean entered his senior year, an updated election law required that all voters re-register, and it added a worrisome condition. Now, not only would he be required to prove an ability to "read and write any passage of the Constitution," he would have to do so *"to the satisfaction of the registrar."* These six simple words gave local Democrats unilateral power to declare anyone, despite their abilities or achievements, illiterate. To no one's surprise, within a year there was scarcely a "literate" black man left in the state.[23]

Lucean and his fellow students read of the new scheme in a *Franklin Times* article. Pronouncing those eligible to vote under the grandfather provision a "roll of honor," *Times* editor James A. Thomas expressed his hope that "all illiterate white men" would go to the polls. He then gloated that "Negroes who register at all must register under the educational [that is, literacy] clause," adding with a wink, "Registrars should remember that they are the sole judges of the ability to read and write." Thomas then tipped his hat to an understanding Democrats had struck with many white Fusionists—their voting rights would be protected in return for switching allegiances. The grandfather clause, the *Times* informed them, demonstrated that "the pledges of the advocates of the amendment are made good."[24]

As they despaired over the loss of voting rights, Lucean and his classmates also feared each year for the well-being of their school. As a state institution, Albion was largely controlled by local Democrats, which included editor James Thomas and also Frank Spruill, the orator who had appeared with Charles Aycock in Carthage. Thomas held a seat on Albion's local board of managers and Spruill a place on the school's advisory board. They, along with other political appointees who oversaw Albion's management, were often at loggerheads with President Savage, who had led the effort in Franklin County to keep a faltering Fusionist partnership alive. Unlike Henry Wood, Savage embraced politics, and as late as 1900 agitated within his party for the nomination of blacks for office, leading a walkout from that year's Republican State Convention when delegates refused to nominate a single black candidate.[25]

Savage's stance gave Lucean a more defiant model. It also placed his school in the Democratic bull's-eye. As students had worried, the State Board of Education hit it squarely in 1905 when it withdrew all state support. Reverting to the control of the Presbyterian Church North, Albion struggled thereafter, saved only by the relentless fundraising of President Savage and his wife Mary.[26]

The bonds Lucean developed with faculty and students in his years at Albion Academy helped him stay positive and rebuild his faith in his abilities. They also boosted his self-esteem. Handsome, from a respectable family, and academically successful, he soaked up the admiration of his peers and quickly drew the attention of female classmates. He was in many ways the proverbial "good catch," a fact soon recognized by Tena Elizabeth Drye of Wilmington. In October 1902, at the beginning of Headen's senior year, Tena arrived on Albion's campus as a teacher in its primary grades. Accomplished, stylish, and pretty, she had briefly been a classmate of Nannie's at Scotia Seminary, so Lucean may already have known her. No evidence exists, however, that the two were romantically involved prior to her joining Albion's staff. The young man, though, now was smitten and by the spring was seriously contemplating marriage. On September 8, 1903, a few months after his graduation, he and Tena exchanged vows at Chestnut Street Presbyterian Church in Wilmington.[27]

Tena was a good match for Lucean. She was the same age and came from a family of equal prominence. Her father, James David Drye, was the proprietor of a thriving tailoring and clothes dyeing establishment, and in the 1890s had helped found a business league and a major charity to serve Wilmington's black community. Drye was also a leading elder at Chestnut Street Presbyterian. The summer before he walked his daughter down the aisle, he had traveled to Los Angeles as a commissioner for the Cape Fear Presbytery to the General Assembly's annual meeting.[28]

In matters of the heart, Lucean and Tena shared a bond that only those intimately acquainted with grief can have. When she was eight, Tena had lost her paternal grandmother Sarah. By the age of ten she also watched death take her mother, Amelia. Although her father remarried in December 1889 and his second wife, Jenny, raised the Drye children, the wound remained. Tena had also experienced trauma as a teenager. In 1893, when she was fourteen, she, her sister Sarah, and her brothers George, James, Oliver, and Edward received news that their oldest brother William had been killed when he fell from a train on his way home from New Bern to visit the family.[29]

Although Lucean and Tena's early introduction to sorrow united them, neither was one to dwell on past afflictions. Of decidedly different personal styles—Tena was outgoing and loved social functions, while Lucean remained more reserved—both looked to the future with a strong desire to explore and to make their presence felt. After graduating from Scotia Seminary in 1899, Tena had spent the summer in Harrisburg, Pennsylvania, with classmate Constance Catus. Her sense of adventure came through clearly on the way home when the two had a long layover on the train in Washington, D.C. Rather than sit idly in the station, Tena and Connie made their way into the unfamiliar city to see another Scotia graduate, Vera Baker, then working in the Recorder of Deeds office. Together the three made a visit to the offices of the *Washington Bee*. By the 1910s, Tena had begun to travel frequently, often without her husband, at a time when a woman alone on a train still raised eyebrows.[30]

In the fall of 1899, after returning to Wilmington, Tena pursued a public role uncommon for a woman. Working on behalf of her father's United Charities Association, she was elected secretary for a one-year term in 1900–1901. The only female officer in the charity's history, Tena regularly interacted with city officials, took minutes at director's meetings, and worked with local business owners to coordinate events such as fairs and boat excursions for the needy. Her position taught her important organizational skills and gave her the confidence to work side by side with men. The following year she left home to teach at Albion Academy.[31]

When Lucean married Tena in 1903, he knew she was a woman modern enough to support the life he had planned, yet conventional enough to be accepted in Presbyterian circles. Although Tena pushed boundaries, her labors were focused on helping the poor, teaching children, and supporting church activities (in fact, much of United Charities' business was transacted through Chestnut Street Presbyterian). Accustomed to the roles that Annie Wood, Susie McRae, and his aunts Jane and Marie Tyson had played at Dayton Academy, Lucean was comfortable choosing a wife with her own aspirations, but whose aims did not step outside the values of education and service so important to those who mattered to him.

As Lucean and Tena after their marriage began to consider where best to pursue their goals, they saw little choice but to look northward. Albion had given Lucean temporary respite, and Tena's family and church had provided her the same. But both recognized the new racial reality in North Carolina. Although Tena had been away at Scotia during the devastating riot in Wilmington, she had agonized from afar for news of her family's fate, and worried especially for her older brother George. A Republican registrar and health officer, George had worked with local Fusionists to elect three black members to Wilmington's ten-man board of aldermen in 1897, and he paid the price. Forced out of government and his life threatened, he soon withdrew from politics to preserve his family's safety.[32]

Lucean was also acutely aware of loosening family ties. His father had already relocated to Aberdeen. Now Nannie was thinking of leaving Carthage. After graduating from Shaw, she had returned to Dayton Academy to become one of its principal teachers. Her heart, though, had taken up residence in Winston, North Carolina. William A. Jones, a fellow student at Shaw who took his doctorate in pharmacy the same year she graduated, had joined his brother John, a medical doctor, there with hopes of establishing a pharmacy. In May 1903, he opened the Jones Drug Store. Once it proved a success, "Will" and Nannie began making plans to marry. They wed in 1904 at John Hall Chapel, and Nannie, retiring from teaching, joined her new husband in his Piedmont home, where she became active in Lloyd Presbyterian Church and the Young Women's Christian Association.[33]

Guy Tyson's family was also on the move. In 1900, George White, disgusted with the political developments in North Carolina, had urged his friends to leave the South. Guy, able to find only poorly paid employment at home, finally heeded his call, moving to Philadelphia in early 1903. Arriving without Marie and the children, he took a position as the foreman of the elevator staff at Wanamaker's Department Store and began looking for housing. Marie remained temporarily in Carthage, where she was desperately needed at Dayton Academy. Annie Wood died suddenly in July 1904, and Nannie departed for Winston a few months later. Moving to Philadelphia, however, remained the goal, and Marie permanently joined Guy in late 1906. Once reunited, the couple settled into the social circles of Philadelphia's First African Presbyterian Church, and it would not be long before Guy obtained better employment with the post office.[34]

Tena's family, too, was despairing of life in the South. In 1905, her brother George accepted the position of in-house tailor at Philadelphia's Hotel Walton, and just months prior to Lucean and Tena's marriage, her sister Sarah and husband Samuel J. Stanley had left for Jersey City, New Jersey, where Samuel went to work as a Pullman porter. In the years that followed, all Tena's siblings, save her brother James, who died from tuberculosis in 1916, left Wilmington for Washington, Jersey City, Philadelphia, or New York.[35]

It thus seems almost inevitable that Lucean would soon find himself looking back down the tracks of the Carthage Railroad to see the water tower of Tyson & Jones and the steeples of Carthage Presbyterian and John Hall Chapel disappear into the distance. Although he must have felt pangs of guilt as he said goodbye to his grandfather, now seventy-six and alone, Lucean was young, newly wed, and eager to begin his own journey. Regret would soon give way to anticipation as he and Tena followed the Stanleys north—to Jersey City.

CHAPTER THREE

A Dream Seeks a Path

When Lucean arrived in his new northern home, he became part of a thriving transportation hub across the Hudson River from lower Manhattan. The eastern terminus for five major rail lines, Jersey City hosted the Pennsylvania, the Lehigh Valley, the Central New Jersey, the Delaware, Lackawanna & Western, and the Erie railroads. As the penultimate leg in the journey for thousands of visitors and suburban commuters that the tracks funneled daily onto ferries crossing the Hudson into "Gotham," it was a perfect Eden for a young man taken with machines. Up and down the river an energetic procession of ferry boats, yachts, barges, steamships, and tugboats churned past the Statue of Liberty. The city's docks brimmed with railroad shops, shipyards, and factories. All beckoned to Lucean.

To his delight, Jersey City also gave him a front-row seat to the nation's most exhilarating new technologies. Less than twenty miles to the west, in West Orange, hummed the laboratories of Thomas Edison, where a staff of experimenters labored to perfect moving pictures and the earliest sound recording devices. To the east, New York's wealthy sportsmen were pushing the new horseless carriage to its limits, trying to turn the vehicle that had so piqued Lucean's interest into something robust and reliable. In 1904, William Vanderbilt established the first Vanderbilt Cup Race on Long Island, drawing an international cadre of drivers to test the designs of the world's most successful automobile builders. The sleek Locomobiles, Panhards, Renaults, and Fiats ogled by racing fans each October could later in the winter be admired by enthusiasts like Lucean at the annual New York International Auto Show in Manhattan.

Long Island was also then emerging as the country's "cradle of aviation." Spurred by the Wright Brothers, flight enthusiasts from every borough of New York came together to form the Aero Club of New York in 1905 and the Aeronautic (later Aeronautical) Society of New York in 1908. Both groups built hangars, workshops, and airstrips on Long Island's flat, undeveloped Hempstead Plains, and staged well-publicized air meets at Morris Park, Belmont Park, Nassau Boulevard, Mineola, and Garden City. Each week Lucean could read in the *Times, American, Tribune, Herald,* and other New York newssheets the exploits of the Wrights, their chief competitor Glenn Curtiss, and pioneers such as François and Bessica Raiche, Henry Walden, Clifford Harmon, Earle Ovington, Leo Stevens, Thomas Baldwin, and a myriad of others whose awe-inspiring, if somewhat wobbly, flights drew Saturday afternoon crowds and reporters.[1]

On occasion, thanks to lower Manhattan's famous landmarks—a magnet for aviators seeking to create a dramatic impression—the figures in the news came into direct view or earshot of Jersey City. The October 1910 international air meet at Belmont Park included a race to the Statue of Liberty and back, attracting clamoring crowds to both sides of the Hudson to cheer on American John Moisant against his British and French rivals. Soon afterward the buzzing of Harry Atwood's plane attracted the attention of those in Jersey City when Atwood circled the towering Singer Building in heavy fog across the water.[2]

Enthralled by the exciting world he had entered, Lucean began to believe that he might share in it. By the time of his arrival, at least two other African Americans were already leading the way. Brooklynite Lewis Latimer, holder of seven patents related to light bulb filaments, had worked since 1885 for the Edison Electric Light Company, which became General Electric in 1896. In 1899, Jersey City's Edward Crabb had been named the Erie Railroad's first black electrical engineer. Local papers also touted the achievement of a host of black inventors, with the *New York Age* noting in 1908 that black Americans had by that date received more than a thousand patents. Editors reserved special praise for prolific innovators such as Granville T. Woods and Elijah McCoy, whose patents encompassed products ranging from telephone devices sold to Bell Telephone Company to railway air brakes and lubrication methods adopted by numerous railroads. Lesser innovators, too, commanded copy. Between 1903 and 1912, the *Age* ran more than two dozen articles on black inventors active across the country.[3]

Lucean would quickly learn, however, the enormity of the task before him, as he sought to develop the skills necessary to emulate those already recognized. *Jersey City of To-day*, a promotional booklet, bragged that "experts in every handicraft" who had "come across the seas" toiled harmoniously in the city's industries alongside native-born workers because skill was "the one language all men understand." The language, though, became garbled when it came to African Americans. White unionists, both native and immigrant, locked arms to protest blacks' entry onto the shop floor. A member of the Brotherhood of Railroad Trainmen voiced the prevalent attitude. Applauding a decision to accept only whites, he claimed that the black worker "should be confined to his place, . . . a 'servant of servants,' not a serf or a slave, but a hired helper." Such sentiments led to an almost complete exclusion of black workers from the city's skilled jobs. In 1910, the Erie's Edward Crabb remained Jersey City's single black electrician, and only 4 of the 2,243 machinists employed by local railroads and factories were black.[4]

Unable to secure a place to develop his abilities or discuss his ideas with others having greater experience, Lucean faced a conundrum. He had no capital with which to finance his inventive pursuits, and prospects were slim for gaining any. Resources his family might have provided had gone up in the smoke billowing from his father's burning sawmill. He also lacked access to northern businessmen who might invest in his ideas. Not being able to envision a clear path forward must have weighed heavily on him as he wrestled over the next decade with how to finance his dreams. Forced to look inward to keep faith in his plans, Lucean would have to bide his time, working gradually toward his goals. He would also have to demonstrate a creativity that encompassed far more than mechanical innovation.

To meet his and Tena's immediate needs, Lucean returned to the Pullman Company. Between 1904 and 1909, he tended sleeper cars on trains in Pullman's New York department. He was not alone. His brother-in-law Samuel Stanley, whom he had followed north, was already a regular on cars headed for Buffalo, and the two men often worked side by side, growing closer from the shared experience. When Lucean left Pullman in 1909 to don the black tie and white jacket of an Erie Railroad dining car waiter, Samuel soon followed. Tena was thrilled to reunite with her beloved sister Sarah (affectionately called "Sadie") when she and Lucean, after address-hopping for several years, began sharing a house with the Stanleys on Kearney Avenue near the Erie's yards. Fellow porter Andrew Davison joined them as a roommate to help pay the bills.[5]

A few blocks from their new home stood Lafayette Presbyterian Church, where Tena and Sarah became leading members. Tena focused on teaching and fundraising and Sarah on the choir. Much like Albion Academy, Lafayette Presbyterian allowed Lucean to stay focused on his aspirations. Founded by Dr. George E. Cannon, who had put himself through medical school on a porter's wages, Lafayette offered a warm welcome to trainmen and their families, often adapting its calendar to accommodate their schedules and repeating services to allow those absent on long cross-country runs to participate. The church provided a steadying and encouraging influence.[6]

The same was true of the railroad, especially after Lucean joined the Erie in 1909. Although reserved, Lucean enjoyed popularity among his dining car coworkers. His ability to anticipate every curve, climb, and dip in the rails between Jersey City and Chicago became legendary on the line, and his tray-balancing abilities, even in the sharpest turns, were "the envy and admiration of all who administered to the wants of the hungry." It was Lucean's ingenuity, however, that sparked real excitement, and many of his fellow waiters deemed him "an inventive genius." Many of them young and educated, they shared his yearning for success, and they bolstered his hopes of overcoming racial obstacles. "Opportunity awaits you at every turn," Chicago-line waiter Cornelius Robinson, less than a year Lucean's senior, heartened his friends, arguing that by developing their minds, they could refute the prejudices of white employers. Reflecting the same surety, and appreciating Lucean's talents, those surrounding him embraced his ambitions and expressed certainty that he would "yet make his mark."[7]

Buoyed by their belief, Lucean seized upon the railroad's limited opportunities, once again maintaining his spirits by taking advantage of the travel and flexibility that train life offered. During his seven-year stint with Pullman, he explored New England and upstate New York. On the Erie's Chicago line, he caught his first glimpses of the forests of New York's southern tier, the mountains of Pennsylvania, the unfurling farmlands of Ohio and Indiana, and the wide boulevards of the Windy City. Working six- to eight-month stretches for Pullman, he took the time he had free to pursue invention. The company seemed unperturbed by his comings and goings. Pullman often laid off workers, only to hire them back months later, suggesting that managers preferred employees to leave during slow periods, saving them money. Capitalizing on these employment gaps, Lucean tasted his first success as an inventor, designing an improved cover for ash carts (used to haul away stove and fireplace ashes). Although he never patented the device, according to one source he sold it to the City of New York.[8]

By the time he began work for the Erie, Lucean had set his sights on something much loftier than ash carts. Captivated by the tiny craft whose motors whined in the skies overhead, he became an early convert to aeronautics. He was soon devouring *Aeronautics, Aero, Aircraft, Air-Scout*, and other magazines, studying their discussions of technical problems and patents and scrutinizing the construction diagrams and photographs of completed machines that illustrated their pages. Through the Aeronautical Society's free bulletin, which reprinted technical lectures given to society members, he gained insight into the thinking of leading authorities on motor designs and the mechanics of flight. Articles such as "Carburetion and Vaporization" and "Gasoline and Lubricating Oils" prompted him to mull in depth the fundamental problems that would shape his later career as an engine designer.[9]

Intensely interested in the mechanics of flight, Lucean began work on the problem of how to allow airplanes to turn in the air without losing stability.

The common approach for biplanes was to install flat, rectangular control surfaces, called ailerons. When a craft flew in a straight line, the ailerons, mounted midway between the upper and lower wings on either side of a biplane, remained in a flat position. To turn the machine, the pilot hand-pulled (or controlled by foot) cables attached to the ailerons, altering their angles. If the pilot raised the angle of one aileron (decreasing the lift under that side of the plane) and lowered the angle of the corresponding aileron (increasing the opposite side's lift), the plane banked in the direction of the upwardly angled aileron. A return to level flight required the pilot to move both ailerons back to a horizontal position. The difficulty with this approach was that the banked wing met air resistance as it rose, tending to pivot the machine from its path. This required the pilot to adjust the ailerons and engage the rudder simultaneously, greatly increasing the likelihood of pilot error.

Between 1910 and 1911, developing an automatic stabilizing device became something of a Holy Grail in the airplane industry. Lucean, joining the quest, developed his "equalizer" as one solution. Patents of the day demonstrate a broad range of such designs, all aimed at adjusting the ailerons in tandem. Some approaches incorporated differential gears, others gyroscopes, and some pendulum-like mechanisms to coordinate the ailerons. We have only a single description of Lucean's device, filtered through the eyes of a reporter, making it difficult to say exactly what his thinking was. We do know, though, that he envisioned a metal ball that moved back and forth, suggesting he may have ascribed to something akin to the pendulum method.[10]

As he sought to develop his equalizer, Lucean ran into the perennial problem of how to finance the testing of his work. On the meager salary of a waiter (as late as 1916 the Erie paid its dining staff only between $25 and $30 a month), he barely had enough spare cash to cover magazine subscriptions and auto and air show entrance fees. He could not afford the specialized tools and materials needed to build models of his ideas, and the purchase of an airplane seemed out of the question. The cost of a Wright biplane ran $7,500, and an authentic Curtiss model commanded $5,000. Building his own plane seemed equally unfeasible. Those who pieced their craft together over time, purchasing parts as their pocket books allowed, eventually spent thousands of dollars as they paid for specialized aviation motors, propellers, and parts, and rented workshop space and storage sheds.[11]

With prospects dim, by 1911 Lucean was also growing restless. He had served on the rails for almost a decade, and travel had lost its luster with repetition. In the words of Erie dining car chef S. H. Gladden, the freedom of the rails could at times seem like an "exile from home in far away lands." This was especially true for Lucean, who now wanted to spend as much time as possible near the technological center of New York.[12]

Outside expectations also pressed on him. Since he was a boy, Lucean had absorbed at the dinner table, in the pews of John Hall Chapel, and at the desks of Dayton and Albion Academies an understanding that the privilege of education came with a duty to serve. Many of Headen's peers had not hesitated to take up the mantle of service. Former Dayton classmates Nathaniel Jackson and Adam David Kelly completed medical degrees and set up practices in Covington, Kentucky, and Laurinburg, North Carolina. Kade Kelly's son Charles, a graduate of Albion Academy, later became a doctor as well, opening an office in Clarkesville, Tennessee. As Headen toiled in the dining cars, Duncan McRae's son James was hitting the books at Howard, also studying medicine. Other Dayton classmates distinguished themselves as educators. By 1910 Charles Foushee had risen to the post of principal at the highly regarded Morningside School in Statesville, North Carolina, and Robert Taylor, after serving as principal for the Dickinson School in Pinehurst, established the Academy Heights School in nearby Taylortown. Offering medical care and education to struggling families in the South, such men commanded enormous respect.[13]

Closer to home, the contrast was starker. Lucean's cousin French, his uncle Henry's son, had by 1912 graduated with honors from Harvard University and Howard Medical School and taken a position as a surgeon at Good Samaritan Hospital in Charlotte. Garnering national attention at Harvard, he won the school's Boylston Prize for Elocution, acted as a distributor on campus of Charles Chesnutt's novels, and in 1907 helped host a visit by Booker T. Washington. Meanwhile, the Jones Drug Store that Nannie's husband Will opened in 1903 had so prospered by 1905 that Washington personally invited him to address the National Negro Business League (NNBL) in New York to explain the secret of his success. Jones and his brother John, a medical doctor, had by 1910 risen to be two of the most prominent citizens in Winston-Salem's black community, together presiding over a wide range of business enterprises and leading church, fraternal, and charity work. They, too, were hosts to Washington when the "Wizard of Tuskegee" visited Winston-Salem in 1910.[14]

The extroverted life of the professional and the organizer, though, was not for Lucean. He preferred what patent examiner Henry Baker called the "patient inquisitiveness, plodding industry and painstaking experiment" of the inventor. Absorbed in his passion, he neglected the call of church and community. No mention of him appears in the *Age*'s extensive coverage of Lafayette Presbyterian's Brotherhood, Christian Endeavor Society, Presbyterian Lyceum, or Altar Guild. Similarly, he made no contribution to the Railroad Porters' and Waiters' Voluntary Subscription Fund, created in 1906 to provide survivor and burial benefits to families of deceased workers. While other Lafayette railroad men spent their free time teaching Sunday school and mentoring Boy Scouts, and while fellow congregants Forrest Hayes and Joshua Gunnell helped found and lead the Voluntary Subscription Fund (nurturing in the process the organization that eventually evolved into the International Brotherhood of Sleeping Car Porters), Lucean pursued what, to the more sober minded, must have seemed an unlikely dream.[15]

And, despite his devotion to his chosen profession, Lucean had not yet met its highest standards. As the year 1911 opened, he had one invention to his credit, but he had not secured the true mark of an inventor's success—a patent. The official seal of the U.S. Patent Office attested to the validity of one's ideas and made it possible to attract investors. It also granted legal protection against those inclined toward intellectual thievery. The Wright Brothers themselves, before patenting their flying machine, conducted their experiments in guarded secrecy to keep others from stealing their ideas. They defended their patents with vigor, often at the cost of the goodwill of the larger aviation community.[16]

As Lucean struggled, he watched innovators around him prosper. In 1910, while he hustled for tips, a machinist in the Erie's shops patented a steam pipe valve which, the railroad announced in its employee magazine, it had adopted. Unable himself to secure mechanical work at the Erie, Headen was forced to experiment in isolation, his intellectual reach limited to developing low-cost items that fit within his budget. It was little solace that many inventors working outside the shops and research facilities of established organizations shared his predicament. As economic historians Naomi Lamoreaux and Kenneth Sokoloff have noted, independent inventors in the age of Edison had typically earned patents throughout their careers. After 1900, however, personal productivity was delayed. Facing stiff competition from well-trained, organized industry researchers, those striving on their own to establish a reputation and raise funds often did not receive their first patents until much later in life. The cause of their deferred achievement, although evident to us now, was not necessarily apparent to those seeking to invent at the time. Most who worked independently, including Headen, likely faced inevitable self-doubt at their slow progress.[17]

Any misgivings Lucean may have felt, however, failed to lessen his resolve. His persistence reflected a personal drive he sequestered deep within himself. Credit is also owed to the influence of mentors and family who had long faced adversity without despairing. As a young man, he had witnessed his grandfather, tested by emotional, financial, and physical losses, bounce back to rebuild his life and home. He had watched his father work steadily toward his goals, despite limited financial resources, and when he lost what he had built, start a new life for himself. Adopting their determined outlook, Lucean came to believe that through perseverance he, like they, could succeed.

Lucean could rely, too, on Tena to provide him social breathing room. Where Lucean was largely absent within the community, she was a leading presence. An officer in the Woman's Auxiliary of the Voluntary Subscription Fund, she also headed one of Lafayette Presbyterian's Sunday school clubs and organized special programs, such as the church's Grand Rally Day. She also worked to finance church projects, helping stage the Ladies Aid Society's annual fair and chairing committees dedicated to increasing revenues. Through her and other lay leaders' efforts, Lafayette was able to purchase a more spacious building at the corner of Summit and Ivy Place in 1909 and to extensively renovate it in 1911–12. Through such efforts, Lafayette soon became "one of the most influential churches among Afro Americans in the city."[18]

Tena's alma mater also benefitted from her unflagging energies. Several members of Lafayette were graduates of Scotia, including Mary Cannon Scraggins, sister of church founder George Cannon. (Another Cannon sister, Clorena, had headed Scotia's Industrial Department during Tena's time at the school.) In 1908, Scraggins, Tena, and the other alumnae organized the Scotia Literary Society. By 1910 this group had founded the more service-oriented Scotia Scholarship Society, which each year paid for one girl from the church to attend the school and raised money to help finance campus improvements.[19]

With Tena's accomplishments lessening the pressure on him to serve, Lucean may have profited similarly from the achievements of other family members. In 1906, Mary Church Terrell, who three years later would help found the National Association for the Advancement of Colored People (NAACP), appeared as a guest speaker at Lafayette in honor of Woman's Day. Terrell and her husband, Judge Robert Terrell, were close friends of Henry and Jane Tyson, working with them in the Bethel Literary and Historical Association and other organizations in Washington. One year after Terrell appeared at Lafayette, George H. White, the former congressman who had served as a delegate to the Presbyterian Church North's General Assembly with Guy Tyson, also arrived to speak. Lucean's connection to such luminaries likely bolstered his status at the church, as he shone in their reflected light.[20]

Through Tena's work at Lafayette, Lucean also gained contacts that would help support his career. Besides teaching classes and raising money, she often played whist with George and Genevieve Cannon, Traverse and Mary Spraggins, and Dr. Walter and Julia Quinn, forging bonds with individuals who would later emerge as important figures in state and national politics and in the black business world. She and Lucean could not afford to join the motor outings the Cannons took with the North Jersey Medical Association Automobile Club in 1911 or jaunts on which they embarked with several New York auto enthusiasts in 1912, but Tena maintained ties with them through church and social gatherings. She also worked alongside prominent women's club leaders, including her friend Lizzie Palmer Berry, president of the Federated Women's Clubs of New Jersey. Berry drew Tena into the orbit of a nationwide network of powerful club women. Through the Presbyterian Lyceum and Christian Endeavor Society, Tena met as well local leaders from outside the church, including Fred Moore, editor of the *New York Age*, and Harold W. Barrett, president of the Metropolitan Mutual Benefit Association. Moore would soon play a key role in giving Lucean publicity, and Barrett would later become an important partner. Walter Quinn, the Cannons, and Lizzie Berry would serve as important character references for Lucean as he sought support for future business efforts.[21]

Tena and others like her kept the network of support Lucean's family had provided him in the South alive, giving proof to an 1892 prediction by Raleigh schoolteacher Tena Nichols, sister of Susie McRae, that educated women would prove a great advantage to others in their communities. For Lucean, that advantage was manifest. Tena not only helped extend his southern network but added new connections to its latticework in the north. Shouldering the demands of "uplift" on his behalf, she allowed him, in the words of Cornelius Robinson, to "strive for that higher plane to which your individuality especially fits you."[22]

As Headen's twenties melted into his thirties, more direct examples of that "higher plane" came into focus. By 1909 a group of black entrepreneurs in Manhattan had begun making forays into the automobile and aviation industries. That year, Benjamin Franklin Thomas, president of the New York chapter of Washington's NNBL, and owner of the well-patronized Hotel Maceo, partnered with Lee Anderson Pollard to open the Cosmopolitan Automobile School. They planned to teach students driving and motor repair. Others, such as J. Albert Robert, who opened a similar facility on West 66th Street, soon joined them. While Thomas and Pollard trained chauffeurs (and Thomas designed and manufactured folding auto tops and other accessories), a few blocks away Ulysses Grant Scott was "doping" engines at the Palmer & Singer Garage for the national Buick Racing Team. Scott soon after appeared at the Aeronautical Society, where he helped members adapt Ford Model T engines to airplanes. In December 1910, he, along with white partner Henry Winter, opened the Aeronautic School of Engineers in Manhattan. Those eager for a peek into their 53rd Street facility, where Scott taught airplane construction and engine mechanics, could then walk eight blocks southeast to view the model of a multipassenger monoplane designed by electrical engineer Charles Ward Chappelle, on display at the First International Aviation Show, which opened at Grand Central Palace that month.[23]

The *Age* closely followed Thomas and Pollard's activities, and in its pages Lucean could track the fortunes of the Meteoric Aeroplane Company, incorporated by Chappelle and seven black businessmen (including Thomas and Pollard) to manufacture his plane. Meanwhile, aeronautical publications and white city papers carried stories on Scott's school, and after his sudden death from pneumonia in February 1911, the *Chicago Defender* memorialized his work. A black-owned publication brought east by porters on the Erie, by 1910 the *Defender* rivaled the *Age* in local popularity, becoming in the words of one writer, "the rage in New York and Jersey City." Thus, the possibility that Lucean missed its front-page, photo-laden eulogy to Scott is slim.[24]

Headen could easily identify with such men, as well as with inventors like Lewis Latimer. They showed the same affinity for innovation. They also shared his artisanal origins. Latimer's grandfather had been a stonemason and his father a paper hanger. Thomas was the stepson of a South Carolina carpenter, and Pollard the son of a Richmond painter. Scott, born in Virginia, hailed from a family of brickmasons and tinners, and Chappelle had himself mastered multiple building trades. Relatable models, these men provided Lucean with inspiration that directly reflected his personal history and ambitions.

Their examples also gave Headen a clear appreciation of what it would take to succeed. Latimer had slipped past the color barrier into Edison's research laboratory only after working in obscurity for more than two decades as a draftsman for other inventors. Even then, many whites resented his presence, and he could exercise only limited control over his work. Chappelle had labored as a building contractor in Atlanta, Chattanooga, and Cincinnati for twenty years before studying engineering through correspondence to become the only black electrician in a Pittsburgh steel mill. A self-taught mechanic, Scott, prior to moving to New York in 1903, had since the mid-1890s operated bicycle and auto repair shops in Newport, Rhode Island, where he catered to wealthy whites such as William Vanderbilt and the other society denizens who summered in the City by the Sea. It had taken Thomas a decade of hotel management to earn the capital needed to open his automobile school, and Pollard had served for equally as long as a chauffeur before joining Thomas. Clearly, Lucean understood, his path would not be an easy one.[25]

As he studied the methods of those in New York, Lucean saw demonstrated the principal options for a black inventor—chase the slim possibility of a position in a corporate environment, rely as Chappelle had on the NNBL model of Washington, in which black investors pooled their resources, or like Scott, build relationships with established white motor and aeronautical experts. At least one of these approaches, he hoped, could help him secure the resources needed to develop his ideas.

Weighing his options through much of 1911, Lucean continued to spend his free time on his equalizer. By the fall he had decided to take a bold step to test it. He turned to Scott's strategy first.

CHAPTER FOUR

A Dream Takes Flight

In early October 1911, Lucean boarded a Pennsylvania Railroad car in Jersey City, traveled through the newly opened Holland Tunnel under the Hudson River to the also newly constructed Penn Station, and then transferred to the Long Island Rail Road. He was on his way to Mineola to ask for flying lessons. The event that likely prompted him to action was a race in late September between James Ward and Calbraith Rodgers. The two were chasing a prize offered to the first person to fly a plane across the country in less than thirty days, and both elected to follow the Erie's tracks to Chicago for the first half of their journey. The railroad's management took pains to aid the flyers. When Ward took off, workers placed white flags on a pilot engine to help him stay on course as he navigated the maze of tracks radiating from the city, and they put similar flags on water towers along the route. For Rodgers, trackmen marked the path by laying large strips of white cloth alongside the rails wherever a track crossing might confuse him. Rodgers repaid their efforts by circling the Erie's Pavonia Avenue Station in Jersey City several times after he crossed the Hudson on September 17 to begin his journey.[1]

Rodgers's sponsor, the Armour Company of Chicago, underwrote expenses for the flight and chartered a special Erie train to follow the aviator. The Pavonia Avenue Station was the point of departure for the *Vin Fiz Special*, named for a new soft drink that Armour hoped to promote. The train included a Pullman buffet-sleeper and an observation car to carry company officials and Rodgers's family, friends, and mechanics, as well as a "hangar" car, painted white to make it recognizable from the air. The latter served as a workshop, and held tools, spare parts, and a Palmer & Singer automobile for use in retrieving Rodgers after each landing. Lucean was not one of the two lucky men chosen to serve the passengers on the *Special* (that honor went to two Pullman employees named Barns and Lawrence). He and others in the dining car department of the Erie, however, stayed informed of the train's progress through regular stories and letters appearing in their employee magazine and in local papers. The Erie's involvement in Ward's and Rodgers's flights allowed the trainmen to feel a part of what would become an historic event when a much-weathered but happy Rodgers at last reached the Pacific Coast.[2]

Lucean appeared at Mineola less than two weeks after Rodgers's Jersey City flyover and experienced for himself there the atmosphere that had nurtured Ulysses Scott. The Aeronautical Society was a unique place, one where a deep passion for the new technology blended with a general disregard for social rules. Unlike its blue-blood Aero Club counterpart, the society encouraged social fluidity. Its egalitarian creed was evident in its first published bulletin, which pledged dedication to "the glorious ideal of each doing his utmost for the service of all and the progress of the art." The bulletin noted that the society had "within its ranks the man of wealth, the scientist, the professional man, the mechanic." As Scott's white business partner Henry Winter (a cabinetmaker and upholsterer's apprentice) later reminisced, "All here were congregated from all walks of life, to experiment, to fly, to swap information, assist one-another, and in some instances to maim or kill themselves." According to Winter, financially flush members provided assistance to promising designers whose ability and desire outstripped their funds, and machine shop owners frequently opened their facilities to others at no cost. In addition, Standard Oil Company provided cheap gasoline and free oil at the field.[3]

The openness of the Aeronautical Society reflected the early fervor that often surrounds technologies before they settle into corporate affairs. It also attracted a range of "free thinkers" ready to challenge social boundaries. E. Lillian Todd, the earliest woman known to design an airplane, rented space in the society's main shed at Mineola, and François and Bessica Raiche flew and offered lessons at the field. In 1909, François, using a motor provided by engine expert Charles Crout, became the society's first member to produce a machine that flew. Bessica, a medical doctor who unabashedly sported knee breeches, advocated for the availability of birth control, and showed a fondness for shooting and swimming, was credited the following year with becoming the first U.S. woman to complete a solo flight. Among those at Mineola when Lucean arrived was also Thomas Baldwin. Not quite a free thinker, he did nonetheless share a broader experience of the world than many of the wealthy scions flying on the island. An orphan, he had run away from his adoptive parents as a teenager to train as an acrobat and balloonist with the circus, later parlaying his aerial experience into a career designing dirigible airships for the U.S. Army Signal Corps.[4]

Some at the Aeronautical Society were also willing to look past racial barriers. Besides Winter, George Russell and Joseph Stevenson, two of the flyers who had worked with Scott, had cared more for his expertise than for protecting the color line, as had Thomas Baldwin himself, who asked Scott to help him maintain his planes. Others at the society, such as Dr. Henry Walden, proved amenable to flying for black spectators. A dentist turned designer, Walden was the first man to build a successful monoplane in the United States. In September 1911, after starting his own exhibition company, he received invitations to fly at state fairs across the country. Walden later noted that there was only a "small number that I could accept." Among those to whom he gave a positive response was the Georgia State Negro Fair in Macon.[5]

The attitudes of men such as Russell, Stevenson, Winter, Baldwin, Raiche, and Walden, and of women such as Todd and Raiche, at last allowed Lucean the opening he had hoped for. He rushed through it. While the identity of his instructor has not been documented, strong circumstantial evidence points to François Raiche. When Lucean arrived at the society, the Raiches were at a turning point in their careers. By February 1911, Bessica reportedly had sunk $10,000 into her hobby, and François likely had spent as much. With funds dwindling, in October 1911 the couple was busy building and selling planes to recoup some of their costs, and François was advertising for pupils. He promised to teach novices to fly a four-cylinder biplane at "terms very reasonable." His terms fit Lucean's budget, and details Lucean adopted to promote himself echo the influence of both Raiches. In January 1912, he showed reporters a medal he had received, inscribed "First Negro Licensed Aviator in the World." Dated November 30, 1911, it had been presented to him, according to the *New York Age*, by the "Francia Aviation Co." at the Aeronautical Society. Of French descent, Raiche had named his school the Française Americaine Aeroplane Cie (or French American Aeroplane Company), and he encouraged a general impression that he was a native Frenchman, although he had been born in Portsmouth, New Hampshire, and had for much of his life gone by the name Frank Wright. When Bessica Raiche first flew in September 1910, the Aeronautical Society had awarded her a gold medal inscribed "First Woman Aviator of America."[6]

In January 1912, Lucean resigned his position with the Erie and announced that he planned to fly exhibitions in the South with his instructor. To publicize the tour, *Age* editor Fred Moore, who only a few months earlier had spoken before the Lafayette Presbyterian Lyceum, ran a front-page article and a photo of Lucean at the controls of a Curtiss-type biplane. The plane fit the general description of a four-cylinder model Raiche had just completed in December. Details of the Southern tour, which was to take Lucean down the Atlantic Coast, are sketchy. The Erie's magazine noted that the destination of the first leg was Richmond, Virginia, where Lucean was scheduled to arrive on December 27. Afterward, black newspapers picked up the trail, although the inability to pay a reporter to follow him and the absence of any strong black press agency for news sharing made their task a difficult one. The *Age* did note

Headen at the controls of a Curtiss-type biplane at the Aeronautical Society of New York in Mineola, Long Island, where he learned to fly in the fall of 1911. Courtesy of the Library of Congress Manuscript Division.

that an early engagement in Norfolk, Virginia, scheduled for the first week of January, was to be for the local white Young Men's Christian Association (YMCA). Aviation history was not to be made that day, however, as the only records broken related to the weather. With temperatures dipping dangerously low, a deep blanket of snow spread over Norfolk and stayed put in the bitterly cold days that followed. Some evidence suggests François Raiche may have pulled out of the venture at this point. The January 20 issue of *Aero* magazine ran an advertisement for a Curtiss-type biplane for sale in Norfolk, and by early February the Raiches had accepted an offer to manage the Standard Aviation School in Clearing, Illinois, southwest of Chicago.[7]

As Lucean trudged on alone by train, not sure where he would obtain a plane for his future appearances, his luck did not improve. "Entire South and Atlantic Coast in Grip of Severe Blizzard," one newspaper announced. By late January, the Baltimore *Afro-American* reported the determined flyer had made it to Charleston, South Carolina. The Great Cold Wave of 1912, however, once again intervened as the Palmetto City, too, fell victim to a rare snowstorm, making takeoff impossible even if he had found a plane.[8]

Discouraged but not willing to give up, by summer Lucean had joined the Raiches at Clearing Field (located on land that today makes up the southern tip of Midway Airport). At work to expand the Clearing facility, the couple was overseeing the construction of two new hangars on the grounds, and Bessica inaugurated a woman's department to attract those of her sex interested in learning to fly. In early June, the *Age* noted that Tena had left by train to visit Lucean, traveling first to Chicago and from there to Clearing. According to the paper, she planned to witness her husband perform at an air show later that month. The exhibition referred to was likely a small one staged by the Raiches and their students, as no official meets were scheduled at Clearing until September, when it served as the site of the Gordon Bennett Cup Races.[9]

One can only imagine what transpired between Lucean and Tena as they discussed the future. Flying was a risky endeavor, both physically and fiscally, and although she wanted to support Lucean's ambitions, Tena could not have escaped worry over them. Her return to Jersey City after the show indicates the couple did not view Lucean's move to Chicago as permanent, but only as an opportunity to make a go of exhibition flying. In November, the *Age* still referred to Lucean as "Jersey City's colored aviator," and in late January 1913, Tena accepted reelection as president of her Sunday school club for the upcoming year.[10]

Meanwhile, Lucean did everything he could to establish himself in the flying world, approaching the organizers of several Chicago events. As he continued his mission, however, he quickly learned the pitfalls of a flyer's life. As new to the task of self-promotion as he was to flight, he was ill prepared for the challenges he faced in the coming months. Unsympathetic spectators, unexpected rivals, reluctant promoters, and hostile reporters would test his fortitude and force him to reassess an effort that, undertaken originally to demonstrate his invention, had soon morphed into a referendum on his personal skills.

Lucean's troubles were already apparent by summer's end. After months of seeking entry into Chicago-area air shows, he complained that he had "received no encouragement from the contest managers." Part of his difficulty was that sanctioned aviation meets rarely featured any but the world's top flyers, and promoters required participants to be licensed. Although Lucean and others often held cards authenticating their training, few had stood examination for the official Aero Club of America or Fédération Aéronautique Internationale certificate that officials desired. As *Aeronautics* magazine noted in March 1912, "The majority of flyers in the U.S. have not bothered to obtain certificates." This included the Raiches themselves. Although they, and many other noted amateurs, had made considerable contributions to aviation, they did not rank among the upper echelon of expert licensed pilots retained by exhibition companies led by the Wright Brothers, Glenn Curtiss, Thomas Baldwin, and a handful of others.[11]

As Lucean's letters to organizers went unanswered or drew negative responses, he quickly learned that breaking into this elite circle was more difficult than he had anticipated. With no license and only two pilots in his corner—New Yorkers who despite their accomplishments were relative unknowns in Chicago—he had little chance of competing for a place in lucrative events such as the Triple City Aviation Meet, organized by the towns of Cicero, Elmhurst, and Wheaton in late May, or the "aviation pageant" staged by the Aero Club of Illinois at Grant Park in July.[12]

Another problem for Lucean was that he did not own a flying machine. This made it impossible to take advantage of the rare openings that would have allowed him to demonstrate his abilities. For example, the international Cicero-Aurora Aviation Meet, held at Cicero Field in September, allotted one day for amateur flyers but stipulated they provide their own craft and offered no prize monies. Lucean had only the Raiches to turn to for a plane, and by September they were experiencing serious difficulties of their own. Faced with stiff competition from instructors at nearby Cicero Field, they struggled to keep the Standard Aviation School profitable. Losing money and prospects, they could ill afford to take chances with the school's three planes without the promise of immediate financial return.[13]

Lucean was also soon to lose the emotional support the Raiches provided. In June, the *Aerial Age*, a newly established publication eager to make a name for itself, set out on a "muckraking crusade" to rid aviation of "near fake flying schools." The magazine complained that many instructors, instead of teaching pupils to fly as promised, instead exploited them as free labor to build airplanes, and it stated it intended to unmask the offenders. The charge targeted a common pedagogical approach that posited a student needed to understand how an airplane was put together before learning to pilot it. By October, the Standard Aviation School, along with close to a dozen other schools, was in *Aerial Age*'s crosshairs, and the publication's muckraker-in-chief, George Bindbeutel, accused the Raiches of being frauds.[14]

Although Bindbeutel, often overzealous in his mission, ruffled many feathers, his allegations reflected a more general movement to professionalize flying. Between 1908 and 1911, a total of 221 flyers crashed to their deaths, and the number increased each year thereafter. Countless others suffered serious accidents or injured spectators through poorly executed antics. Determined to reduce the casualties, reformers sought to restrict all exhibitions, large and small, to those who secured licenses and completed specialized training in stunt flying, and they declared anyone without a license unqualified to teach others.[15]

The incensed owner of the Standard Aviation School filed suit against the *Aerial Age* for $25,000 in damages, but the Raiches, broke and disgusted, had little heart to stay and fight. By late autumn they had decided to quit aviation altogether, departing for Newport Beach, California, where François restarted his law practice and Bessica opened an obstetrics and gynecology clinic. Their move left Lucean without aviation contacts and without a flying field.[16]

In addition to these setbacks, Lucean also encountered Chicago's color line. While his lack of a license had blocked his entry into organized aviation events, membership in the Aero Club of Illinois was denied because of his race. In August, Lucean told the *Chicago Inter-Ocean* that he had applied for admission and been refused.[17]

Making little headway in his efforts, Lucean was forced to develop a new strategy. By late summer he was exploring the possibilities of black audiences. Aware of the Macon Fair's desire to hire a pilot the previous fall, he now learned of promoters in Chicago who were making plans to sponsor a Jack Johnson Gala Day at Hawthorne Race Track near Cicero. The event was to feature the heavyweight boxing champion in his attempt to break an automobile speed record. Other competitors would participate in foot, motorcycle, and auto races throughout the day, with musical interludes as a bonus. With Lucean's arrival, the sponsors, eager to attract spectators, could not resist the novelty of pitting a black pilot in his airplane in a contest around the track against the noted black boxing hero in a Chalmers-Detroit. Thus in early August they offered Lucean his first paying contract in the city. He soon after thrilled at seeing his name headlined in newspapers across the country next to that of the famous pugilist. He could bask, too, in a bit of local prestige, as the *Inter-Ocean*'s publicity prominently highlighted his planned appearance.[18]

By early September, Lucean had gained sufficient recognition to put together a schedule of flights across the Midwest, including events in St. Louis, Kansas City, Louisville, and Memphis. Where he obtained the Curtiss-type biplane he used in his exhibitions is unknown, but the Raiches are a good possibility. Desperate for cash, by September they may have been willing to sell him one of their planes, perhaps on an installment plan, stipulating that he pay them as he earned commissions from his appearances.[19]

Lucean's hopes of turning a profit, however, were quickly dashed. Promotion of the Hawthorne Track flight created enormous expectations and when the Gala Day arrived, thousands who had paid the fifty-cent admission fee shifted restlessly in the stands, eagerly awaiting the clash between their idol Jack Johnson and "L. Arthur Headen, Only Negro Aviator in the World." Headen, however, did not complete the contracted flight, enraging spectators. One "longed to see the promoter of the event" and complained bitterly that "many persons were faked out of the price of admission." In Headen's defense, evidence indicates he may have been injured. *The Freeman*, a black weekly in Indianapolis that printed news from Chicago, noted on its August 10 editorial page that, "An aviator was hurt this week by flying into a chicken coop. You need not tell us his nationality." Jokingly referring to the common stereotype of blacks as chicken thieves, the remark insinuated the pilot was black, and the paper was likely referring to Lucean. The only other African American pilot in the city was Fred Bradford, and *The Freeman* never referred to him in any other than glowing terms.[20]

The Freeman was not kind to Lucean, in fact, in part because of the rivalry he had developed with Bradford. A professional balloonist, Bradford had for many years wintered in Chicago between tours and had developed a close relationship with Sylvester Russell, an entertainment writer for both the *Chicago Defender* and *The Freeman*. When promoters claimed Bradford was to ascend as part of the Johnson gala, without consulting him first, the aeronaut complained to Russell that he had been "advertised to appear without authority" and that he "did not even know who the promoters were." Bradford's justifiable chagrin was heightened by the fact that Lucean had stolen his thunder. When Lucean arrived, Bradford claimed to have just completed his own flight training with the Mills Aviators, and he harbored hopes of making his living through flying. He may have felt that the East Coast upstart, new to his territory and claiming to be the country's sole black pilot, had ruined his opportunity to appear at the gala as a flyer rather than as a balloonist. The rift would sour Lucean's relationship with both Bradford and Russell, and the latter afforded him no further mention in either paper he served.[21]

A month later, Lucean was visited by new troubles in St. Louis when he arrived for a scheduled performance at Handlan Park. To promote his flight, which was to be the highlight of a program to celebrate the fiftieth anniversary of Lincoln's Emancipation Proclamation, he further emphasized the obstacles he had encountered in his efforts. In doing so, he was building on a growing disillusionment among African Americans in the North. As a Lexington, Missouri, resident proclaimed in 1911, "The white race is crushing us on every hand, and if we fail to help ourselves no one else will do it for us, so be a man and fight for your rights." The new mood expressed anger over Jim Crow's creeping presence beyond the South, but it also conveyed the dismay many felt over recent attacks. In Springfield, Illinois, in 1908, would-be lynchers, thwarted in their efforts, had set fire to black homes and businesses and killed two people. Two years later, in 1910, spontaneous riots broke out in cities across the North as whites vented their fury over Jack Johnson's defeat of Great White Hope Jim Jeffries. Determined to fight back, many within black communities had begun to adopt a more militant tone, expressed in a flood of letters to the editors of black newspapers.[22]

The growing push for resistance affected the portraits of heroes that black editors offered the public. Headen had seen an example of this in the *Defender's* portrayal of Ulysses Scott upon the latter's death in February 1911. In its paean to Scott, the paper had taken great license with the facts of his life to fashion him as a man with whom readers could readily identify. It described Scott as a pioneer who had "forced himself to the front" against a tide of Southern white migrants and Irish immigrants in New York, and it praised his racial loyalty when, according to the paper, he had on his deathbed left the secret of a new plane he had invented to a "colored friend" (rather than, one presumes, to his white business partner). "Tho Black He Rose," the paper asserted.[23]

Scott's life was not unmarked by discrimination. In Newport, he had been assaulted by an Irish immigrant, and when he opened the Aeronautic School of Engineers in 1910, his first question to his business partner was how he thought white students would "react to a colored instructor." He had, however, generally enjoyed an equity seldom afforded a black man. Not only did Newport County's District Court heavily fine his Irish aggressor, but Scott also prevailed in other legal matters brought before the court, and he competed against whites without incident in high-profile motorcycle and bicycle races in Newport and New York. Perhaps the best evidence of his acceptance in Newport is found in a 1903 story in the *Newport Mercury*. When a white woman cyclist crashed into his car, the paper reported the story from Scott's point of view, describing his "exciting experience" and praising him for helping the woman. For a white journalist to adopt the perspective of a black man in relation to a white woman in any scenario was remarkable for the time. This more nuanced story, however, did not reflect the experience of most black Americans, and the *Defender* instead focused on the portion of Scott's story that spoke to its readers.[24]

Eager to take on the persona of the more assertive hero, in St. Louis Headen began to tell his story with a new directness, at times resorting to embellishment to make his point. Informing the St. Louis *Globe-Democrat* that "the color line has been drawn even in the air," he claimed that after being refused a place in American schools, he had gone to Le Havre, France, to learn to fly. The statement, though untrue, conveyed the defiance desired by the public. It also drew on the popularity of the French among black Americans, who appreciated the welcome France had given sportsmen such as Jack Johnson and cyclist Major Taylor, an idol in the bicycle-infatuated country. Headen's invoking of France as a land of opportunity resonated with an audience battling segregation and economic hardship.[25]

The strategy, though, backfired. As the crowd waited, excitement built, and spectators found it difficult to concentrate on the featured speakers. Despite ominous clouds looming overhead, eyes repeatedly wandered to Headen as he made a last-minute check of his plane. Before the speeches were done, however, rain set in, quickly escalating into a thunderstorm. Headen decided not to risk the menacing clouds and lightning, and the crowd was furious. Circling the box office and threatening to swarm it, they were dissuaded from rioting only by the organizers' promise to reschedule.[26]

Every aviator of the time dreaded the hostility of incensed crowds, who having parted with their hard-earned money, had little patience for excuses. The previous year, exhibition flyer John Frisbie had crashed to his death after taking off in a damaged machine to placate jeering Kansans who accused him of being a "faker." His experience was not uncommon. In December 1911, Mills Aviators flyer Art Smith had to request the escort of armed sheriff's deputies to escape an upset throng in Bay City, Texas, after rain forced him to cancel a flight.[27]

As a pilot who had appealed to his audience's race pride, Lucean evoked even deeper resentment. He had stirred not only a feeling of being "taken" and the keen disappointment of missing seeing an airplane fly, but also embarrassment. Those awaiting the flight at Handlan Park were well aware of the idea long promoted by whites that blacks were incapable of flying. Popular accounts by white balloonists and aviators unrelentingly poked fun at blacks, portraying them as terrified of the craft that appeared above them, and minstrel shows and popular songs reinforced the notion. Doubtless many white St. Louisans had hummed along to the popular 1906 tune "Let Me Down Easy," enjoying its derisive lyrics:

> Sam Johnson was a machinery man with ideas of his own. . . .
> His bump of inventerology stuck out like a big ham bone;
> He built himself an airship that he cert'ly tho't would fly,
> And said, "I'll show them common coons a new way of living high."

When Johnson's airship crashed, to the delight of white listeners, he exclaimed, "I'll never make no more machin'ry things, till the good Lord gives me a pair of wings."[28]

Blacks in the crowd knew that Lucean (and they) would now endure the slings of racists. It would not be long before the insults began. The *Globe-Democrat*, mocking Lucean and the Emancipation celebration, joked that he had failed to "emancipate" himself from the ground and gloated that he had been unable to "cast off the shackles" of earth. In a similar tone, Chicago's *Aerial Age* titled its notice of his nonperformance, "An Eclipse for St. Louis," and it later labeled an announcement that Lucean would appear in a rain-check exhibition, "A Dark Cloud A Rising." For those at the celebration, Lucean had brought ridicule to what was for many an almost sacred event.[29]

Headen, though, would have an opportunity to redeem himself. Two weeks later, on Sunday, November 3, he appeared at South Kinloch Park to undertake his makeup flight. His appearance was underwritten by Olive Street Terrace Realty Company, a white firm then engaged in building a black subdivision near what is today Ferguson, Missouri. Its owners were eager to jump-start sales of their lots, located not far from the flying field. The lack of any coverage of the actual flight in white papers, which had heavily advertised it, suggests Headen completed it without incident, given that white reporters would not have squandered the opportunity for more fun at his expense. The *Age* reported that the flight had been successful. It also evidently did its job. Over the next decade, more than 2,000 new black residents made the area their home.[30]

Headen's itinerary after St. Louis is not well documented. No confirmation has been found of the flights he had planned for Kansas City and Louisville, although according to the *Age* by late November he was on his way to Memphis, Tennessee. Arriving back in Chicago as winter set in, low on funds and having achieved mixed results, Lucean had to come to terms with the unlikelihood of earning a living (or of financing his invention) through flying. According to one aviation commentator, fewer than 20 percent of those in the profession were able to profit, or even cover expenses, from their labors. Like hundreds of other aspiring pilots dreaming of escaping humdrum jobs to seek the freedom of the air, Headen had underestimated the obstacles. Foremost, he had failed to recognize that in the early 1910s flight was as much an entertainment as a technological pursuit. Although he easily grasped the mechanics of flight, he remained relatively unschooled in the press management and audience mollification skills vital to the showman.[31]

Still, Lucean's efforts were not for naught. His successes had been qualified, but the same was true of most early aviators, and it did not prevent many from embracing him. While the *Defender* ignored Lucean, the *Age* praised him as a positive symbol of achievement. "The Negro is being represented in the field of aeronautics by Lucian Headin [*sic*]," the paper declared with satisfaction, arguing that his actions proved: "Wherever the white man is there also is the Negro." A major East Coast organ, the *Age* had a long reach, and smaller papers from Cleveland to Denver reprinted its coverage of Lucean's activities. The *Age*'s notice also brought Lucean to the attention of Monroe Work of Tuskegee University, publisher of the *Negro Year Book*, which each year chronicled the accomplishments of black Americans. Work noted Lucean's development of his aeronautical equalizer in the 1912 edition, raising him into a national pantheon of black heroes.[32]

The most gratifying affirmations of all, though, would come from home. Will Jones proudly informed the *Winston-Salem Journal* that the now nationally known flyer was his wife's brother, and Albion Academy later relished "the honor of having one of her students become the first colored aviator." At last Lucean stepped out from the shadow of more accomplished family members.[33]

In addition, Headen's time on the road had given him his first opportunity to test financial strategies. He had quickly learned the limits of partnering with a single technical expert. He had also discovered the vicissitudes of appealing solely to black audiences. His attempts to interest investors across racial lines had similarly proved problematic. By the end of his tour, however, Headen was intrigued by this latter strategy. Ironically, just as he assumed a more assertive voice, rejecting the measured tone of Henry Wood, it was toward his minister's methods that he was beginning to gravitate. As he moved forward, he would rely on various financial models, depending on the possibilities that presented themselves, but his struggles on the road had impressed upon him that Wood was right—an individual needed allies in every corner. The next decade would bring that lesson home again and again as he began to formulate a new strategy for invention, one perhaps unique among his peers, but very much rooted in his past.

CHAPTER FIVE

A Dream Finds Allies

"The secret to advancing is to know men," railroad president Martin Hughitt once noted. Henry Wood had demonstrated for Headen the need not only to know men but to know *as many* men (and women) as possible to ensure success. Individuals could help one get a foot in the door, and to find one's way inside, but a diversity of allies provided options should the door suddenly close. Headen had now discovered for himself the value of having a backup plan. As he developed his next ideas, which included a "spring inner tube" for commercial vehicles and a "cloaking device" that obscured small boats from the view of submarines, he remained flexible, taking what opportunities came his way. It was when he began to master the approach he had observed as a child, however, that he prospered. Learning to leverage old connections to good effect, to create new ones, and to draw them together when needed, he would by 1918 establish himself as a well-known figure on Chicago's South Side.[1]

In laying the foundation for his career in Chicago, Headen used as his cornerstone white patent lawyer Wilmot Comfort Hawkins and members of the powerful McCormick family. It is unclear how Headen met Hawkins, but the fellow Presbyterian became a steady advocate. Headen found employment with Hawkins just as his flying career faltered. Working in the capacity of "expert mechanic," he helped evaluate prototypes of inventions Hawkins had been engaged to promote. Although the work was not full time, it gave Headen a foothold in Chicago. It also allowed him to see the inner workings of the patent process up close.[2]

To supplement the income he earned with Hawkins, in 1914 Headen began advertising his services as a chauffeur, an activity he likely had pursued on the side while still in Jersey City. His ad claimed twelve years' experience. Almost immediately, he secured the coveted post of driver for *Chicago Tribune* publisher Robert R. McCormick. This development was likely not an accident. McCormick was the grandnephew of inventor Cyrus McCormick Sr., who had amassed a fortune after developing the McCormick reaper. The elder McCormick and his wife Nettie were leading donors to the Presbyterian Church North, and their generosity had extended to a number of black schools in the South. Key for Headen, their son Cyrus Jr. had taken a particular interest in Albion Academy. A member of the church's Board of Aid for Colleges and Academies, which took Albion under its wing, Cyrus Jr. also opened his personal pocketbook to support the school. In 1884, he joined Albion's board of trustees, attending meetings alongside Henry Wood, then the board's vice president.[3]

Nettie McCormick was close to her nephew Robert, and Cyrus Jr., president of International Harvester, often visited with his cousin or dined with him at the exclusive University Club. Thus, it is likely one of them recommended Lucean to him. They often helped students from the schools they supported find positions, and Headen was at the time living only a few blocks away. Residing on West Hill Street in Near North, just above the northern branch of the Chicago River, his quarters stood across the elevated (El) train tracks from the tree-lined neighborhood known as "McCormickville," where Robert, Nettie, and Cyrus Jr. all resided. Home as well to the Rockefellers, Medills, Fields, and Pattersons, with whom they had intermarried, the area was a sought-after workplace for those in the service trades.[4]

With Headen finding steady work in Chicago, Tena left her sister and friends in Jersey City to join her husband. Soon after her arrival, the couple moved to 1507 South Dearborn Street just below the river. The change in residence reflected Robert McCormick's decision to relocate closer to the *Tribune*'s offices at Madison and South Dearborn. To meet the needs of his employer, Lucean selected a residence a few blocks away so that he could be at the ready for McCormick, who often stayed at work until well after midnight.[5]

Headen's experience working for McCormick differed greatly from that of many who were hired to drive the rich. Edith Rockefeller McCormick, married to Cyrus Jr.'s younger brother Harold, represented the extreme in snobbery. Refusing to address her driver directly, she provided him written directions through her household secretary to avoid interaction. Robert, on the other hand, was on a first-name basis with those who delivered him about town. Once, on a visit to the theater to see *Hamlet* with a chauffeur, he decided not to stay and, only minutes after the curtain rose, stood up and announced loudly, "Come on, Bill, let's go. I saw this play in college."[6]

Headen also found in McCormick someone compatible in personality and interests. The men differed in age by only a year, and both projected the stoic, unemotional demeanor that was the Presbyterian Church's cultural legacy. In 1917, the *Defender* characterized Headen as a "man of very few words," adding, "No one knows where he came from, where he is going or what he knows as he says nothing." In a similar assessment of McCormick, the *Tribune*'s Washington bureau chief described him as "cryptic as the Delphic Oracle." Despite adopting the persona of their childhood religion, however, neither Headen nor

McCormick was inclined toward piety. Headen, in Chicago for more than a year before Tena's arrival, made no attempt to join a fellowship, and McCormick, according to one biographer, "assumed God to be a Presbyterian, but almost never tested the theory by going to church."[7]

Most exciting for Lucean, the man for whom he was now personal driver shared his passion for flight. McCormick was an avid pilot, having fallen under aviation's spell after witnessing the Wright Brothers demonstrate their Wright Flyer at Fort Myer in Arlington, Virginia, in 1908. While Headen was learning to fly at Mineola, McCormick was working on experimental planes in a hangar he built on land owned by his grandfather Joseph Medill in San Antonio, Texas. He spent as much time there as possible, curtailing his visits only when growing responsibilities at the *Tribune* demanded he live full time in Chicago and limit flying to weekends. He and Headen, in fact, may have flown together at Cicero Field (a facility financed by Harold McCormick). According to logbooks in the possession of aviation historian Carroll Gray, an African American pilot flew and took up passengers at Cicero sometime before the field's closure in 1915. McCormick also had Lucean's itch for a patent, eventually receiving seven, most related to printing presses.[8]

No end of topics thus presented themselves as the two sat in city traffic or left on regular weekend trips to Lake Forest. It is unlikely Headen and McCormick ever spoke openly, however, of the reason behind the Lake Forest jaunts, except to agree that they were not to be mentioned. Robert's lover, Amy Irwin Adams, lived in the exclusive suburb, and the circumstances surrounding their relationship were socially explosive. Although Amy had legally divorced her alcoholic husband, Edward Adams, in March 1914, the following August Adams brought suit against McCormick for "trespass" and in September asked that the divorce case be reopened. He also filed an "alienation of affections" suit, claiming, quite correctly, that Robert and Amy had long been intimate before the divorce. McCormick in turn sued Adams for repayment of a $38,000 loan and several notes of smaller amounts.[9]

For Lucean, the legal melee that followed illustrated the precarious position inhabited by a chauffeur, no matter how warm the relationship. A former McCormick driver was arrested in the midst of the proceedings and charged with having extorted kickbacks from garage owners for purchases of oil, auto parts, and tires while in McCormick's employ. Once in custody, he was pulled aside by a private detective and a *Tribune* attorney and grilled for hours to determine what damaging information he might possess on Robert and his paramour. Convicted, he filed his own suit against McCormick for defamation of character, asserting that the charges had been fabricated to find out what he knew, and claiming that McCormick had gone so far as to pay his sister-in-law to spy on him using a "dictagraph."[10]

Now occupying the same seat, Headen was acutely aware that discretion was as much a part of his job as plotting routes, tuning and repairing the engine, and changing tires. In this instance, being a "man of very few words" was a very good thing, and he took pains not to expose McCormick. While Robert and Amy visited on weekends, he discreetly disappeared into Lake Forest's small black community, where he made friends with Clifford and Mollie Sloan. Clifford, a wheelwright and blacksmith, owned the town's leading wagon-making business, and Headen was right at home among its hearth fire, anvils, and wheel loaders. He also talked cars with Sloan, who made frequent trips to Chicago in his six-cylinder Pierce-Arrow, and had been learning to repair engines in hopes of opening a garage.[11]

If this was not enough to make Headen's time in Lake Forest enjoyable, he could also socialize there with recent migrants from North Carolina, including William and Cora Franks, whose daughter Laura was preparing to leave that fall for Scotia Seminary. The Franks and others treated him as a local celebrity. As one resident told the *Chicago Defender*, "Lake Forest is highly honored by having Mr. Headen, the only Afro-American aviator, with us. We feel very proud of him." Since white Chicago society was the most unlikely group to read the city's black newspaper, Headen could enjoy the praise of his peers without threat of giving away McCormick's location.[12]

By the winter of 1915, his circumspection had earned Headen a place of trust in McCormick's household, and it would be to his chauffeur that the newsman turned as he began plotting an elaborate intrigue. In January, McCormick's mother, determined to separate him from Amy, approached Russia's ambassador to the United States to ask a favor. Knowing her son longed to be a war correspondent, she sought an invitation for him to visit the Russian front. The ambassador agreed. Robert was ecstatic and, using political clout of his own, obtained a commission in the Illinois National Guard in order to make the trip as a military man. He then pocketed a $50,000 bribe offered by his mother in return for a promise to stop seeing Amy and boarded a ship for Europe, his valet, a reporter, and a cameraman in tow.[13]

Not to be outdone by his conniving mother, however, before leaving in early February, Robert asked Amy to follow later in the month and secretly meet him in London. He tapped Lucean to accompany her. Per McCormick's instructions, Headen recorded on his passport application that he was going to Europe "As chauffeur to Mr. Robert R. McCormick," and he informed friends in Lake Forest that he was traveling with McCormick to the front.

Headen poses tentatively for the camera while being photographed for his passport application in February 1915. Photo from U.S. State Department records housed at the National Archives in Washington, D.C.

The application date told a different story. It was two weeks after McCormick had sailed but only three days before Amy applied for her passport, revealing that his real job was to act as Amy's driver around the English capital.[14]

For Headen, his studies of English driving rules and etiquette, for the time being at least, would disappointingly go unused. It appears Amy decided she would not need a chauffeur. When she and her sister Ida Small embarked together on the R.M.S. *Lusitania* on February 28, Lucean's name did not appear on the ship's manifest or on that of other ships departing near the time. Likewise, there is no record of a return trip for him, and he was not among the party of the now clandestinely married Robert and Amy when they left England for Malta aboard the R.M.S. *Kaisar-i-Hind* in mid-March.[15]

By May, in fact, McCormick was beginning to regret that he had not brought Headen along. Early that month he wrote his cousin Joseph Patterson, who shared control of the *Tribune*, that the paper's newsreel cameraman had proved unreliable and developed a "big head," and that despite his conceit had shown himself entirely incompetent in using his equipment. The next time he traveled, he declared, he would bring instead a mechanic, "viz. Frank Dean or my chauffeur Arthur Heyden [sic]." He had complete confidence, he wrote, that either Dean (a Chicago garage owner) or Headen could have readily learned the technical aspects of the "art of photography."[16]

While his employer traveled to film the war, Headen remained in Chicago, where a November article in the *Defender* referred to him as a "machinist for the McCormicks" rather than as a chauffeur. The term "machinist" commonly denotes someone who designs and fabricates parts or builds machines. This suggests that when McCormick left for Europe and Russia, Headen may have filled his time by working in the *Tribune*'s machine shop, which built and repaired delivery wagons and serviced a small fleet of cars and trucks used by reporters. Workers in the shop were known for their skill and for their original fabrications, including a "disappearing tower" appended to the back of a specially reinforced Ford Model T. The press of a button activated a jack-like device that raised a narrow platform into the air, lifting a photographer above the crowd to obtain better views. When done, another push retracted the platform.[17]

Whatever the nature of Headen's work at the time, through his employment with McCormick he had already gained regular access to the latest model automobiles, and he reveled in investigating the intricacies of their powerful engines. He was responsible as well for maintaining his employer's other vehicles, having, he later claimed, "tak[en] charge of all machinery, including planes, automobiles and yachts." McCormick offered in addition continued access to powerful individuals. In the coming years Headen would rely on several McCormick family members to help support his career as an inventor.[18]

Wisely, Headen also cultivated other champions, once again drawing on family relationships to do so. One of the first people he had contacted in the city was Dr. George M. Porter. An established pharmacist, Porter was a colleague of Will Jones. The two men often worked closely together as members of the Pharmaceutical Section of the National Medical Association. Porter, described in a local business directory as "one of Chicago's most successful and substantial businessmen," was in a good position to introduce Headen to the South Side's growing black professional class, and he would remain a longtime friend.[19]

While Lucean strengthened ties with Hawkins, the McCormicks, and Porter, Tena once again forged important social and church bonds. After joining Lucean in the city, she surveyed the local religious landscape and settled on membership in the prestigious Grace Presbyterian Church. Located at 3407-09 South Dearborn, its congregation included many of the South Side's most eminent politicians, professionals, and business leaders, including *Defender* publisher Robert Abbott, 8th Illinois Infantry commander John Randolph Marshall (Ulysses Scott's uncle), successful bandleader Joseph Jordan, noted surgeon Dr. George Cleveland Hall, who became the Headens' personal physician, and reformer Ida B. Wells-Barnett. After attending services for several months, Tena approached Grace Presbyterian's minister with a letter from Lafayette Presbyterian to request membership for both herself and Lucean. The couple was officially welcomed into the congregation at the next communion.[20]

Headen would quickly tap into Tena's new circle, which ultimately produced a number of important investors and supporters. More immediately, it afforded him the chance to repair his relationship with the *Defender*. Since his troubled start with Sylvester Russell, the paper's reporters had made no mention of Lucean, despite his exhibition flying. This fact illustrates how important personal contacts were in the world of early journalism, when newspapers had limited resources and staff, and individuals held great sway over content. Without a friendly advocate, Headen had not rippled the *Defender*'s consciousness. At their new church, however, Lucean and Tena became friends with Robert Abbott. Soon after they began to receive regular note in the paper's society pages, where Headen became "Aviator Headen" and Tena a "prominent figure in North Side society and well-known in Chicago."[21]

In 1916, when McCormick left to serve with the National Guard in Mexico, Headen, gaining recognition for his expertise and enjoying increased social ties, was ready to take another risk. He appealed to investors to help him perfect and market a "spring inner tube" for tires. In 1915, Headen had applied for a patent on his new device, and in May 1916, taking a leaf from Charles Chappelle's New York playbook, he attracted to his venture several black professionals. When the Headen Spring-in-a-Tube Company incorporated that month, it listed Headen as president and treasurer, Walter B. Anderson as vice president, and Walter D. Allimono as secretary. Soon afterward James S. Nelson and John F. "Jack" White joined the board of directors.[22]

Each of Headen's backers had sterling credentials. Allimono, a certified public accountant, held degrees from Straight University, Bryant & Stratton Business College, and Northwestern University and was already a partner in a local contracting business and a State Street confectionery. Anderson, along with William Terrell, operated the South Side's most prosperous real estate agency. Headen may have met Anderson through Terrell's previous partner, Walter

Quinn Jr., the son of Lafayette Presbyterian's Dr. Walter Quinn Sr. (the younger Quinn had moved to Chicago a year before Headen), or through George Porter, Anderson's next-door neighbor. James S. Nelson, formerly a stonemason, was now a noted attorney and a major in the 8th Illinois Infantry, and White, a successful pharmacist, co-owned Rankin & White Drugstore.[23]

Renting space at 3701–03 South Wentworth Avenue, the incorporators of the Spring-in-a Tube Company capitalized the new venture at $50,000 and began selling stock. By the following year, however, it became clear that Headen's first attempt to enter the business world was not destined for success. During late 1916, the company brought in cash by selling auto supplies, but it never successfully marketed his spring-fitted tube. The *Defender* claimed that the U.S. Army had ordered tires using his tube for 4,000 trucks, but other evidence contradicts this assertion. Allimono, in his annual report to the secretary of state, dated May 1917, noted that the company "was not now engaged in active business." He did not indicate that he and the other principals had given up their plans, but stated they were only waiting until the tube was perfected. It would be put into production, he wrote, "when ready."[24]

Allimono's choice of the words "when ready" suggests that Headen may have been having trouble convincing the Patent Office of the originality of the ideas outlined in his application. In the patent process, an examiner searches published patents to verify that each element of an inventor's design has not previously been claimed. When challenged on any point, the applicant must clarify how the proposed invention differs from that of his or her predecessors. Headen appears not to have swayed the Patent Office from a negative assessment of his claims, for he soon afterward abandoned his application.[25]

By the time of Allimono's report, in fact, he was hard at work on another project, this one related to the war continuing to rage in Europe. Headen was keenly interested in the growing problem of the submarine. German U-boats posed a grave threat in World War I, as the American public became intensely aware after the torpedoing in May 1915 of Britain's *Lusitania* with 120 Americans onboard. Pondering how to neutralize their menace, Headen spent the winter of 1916–17 designing and testing a unique approach. On May 6, 1917, McCormick's *Tribune* announced that Headen had devised a means of cloaking submarine chasers (small ships designed to search for and destroy U-boats) so that they could not be detected by the enemy. Headen's idea was to bevel glass at calculated angles on its back, with each beveled edge silvered to refract light, so that the glass reflected to an observer only images of sky and water. Placing this specially prepared glass on a boat's hull could mask its presence on the water.[26]

In early 1917, Headen sketched plans for a model submarine chaser fitted with an array of his angled mirrors and began recruiting backers. Having turned to the black business community to fund the Headen Spring-in-a-Tube Company, this time he tested Henry Wood's coalition approach, soliciting proponents from the South Side and Hyde Park communities, as well as McCormickville. Among the earliest champions of Headen's idea was white financier George F. Liebrandt, president of the Lincoln State Bank located at 31st and South State Street. Liebrandt, the son of German immigrants, was a strong advocate for black businesses, including the Liberty Life Insurance Company, of which he was a major stockholder. University of Chicago physics professor Harvey Brace Lemon, representing a faculty consortium focused on developing war technologies, soon joined Liebrandt. He was followed by black composer and bandleader Joe Jordan. Jordan was a prominent member of Grace Presbyterian who had translated early song royalties and European tour profits into lucrative real estate holdings on the South Side and may have viewed Headen's invention as an alternative investment opportunity.[27]

In April, Headen had convinced Jordan and Liebrandt to provide the initial outlay for his model boat and for tests on Lake Michigan to demonstrate the efficacy of his cloaking device. The experiments proved that the craft (measuring 12 by 4 by 3 feet), when moored 200 yards from shore, could be rendered invisible to boats launched to search for it. Confident after successful trials, Headen attempted to interest the military in his "Invisible Boat." Records of the Naval Consulting Board, a joint military-civilian body tasked with reviewing inventions proposed by the public, show that Headen wrote Secretary of the Navy Josephus Daniels on March 5, 1917, offering to demonstrate his invention.[28]

The self-assured, at times presumptuous tone of Headen's letter is worthy of comment, especially considering its recipient. Daniels, a native of Wilmington, North Carolina, had in the 1890s and early 1900s been publisher of the Raleigh *News & Observer*, a leading organ in the "Redemption" movement that brought Jim Crow and disfranchisement to North Carolina. Headen, however, was not intimidated. Adopting the legal language of Wilmot Hawkins, he asserted himself without a hint of nerves. "[M]y mechanical ingenuity," he wrote Daniels, "has devised an effective remedy for this form of modern warfare." "Knowing this INVISIBLE BOAT solves the Submarine menace, and believing you are intensely interest[ed] in safe guarding our Navy and Merchant Marine in times of war, I respectfully submit my proposal to give you or your Naval Committee a demonstration at any time within a period of three weeks." After that time, he stated, he would consider his obligation to offer his invention to the United States null and void. He then laid out his terms. "In the event no favorable consideration is given me," he wrote, "I hold that my duty as a citizen of these United States has been discharged and I am free to deal with any other nation whom may desire to secure this protective device wherever they may deem it necessary to use same."[29]

The tiny Naval Consulting Board staff, swamped with letters from inventors across the country, did not respond to Headen immediately. Thus he sent Daniels a follow-up letter two weeks later. When that too failed to evoke a response, in a move worthy of his uncles Henry and Guy, Headen turned to political channels. The series of events that followed would reveal the wide range of backers he was able to rally behind him.[30]

In late March, Headen approached black minister Archibald J. Carey of the Institutional Methodist Church in Chicago. Noted for his strong Republican ties, Carey recommended Headen to British-born Illinois congressman Martin B. Madden, for whom Carey had heavily campaigned on the South Side. Madden was popular among his black constituents and was known as someone who could be counted on to promote their interests. Headen wrote to Madden on March 31 to ask him to intervene with Secretary Daniels, and Madden subsequently sent a note on April 7, the day after Congress declared war on Germany, requesting that the navy consider Headen's invention. On April 17, Daniels responded, instructing Madden to inform Headen that he should submit a more detailed description of his plans for consideration. Headen then supplied a blueprint through newly seated Illinois congressman Medill McCormick, Robert McCormick's older brother. Although the exact role Medill McCormick played thereafter is unclear, his interest in Headen's invention is not surprising. He would soon be exchanging testy correspondence with Josephus Daniels charging the navy with paying too little attention to the issue of building and outfitting submarine chasers.[31]

When no further action was taken on his device, Headen, who often struggled to see the virtue in patience, appealed directly to "his old friend, Mrs. McCormick" and to George Liebrandt for help. The *Defender* reported that Mrs. McCormick responded by enlisting the aid of Julius Rosenwald, owner of Chicago's Sears & Roebuck Company. Nettie McCormick and her children often worked with Rosenwald on philanthropic projects, and Rosenwald was then a sitting member of the Advisory Committee to the National Defense Council. On her recommendation, Rosenwald personally interviewed Headen and was sufficiently impressed to approach fellow committeeman Howard Coffin. He persuaded Coffin, who was dually a member of the Naval Consulting Board, to provide Headen a letter of introduction to Daniels's private secretary, Captain Frank Smith. Meanwhile, George Liebrandt worked through Illinois senator James H. Lewis to obtain a meeting with another Captain Smith, this one William Strother Smith, the Navy Department's liaison to the Naval Consulting Board. On May 1, Senator Lewis's office officially requested the meeting.[32]

The political lubricant applied by the McCormick family, Rosenwald, and George Liebrandt succeeded in unsticking the bureaucratic gears. In late April, Headen traveled to Washington, accompanied by Liebrandt and Joe Jordan, to present his idea in person to William Strother Smith. Excited by the possibilities of what he saw, Smith declared the device feasible and referred it to the Naval Consulting Board. On April 28, the board, one of whose members was Hudson Maxim, president of the Aeronautical Society of New York when Lucean learned to fly there, recommended that Headen transport his model to the Navy's Great Lakes Naval Training Station outside Chicago for testing.[33]

Accompanied to Great Lakes by professor Lemon and Jordan, Headen met with the station's commandant, William A. Moffett, on Friday, May 5, and they agreed to a demonstration the following week. The test succeeded. Moffett wrote Josephus Daniels that the model had yielded "excellent results" and that he believed the mirrors could be applied to a ship's hull to effectively reflect its surroundings without producing glare, allowing the ship to remain unseen. He then recommended that Headen's idea be examined more closely by the Naval Consulting Board. A few days after Daniels received Moffett's letter, Headen elatedly accepted an invitation back to Washington. There he made his uncle Henry's home his base for the next several weeks while he awaited a final decision by the board.[34]

As Headen paced in anticipation, members of the Naval Consulting Board weighed the advantages and disadvantages of developing a beveled-glass hull covering. Ultimately, the board decided to forego investing in Headen's invention. In a letter dated June 18, Daniels pointed out that the weight of the glass was a drawback and that the board felt it could protect chasers sufficiently through cheaper means already available. Daniels was alluding to "dazzle painting," in which ships' hulls were painted in irregular, intersecting geometric patterns to make it difficult to determine their heading and distance. Although this means of camouflage did not protect a vessel from being seen, in the navy's thinking the downside of increasing a ship's load trumped the benefits of invisibility. As a history of the Naval Consulting Board later noted, the navy believed "it was better to lose a few ships" than to "reduce the carrying capacity" by adding weight. Headen thus joined the ranks of the 110,000 other hopefuls whose ideas were rejected by the board during the war.[35]

It was never in Headen's plan, however, to give up. He had advanced into the tiny elite (0.1 percent) whose inventions were deemed "of requisite standard" to be seriously considered, and he still had every belief in his device. Returning to Chicago, he responded to Daniels with the same lack of deference he had assumed from the beginning. Writing that he had not been returned plans and specifications he had earlier submitted to Frank Smith, he directed Daniels to "Kindly look into the matter and have him send them to me *immediately*."[36]

Headen then began to explore his options. His initial letter to Josephus Daniels indicated that he viewed not only the United States but all the Allied Powers as potential buyers. Raised on Henry Wood's tales of traveling abroad, he had long been aware of the opportunity that beckoned beyond America's shores, an awareness that had been reinforced by years of reading editorials in the *Age*, the *Defender*, and other black publications about the racial openness of Paris, London, and other European capitals. He himself had appealed to the popularity of the French to promote his Emancipation Day flight in St. Louis. Now, two years after his aborted trip to England, he revived his hopes of seeing London.

The timing was auspicious. In the summer of 1917, the British were desperate to solve the submarine problem. Germany had begun carrying out "unrestricted submarine warfare" against civilian and military vessels in British waters, and casualties were mounting. In April 1917 alone, the Germans sank an astounding 354 ships, while the Royal Navy managed to eliminate only two enemy submarines. Fearing the U-boat could turn the tide of the war, British officials were scrambling for answers. While Headen was still in Washington, a delegation of British and French scientists, including members of the British Admiralty's Board of Invention and Research (BIR), had arrived to discuss antisubmarine measures with the Naval Consulting Board. In a report of the visit, Sir Ernest Rutherford noted that the delegation had met on the trip with the board's leading scientists as well as "numerous inventors of the general public."[37]

Headen was undoubtedly among this number. That summer he began seeking financial backing to help him market his invention to the British. He turned to Wilmot Hawkins for help. Hawkins, then working for the Strauss Yielding Barrier Company of Chicago, obliged, presenting the idea to chief operating officers Charles Cook and Joseph Strauss. Strauss, who also owned the Strauss Bascule Bridge Company, would later become the celebrated builder of San Francisco's Golden Gate Bridge. At the time, however, he was a businessman looking for opportunities, including the wartime government contracts that an invention such as Headen's promised.[38]

A confident Headen, encouraged by the British Admiralty's interest in his camouflage mirror array, sits for a second passport photo in 1917. This time he would put his passport to use. Photo from U.S. State Department records housed at the National Archives in Washington, D.C.

In late September, the company agreed to finance a trip by Headen and Hawkins to England. Strauss informed the Bureau of Citizenship in Washington that the two would be traveling on business "pertaining to our present war with the central powers" with the "purpose being to make a demonstration to the British government." Headen was to be well compensated for the trip, receiving a salary of $50 per week beyond his transportation costs and expenses. Sailing aboard the S.S. *Lapland*, Headen, Hawkins, and Hawkins's wife Anna, who accompanied them as secretary, arrived in England on October 9.[39]

The trio spent six weeks abroad, during which time Headen was afforded space in an Admiralty office overlooking Trafalgar Square, and he carried out demonstrations of the "Headen system of mirror Camouflage." The course of invention, however, seldom runs smooth. Just as Headen made his pitch, the BIR fell victim to a reorganization. Between November 1917 and the end of January 1918, many of the duties of the BIR, including the examination of new inventions, were reassigned to a new entity in the Admiralty—the Director of Experiments and Research (DER). In the shuffle, as the BIR and the DER worked to clarify their respective roles, decisions on Headen's and others' projects were delayed.[40]

The Admiralty, however, was interested enough in Headen's means of camouflage and in his mechanical skills that it acted to keep him within its orbit while considering his invention. Headen was thrilled when officials offered him a position in the recently militarized British Ministry of Shipping. Assigned to the ministry's New York headquarters, he was tasked with inspecting and testing vehicle and marine engines. Before posting Headen to his assignment, the Admiralty may have sent him to Pau, France, for the specialized training that would be needed for the position. Headen would later state that he had studied mechanics at Pau.[41]

Concrete action was finally taken on Headen's idea in September 1918. The trigger for the revitalized interest was a mission led by Sir Richard Paget to the United States over the summer. Between May and July, Paget and his team met with members of the Naval Consulting Board and the British Embassy's naval attaché in Washington, as well as war mission personnel in New York. Almost immediately after his return to England, Paget produced BIR Report No. 14,966d, which outlined his personal assessment of Headen's camouflage method. Although the report itself, like the bulk of BIR reports, has not been preserved, it is known to have been positive. In November 1918, E. W. Nelson of the Admiralty noted that Headen's invention had, based on the report's recommendation, been referred to the DER for further development.[42]

That development, however, would never occur. Just as his idea received Paget's blessing, the war abruptly ended. Caught unawares, the Admiralty was forced to shift its energies to peacetime concerns, leaving experiments to hang in the balance. As the Admiralty's Albert B. Wood noted, the signing of the Armistice effectively brought wartime research to a halt, as funding, even for the highest priority projects, quickly "dried up." Only months after the hostilities ceased, the research station that Wood led, as most others, was permanently closed.[43]

Although Headen's demonstration to the Admiralty did not ultimately produce the results he had hoped, his time in England reinforced his belief in his abilities. Crucially, it also raised his sense of possibilities. On British soil, he had felt the first inkling of what life without American racial restrictions could be like. He reveled in it. Eleven Londoners were killed the day after he boarded his ship for the journey to England, and the threat of zeppelin attacks loomed over London throughout his stay, but it was not the dangers of war Headen remarked upon in his first letter home to Robert Abbott. As he enjoyed the liberty of a culture less dominated by the dictates of race, it evoked in him a sense of his full humanity. "A man is a man for a' that," he wrote after touring the city. It was no accident that the words he chose were from Robert Burns's 1795 Scottish paean to the equality of all men.[44]

Headen's time in England also enhanced his public stature at home. When he arrived back in New York in the late fall of 1917 to await a decision on his invention, Harlem had embraced him. A black man whose intellect had drawn the respect of some of the world's most powerful military officials, he became a hero to many in the community. Invitations flowed in. Using the home of former Jersey City housemate Andrew Davison, now a local café owner, as his base, he set out to make the public-speaking rounds, appearing first in December 1917 before the congregation of St. James Presbyterian Church, where he described "his recent experience in London and Europe." He later spoke before the church's Brotherhood.[45]

When Robert Abbott visited the *Defender*'s New York offices the following summer, the paper's staff treated Headen to the theater and dinner alongside Abbott, then called upon him to address the group. The next day Headen invited Abbott to accompany him as his guest to "Villa Lewaro," the newly built Irvington-on-Hudson mansion of black hair and cosmetics entrepreneur Madame C. J. Walker. Walker and her daughter A'Lelia often entertained Harlem society, and Headen clearly was now considered part of it. Tena must have been pleased at her husband's new status in the social realm in which she thrived, and she joined him regularly in New York, taking advantage of the opportunity to visit her brother George, who had recently relocated there. August 1918 would find Lucean and Tena motoring to Philadelphia, where now not only Guy and Marie lived, but Sarah and Samuel Stanley as well. Stopping along the way in West Chester, Pennsylvania, the Headens stayed with building contractor Joseph Gibbs, whose daughter Alberta Johnson was an acquaintance in Chicago.[46]

Enjoying his new popularity, Headen relished the role of hero. He had first demonstrated this penchant in 1912 as an aerial showman. Now, even more than before, he sought recognition, demonstrating a willingness to stretch the truth, or at least to allow others to do so, to achieve it. Reporters from the *Defender* and *Age* published claims that Headen had been commissioned a lieutenant in the Royal Air Force (RAF), and that the RAF had stationed him on Long Island to train aviation recruits in the use of his earlier airplane equalizer. Both claims were fantasy. The RAF has no enlistment record for Headen, and it maintained no training facility on Long Island. The resulting press coverage, though, boosted Headen's growing celebrity, and he made no attempt to clear up the misconceptions. "Lieutenant" had a nice ring to it, and Headen, now forty years old, seems to have enjoyed the veneration it stirred.[47]

War's end, though, forced Headen to pack for home, and once again to face the challenge of how to parlay his skills and prestige into a conduit for his experiments. He had learned much from his application of Henry Wood's coalition approach. It had proved a vehicle to social prominence, and it had gained him temporary entry into institutions from which he otherwise would have been excluded. Going forward, however, he had few hopes of joining the white inventors who were to become the vaunted "industrial scientists" of DuPont, Ford Motor Company, and Bell Laboratories. Idiosyncratic allies and the exceptional demands of war had cracked the door open, but the conflict's end firmly closed it. As the experience of Lewis Latimer, the only black inventor ever to work for Edison, illustrated, men of color were a rare presence in the collaborative research world that was increasingly shaping American invention.

Still, Headen was not ready just yet to discard Wood's model. Despite its limits, its vulnerability to changing circumstances, and his immediate inability to create a new alliance, he had come to appreciate the approach's potential. As he built a new career for himself in the 1920s as an automotive designer and entrepreneur, he would temporarily return to a full reliance on black capital. It would not be long, though, before he again was taking steps to attract a more expansive support base. The results would be impressive.

CHAPTER SIX

A Dream Becomes a Company

When Headen returned to Chicago in early 1919, he announced the opening of the Headen Repair Shop, an auto garage located near the corner of East 36th Street and busy South Michigan Avenue. Slowly building up his business, he had a larger goal in mind. He hoped to raise the capital needed to produce his own automobile. It did not take him long. By 1921 his thriving firm had generated profits sufficient to launch the Headen Motor Company, the first manufactory in the country to produce both a body and a motor developed by an African American. The firm, which between 1921 and 1924 built and sold a touring car, a sport model roadster, and a racer, elevated his national stature, especially after he began to travel extensively to market his cars and to assemble a broad coalition of investors. The support he garnered from multiple sources and the press coverage his actions sparked made him one of the most influential voices on the automobile in black communities across the country.[1]

Pulling together necessary funds for the Headen Repair Shop, however, proved a challenge. To supplement his own savings and monies that Tena earned by taking in roomers, he seems first to have sought support from a Hampton Institute classmate of Robert Abbott. Just days after the Armistice was signed on November 11, instead of heading home to Chicago from New York, Headen traveled to Richmond, Virginia, where he spent a week with Walter D. Jones. Jones was a prominent wheelwright and carriage builder in the city and had recently helped revive the local chapter of the NNBL. Earlier, he had been among those who founded the Young Men's Investment League in Richmond, and he often sank profits from his firm into entrepreneurial efforts. Although no records confirm a financial connection (paperwork for Headen's incorporation of his new garage has not survived), Headen's trip is otherwise difficult to explain. He had no family, church, work, or other ties to Jones, and he had no known personal connections to Richmond. If Jones did become a backer, it would represent an unexpected flow of black capital from South to North.[2]

To collect the remainder needed, Headen resorted to more drastic measures. December found him in Monroe, Michigan, engaged in the illegal, if increasingly common, practice of bootlegging. Long before national Prohibition took effect in January 1920, many states had outlawed the sale of alcohol. Michigan joined them on May 1, 1918, and the state legislature's action opened opportunity for Headen. While Michigan had gone dry, its neighbor Ohio had not, and a thriving trade in contraband liquor soon kept the newly paved Dixie Highway between Toledo and Detroit brimming with cars. Headen joined the steady stream of drivers ferrying illegal supplies northward for quick payoffs. His career as a "rum runner," however, was short lived. Two days before Christmas, the Michigan state constabulary pulled him over outside Monroe, just twenty miles north of Toledo, and charged him with carrying ten gallons of whiskey concealed in a false gasoline tank. Like most of the more than four-thousand bootleggers arrested in the county in the ten months between May 1918 and February 1919, he paid a high price. On Christmas Day, and for the two months that followed, he shivered in the damp, vermin-infested Detroit House of Correction.[3]

Fortunately for Headen, no whiff of his arrest, though published in several Michigan newspapers, made it into the Chicago press, and he likely disguised his absence from the city as an extended fund-raising trip. By spring, he was home and, rebounding quickly, finally scraped together enough money to finance his small enterprise. He soon also secured a favorable spot for it. Located in a converted carriage house of a former Michigan Avenue mansion, the garage stood at the southernmost boundary of Chicago's three-mile automotive district, which stretched down South Michigan from 12th to 36th Streets. From its beginnings, it catered to the South Side's black middle class, which had expanded during the war years. The promise of munitions, stockyard, and factory jobs, combined with Jim Crow and the appeal of fiery editorials in the *Defender* encouraging black southerners to abandon the states of the former Confederacy, had drawn a flood of migrants to Chicago, almost tripling the city's black population. The influx created a bustling South Side city center, later known as Bronzeville. This developing metropolis was anchored by the *Defender*'s offices on South State Street. Called the Black Wall Street, South State and the thoroughfares that surrounded it were filled with nightclubs, restaurants, theaters, tonsorial parlors, drug stores, grocery stands, and five-and-dime stores that sprang up to serve the needs of the new arrivals.[4]

Along with cooks, factory laborers, domestics, laundresses, and bootblacks came barbers, doctors, shopkeepers, dentists, lawyers, real estate and insurance brokers, teachers, and undertakers. This burgeoning professional elite had money to spend, and "motoring" quickly gained popularity. In 1915, the *Defender* announced proudly, "Dr. A. W. Williams Purchases Big Car." By the beginning of the 1920s, many who could afford it had joined Williams, clambering into Model Ts, Pierce-Arrows, and Studebakers to picnic in the forest preserves on Chicago's outskirts, to visit family and friends, and to vacation in emerging all-black resorts such as Lake Michigan's Idlewild. Courting this element, Headen Repair built a steady clientele.[5]

Neither his customer base nor the enduring status he had earned from his wartime activities, however, could protect Headen from the specter of racial hatred that ever loomed over his life. Less than a year after he first hoisted open his new garage's doors, trouble appeared outside them. In July 1919, a bloody riot rocked the South Side, putting Lucean and Tena in danger and jeopardizing the new business. The riot capped a wave of postwar racial aggression in the "Red Summer" of 1919, which saw more than twenty major conflagrations, and many minor ones, break out across the United States. The violence in Chicago did not surprise Headen. The storm clouds had been gathering for months. The day he arrived in Richmond, the *Richmond Planet* had greeted him with headlines announcing a deadly conflict in Winston-Salem. Thwarted by police from lynching a black prisoner, a furious mob had turned its sights on his sister Nannie's neighborhood. Five lay dead before National Guard troops brought in from nearby Charlotte and Greensboro could stop them. It would be these soldiers who rescued a man shot while he was walking "half way between the depot and the Jones Drug Store."[6]

Worried for his sister and brother-in-law, Headen was also alert to the growing threat in his own city, as frictions wrought by wartime changes gave rise to conflict. White Southerners and European immigrants had streamed into Chicago alongside blacks, all looking for work. Many of them resented competing for jobs and living space with those they considered inferior, and they were determined to assert Jim Crow. African Americans, especially soldiers from the 370th Infantry, recently returned from risking their lives to defend democracy in France, were equally resolved not to let inequality take root. Some began to openly challenge whites, competing head to head for jobs, going to the ballot box, and balking at social norms devised to belittle them. Whites fumed, and gangs, often Irish or Italian, assaulted blacks on streets and in alleys. Others dynamited the homes and businesses not only of black residents but of whites willing to rent to black tenants. By mid-1919 such attacks had become almost weekly occurrences.[7]

Focused on getting his new business up and running, Headen tried to stay calm in the midst of the deteriorating situation. Whatever personal peace he found, however, did not last long. In mid-July, word reached Chicago that a racial melee had broken out in Washington, D.C. For three nights a group of white army and navy veterans, incensed by a rumor that a black man had assaulted the wife of a white sailor, roamed through black neighborhoods across the city, brutally beating random men, women, and children. On the third day, blacks began to fight back, taking to the streets and shooting from cars. The conflict raged for another two days. As he had feared for Nannie, Headen now dreaded harm to his uncle Henry and aunt Jane, remaining uneasy until he learned that they were not among the four killed or the thirty hospitalized during the riot.[8]

A week later, the storm finally broke in Chicago. Tensions peaked on July 27 at Lake Michigan's 29th Street beach, a few blocks northeast of Lucean and Tena's East 38th Street home. The mayhem began when a group of black bathers arrived at the whites-only beach and were pelted with rocks. After they retreated, a white man, still angry over the defiance of segregation's rules, walked down the shoreline until he came upon a group of unsuspecting black teenagers frolicking in the water. Considering them too close to white territory, he heaved bricks toward them until he struck fourteen-year-old Eugene Williams in the head, knocking him unconscious. Williams drowned, and the chaos that followed cost another thirty-eight people, two-thirds of them black, their lives. It also reduced more than a thousand black homes and businesses to ashes.[9]

Like his neighbors on East 38th Street, Lucean could do little but lock his doors and strain to hear the sounds of peril above the thumping of his heart. His street and those close to him became a battleground as whites drove through shooting randomly from their automobiles. In the riot's second night, a white gunman and a black knifeman found victims only two blocks from his and Tena's doorstep. A white insurance agent making his rounds also soon lay dead, killed by a black mob gathered on a nearby corner seeking retaliation for black deaths across the city. For seven long days the riot kept Lucean in a constant worry. Not until the sun rose on the hot summer morning of August 2 would the siege finally end, allowing him to breathe freely again. Emotionally exhausted residents surveyed the riot's devastation, dazed but counting themselves lucky that they had been spared physical harm. Many, however, mourned the death of friends. Grace Presbyterian's congregation remembered Oscar Dozier, who had been viciously clubbed and then stabbed to death while walking home from work.[10]

After the riot, Lucean, like others on the South Side, was faced with picking up the pieces. Determined not to be defeated, he turned his attention back to his business, where he found an unexpected silver lining. His garage, tucked behind a former mansion that fronted Michigan Avenue, had escaped notice. In the still tense environment of the post-riot period, it would thrive. The explanation was simple. White vindictiveness lingered long past August, and many white businesses refused service to black patrons. This included many repair shops and filling stations along South Michigan. Dislodged customers rolled up to Headen's door. Regardless of whether his new patrons were responding to immediate necessity or to the urgings of men like R. W. Hunter—a local bank owner who hoped the riot had "taught the race a lesson" and advised blacks to support race-owned businesses—Headen and others like him benefitted. The new enthusiasm for self-help efforts that followed in the wake of the violence catalyzed the chartering of the city's first black-owned state and national banks less than two years later.[11]

With growing income, Headen hired several talented mechanics who would help him increase his business. By late August he had put his best worker, Henry J. Poindexter, in charge of the garage's day-to-day activities. When Poindexter left five months later to start his own concern, Headen replaced him with Fred Walls, an equally capable manager who continued to pad the firm's profit margin, so much so that by early 1921 Headen had begun searching for a larger space. Convincing Edward G. Shaw, a local black grocer, to provide an infusion of capital, he began to plan new services. When Shaw came on board, Headen moved his garage to 4007 South Wabash Avenue, six blocks away. The new Headen & Shaw Machine Works, which opened in March 1921, occupied two floors, employed twenty-two mechanics, and offered not only repairs but auto painting and twenty-four-hour towing assistance.[12]

The name that Headen chose for his expanded concern signaled his intention to operate more than a garage on Wabash. Besides grease pits, winches, and tire mounters, his new works housed machine tools needed for the construction of automobiles. Although by this date the assembly line had established Ford Motor as the dominant force in American auto production, opportunity was still open. Hundreds of plants, large and small, hummed across the country, housing the creative efforts of manufacturers that ranged in size from direct Ford competitors such as General Motors, Cadillac, and Packard to firms like the Wizard Automobile Company in Charlotte, North Carolina, producer of several hundred cars per day, to smaller firms such as Atlanta's Hanson Motor Company, which turned out only five. Small, independent constructors were feeding a steady demand across the country for autos that could stand out. Many drivers valued speed and luxury over the slow-but-steady utility of a Ford "Tin Lizzie." Others aspired to the status that owning a unique vehicle conferred. Appreciating the desire for more personalized cars, Headen hoped to join the effort to supply them.[13]

Headen, in fact, was not the first African American to recognize the demand for custom cars. He was preceded in the manufacturing business by Fred D.

Patterson, of Greenfield, Ohio. In 1915, Patterson expanded his father's long-standing carriage-making business to produce both a Patterson-Greenfield roadster and a touring car, and he sold his cars until 1918. Patterson's interest seems, however, to have been primarily business rather than mechanics. He did not equip the auto bodies his factory produced with a motor of his own make, instead purchasing the engines he used from the Continental Motor Company.[14]

Headen likely knew about Patterson. The *Defender* had publicized the manufacturer's first cars in 1915 and had run a follow-up story the next year. His immediate inspiration, though, seems to have been a local white designer named Adolph Monsen. Monsen had raced in Chicago for several years before moving to Indiana in 1918 to begin building his signature ReVere, one of the highest performance road cars of the day. Headen bought a ReVere in 1921, paying $3,850 (five times the price of the most expensive Ford) for the privilege. With his purchase Headen became the owner of one of fewer than 200 ReVeres sold between 1918 and 1926, when Monsen's company folded. The purchase revealed the profits Headen's garage was generating, as well as his growing love of speed. Itching to test the capacity of the ReVere's four-cylinder Duesenberg engine, Headen drove it south in June to attend the Indianapolis 500. He was accompanied on the trip by friends George Porter, Eddie Williams, Dr. J. Pratt, and *Defender* general manager Phil Jones. The camaraderie the men shared was evident in the nicknames they selected for each other en route, including "The Secretary," "Lookout Pratt," "Good Rubber Eddie," and "Silent Jones." Headen would earn his own moniker, "Speedway Headen," after the race ended. Convinced his ReVere could outdo the cars they had observed blurring by, he took to the empty track and maintained a reported speed of eighty-four miles per hour for two full circuits, an impressive feat for both man and machine.[15]

Hoping to surpass the ReVere, in reliability and endurance if not in swiftness, Headen began sketching plans for a touring car. In the fall he recruited partners for a new company to produce the "Headen Pace Setter." To fund its manufacture, he cast his net wide, starting locally but soon looking beyond Chicago to amass a national army of supporters. Over the next three years the roster grew impressively, and it included men and women from almost every walk of life. They would be black and white, young and old, northern and southern, rich and poor, churchgoing and (in the case of at least one) socially marginal.

Headen first obtained backing from two white Chicagoans, Charles Stretch and Patrick J. Dwyer. Stretch, a veteran North Side salesman, knew a marketable idea when he saw one. The success of Headen's repair shop had demonstrated the profits to be made from black auto enthusiasts. Dwyer, a resident of the West Side, represented an entirely different kind of investor. The son of Irish immigrants, he was part of Chicago's notoriously corrupt machine politics. Secretary of the Eighteenth Ward's Regular Democratic Organization and clerk of the Chicago Election Commission, he also had ties to organized crime. Between 1918 and 1923 Dwyer was indicted for burglary, safecracking, and murder, though he spent no time in prison for any of the charges. Dwyer's support of Headen could be explained as a move to curry black votes on the South Side, traditionally solidly Republican, or even an attempt to use the business as a means to launder ill-gotten monies. Either way, for Headen, inclusion of Dwyer likely represented his lack of other options and the pressure small business owners often felt to accommodate the demands of powerful gangsters.[16]

The initial business plan for Headen Motor Company was to sell used cars and auto supplies to South Side drivers to generate income while Headen built a prototype of his Pace Setter. The company hoped eventually to sell the car to black society leaders across the country. Just as the middle class had expanded in Bronzeville, it was growing in urban areas elsewhere. New York, Philadelphia, Detroit, Kansas City, Los Angeles, Denver, San Francisco, Seattle, Richmond, Houston, Tampa, Durham, Atlanta, and a host of other cities witnessed a boom in the building of business districts to serve segregated neighborhoods. Although the well-to-do in these locations never exceeded a tiny percentage of the black population during the 1920s, they were numerous enough to provide Headen with a viable market.

Headen, Stretch, and Dwyer officially incorporated Headen Motor Company on December 1, 1921, and began operations at Headen & Shaw. As president, Headen retained the controlling interest in the common stock venture, capitalized at $40,000. He put up his inventory and tools (appraised at $7,900, equivalent today to somewhat over $100,000) to satisfy the bulk of the legal requirement. Stretch, as treasurer, purchased twenty shares of the $100 stock for a $2,000 investment, and Dwyer, who served as secretary, held a single share, his small outlay reinforcing the idea that his interest was more political than monetary.[17]

Headen Motor made its debut at the city's annual auto show, held at the Chicago Coliseum between January 28 and February 4, 1922. During the eight-day event, Headen and his partners rented a booth in the Greer Building just off the coliseum, where they displayed their wares alongside those of other "accessory and equipment" companies. Afterward, the firm elected new officers.

Despite Stretch and Dwyer's investment, and the fact that Dwyer as late as March 1923 was still filing the company's annual reports, Headen Motor after 1921 would always have black officers, reflecting a desire to reach the company's primary market. In the 1922 company election, Headen retained the presidency. John F. "Jack" White, who had been an investor in the Headen Spring-in-a-Tube Company, became vice president, and Alphonso C. Wilson, an Omaha, Nebraska, businessman, assumed the position of secretary.[18]

By summer Headen had completed his first Pace Setter, fitting it with his own four-cylinder side-valve engine. The specifications published in the company's promotional brochure reflect the customer Headen had in mind. Relatively powerful compared to mass-produced Fords, the Pace Setter had a 211.6-cubic-inch cylinder volume and could produce fifty-seven horsepower, more than double that of the Model T. Although Headen never advertised how fast his Pace Setter could run, it would easily have surpassed the Model T's maximum speed of forty-five miles per hour. Falling somewhere between the Ford and Monsen's ReVere, which was capable of reaching eighty-five miles per hour, the Pace Setter was meant to appeal to the wealthy looking for a reliable but fleet ride.[19]

To provide the style and comfort he knew such drivers would demand, Headen fitted his prototype with silver-plated road lamps and the recently introduced Temme Heater. This much-desired amenity routed the heat from exhaust gases beneath a floor-installed radiator to keep passengers warm. Headen also emphasized his Pace Setter's easy maintenance, reflecting his own hours struggling beneath a hood. He noted that he had nickel plated the interior of the motor head to prevent corrosion and carbon deposits, spaced engine components so they were readily accessible to the mechanic, and installed a safety device to ensure continuous lubrication of wheel bearings and other parts.[20]

Ready to prove his car on the road and make his first sales, Headen turned to Robert Abbott for help. In June, the publisher sponsored a long-distance road trip to publicly unveil the Pace Setter. Kansas City, Missouri, 510 miles away, was selected as the destination. Kansas City was home to Homer Roberts, the country's only black auto dealer, whom Headen hoped would manage sales of his car in the Midwest and West. Roberts at the time operated a single-vehicle showroom, but he was preparing to break ground on the Roberts Company Motor Mart, a sixty-car dealership he completed the following year. Headen also planned to take advantage of the *Defender*'s contacts among the Kansas City sporting set. A year earlier, managing editor Cary Lewis had helped found baseball's Negro National League in Kansas City.

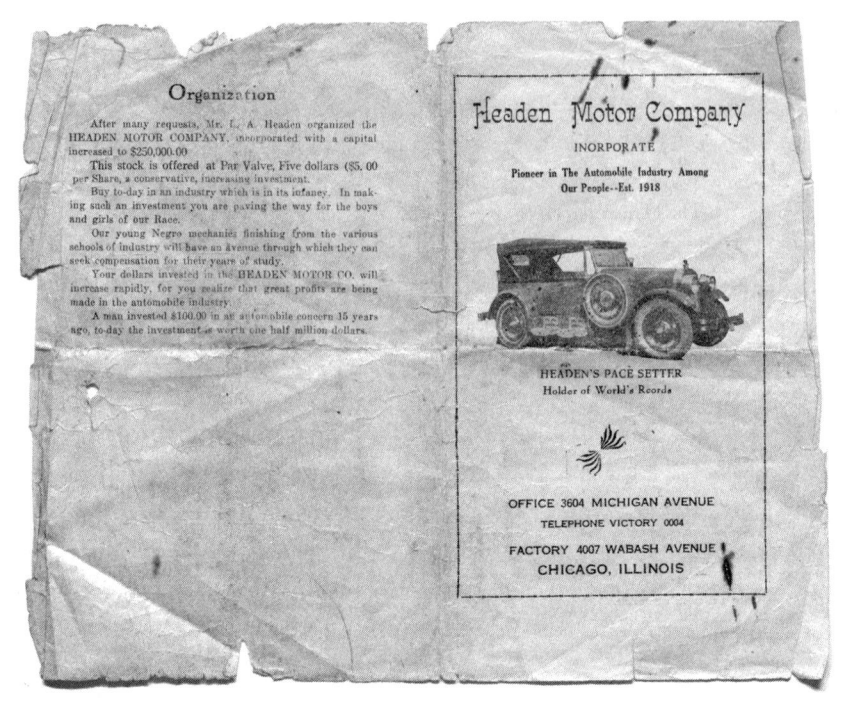

The cover of the 1922 advertising brochure Headen distributed as he traveled the country to sell stock for Headen Motor Company. Featured on the cover is his Pace Setter touring car. Courtesy of the Library of Congress Manuscript Division, Green-Driver Collection.

Elected secretary, Lewis was one of three men who wrote the new entity's constitution. Other *Defender* writers were instrumental in providing publicity to the league's members, including the Kansas City Monarchs. On his trip, two Monarchs principals, Dr. Howard Smith, the team's public representative, and Felix Payne, one of its earliest promoters, acted as Headen's hosts.[21]

The trip was a success from start to finish. Setting out for Kansas City on Thursday, June 29, 1922, Headen pulled away from Chicago at midnight. Occupying the Pace Setter's other seats were *Defender* general manager Phil Jones, editorial cartoonist Leslie Rogers, Headen Motor secretary Alphonso Wilson, and mechanic Charles Thomas. Wilson served as navigator on the arduous trip, which was marked by unexpected road closings, a torrential rainstorm, and crowds of curious onlookers wherever Headen pulled off the road. When the group finally rolled into Kansas City at 8:46 P.M. on Saturday, July 1, they were dog tired but exhilarated. Subtracting time for stops in Danville, Illinois, one unidentified spot along the road to take refuge from the downpour, and

St. Louis, the trip had been accomplished in only 20.1 hours, which the *Defender* claimed was a new record. To his great satisfaction, Headen also encountered no mechanical difficulties on the trip, proving his motor's viability.[22]

The next two days were a swirl of activity for the company's officers. Once in the city, Headen's party was joined by Jack White, who had traveled separately. The entire group was properly feted. Jones and White, house guests of Felix Payne, were shown the city and treated to a tour of the farm of white millionaire lumberman Robert A. Long. Headen and Wilson, staying with Dr. Howard Smith, were entertained at dinner by Smith's wife. Afterward Headen got quickly down to business, meeting with Homer Roberts. By the end of the negotiations, Roberts had agreed to put the Pace Setter in his showroom. Relieved, Headen joined the others on Sunday evening at an American Woodmen banquet honoring visiting national Supreme Commander Cassius M. White. Headen received a "splendid ovation" at the gathering and was called upon to speak. By night's end, James E. Baker, founder of the local American Woodmen Camp, had pledged to be Headen Motor's "western representative." While Roberts handled sales, Baker would sell stock and promote the company.[23]

Returning to Chicago with commitments pledged, Headen worked to make the most of his new connections. When Howard Smith's colleague Dr. Lucian Richardson arrived in Chicago in early August to spend the week with fellow medical man Chester Brewer, Headen drove Richardson on a tour of Chicago's main boulevards. Later in the month, socialite Sarah Rector, one of Kansas City's newest residents, visited the Windy City, and Headen quickly approached her as a customer. Pulling out all the stops, he had by month's end persuaded her to order a roadster version of his Pace Setter, called the "Headen Six." Rector was not a difficult sell. Heir to a fortune from oil discovered on land she and her mother held in Oklahoma, she already owned two automobiles and was well known for her love of speed and spending. Her mother, Rosa Rector, also loved cars, already owning three in 1921.[24]

To clinch the deal, Headen accompanied Rosa, who had traveled to Chicago with her daughter, and a friend known only as "Mrs. Williamson," back to Kansas City. Each woman drove separately, and the convoy made overnight stops in St. Louis and Columbia. To dispel any suspicion that her husband's trip with two female companions was for other than business purposes, Tena boarded a train for Kansas City to greet the trio upon its arrival. She then traveled the 190 miles north with Headen to check in with Alphonso Wilson in Omaha. Finally, in late September, the couple set out over the rolling hills and plains for the 470-mile trek home through Iowa and western Illinois. Tena's presence on the trip helped reassure those who lived in small towns along the way, or who read of the adventures in the *Defender* and other papers, that black women could be safe on the open road.[25]

In promoting his company, Headen did not extend the hand of welcome to the wealthy alone. He also approached investors of modest means, including many in the South. In August, he announced that the Headen Motor Company was "placing its proposition before the public," and he hired William Johnson as his representative in the southeastern states. Little is known about Johnson, but by early September he was already at work in Birmingham, Alabama, where a local reporter noted he was in town "on business" for the firm. Headen priced shares to keep them "within the reach of every man, woman, and child." Setting the cost initially at $5, by late fall he had reduced it to only $2 to accommodate small investors such as Baptist minister Rev. John Benjamin Green of De Soto County, Florida, who paid $10 for five shares in November 1922.[26]

After returning to Chicago from Omaha, Headen remained only long enough to swap his Pace Setter for a Headen Six roadster and to confer with the company's officers. The following week he departed on a sales trip through the Mississippi Valley and into Texas, accompanied by the Reverend Harold W. Barrett. Headen likely met Barrett through Tena. Barrett, the former head of the Metropolitan Mutual Benefit Association in New Jersey and a founder of the Combined Christian Churches, had appeared as a speaker at Lafayette Presbyterian several times in the early months of 1913—after Headen had left for Chicago, but Tena remained in Jersey City. Relocating to Chicago in 1921, Barrett made the Grace Presbyterian Lyceum, where he spoke in October, one of his first stops.[27]

As Headen and Barrett set off that month, the pair planned major stops at Nashville, Chattanooga, Shreveport, and Dallas. On the way they paused in Indianapolis, in part to refuel, but also to reconnect with acquaintances Headen had made during his trip to the auto races there the year before. They also dropped in at the offices of *The Freeman*, where Headen received a far kinder reception than he had a decade earlier. A *Freeman* writer, marveling at Headen's gleaming green car, praised its "mechanical workmanship," and in a fit of enamored enthusiasm gushed that it represented "the world's greatest Negro achievement." The flattery warmed the earlier chill left by Sylvester Russell's shoulder. Coupled with praise for his "Green Dragon" from the St. Louis *Globe-Democrat*, the white paper that had mocked him in 1912, Headen could now feel confident in his ability to woo the press, black and white.[28]

During the journey, Headen relied on networks of local community leaders to reach potential customers. In Nashville, he was hosted by the city's

Superintendent of Colored Schools, Dr. John P. Crawford. A popular administrator, Crawford was also a well-known fraternal figure, having served for at least a decade as Grand Chancellor of the Tennessee Jurisdiction of the Knights of Pythias. Headen's connection to Crawford may have been through his brother-in-law Will Jones. Nannie's husband was a longtime officer of the Pythians in Winston-Salem and his older brother, Dr. John W. Jones, served as Grand Chancellor of the North Carolina Jurisdiction. As contemporary state leaders, Jones and Crawford undoubtedly knew each other. Barrett, too, was a long-time Pythian. Crawford's status in Nashville and his broader Pythian connections, like James Baker's Woodmen ties in Missouri, presented Headen with a promising roster of buyers and shareholders.[29]

It is unclear who Headen's contacts were in Chattanooga, but he was observed in the city promoting his company in late November by entertainer Joseph "Jonesy" Jones, then appearing at the local Liberty Theater. Headen's contacts in Shreveport are also difficult to confirm, as no black newspaper from the area has survived. In Dallas, however, *Dallas Express* editor James R. Jordan, also active in civic and fraternal affairs, took up his cause. Jordan published a front-page, congratulatory article on Headen that relied heavily on information lifted from the company's promotional brochure. The brochure Headen supplied the *Express* and other papers along his route, in fact, demonstrated his growing sophistication in regard to publicity. Through his friendship with Robert Abbott and his time traveling with *Defender* writers, he had seen firsthand the pressures journalists faced. Even a leading national paper like the *Defender* had a tiny staff, and its reporters, as those everywhere, struggled to find good copy and meet short deadlines. Headen recognized that to gain the help of writers he needed not only to be newsworthy but to make their jobs easier. He crafted his advertising narrative so that, in addition to providing design and engine details, it could easily be converted into a feature story. Papers like the *Express* clearly appreciated the gesture.[30]

By the time Headen and Barrett returned to Chicago, Headen's experience on the road, his improving business savvy, and the respectability lent his firm by Rev. Barrett began to pay off. At the annual directors' meeting in January 1923, he reported that orders had been placed for 161 cars. Company accountant Walter B. Allimono also announced that new machinery had been ordered to allow for large-scale manufacturing. In response, the board voted to increase the firm's capital to $250,000 to help pay for the anticipated costs of materials and labor. The final item on the agenda was to choose new officers, and when the results were tallied, Headen and Jack White were reelected to lead the company. They were now joined by S. W. Sawyer, who replaced

Alphonso Wilson as secretary, and Barrett, who was now officially elected to the general manager's role he had held throughout the previous months. Sawyer's identity is unclear, but it may have been Searetta Sawyer, a local restaurant owner whose cousin, actor and poet Samuel Tutt Whitney, regularly wrote for the *Defender*. If so, this would mark the first appearance of a woman among the company's directors.[31]

At the board meeting's conclusion, Headen set out on another tour, this one to the Southeast. Traveling in late January to South Carolina, he arrived in the state capital of Columbia in early February, where he was hosted by undertaker and barber Thomas H. Pinckney. Headen's companion on the trip was former South Carolina Congressman George W. Murray, whom Columbia's *Southern Indicator* identified as an agent for Headen Motor. Murray was a fellow Chicagoan, having moved there in 1905, but his ties to Headen's family were much older. Between 1893 and 1897, when Murray served in the U.S. House of Representatives, he had been a leader in the circle of black Republicans in Washington to which Henry Tyson belonged. Tyson was instrumental in inviting Murray to speak before the Bethel Literary and Historical Association in 1893, and the two men had stayed in touch, working together on charity and other events and serving together in 1914 on a committee to honor Judge Robert Terrell. Immensely popular among his former Palmetto State constituents and himself an inventor, the sixty-nine-year-old Murray was the perfect front man for Headen Motor. He was still traveling with Headen in April when the pair visited Camden, North Carolina.[32]

Although no confirmation has been found, Headen's trip south must also have included a visit to Tampa, Florida, to see his half-brother James L. Street. James by this time was a well-known figure in Tampa. Vice president of the Central Industrial Insurance Company, he also helped establish the city's chapter of the National Urban League. When the Headen Motor board of directors met in January 1924, it reelected Headen and White and added Walter Allimono as secretary. Street joined them on the board, along with several Tampa professionals connected to him. In 1900, Street had married Idella Armwood, a shopkeeper who hailed from one of Tampa's most prominent black families. Idella's sister, Blanche Armwood Beatty, was the superintendent of Tampa's Colored Schools and a national political and women's club figure. She now also became treasurer for Headen Motor Company.[33]

Other Tampans joining the board were Dr. A. Jerry, who lodged with one of the teachers under Beatty's supervision, and D. A. Larramore, about whom little is known. Beyond family ties, Beatty was also part of Tena's network, having close connections with George and Genevieve Cannon and Tena's close

Headen's half-brother James Lillie Street, ca. 1915–1920, in Tampa, Florida. In 1924, James joined the board of the Headen Motor Company. Courtesy of Special Collections, Tampa Library, University of South Florida.

friend Lizzie Palmer Berry through the National Republican Party and the National Federation of State Women's Clubs. Had Beatty harbored concerns over the enterprise being undertaken by her sister's brother-in-law, she had a host of Tena's friends to put her at ease.[34]

As he crafted his appeals while on the road, Headen for the first time was forced to articulate a cohesive vision for the technology he loved. That vision would express a growing faith in machines and a belief in their ability to foster a better life for black Americans. His brochure, disseminated widely, initially echoed older themes. Recalling early encounters with racial limits, Headen decried in his new narrative, as he had in 1912, his exclusion from aviation meets. He also again invoked the symbol of France, although he now created an alternative back story. In this version, he stated that after being rejected in the United States he had, before taking up flying, gone to Pau, France, to study automotive engineering. No passport record or shipping manifest supports Headen's claim. If he did go to Pau, a much more likely scenario is that the British Admiralty sent him there for coursework related to his work at the Shipping Ministry. He knew, however, that the veracity of his assertion, as that of his claim to have learned to fly in Le Havre, was irrelevant. What mattered was that he express the defiance so many felt and the hope France represented. In the years since his flight, the land of liberté had only gained power in the black public's imagination, especially after French officers praised black

American troops for helping defend France in the war, and Parisians welcomed the soldiers with open arms, ignoring vociferous objections by white Americans.

Assuming the mantle of racial defender, Headen also now addressed the growing desire of black boys and men to resist intimidation and assert their manhood. Portraying himself as a technically brilliant adventurer, he boasted in one fanciful passage that "when the Wright brothers were going thru the experimental stage, he [had] hung up records in a plane of his own design and construction," and he referred to his Pace Setter as a "master-piece" of engineering. Through braggadocio, backed up with the real accomplishment and courage required for a black man to brave Southern roads in a unique car in 1922, where any sign of "uppityness" carried significant risks, Headen embodied for prospective male buyers the promise of masculinity and self-respect that the automobile offered.

Significantly, however, Headen's brochure moved beyond recounting grievances and asserting black men's strength. It also offered a racial blueprint for solving broader social and economic ills. In doing so, it laid out bold claims for the automobile. Economically, Headen argued, participation in the automotive industry could serve as an antidote for the hopeless search for skilled work and could improve black employment prospects. "Buy to-day in an industry which is in its infancy," he told investors. "In making such an investment you are paving the way for the boys and girls of our Race." His company and others like it, he insisted, could provide jobs for those training in industrial schools across the South.

The latter promise resonated strongly for gifted students aware of their slim chances of gaining positions in white-controlled machine shops. Headen's arguments also opened a ray of hope for parents and civic leaders, who feared that the rapidly modernizing world would leave black youth behind. And, despite his focus on men, his mention of "girls of our Race" reassured young women that they, too, occupied a place in the world he imagined.

Finally, for the purely pecuniary minded, Headen dangled the possibility of riches. Referring to Henry Ford without naming him, he told of how one auto manufacturer's $100 investment in 1908 had yielded a half-million dollars. "Your dollars invested in the HEADEN MOTOR CO.," he assured them, "will increase rapidly."[35]

In 1924, two years after producing his brochure, Headen added another expectation—that the automobile could help circumvent segregation. Since the auto's first appearance, many had understood its potential for escaping white control. In 1905, to protest Jim Crow streetcars, a group of businessmen in

Nashville had formed the Union Transportation Company and purchased five "horseless carriages" to equip passengers with an alternative. Throughout the 1910s and 1920s, city dwellers established "jitney" or bus companies to serve black communities, often ignored by local transportation authorities, and newspapers published features on convention-goers in the South, who purchased automobiles and drove long distances to avoid the humiliation of riding in segregated train cars. Though some journalists warned money might be better invested in homes and farms, many were adamant that blacks embrace the new technology. As a writer for the black nationalist *Negro World* asserted, in praise of car buyers in 1924, "The jim-crow abominations and horrors in Southern travel have got to go . . . Let us use all the weapons we can command to help them to go." Conservative columnist George Schuyler agreed, urging, "All Negroes who can do so purchase an automobile as soon as possible in order to be free of discomfort, discrimination, segregation and insult."[36]

American highways, however, posed their own difficulties. Roads were rough and poorly marked, maps sketchy and often out of date, and overheating engines and blown tires were frequent headaches. And segregation on the road could at times rival that on public conveyances. Restaurants, hotels, and filling stations often refused service, and physical safety was always a concern. White auto owners resented blacks on the highway, and state and local police often shared their surly attitude. For protection, many travelers drove in convoys and inquired along the way which towns were "friendly" or "unfriendly." They also relied on institutions such as black YMCAs, which offered rooms when hotel accommodations were not available and could be called ahead to obtain information on local services and weather. In Tampa, James and Idella Street approached the problem by soliciting the help of the Traveler's Aid Society. The branch of the National Urban League they helped lead reached out to the international volunteer group, dedicated to protecting those, especially women and children, stranded on the road, in early March 1924 with a request to work "among the colored people."[37]

In September 1924, Headen and a group of Chicago businessmen founded the Afro-American Automobile Association to create a more reliable source of aid for black motorists. The "Four As," as it became known, proposed a nationwide network of car owners and businesses to serve black drivers, and it announced it would establish branch offices in major cities that could answer calls for help.[38]

Headen's vision was, for his era, the most comprehensive expressed in African American writings on the automobile. Not all his ideas were original. They built on those of predecessors and contemporaries. As seen by the efforts in

Nashville, the possibility that motorized vehicles could free blacks from Jim Crow had been discerned almost as soon as the first sputtering two-seaters began startling horses on America's streets. It did not take much longer to discover their economic potential. In 1909, John Gannaway, when he opened a driving school in Denver, Colorado, promised prospective students that "many positions await competent Colored chauffeurs." A year later, Cosmopolitan driving-school manager Lee Pollard added that those who trained as chauffeurs would also be guaranteeing themselves a chance to become airplane mechanics and pilots, when their employers eventually bought airplanes. A decade later, in 1921, William McDonald Felton sought to make Pollard's prediction a reality, opening the Auto and Aero Mechanical School in Harrisburg, Pennsylvania, where he not only taught chauffeuring and engine work but hired a local white pilot to give students flying lessons.[39]

Headen brought together then existing economic and social strains of thought on the automobile. Departing from many of those who preceded him, however, he deemphasized service positions, revealing the growing expectations of educated blacks. He had seen Charles Chappelle reject the idea of spending his life in construction, studying to become instead an architect and electrical engineer and manufacturing his own airplane. He had witnessed Ulysses Scott, not satisfied to work for others, start an airplane construction school. Now Headen, one month after he founded the Four As, publicly encouraged black youth in New York to look beyond being chauffeurs to train as engineers. "There is a big field for the ambitious colored youth as automobile mechanics, engineers and eventually manufacturers," he told them. The automobile and aviation industries, he argued, were not yet plagued by well-developed color lines, and thus opportunity was still open. Moreover, where obstacles were encountered, blacks could develop independent businesses and organizations such as his own. Finally, reflecting the changing role of women, Headen opened a new discussion of how the automobile might help challenge the "place" black women had been assigned.[40]

Crisscrossing the country between 1922 and early 1924 to market his company, and in late 1924 and early 1925 to promote the Four As, Headen spread his narrative widely, eliciting positive commentary from journalists and businessmen pleased that he was proving "a big stimulus to young Negroes." And if imitation is the sincerest form of flattery, then he could take pride in the influence he had on at least two emerging black aviation pioneers in Chicago.[41]

In 1922, a young woman named Bessie Coleman was listening as Headen promoted his car company. A native Texan, Coleman had arrived in Chicago in 1914, and after finishing a course at the Burnham Beauty College, had obtained work as a manicurist at the fashionable Goins' Tonsorial Parlor, a barbershop a few storefronts from the *Defender*'s office. Inspired to fly, perhaps by balloonist and pilot Fred Bradford, who lived in a flat above the shop, Coleman had by early 1921 made the acquaintance of Robert Abbott and banker Jesse Binga. She soon convinced them to send her to France for lessons.[42]

When Coleman returned in September 1921, newly licensed by the Fédération Aéronautique Internationale, she began to speak about the importance of aviation for blacks. Her early comments, however, did not address flying as an economic activity. Reflecting the chill many still felt after a riot in Tulsa, Oklahoma, that summer, in which white pilots buzzed over the city, shooting at those on the ground and dropping incendiary liquids onto burning homes, she warned of the dangers of falling "so far behind the white man." Pressing the need to "keep up with the times," a few months later Coleman returned to Europe to train as a stunt flyer. When she arrived home again in October 1922, just as Headen published his brochure, her rhetoric began to change, reflecting his influence. Jobs replaced self-protection as the centerpiece of her rhetoric as she promoted flights she made between 1922 and 1926 in New York, Chicago, Memphis, Savannah, Los Angeles, and Houston.[43]

Two years after Coleman's death in a 1926 crash, William Jenifer Powell, a young Chicago businessman picked up the refrain. Powell, born in Kentucky, had grown up at 65 E. 36th Street, where his mother, beautician Lula Jenifer Powell, and her second husband, barber Louis Powell, operated their businesses from their home. When the younger Powell returned from the war after serving as a lieutenant in the 365th Infantry, he must have spied with interest the new garage opening only three doorsteps away at 71 E. 36th.[44]

Powell would leave Chicago soon after to complete an interrupted degree at the University of Illinois, but he returned in the summer of 1922, just as Headen announced the opening of Headen Motor Company and began distributing his brochure. It did not take Powell long to follow Headen's lead. The following year he invested in a gasoline station located six blocks south of Headen Motor on Wabash Avenue, and he soon afterward opened two additional locations. By 1925, he was ready himself to enter the garage business, building Powell's Auto Service on Wabash across from his first station.[45]

Bitten by the aviation bug, Powell moved to Los Angeles in 1928 to learn to fly and open a flight school, but he would carry Headen's influence with him. To promote his school, he wrote an autobiography, *Black Wings*, in 1934, and a year later produced a film entitled "Unemployment, the Negro, and Aviation." Powell's works applied Headen's sweeping vision directly to the airplane and repeated his arguments wholesale. He promised his readers and the viewers of his film unrivaled economic opportunity in the new, not-yet-white-controlled industry of aeronautics, and he called on blacks to train not only as mechanics but in all aspects of airplane construction and engineering. He also encouraged black leaders to develop a national network of airports and businesses to bypass Jim Crow, and like Headen he depicted the technology as a path to advancement for women as well as men. Although Powell attributed his aeronautical enthusiasm to Coleman, founding the Bessie Coleman Aero Club in 1930, he clearly had absorbed much from his forerunner in the South Side mechanical community.[46]

As Headen's thinking gained adherents like Coleman and Powell, however, his direct influence in the African American automobile world was about to suffer a serious blow.

CHAPTER SEVEN

Dreams Collide

In September 1924, with the Afro-American Automobile Association uppermost in his mind, Headen began to travel the eastern United States as its principal representative. By the following April, however, the organization, by then renamed the National Colored Automobile Association (NCAA), would have new officers. Many of them were new rivals from Indianapolis, and they acted to sideline Headen. Accusing him of assuming credit for others' efforts, they unceremoniously expelled him and banned him from future membership. The attack was personal, and the exile bitter. With the ouster, Headen lost the platform he had worked so long to build, and he was forced to cede his vision to that of others. Although he would make attempts to regain his status as a national spokesman on black automotive affairs, he would never again be celebrated as such.[1]

The narrative of the self-aggrandizing promoter, punished for stretching the truth, does not fully explain what happened to Headen. While egos certainly played a role, the split more accurately reflected the ramifications of a key decision that Headen and the Four As made in its earliest days—to sponsor automobile races. Ostensibly created to support the general motorist, the organization funneled most of its energies into the promotion of dirt track events. That choice replaced a cooperative model with a competitive one, and in the long run alienated important sectors of Headen's coalition, damaging his company (and his marriage) in the process, and ultimately forcing a showdown for control. For Headen, it would provide a lesson in the limits of Henry Wood's coalition approach.

Warning signs were present early, but Headen and his supporters can be forgiven if they did not see the collision around the turn. Like many, they were caught up in the wave of enthusiasm for fast cars that swept America. In 1924, the Indianapolis 500, then in its thirteenth year, drew a record 140,000 spectators to the stands. Across the country thousands flocked to smaller challenges sponsored by the American Automobile Association.[2]

Competition's siren song proved irresistible to "Speedway Headen" and to many black Americans, especially men, for whom racing became a point of pride. Excluded from most white-controlled contests, black drivers had long settled for challenges carried out on rutted, makeshift ovals or country backroads. But in the early 1920s promoters were beginning to create new opportunities, staging races at local fairgrounds and at tracks in cities north and south. By 1924, black speedway groups were active in Indianapolis, Detroit, Chicago, and Savannah, and the public was clamoring for more, eager to watch black daredevils rival the feats of acclaimed white drivers Barney Oldfield, Ralph DePalma, and Eddie Rickenbacker.[3]

A month before the Four As was born, the Colored Speedway Racing Association in Indianapolis had upped the ante, bringing "big time" racing to black audiences when it staged the first Gold and Glory Sweepstakes. The 100-mile sweepstakes featured drivers from multiple states and offered large prizes. The winner of the inaugural run in August 1924 claimed $1,200 and a silver trophy (presented by boxer Jack Johnson). The runner-up took home $500. Inspired by what they saw, a group of Chicago businessmen hurried home to form the Chicago Colored Auto Racing Association, and announced that they would sponsor a similar race in the Windy City. The "Dreamland Derby," named for a popular South Side café and night spot, would never reach the status of the sweepstakes, which reigned as black racing's premier event until the Depression doomed it in 1933, but it whipped up enormous interest.[4]

Headen saw little downside to the sport. He looked forward to competing and testing his engine against some of the best. He also seized upon the track as a natural setting for furthering his vision, believing that his actions on the oval could encourage a new group—men and boys of limited means but passionate about cars—to recognize the economic promise of the automobile. The dirt track also gave Headen a highly visible stage for his company. Invited to participate in the pre-run activities for the 1924 Gold and Glory event, he led a convoy of South Siders to Indianapolis in his Pace Setter, and in prerace festivities he carried Speedway officials at the head of a parade that wound through the city to the State Fairgrounds. Riding next to him were Speedway Association founders William Rucker, a well-known Indianapolis civic leader, and Harry Dunnington, owner of a local billiards parlor, along with the organization's two white financiers, Harry Earl and Oscar Schilling, both executives of the Cincinnati, Indianapolis & Western (CI&W) Railroad. Schilling also owned a small local track.[5]

That same month Headen assembled his first "Headen Special," a racer specifically designed for speed. The *Defender*, confident that auto racing would be good for the cause of black Americans (and for its own bottom line), praised his latest step, declaring that Headen "caused stock in the race to jump 50 per cent when he shot up State St. early Monday morning in his newly built green special of the Headen Motor Car Company." When September arrived, Headen sought to test his Special by entering it in the first Dreamland Derby.[6]

The *Defender* and other papers heavily publicized the derby. "Chicago is looking forward to this event, which marks a new era in the local sport world," the *Defender* noted. "There are thousands and thousands of people who have never seen an automobile race before who are glad of the opportunity." The paper's claim was an understatement. Famed trumpeter Louis Armstrong described the wild enthusiasm the contest aroused. "Everyone was so nervous the night before they could hardly wait for the day to come," he noted. "I was really out of my mind with excitement."[7]

On Sunday afternoon, a crowd of 15,000 jammed into the bleachers to watch entrants from Chicago, St. Louis, Detroit, and Indianapolis jockey for lucre and bragging rights. During a sprint that served as a warm-up for the main fifty-mile derby, Headen drove his Headen Special to a second-place finish, winning $50. If not particularly remunerative, his effort did at least cover his entry fee. Looking forward to driving in the main event later in the day, he joined the crowd to watch another preliminary race, this one a twenty-mile run. All around him the crowd cheered with abandon, rising to its feet to better see the cars fight for position, churn up clouds of dust, shred tires, pop piston rods, and careen desperately to avoid colliding.

Then, suddenly, tragedy struck. As Chicago cabbie Norbert Wiley barreled down the straightaway at 72 miles per hour, spectator Fred Shaw, misjudging the speed of the cars, attempted to run across the track. Startled, Wiley swerved but could not miss the darting fan. The impact carried Shaw on Wiley's radiator for forty feet before he was crushed beneath a wheel and killed. The car then flipped, throwing Wiley out. He would die at Provident Hospital the following morning.[8]

After the accident, a pall fell over the formerly gay atmosphere, and some fans left. Among them was Armstrong and his wife Lil, both of whom also decided to forgo the post-race ball scheduled for that evening at the Dreamland. Sickened by what he had witnessed, Armstrong descended the stands vowing, "From now on I don't want to see a foot race let alone an Automobile Race." Headen forced himself to shake off his own feelings about the loss of Shaw and Wiley. Hiding a heavy heart, he lined up with the other competitors for the main derby in the late afternoon. Only nine laps in he would be back among the crowd after his Special suffered a broken crankshaft. He could only watch as the afternoon stretched into the evening hours, and another Chicago driver, William Carson, took home the top prize.[9]

The horrible deaths of two men might have led some to question the judgment that the track was an appropriate place to promote an economic and social vision. Prerace events also offered a cautionary tale. During planning for the race, squabbles erupted between the leaders of the Indianapolis Colored Speedway Racing Association and the Chicago group. The principal Chicago organizers were William Bottoms, owner of the Dreamland and known locally as a policy runner, and William "Wild Bill" Jefferies, a bootlegger who laundered his income through a real estate business. Both men decided to enter their own contest, with Jefferies, who had been forced out of the Gold and Glory Sweepstakes by a broken water jacket, especially eager to prove himself. When the pair, just after signing the contract to use the Hawthorne Race Track, announced they would drive, Indianapolis Speedway Association general manager Harry Dunnington jumped to criticize their decision.

Concerned over propriety, Dunnington worried the men's participation might damage fans' faith in the legitimacy of the competition. This was understandable given that Jefferies was to pilot a $12,000 Ford Frontenac and Bottoms a $10,000 Duesenberg. These top-flight race cars posed quite a challenge to the majority of drivers, reliant on self-built racers cobbled together from parts, or modified road cars "doped" to increase their speed. The conflict sparked a bitter exchange of words between the *Defender*, which defended Jefferies's and Bottoms's right to compete, and *The Freeman*, which sided with Dunnington. Resenting attempts by Dunnington "to show" those in Chicago how to run their race, the *Defender* mocked Indianapolis drivers as "scared stiff" to face the Windy City drivers and pointed out that while organizers in Indianapolis had depended on white promoters, the Chicago race was being financed by "business men of Color."[10]

Despite the evident dangers and fierce rivalries, Headen displayed few reservations about racing, facing the jeopardy that the track posed to life and limb with curious unconcern for a man of forty-five. Long fascinated by speed, he had refrained from pursuing it openly, channeling his energies instead into building his more staid Pace Setter and his roadster and attending competitions only as a spectator. Now he embraced the breakneck abandon the track demanded. Forming the Afro-American Automobile Association only days after the fatal derby, he eagerly announced his plans to participate in the events it planned to sponsor.

From the start Headen allowed racing to overshadow the Four As' commitment to black motorists. This was in part due to timing. Public interest was high and capital available. Events closer to home, however, may also have influenced him to push the organization in that direction. He had recently assumed a new relationship to death. Its specter had thrice visited in the months before he established the Four As. In March his brother James, who had only that year joined Headen Motor, fell suddenly ill with pneumonia. He died ten days later at the age of forty-nine. The following month, Harold Barrett, who had accompanied him on his Mississippi Valley trip, died at the age of fifty-five. Only weeks after Headen buried his brother and his friend, his twenty-year-old nephew Roland Tyson, the youngest of Guy and Marie's children, drowned in June on holiday at the shore in Asbury Park, New Jersey. To deal with her grief, Marie Tyson retreated to North Carolina to spend several weeks with her daughter Guyrene, now the wife of a Greensboro dentist. After attending the funeral in Philadelphia, Headen returned home to build a race car. Forced to confront his own mortality, he had clearly resolved to throw caution to the wind.[11]

Headen could not, however, ignore the discomfort the riskiness of racing aroused in others. As he traveled for the Four As as its president and promoter, he had to work to quell nerves. Journeying to New Jersey in October to bring the state its first all-black contest, he spoke before commercial gatherings and with reporters to stress that his ultimate goal remained to "develop the auto industry among Negroes." If blacks intended to obtain a place in that industry, he argued, then they had to participate in all its aspects. Familiar with the Headen Motor Company, many seem to have trusted its owner to emphasize a positive, economic uplift approach in competitions, despite the dangers.[12]

The press continued to serve as Headen's ally. As he worked to handle logistics for the New Jersey race, the *Defender* was his principal partner. Headen made the paper's New York offices on Seventh Avenue his headquarters, and shortly after announced he had arranged for the use of the Ho-Ho-Kus Race Track in Ridgewood as the event's venue. A stop on the Erie Railroad a few miles north of Jersey City, Ridgewood was a familiar landmark to Headen. While he worked to finalize contracts with drivers and to obtain security, concession, and other personnel, *Defender* office managers William White, Archie Morgan, and Albert Mordecai began to pump out publicity. The *New York Age*, the *Negro World*, and the *Pittsburgh Courier* picked up their stories as anticipation built for the Election Day race. "Wonders will never cease," declared the *Courier*, as it touted a program that promised to feature "the pick of the greatest auto racing drivers of our group in America." The coverage highlighted Headen's involvement and encouraged fans to come get a look at the man and his car. "If for no other reason," the *Defender* told ticket buyers, "attend the automobile races at Ho-Ho-Kus, N.J., to see Lucien [*sic*] A. Headen, the only automobile manufacturer of our group in the world, drive his Headen Six car in the 50-mile derby."[13]

With the preliminary arrangements made, Headen swung back west, making a strategic stop in Indianapolis, where he appeared before the businessmen's Monday Luncheon Club. Sharing the podium with such luminaries as former Assistant U.S. Attorney General William H. Lewis and NAACP secretary William Pickens, Headen impressed at least one listener, a reporter for the *Courier*, as an "interesting speaker." If he intended his appearance as a peace offering to those in Indianapolis, however, it had little impact. Headen was unable to persuade any of the city's drivers to come to New Jersey, suggesting the Illinois-Indiana feud remained alive and well. Fortunately, however, Headen was able to sway twelve other entrants, representing Chicago, Minneapolis, Philadelphia, and New York City. This was a field as diverse as that offered by either the first Gold and Glory Sweepstakes or the Dreamland Derby.[14]

On race day, the weather cooperated, and as track officials (with few exceptions members of the *Defender* staff) took their positions, the drivers maneuvered into position and revved their engines for the first of the day's heats. The crowd eagerly strained to get a closer look at the cars and those commanding them. They also scanned the sidelines in hopes of catching a glimpse of vaudeville star Bill "Bojangles" Robinson, whom the *Defender* had convinced to serve as a timer. Robinson's presence may in part explain the fact that a "large percentage" in attendance consisted of "ladies and children." Another attraction luring women to the track was what the *Courier* described as "the most charming event of the day," a five-mile race between New York's Mattie Hunter, who drove a Headen Special, and Long Island's Annie Stovall, operator of a Dover Special.[15]

In the warm-up races, William Carson (winner of the Dreamland Derby), James Burgess of Philadelphia, and William Morgan of New York dominated, each trading places crossing the line first in the various contests. As twilight approached, Morgan took top honors in the main event. The only factor marring an otherwise perfect day was a serious accident that occurred during an early ten-mile race. In a repeat of the Chicago tragedy, a man named Henry Baker attempted to cross the track. Burgess, blinded by a cloud of dust, did not see the scurrying figure and struck him while going 62 miles per hour. Baker would die in the hospital several days later, but many in the crowd were blissfully unaware of the seriousness of his injuries, and the spectators who filed out of the gates that evening, the *Age* declared, had "enjoyed themselves to the highest degree." The celebration continued into the evening as the drivers and their guests made their way back to Harlem for a banquet at the Manhattan Casino.[16]

With the revelry over, Headen turned his Special southward. As he left Ho-Ho-Kus behind, he could take great pride in his accomplishment. The *Age* had described his Election Day events as "first class motor races in professional style." The races had proved so popular, in fact, that they inspired a group of black businessmen in New York, with the encouragement of nearby Ridgewood shopkeepers, to form the Eastern Automobile Association. They immediately set out to sponsor a second series of contests in late November, with plans for additional runs in May and July.[17]

Headen had also succeeded in building a new racing team. Agreeing to travel south with him was Tena's younger brother Oliver (Ollie) Drye. Drye had learned to drive while working at the Benning Racetrack (near Benning Road and Kenilworth Avenue) in Washington, D.C., where he had shoed and cared for race horses until autos began to take over the track. Bill Blackman, one of the most respected drivers in the country, had also promised to join them after driving in the later New York races. Hailing from Shreveport, Louisiana, Blackman had traveled across the United States, Mexico, and Canada in search of opportunities to test himself, and earlier that fall had won the open race at the St. Louis County Fair in Hibbing, Minnesota. He had also lined up next to Headen in the Dreamland Derby in August. When the three men met up in Georgia in December, their itinerary already included races in Savannah, Jacksonville, Miami, and Havana, Cuba. These locations suggest Headen was taking advantage of a racing network already put in place by a group known as the Negro Men's Racing Association. Based in Savannah, the association had been conducting dirt track events throughout Georgia and Florida since 1921.[18]

Headen's Ho-Ho-Kus success and the inroads he was making into the southern black racing market seem finally to have convinced those in Indianapolis of the need for an alliance. In December, the officers of the Indianapolis Colored Speedway Racing Association came to an agreement with Headen to merge their efforts. The result was a new organization, the National Colored Automobile Association (NCAA), founded at the Association's offices in Indianapolis on January 1, 1925. Like the Four As, the NCAA purported to "protect the motorist and private owners of automobiles," but it focused primarily on "the interest of the Race in the auto racing game." Reflecting the original Indianapolis group's emphasis on professionalism, the NCAA stated it intended to establish standard rules and to provide drivers with accident insurance. It also spoke directly to a desire to break free of reliance on whites, so that soon races could "be put over entirely by colored men." Headen became "joint promoter" for the NCAA, which meant the organization would assume sponsorship of the races to which he was already committed, and during the winter of 1925 he would organize additional ones solely under the NCAA's auspices.[19]

Headen's Savannah race was scheduled for New Year's Day, the very day the NCAA was established. It thus became the new organization's first official event. The group would have to wait for more than a week, however, to claim an appearance in the South. Postponed twice because of torrential rainfalls, the competition did not come off until January 10. Even then the water-soaked condition of the Tri-State Exposition grounds' half-mile track forced Headen to cancel planned motorcycle races and to shorten the three main events from ten to five miles. The crowd left happy, however, as local hero Joe Bruen, described as "the best known Negro automobile driver in the South," "romped away" with two of the three races. Headen also left satisfied. He had won the third.[20]

Before leaving Savannah, Headen added Joe Bruen and several other local drivers to his team. With familiar names as drawing cards, he was able to supplement the NCAA's schedule with races in Macon, Albany, and Atlanta, Georgia. Headen's own driving would improve dramatically as he competed with top drivers. Steering his Headen Special to victory at Macon in February, he captured the $500 prize in the meet's open race. Reporter Garland Ashcraft, who covered the event for the *Macon Telegraph*, acknowledged Headen's prominence (albeit in the minstrel dialect that permeated white descriptions of black events). After listing the humorous monikers of the other drivers, which included "The Vamp from Savannah" and "Dare Devil Zeke," Ashcraft remarked that "'Mistah' L. A. Headen of Chi," was "a ge'man who am so 'potant he doan need no nick name." The race in Macon, held at Central City Park's one-mile dirt track, was such a hit that Headen and the others were requested to do a repeat performance, staged for blacks and whites, although they sat separately in the stands.[21]

Headen worked tirelessly to promote his races. Despite the NCAA's desire to unfetter itself from white control and to professionalize the sport, he recognized that white spectators and promotional help were necessary and that races needed to answer not only the organization's needs but those of the sponsoring communities. New York had been a large enough market to command a crowd with moderate effort, but unexpected layover expenses and a smaller than anticipated gate from the rain-interrupted races in Savannah had made it critical that Headen broaden his appeal. Once in Macon, he began to reach out to locals. The second race he organized in the city was conducted to benefit the city's Parent Teacher Association.

Headen continued this strategy a month later in Albany. As he advertised his team's competition there, scheduled for March 29 at the local fairgrounds, he made visits to schools, churches, and public rallies in every town within a fifty-mile radius to build interest, and he announced proceeds would go to the Georgia Normal and Agricultural College. The college, a black Presbyterian school today known as Albany State University, had been heavily damaged by floodwaters escaping the Flint River, swollen by the same rains that had dogged Headen in Savannah, and putting much of the campus under water. Headen's pledge was a balm to president Joseph W. Holley as he struggled to figure out how to finance the extensive repairs his school needed.[22]

Headen's efforts bore fruit. In the weeks leading up to the race, the *Albany Herald* reported that he had elicited "deep interest" "from all over South Georgia." The towns of Thomasville, Warwick, Sylvester, Cordele, Vienna, and Americus, the paper noted, all intended to send contingents of blacks and whites to the races. When the big day arrived, Headen's team rolled onto a newly upgraded oval that had been described by white drivers who competed on it earlier in the year as the "best half-mile dirt track in the South." The results of the day's events, however, unfortunately have been lost to time. The issue of the *Herald* for the week of the race has not survived.[23]

Whether the race ended in glory or disappointment, it would mark an important turning point for Headen. Two weeks after its running, the harmony he had achieved with those in Indianapolis disintegrated. When the NCAA met in April, it elected a new board of directors, composed almost entirely of members of the Indianapolis Colored Speedway Racing Association. The group considered one Chicagoan (ironically, the original source of conflict, William Bottoms) for board membership, but it voted to ban Headen permanently. Its stated reason was "alleged statements" Headen had made "giving himself credit for promoting the first Indianapolis races last year." A week later, the spat got ugly when William Rucker claimed Headen had given auto racing "a black eye," and insinuated Headen had been unable to pay his drivers. Indianapolis-based sportswriter Alvin Smith, one of the original founders of the Indianapolis group, reported that Rucker wished to warn drivers against Headen and to reassure anyone registering for an upcoming Louisville race to be sponsored by the NCAA that the contest would have "strong" financing.[24]

The dispute likely had multiple roots. Those in Indianapolis could have been unimpressed by the profit margins from the races Headen promoted, and it is unclear if Headen's decision to donate proceeds to local causes had been fully approved by the board. The extent of white involvement also may have been a source of contention. The NCAA wanted to create a self-contained organization. Headen was looking to build alliances.

The personal nature of Rucker's attacks also suggests that old rivalries had never completely healed. While in Albany, Headen told reporters that he was considering the idea of moving his auto manufacturing business to the South, and the announcement may have rankled the NCAA, causing members to wonder if Headen was simply using the organization to further his own interests. Those in Indianapolis also likely did not relish seeing Headen's growing status overshadow their own, especially as coverage in white papers gave considerable attention to Headen, without acknowledging the NCAA. Articles in both the *Macon Telegraph* and the *Albany Herald* prominently featured Headen, focusing on his status as an auto manufacturer and racing promoter. The *Herald*, praising Headen as an "expert driver" piloting a car "of his own invention," failed to mention not only the NCAA but Bill Blackman and Joe Bruen, more experienced drivers who should have figured as major attractions.[25]

Whatever the sources of the rancor, the split between Headen and the NCAA spelled the end of anyone's hopes for a lasting national black auto racing circuit. If the NCAA believed it could succeed in the South without Headen, it was mistaken. By midsummer 1925 the group had extended its reach north to Windsor, Ontario, across the Detroit River from the Motor City, but it never again sponsored a race south of Louisville, Kentucky. Headen, without the association's backing, did not have the personal funds to operate alone. Racing was an expensive proposition. It required large amounts of cash upfront for prize monies, track rentals, payment of race officials, advertising, and the hiring of security officers. Financially strapped and ostracized, he saw no way to build a rival organization.[26]

Headen was in fact in an especially tough spot, forced to reckon with the collapse of a coalition that had proved unwieldy from the start. When he launched his car company, he had been admired for his technical prowess and for his championing of black aspirations. As he traveled to promote races, however, Headen began to neglect his obligations to investors. The Headen Motor Company had financed his dream, allowing him the opportunity to build his designs, but it did not produce promised riches. Racing had also not delivered any substantial employment opportunities. Most positions on the racetrack were honorary, assumed by already employed businessmen and journalists, and profit margins were thin. In fact, if William Rucker is to be believed, they may have been insufficient to cover costs, especially after donated monies were subtracted. Although his attempts to mold racing into a community-focused activity had boosted revenues, this approach ironically seems to have backfired by pushing away his Indianapolis peers.

Besides failing to fulfill monetary pledges and sustain racing-world partnerships, Headen had also at times challenged the politics and offended the moral sensibilities of important parts of his coalition. The financial exigencies of racing often brought him into close association with organizations and individuals that set middle-class reformers' nerves on edge. Joining Headen after the Ho-Ho-Kus race had been Henry Vinton Plummer Jr., a black nationalist prominent in Marcus Garvey's Universal Negro Improvement Association (UNIA). Before meeting Headen, the lawyer and real estate agent had helped establish the Newport News, Virginia, division of the UNIA. After moving to New York, he headed the Publicity and Propaganda Bureau for the Black Star Line, a fleet of ships Garvey hoped to use to develop African commerce and provide passage for blacks wishing to repatriate. A leader in Garvey's paramilitary African Legion, Plummer supported the purchase of automobiles (the UNIA even featured a Ladies Motor Corps) as well as airplanes and other technologies that could protect countries on the continent from white aggression.[27]

Headen, although politically conservative, found common ground with Plummer and the UNIA. He, like they, hoped to champion black capitalism. Both also shared the belief that transportation technologies were critical to success in a modernizing world. The UNIA had praised Headen for his initiative in becoming a car manufacturer, and it encouraged its members to attend the Ho-Ho-Kus race. When Headen left New York, Plummer joined his team as publicity agent. He was to prove an important asset. Garveyites had organized heavily in the towns and farmlands of southern Georgia, and two years earlier, Plummer had been received warmly after touring Savannah's black business district on behalf of the UNIA's *Negro World*. His presence was a particular boon in Albany, a city with fourteen UNIA divisions flourishing within a forty-mile radius, almost the exact area in which Plummer and Headen vigorously promoted their March contest.[28]

Plummer's participation, however, offered an affront to Headen's longtime supporters, many of whom considered both Garvey and Plummer charlatans. Robert Abbott, a bitter enemy of Garvey, had exchanged barbs with the Jamaican-born leader for years, calling him a buffoon who led his people astray, and mocking his "Back to Africa" platform. Joined by mainstream journalists across the country, Abbott applauded when in 1923 the U.S. government convicted Garvey of mail fraud for selling stock in the ill-fated Black Star Line, which by 1924 had been sunk by a combination of UNIA inexperience and determined government persecution. Plummer, too, had legal troubles, having served time in Leavenworth for embezzling and check fraud, and having been convicted in Washington, D.C., for similar infractions. Many supporters believed the charges had been concocted to blunt Plummer's political effectiveness. Whether his convictions stemmed from harassment or his own misdeeds, however, Plummer held little appeal for those hoping to achieve black economic development through unimpeachable means.[29]

Headen's new association may have led to a cooling of Abbott toward him. Despite the *Defender*'s strong support for the Ho-Ho-Kus event, the paper did not cover any of the races Headen organized after that date or his later activities in the South. The distance would not prove permanent, but the two men's friendship seems to have suffered for the moment.

Racing's economic exigencies also led Headen afoul of those fearing for the fate of public morality. For blacks and whites, the high costs of staging races often meant reliance on underworld figures. Although Harry Earl and Oscar Schilling in Indianapolis were businessmen with good community standing, the individuals from whom they raised the $50,000 needed for the 1924 Gold and Glory Sweepstakes were of less sterling character. The Dreamland Derby and later events sponsored by William Jefferies and William Bottoms in Chicago were bankrolled using illicit gains, and the Four As itself had relied heavily on backroom gambling monies. The association's roster included Headen as president, the ever-steady Jack White as his second-in-command, and respected real estate developer Fred D. Morris as treasurer, but the remaining officers raised eyebrows. Virgil L. Williams, former owner of the Royal Gardens dance hall, served as general manager, and Clarence R. McFarland, proprietor of the Pioneer Garage and the Pioneer Club, assumed the position of secretary. Williams and McFarland had long been identified as part of the "graft syndicate" in Chicago. In exchange for political donations to Republican Mayor William Thompson (demonstrating that corruption knew no party), Williams had ensured his illegal policy game could "run all night without police interference." Some citizens complained that the club also admitted underage girls for the edification of predatory men. McFarland's Pioneer Club on South State Street was regularly raided as an illegal gambling house.[30]

Many business owners and churchgoers on the South Side found organized crime (rampant after mobsters took over bootlegging under national Prohibition), as well as what they perceived as a general decline in moral values, deeply disturbing. In 1923, the Associated Business Club struggled with the ambivalence felt toward nightclubs, the main distributors of illegal liquor. At a December meeting, it debated the question "Are Cabarets an Asset or Liability to Our Community?" As entrepreneurs, the ABC's members understood that the income such places generated was important to black businesses, serving as a scarce source of capital. Still, this did not free them from worry over the encouragement of vice. The *Defender* and smaller black Chicago papers such as the *Broad Ax* and *Chicago Bee* frequently ran editorials lamenting falling church attendance, drinking, and public disorder, and many attributed these ills to night spots.[31]

The culture of the racetrack only added to public discomfort, especially for society women. A fiercely competitive, profanity riddled place, the track was the purview of men such as driver Bob Wallace, whose nephew remembered was "no angel," adding, "Few of them were really." Many drivers, including Wallace, honed their skills by outrunning police to deliver whiskey to small-town distributors. Paid handsomely by mob bosses based in Chicago, Indianapolis, Kansas City, and St. Louis, they often invested the proceeds in faster cars. Alcohol also permeated race-day festivities. Louis Armstrong remarked that at the Dreamland Derby, "Everyone had their bottle—I mean everybody, even had a little bottle on my hip myself." Many women found the hypermasculine swagger of the track equally disagreeable. Although she dutifully attended races, Indianapolis social leader Roberta Wiggins, whose husband Charlie was among the most successful Gold and Glory drivers, often grew upset over "greasy, rough-talking men hanging around" her house, and she expressed a hearty dislike of the boastful William Jefferies, disapproving of his "always talking big and flaunting about."[32]

Although Headen had flirted with "rum running" to raise money for his garage, and provided Patrick Dwyer a figurehead position in his firm, his immersion in the racing world brought him into more regular contact with unseemly individuals. This growing association distanced him from supporters such as Walter Allimono, a business partner since 1916. Although Allimono was still part of Headen Motor as late as 1924, he declined to follow Headen into his track venture. An evangelist with ties to the People's Forum, founded to reach "men, women and children who are not identified with any church in Chicago," Allimono could identify with a business effort that touted the goals of black economic and racial advancement. He found less to admire in a Sunday activity that left so many church pews empty.[33]

Tena as well seems to have had little affinity for Headen's choice. Lesta Bottoms, wife of William Bottoms, and Henryene Stevens, wife of Chicago driver Ernest Stevens, often cheered for their husbands from the stands and accompanied them to races in which they were not competing. A few socialites like Mattie Hunter and Annie Stovall even joined in the fun on the track. But while Tena had gone on the road with Headen to support his car company, she was not willing to do so for his racing promotions. Her presence was never noted in coverage of track events. The profane machismo of racing seems to have held little appeal for a Presbyterian churchwoman dedicated to the ideals of temperance and community.[34]

Headen's emergence as a leader on the dirt track, in fact, seems to have shifted the balance of power in the couple's relationship, a balance that had been eroding for some time. Since the day Tena had left the tight-knit railroad community and appreciative circle of friends at Lafayette Presbyterian, she had increasingly lived in Headen's shadow. In Jersey City, she had been recognized by the *Age* for her hard work and service. In Chicago, she gradually became simply the "wife of the famous aviator," defined not by her abilities but by her role as a society spouse. Journalists, ignoring her strength and perseverance, now attributed to her an emotional shallowness she had never demonstrated.[35]

On a return trip from visiting her family in Wilmington in late 1915, for example, she left the train during a station stop at Pittsburgh to chat with an acquaintance, perhaps old Scotia schoolmate Connie Catus, who had married a Pittsburgh physician. Lost in conversation, she did not notice that the train had begun to pull away. The *Defender*'s description of the event was telling. Tena, according to the paper, ran screaming after the train, fainted four times, and fretted, "My, my, what will my 'dearie' think of me getting left. Oh! I can't go home." Then, realizing she had left her cosmetics bag on the train, she swooned and exclaimed, "I left my powder puff and fancy mirror. What will I do, what will I do?" The vain, hysterical caricature bore little resemblance to the woman who had organized charity events, worked to provide death benefits to railroad families, and raised funds for her church. She now had to be rescued by the station master, who supposedly after learning she was the famous aviator's wife, "wired him and gave her a room in the best hotel in the city." A much likelier scenario is that she simply went home with her friend.[36]

Even reporting on visits within her social circle, the *Defender*'s society pages emphasized Tena's relationship to Lucean rather than her accomplishments. When Lizzie Palmer Berry dined with the Headens in 1919, for instance, the paper made no mention of Berry's women's club or Tena's church work, noting instead, "Mr. Headen is the well known aviator of our group, now conducting a machine and repair shop." Having entered "society," Tena felt mounting pressure to serve as a lady of leisure and a symbol of her husband's status.[37]

Still, during the couple's years in Chicago, Tena had remained a key element in Headen's business strategy. To build support for his inventions and develop a national coalition for Headen Motor Company, he had needed her. Through Grace Presbyterian, she connected him with journalists Robert Abbott and

Cary B. Lewis, whose wife was president of the Grace Lyceum, and to key investors such as Joe Jordan and Harold Barrett. She had also helped facilitate Headen's outreach to women, assuring them of the road's safety and offering Headen the cover of respectability when he traveled with female customers. Her network of friends had helped vouchsafe Headen's trustworthiness with significant national figures.[38]

With Headen's pursuit of motor sports, however, Tena and her network became less and less relevant to his goals. Racing welcomed women as spectators, but it remained a man's world, where speedsters hoped to prove "beyond a question of doubt that the black man has the nerve of a lion." In this scenario, Mattie Hunter and Annie Stovall became what the *Defender* called "local color," offered as entertainment before the "real drivers" took the course. Ironically, while Headen's car company had expanded the opportunity for women to travel and to participate in the business world, the races he organized reinforced their subordinate status. Dirt track hoopla offered Tena little, and as her husband moved from a cooperative effort that relied in part on women to a business model dominated by men and profiting from graft and danger, she could not help but feel alienated.[39]

Thus, though Headen had moved to recommit himself to larger community needs in the South, donating monies to Macon's PTA and Joseph Holley's school, it was too little, too late. His coalition had been strained past its breaking point. With the withdrawal of the NCAA's backing, the loss of northern supporters, and shrinking common cause with Tena, he saw little left for him in Chicago and did not relish returning home to face former associates. His statements to the *Albany Herald* indicated that he had already begun to contemplate relocating, and with little left to lose, he made a fateful decision. Though he had fled the South more than twenty years earlier, he now once again embraced it, as a place to start over.

CHAPTER EIGHT

A Dream Begins Anew

Picking himself up and dusting himself off as he had so many times before, Headen settled in Albany. Hoping to continue his engine experiments, he set about to rebuild the company that had made his past progress possible. The Southern locality he chose as his new base of operations had much to recommend it to a business-minded engineer. Long the commercial center of southwestern Georgia, Albany was in 1925 a city on the move. When Headen drove through on his way to look over the local track in late February, he observed signs of economic health everywhere. On Pine Street, painters were putting the finishing touches on the just-constructed six-story Hotel Gordon. Blocks away, at the corner of Pine and Jackson, crews were adding 150 rooms to the fashionable Albany Hotel. Talk on the street was of a new municipal golf course, a planned mineral springs and casino resort, a booming convention calendar, and the recent cultivation of peach orchards, pecan groves, and tobacco fields just beyond the corporate limits.[1]

The bustling county seat of Dougherty County, with its sunny skies, aromatic smell of pine, and echo of construction hammers, must have evoked memories of Headen's childhood. But it was Albany's favorable climate for car manufacturing that spoke to his present needs. Seven railroad lines intersected in the heart of town, and a plan to increase the number of through trains was on the drawing board. More trains meant easier shipping for finished cars, a fact other local car makers were already turning to their advantage. Home to the lowest tax rate in the state, Albany also had an aggressive "good roads" movement underway, led in part by *Herald* editor Hugh McIntosh. Inspired by Florida's nearby land and tourism boom, promoters like McIntosh hoped to position the city as an important stopover for the motor herds making their way to the Sunshine State. Progress was being reflected in the sheen of a newly surfaced Dixie Highway through the county, and funds were committed for paving fifty-nine business and residential blocks in Albany.[2]

Albany also had a thriving black business community. To meet the needs of black residents, who made up almost half of the city's population, local entrepreneurs operated an array of cafés, barbershops, funeral homes, and dry goods stores, and formed a large number of fraternal organizations, a boon for Headen, for whom such groups had always been a source of support. The

Pythian network of Will and John Jones was, in particular, alive and well in Albany, with Joseph Holley serving in 1925, as he had for more than a decade, as Vice Grand Chancellor for the Georgia Jurisdiction of the Pythians. Other groups, including the Supreme Circle of Benevolence and the Improved Benevolent and Protective Order of Elks of the World (IBPOEW), were also active, with the Supreme Circle owning its own modern office building downtown.[3]

Albany's racetrack was a final selling point. A good place to test engine refinements, it had the added benefit of attracting local mechanics, speed enthusiasts, and railroad shop machinists, all eager to experiment. Like flyers at the Aeronautical Society, many of these individuals, despite Albany's well-known insistence on keeping the races separate, were willing to ignore social strictures. Henry A. Petit, a locomotive engineer for the Atlantic Coast Line Railroad, was one of them. A long-time Savannah resident before relocating to Albany in 1921, Petit had recently developed an interest in automobile engines and had begun to dabble in auto sales. Bonding over a love of motors, Headen and Petit would soon become fast friends.[4]

The five years Headen spent in Albany, from 1925 to 1930, would be an important turning point in his career. He achieved a lifelong goal in 1930, when he and Petit received a patent for the "Headen-Petit Spark Ignition" device. Additional solo patents would come in the years that followed. After 1929 Headen also adopted a new business model, embarking on a series of one-to-one partnerships with professional financiers. Access to deeper pockets and established business networks opened broader opportunities and ultimately set him on a new path for his future.

No hint of this transition, however, was yet visible in 1925. As he laid the groundwork to restart his car concern, Headen initially reaffirmed his commitment to the coalition idea, despite the difficulties he had encountered in implementing it. With no solid foothold in the South, it was his best hope for continuing his motor work. As earlier, he began by anchoring his efforts among a small group of supporters before leveraging wider networks. He mastered the method in his new home as he had in the North, and it would buy him the time he needed to find a more independent path.

Headen quickly found friends in Albany, and he immediately identified pockets of enthusiasm for the automobile within the local community. He made his home with entrepreneurial couple Emma and William Wynn in the segregated southern portion of town. Emma had for several years owned the Madame E. V. Wynn Beauty Parlor, and locals also knew her for the charity events she organized and for her energetic efforts as a state organizer for the City Federation of Colored Women's Clubs. By 1919 William, who had previously worked as a cook for a white family in Thomasville, Georgia, had opened his own cafe. A founding member of the Albany chapter of the NAACP and steward for the IBPOEW, he, like Emma, offered Headen access to multiple local networks.[5]

By midsummer Headen had brought Emma Wynn into the firm with him, as well as Albany resident Edward E. Harris, driver for a local building supply company. Henry Plummer also decided to stay in Albany, becoming the firm's general counsel and moving into an office in the Supreme Circle's building. On June 30, 1925, Plummer petitioned the county on behalf of Headen, Wynn, and Harris to incorporate the Headen Motor Car Company at a capital stock of $50,000. Shares were to be sold at $100 apiece, and the new partners placed 10 percent of the stock value down as earnest money.[6]

In the figures of Harris, Plummer, and Wynn, Headen wedded important lines of support needed in his new home. Harris and Plummer's participation reflected the economic interest artisans and their children often had in transportation technologies. Harris's father had been a carpenter, and Plummer's a teamster, before becoming a well-known chaplain in the U.S. Army. Both readily saw the economic potential in motor vehicles, as well as the promise of self-help. Speaking to these dual concerns, Headen continued to cast his company as a source of black employment. As he recruited supporters, he announced that his factory would hire an all-black workforce. The formula was effective for Harris, who leapt in to help promote the new company. It also proved compelling for Plummer, whose presence assured Headen continued legitimacy among the many holding nationalist sentiments in the countryside around the city.[7]

The prospects of economic gain and self-determination also appealed to Emma Wynn. Her interest in Headen Motor made perfect sense. Wynn was not the first beauty culturist to embrace the automobile. Madame C. J. Walker, the hair products and cosmetics manufacturer who had entertained Headen during World War I, had purchased a Model T Ford in 1912, arriving in it with her chauffeur at the NNBL's annual meeting that year in Chicago, and before her death in 1919, she traveled extensively in a Cole model to sell her products and meet with sales agents. Walker's own mentor, Annie Malone, who founded the Poro College of Beauty in St. Louis in 1917, purchased one of the first Rolls-Royces owned in that city, and her school operated a fleet of cars and trucks to deliver her hair pomades and styling implements. The automobile allowed both women to transact sales and recruit agents in rural areas and in small towns across the country where trains did not run.[8]

Wynn seized upon the same advantages. Needing to visit numerous out-of-the-way places in Georgia to encourage new members for the City Federation, she was also an agent for "Pearl Drops" cosmetics, produced by the United Manufacturing Company of Jacksonville, Florida. Like Walker and Malone, she valued the automobile as a tool for achieving her business and social aims. Going a step further, however, she plunked down hard-earned profits to become a direct investor in the growing technology.[9]

Headen's ability to interest new partners helps explain how he stayed positive in his pursuit of the technology he loved, even after he lost earlier supporters and even as the voices raised against automobiles grew louder. As he resurrected his company, he heard all around him criticisms of the car, not just in relation to the unsavory elements the "racing game" could attract but in terms of personal ownership. In the 1910s, skepticism had lurked in nervous comments from the pulpit and in expressions of annoyance in editorial pages, whose writers often assailed joy riders for startling horses and endangering pedestrians. By the 1920s, as cars became more widely adopted, resistance surfaced in open complaints against the supposed menace auto ownership posed to the moral fiber and financial welfare of black Americans.

In 1924, the conservative *Atlanta Independent* warned that, "Automobiles are sending more people to hell, married and not married, than many causes of social degradation." Months earlier, the *Savannah Tribune* had attributed a man's loss of his home and family to his determination to purchase a car he could not afford. And, just as Headen began promoting his new company, the *Norfolk Journal and Guide* challenged his and others' claims of economic gain, asserting that, "If one-half of the people who are buying automobiles and do not own their homes would transfer their payments from cars to real estate or educational refinements, great would be our jump in economic standing." In a pithy summary of such objections, the *Richmond Planet* quipped, "AUTOMOBILE TRAVEL is speedy and gratifying, but the expense is speedy and disappointing."[10]

Headen ignored the doomsayers, taking heart that his supporters in Albany valued his automotive work and that many of his peers were quietly disregarding the skeptics. The number of black car owners in Georgia, according to registration records for 1925, showed a "decided increase" over the previous year, and enthusiasm was not contained to the state. And, although some editors fretted, many of those contributing to their papers expressed less ambivalence. To appeal to migrants eager for information about the goings-on back home, many larger newssheets in southern and northern cities printed columns of local news, written by volunteers in small towns and cities across the country. "Motoring" occupied a prominent place in such columns, and their content makes clear that large numbers were finding in the automobile not only business and entertainment possibilities but family and community good.[11]

Individuals drove between cities, and between the countryside and cities, to care for sick relatives, attend weddings, graduations, and funerals, or to simply spend time with old friends. Arthur Carter of Philadelphia, the *New York Age* commented in 1925, had recently gone by car to Plainfield, New Jersey, to visit his sister, Mrs. J. B. Whiting, and the two then took to the road together to Bayonne to see their ailing brother Theodore. Similarly, Mr. and Mrs. William Matthews of small-town Brentwood, Maryland, motored to Baltimore to spend a week "visiting friends and relatives of Mrs. Matthews." At times, such trips covered long distances. Sultana Cannon, George Cannon's sister-in-law, with her daughter Vivian in tow, in August 1924 drove from Jersey City to Greensboro, North Carolina, to visit Sultana's sister, Mrs. William McBryan. That same month, Dr. and Mrs. George Evans of Greensboro, along with several of their relatives, made the reverse car trip, autoing from Greensboro to Plainfield, New Jersey, and then to Boston to see "relatives and friends."[12]

In the new migratory world, where jobs and opportunity were always another destination away, those who could afford the cost of automobiles were using them as a social adhesive for their scattering families and communities. Headen knew this from his own experience. While in Chicago and New York, he and Tena had often driven southward to see family in Philadelphia and Washington, D.C., maintaining old, and building new, relationships along the way as they stayed with friends or with the families of friends. Other relatives followed suit. Levin Armwood Sr., grandfather of James's wife Idella, had as early as 1918 (nearing the age of ninety), purchased a car to visit his children and grandchildren, who were split between Tampa and its suburbs. The automobile allowed the elderly man, who resided in Seffner, thirteen miles east of Tampa, to avoid the indignity of being forced to sit separately on the train into the city, and at the back of the streetcar once there. It also gave him control over when he visited and for how long.[13]

For a busy surgeon like French Tyson, the auto provided the flexibility to combine family and pleasure trips, rather than being forced to choose between destinations because of train schedules. Driving north from Charlotte in 1924, he visited his parents in D.C., then paused at Guy and Marie's to attend his cousin Roland's funeral, before going on to spend time with friends in New York and vacation in Canada. Nannie and Will, meanwhile, in the 1920s set out on car trips to Greensboro and Charlotte to maintain ties with cousins French and Guyrene, and they motored to High Point and Raleigh to see old school friends, Will's fellow Pythians, and his medical colleagues. Nannie and her sister Louise (attending school in Winston-Salem) often drove to Aberdeen to see their father. He, in turn, made the car trip to Winston-Salem. Nannie's keenness for cars did not wane even after a frightening incident in 1926, when an out-of-control driver felled a telephone pole and sent it crashing into her Liberty Street home.[14]

And while ministers bemoaned that automobiles meant a loss of parental control, for Jerry Headen it provided the opposite—a way to keep a loving and watchful eye on his daughters. This would be especially true after Louise, now a graduate of Winston-Salem Teachers College (today Winston-Salem State University) and Brooklyn's Pratt Institute, began teaching in Statesville, North Carolina. The train trip between Aberdeen and Statesville was arduous. It required travel on multiple railroads, none of which synchronized their timetables, and included the discomfort of Jim Crow cars, increasingly difficult for an aging man to endure. By car, in contrast, Statesville was a drive of 120 miles, primarily along two major highways, and Jerry took advantage of the convenience.[15]

Headen could also feel the enthusiasm of many young people. "The possibilities of the automobile industry," the principal of the Bordentown Manual Training School noted in 1925, "have seized upon the imaginations of the colored boys of New Jersey." More than half of the 148 who entered the school that year enrolled for instruction in auto mechanics. With an eye to the future, Headen hoped to keep such interest alive, even among constituencies that could not yet afford the automobile's costs. Leaving no group untapped, in August he made overtures to local black farmers, many of whom had little disposable income but desired to better their lives. Early that month he volunteered to organize an agricultural and industrial fair in Albany. Such fairs had been popular across the South since the mid-nineteenth century and were prized by blacks and whites eager to learn new agricultural techniques, promote mechanical progress, and build relationships between farmers and businessmen.[16]

Assisted by Harris, Headen led the committee to stage the successful exposition. Held at the Albany-South Georgia Fair Grounds in October, it put the spotlight on the products of black growers, livestock raisers, craftsmen, quilters, dressmakers, and cooks, giving them a place to showcase and celebrate their skills. It also allowed Headen the opportunity to display the automobile he hoped to promote. Although no detailed description of the event has survived, it does not take a stretch of the imagination to believe that he had a Headen-built car on display, or at least parked strategically close by the exhibits.[17]

The fair also revealed other ambitions. Headen hoped it would show local economic and civic leaders he was committed to Albany's development. An astute observer, he had noted alarm among business owners of both races over the growing exodus of black workers from the city and its surrounding counties. A decade earlier, when 500 blacks had left Albany for wartime jobs, they had been replaced by others moving in from the countryside. In 1920, the *Herald* optimistically declared that better agricultural methods and the arrival of modern conveniences such as the telephone and electric lights made the city's outlook "full of promise," and it predicted that local cultivators would have little difficulty "keeping the boys on the farms." Optimism turned to dismay, however, as 46,000 black farmers and field hands, an average of almost 300 per county, left Georgia between 1920 and 1925.[18]

When Headen arrived, the exodus was in high gear, threatening to decimate the low-cost labor supply that underpinned Albany's economy. Working the fields, harvesting pecans, peanuts, berries, cotton, tobacco, and produce, caring for livestock, and making bricks (a key industry in Albany) were all labor-intensive activities. But by 1925, so many farms had been abandoned in Georgia, many of them in the counties surrounding Albany, that Congressman Thomas Bell requested $500,000 in disaster relief. The city's plan to develop itself as a tourist destination also demanded a large pool of railroad, hotel, and restaurant workers, now rapidly disappearing. Throughout the mid- to late 1920s, large numbers continued to abandon the area. Eventually among them would be Henry Plummer, who felt great sympathy for the farmers who had made up much of the UNIA's membership.[19]

Albany's black entrepreneurs felt the pinch of the exodus as fewer and fewer customers came through their doors. With livelihoods threatened, they had already begun strategizing how to stem the tide of migrants. They were well aware that it was not simply the recent decimation of cotton crops by the boll weevil or the draw of northern industrial jobs that accounted for the departures. Jobs abounded in Albany. The labor shortage was so acute that local orchard owners were bringing in unemployed white workers from the northern reaches of the state to fill empty positions. Black leaders knew that people opted to leave because of unfair work relations, a general climate of fear spawned by unprosecuted attacks and lynchings, and the daily humiliations of Jim Crow.[20]

Joseph Watson, editor of the *Supreme Circle News*, official organ for the fraternity, attributed the fields "going to rack and ruin" to the peonage-like sharecropping agreements into which farmers were often forced, as well as the lack of voting rights, segregation, and brutal attacks by the Ku Klux Klan. With white control enforced by capricious violence, Albany since the early 1900s had witnessed regular outbursts of lawlessness, including a 1908 reign of terror, when hooded torchbearers ensured that "Every negro church and school-house in an area of ten square miles" was burned in a single night. Mobs in neighboring Colquitt County had torn down schoolhouses in 1920, posted signs warning teachers of dire consequences if they dared hold classes for black students, and severely beaten a local minister who planned to enroll his son in Atlanta University. Although grand juries were convened in each case, they failed to indict any of the perpetrators.[21]

In 1923, black leaders convened to discuss the problem, inviting white community leaders to sit in and confronting them with unusual frankness. Their efforts would pay off, as whites interested in Albany's economic development eventually came to appreciate Watson's assessment and to understand that racial assaults had to be quelled if the city planned to grow. Editor McIntosh had come to this realization much earlier, stating during the 1916 exodus that, "The Negro is leaving because he thinks he is not getting a square deal; and he is not. We have got to treat him better." Now others joined him. In 1924, in a politically unpopular move, the Albany council refused to allow the Klan to use the municipal meeting hall for an initiation ceremony. A year later, just as Headen arrived, local Rotarians sponsored the city's first "Lincoln Day" to honor President Lincoln, and invited the former governor of Michigan, Chase Osborn, to deliver the keynote address. The move was remarkable in a conservative stronghold where Lincoln's election in 1860 had prompted immediate demands for Georgia to secede from the Union. It spoke to the depth of local boosters' desire to create bridges with northern white business interests (a desire evident the following September when the local Chamber of Commerce elected another Michigan native, Paul Dierberger, as its secretary-manager). The move also reflected the need to acknowledge Albany's sizable black community, for whom Lincoln was a supreme hero.[22]

Augmenting the appeals of men like Joseph Watson, Headen's agricultural fair had thus been a gesture not only to illustrate the possibilities Albany could hold for blacks but to reassert the promise to whites that blacks could be convinced to stay *if* given an atmosphere in which they could thrive. As someone who had seen firsthand that violence knew no region, Headen seems to have held out hope that whites could reform, or at least be cajoled into a position of restraint. Dierberger's arrival was likely an encouragement.

As Headen made his manufacturing plans, he began to advocate directly for the advantages of a commercial alliance. In late 1925, when the city initiated an ambitious development plan to promote the Skywater Mineral Springs Resort, now open outside Albany, along with other local attractions and agricultural opportunities in neighboring counties, he was ready. As soon as the Chamber of Commerce announced a massive advertising campaign for the purpose, to be financed by public subscription, he agreed to raise funds in the black community.[23]

Rallying helpers and tapping the fraternal, business, political, and club women's networks of the Wynns, Holley, and Harris, Headen appealed directly to black citizens to support the project. They responded, and in late February Headen handed the Chamber's appreciative president a check for almost $3,000. The drive, carried out under the auspices of the American Community Advertising Association, a national organization dedicated to local development, was a decided success, motivating the *Macon Telegraph* to congratulate the "example in community spirit." The secretary of the association, engaging in more than a bit of hyperbole, even declared that it "loomed large in community building history." For Headen, it cemented the goodwill of the white political and commercial class whose blessing his business required, a fact corroborated by praise his car company would receive in the *Herald*.[24]

With his credentials secured, Headen focused on obtaining adequate quarters for his company. Locating an empty pimento canning factory on Dawson Road in the northwest corner of town, he purchased the 52-foot by 200-foot structure and the half-acre of land on which it sat. The price he paid was a bargain, as prime land along Dawson was then selling at only $150 an acre. By February 1926 Headen had engaged Walter Armwood of Tampa to create a design for expanding the space to allow for manufacturing. Armwood, the older brother of Idella and Blanche, was then a teacher and school administrator, but his training was as an architect. Like Headen, Armwood had struggled early to find a job commensurate with his skills. Leaving Tampa for Trenton, New Jersey, in 1917, he had hoped to obtain work as a carpenter, but encountering "a curtain of prejudice," he returned home to piece together a living through short-term government and teaching positions and started a drugstore with his father. He still hankered, though, to build. Thus Headen's offer to work on his plant was likely a welcome development. Headen in turn must have felt gratified to be able to give back to his brother's family for their support of his earlier company.[25]

Working with Armwood, Headen applied for permits to install an array of drill presses, lathes, forge equipment, bench tools, air compressors, and other essential machinery. Finally, with lumber "on the ground" and construction on the addition underway, he once again hit the road to sell his vision, appearing "on business" in Columbus, two hundred miles away, only two weeks after the first nail was driven. As he promoted his revitalized concern, Headen carefully tailored his words to his multiple audiences. To potential black investors and northern journalists, he displayed supreme confidence, boasting to Baltimore's *Afro-American* that his work in Chicago had constituted only a testing period, and that he now was ready for full-scale manufacturing. He had, he stated, more orders for his cars than he could fill, and he had gone south, where space and labor were cheaper, to build a more expansive factory to keep up with demand. Although Headen's claim of pressing orders was exaggerated, he was aware he had to project an air of success to draw support.[26]

Headen assumed a different demeanor in speaking to whites. Having absorbed the language of the New South, he knew how to flatter the beliefs of white capitalists. Thus he informed the *Albany Herald* that he had left Chicago because the South was the "one place in the world where the negro has the fullest opportunities to grow, to develop and to expand." His words could have come straight from Henry Wood, or from Booker T. Washington, who had famously advised blacks at the Cotton States and International Exposition in 1895 to "cast down your bucket where you are," because "it is in the South that the Negro is given a man's chance in the commercial world." The degree to which that was or was not true, all three men knew, was less relevant than the reality that in the South one had to show deference and present a plan of cooperation to ensure the safety of any enterprise, whether it be a church, a school, a university, or a business.[27]

Headen would never develop Headen Motor Car Company into a large-scale manufacturing firm. Despite the breadth of his coalition, without a range of well-to-do backers, he no longer commanded the capital needed to undertake the extensive travel needed to promote stock sales. He did, however, establish a viable business, earning profits not solely from automobile assembly but from repairing cars and motorcycles, selling auto accessories, and servicing the tractors of local farmers. Between 1926 and 1929 the company provided him with steady income. It may also have finally fulfilled its promise of jobs. In his autobiography, *You Can't Build a Chimney from the Top*, Joseph Holley later referred to an automobile repair shop owner who had asked for help in educating "six Negro boys who were being paid from $25 to $50 per week repairing tires, etc.," explaining that "not one of them could read or write and one of them could not tell the time on a clock." It is unlikely a white garage owner would have hired so many black employees or taken such an interest in their welfare, so that owner may well have been Headen. Holley agreed to tutor the young men in his home.[28]

Headen's business also gave him the all-important personal workshop he desired and the tools needed to continue trying out new ideas. His work at the

Headen Motor Car Company quickly established his local reputation among blacks and whites as, in the words of the *Macon Telegraph*, a "noted Negro automotive engineer." The experiments he carried out on its premises would yield engine-related patents and draw the financial commitments required to develop, build, and market them.[29]

It was in his shop in early 1928 that Headen began the work—tinkering with a new kind of engine—that would change his life yet again. Prompting his interest was the appearance in his doorway of Henry Petit, who had come to ask help in developing a motor for cars and trucks that could burn oils with higher densities than gasoline. Traditionally, gasoline was the fuel of choice for the spark-ignition internal combustion engines installed in almost all vehicles on America's roads. Petit, however, believed that kerosene, paraffin, and tractor vaporizing oil (TVO) could replace it. Grades of "crude oil," such fuels were actually products of the distillation process. When refineries boiled the crude, the individual grades separated out at different temperatures. The sludge remaining at the end was considered waste oil.

Petit was not alone in seeing the value in these heavier distillates. Stationary industrial engines and tractors had been burning kerosene and paraffin since World War I, and the competition was on in the United States and Britain, and across continental Europe, to design an engine capable of using them in personal vehicles. Petit, however, was having difficulty creating a workable design. Determined not to give up, he revived his hopes after observing Headen's skills. Headen, for his part, was immediately intrigued. He had seen oil-burning ship motors, as well as smaller marine engines, while an inspector for the British Shipping Ministry, and he relished a challenge. He agreed to work with Petit, and the two men embarked on an eighteen-month journey of "sleepless nights," hunched over a Ford Model T, and later a Studebaker, in the back of Headen's garage.[30]

Headen did not have to be convinced of the advantages of heavier oils. Having low volatility, they could be stored in intensely hot climates like Georgia without evaporating, and unlike gasoline they had little probability of catching fire in the case of an accident. More to their credit, they were cheap. Kerosene, paraffin, and TVO cost significantly less than scarcer gasoline, the smallest product in the distillation process. It was this latter characteristic that captured the interest of farmers, motorists, and trucking executives on both sides of the Atlantic. All were wincing at the high cost of filling their tanks. In Georgia, tempers flared over gas prices, and in 1925 the governor asked the state courts for an injunction to forbid fuel companies from raising prices. When the court rejected the appeal, the *Macon Telegraph* complained bitterly that car owners, who represented one in every six people in the state, were being "sucked of blood by a parasitical monopoly." The pain was even greater in Britain, where gasoline, known there as petrol, in 1926 reached 1s. 7½d. (41¢) per gallon, the equivalent today of almost £4.25 (or near $5.50). This was compared to the 27¢ per gallon being charged in Georgia, and the 18¢ paid in most other states.[31]

Anxious to join the search for a solution, Headen and Petit knew they faced an uphill climb. For two decades a cost-effective heavy-oil engine for road vehicles had proved the proverbial hard nut to crack for engineers. Lightweight and needing to continually stop and start, as well as to idle for long periods in traffic, trucks and automobiles were unable to maintain the high engine temperatures required to turn viscous heavy oils into a vapor that could be easily exploded in the engine's cylinders. The pair, however, soon developed a plan to change the equation.

Once Petit posed the problem, Headen weighed the then prevalent approaches. He first considered, and rejected, the efforts of contemporaries to perfect the diesel oil engine, invented by German engineer Rudolph Diesel in 1892. Unlike gasoline engines, which turned gasoline into a vapor, then ignited the vapor in the cylinders using a spark plug, diesel engines dispensed with spark plugs and instead compressed air in the cylinders at extremely high pressures until the intense heat that resulted forced oil (injected into the cylinders as a liquid spray) to spontaneously ignite.

While the diesel compression engine, some believed, was the "economical power unit of the future," in 1926 this was not yet the consensus. Diesel road vehicles still faced a litany of problems, most of which would not be solved for another three decades. Chief among them were cost and performance. Unlike mass-produced gasoline engines, diesel motors had to be custom built. To withstand high compression pressures, they also had to be constructed from heavier materials, lowering their horsepower. Neither trait endeared them to buyers. The engines also suffered from noisiness, noxious exhaust, difficulty starting in cold temperatures, "knocking," and their Achilles heel, "dilution." The latter occurred when unburned fuel ran down the cylinder walls, then seeped into the crankcase, where it diluted the thicker oil vital to lubricating the engine.

Present minded, Headen had little inclination to invest in an engine type he knew was so far from being marketable. Thus, he took an experimental path more in line with his practical philosophy—and his limited pocketbook—setting about to convert existing gasoline engines so that they could operate on heavier oils. Although he would also have to solve difficulties related to incomplete fuel combustion and problems starting in the cold, the approach seemed to him a better bet for an immediate resolution. He could begin with a cheap, lightweight gasoline-engined automobile and, through a series of modifications, offer an affordable vehicle within the reach of the average consumer.

As he began his work, Headen followed in the footsteps of earlier mechanical engineers who had in World War I begun developing "bi-fuel" engines for tractors. Tractors engaged in heavy plowing tended to run hot, making them suitable for burning oil. Taking advantage of this characteristic, Ford Motor, John Deere, and other agricultural machinery makers had developed what many called "gasoline-kerosene" engines (known as petrol-paraffin engines in Britain). These engines could start normally on a small amount of gasoline, then switch to burn kerosene, paraffin, or TVO. To make the denser fuels suitable for burning, the designers added a special "vaporizer" that heated the oil and introduced turbulence to help break it up more quickly and thoroughly. The vaporizer turned the oil into a sparkable vapor.

The bi-fuel engine had been a hit among farmers ready to experiment because it took advantage of the quick-starting properties of gasoline, which ignited easily even when the engine was cold, and the low cost of crude oil products, which could be burned after the engine was hot. Surveying the state of these engines in 1926, Headen believed he could improve on their design to make them adaptable for trucks and automobiles.[32]

The innovations Headen and Petit offered focused on the two principal failings of bi-fuel engines—irregular ignition and insufficient vaporization. They addressed the problem of ignition first. Recognizing that spark plugs were not optimal for igniting oil vapor and that, once ignited, the vapor did not burn evenly like gasoline vapor, they resolved to develop a new ignition method. By 1929 the pair had produced a new "multipoint" ignition system. Their invention consisted of a copper plate and a series of conical, porcelain bodies that were screwed into the head of each cylinder and protruded slightly down into the combustion chamber. The copper plate sat between the cylinder head and the porcelain bodies, trapping heat from the engine and concentrating it in the bodies' tapered ends. These intensely heated ends created "hot spots" across the top of each cylinder's combustion chamber. Well spaced, they provided multiple, regular sparking points for the vapor as it entered the cylinders, making ignition more efficient and reliable.

With ignition addressed, Headen tackled the issue of vaporization. He began by considering the basic workings of a spark-ignition engine run on gasoline. In traditional internal combustion engines, fuel is pumped into the carburetor, where it is broken into droplets and mixed with air. Suction from the engine then pulls this fuel-air mixture through an intake manifold (a series of tubes that route the mixture into each cylinder). Once the mixture enters the cylinders, the spark from the plugs, aided by heat created as the pistons rise and compress the air in the cylinders, ignites it, creating an explosion that pushes the pistons back down. When this combustion "stroke" is complete, fumes are routed out of the cylinders through an exhaust manifold (another series of tubes that trap the fumes as they escape from each cylinder and direct them out the exhaust pipe).

Previous vaporizers had most often sat between the carburetor and the intake manifold, and they relied on a variety of means to heat and atomize oil. Headen introduced a simplified arrangement. He created a one-piece cast-iron manifold in which the intake manifold was surrounded by the exhaust manifold, allowing the exhaust heat to raise the temperature of the air-fuel mixture entering from the carburetor. His design also relied on the principle of complete lifecycle heating. He added a "preheating" chamber, warmed by heat from the exhaust, to raise the temperature of the oil before it ever entered the carburetor, thus allowing it to more easily mix with air. Once the warmed droplet-air mixture produced by the carburetor was sucked into the vaporizing manifold, it followed a path made tortuous by a set of metal obstacles, or baffles, which created the turbulence he needed. Set at sharp angles, tapered at their ends, and intensely hot, the baffles forced the oil droplets into a whirling motion that crashed them against the manifold's exhaust-heated sides and instantly vaporized them. Even if the engine cooled when idling or when starting and stopping in traffic, the baffles held enough heat to allow vaporization to continue unabated, preventing the droplets from returning to liquid form. This compact, space-saving design allowed heavy oils to be burned with higher efficiency. By reducing the number of oil droplets reaching the cylinders, it also lessened fuel waste and reduced the dilution of the crankcase's lubricating oil.

On August 1, 1929, Headen and Petit applied for patent protection on their ignition device. Three weeks later, they unveiled Headen's vaporizing manifold to a group of interested friends at the Headen Motor Car Company plant. In the demonstration they equipped a gasoline tractor with both their sparking mechanism and the manifold, converting the machine to use low-grade oil. The result proved the design's efficacy and impressed all present, including a reporter from the *Albany Herald*, who watched the tractor successfully complete sustained plowing with no difficulty. With the spark-ignition/vaporizer combination proving a success, word of the demonstration quickly spread, and newspapers across southwestern Georgia began to remark on the vaporizer's larger implications, especially as Headen and Petit made known their plans to adapt it to passenger cars. It would, an admiring *Macon Telegraph* reporter predicted, "revolutionize the automobile industry."[33]

After the demonstration, Headen must have been pleased by the praise of at least one writer. "Headen is a native Southerner," a *Macon Telegraph* reporter told readers, "but for many years lived in the North, where he developed a remarkable mechanical genius." Chagrin likely replaced satisfaction, however, when many white newspapers, including the *Telegraph*, attributed his motor primarily to Petit. Muddling its facts, the *Thomasville Times Enterprise* erroneously stated that both the men's ignition device and the manifold had already been patented, and it declared that "The patents were granted to H. A. Petit, a locomotive engineer, and L. A. Headen, a negro." In fact, the ignition device was principally Headen's creation, as indicated by his name appearing first on the patent, and although Petit had worked on the vaporizer, the Patent Office rejected his contributions to the completed item as unoriginal, and he thereafter signed an affidavit recognizing Headen as the sole inventor. Headen would receive a British patent on the manifold in 1933 and a U.S. patent in 1935.[34]

Shaking off the *Times Enterprise's* slight, Headen focused on attracting investors. Success would come quickly. George P. Koelliker was the first to step forward. Former vice president of the Union Trust Company Bank in Cleveland and a director of the Canfield Oil Company, Koelliker had recently retired and moved to Tallahassee, Florida, where he had begun speculating in inventions. By the time he met Headen, he had already purchased rights to a storage battery and an electrolytic rectifier. Koelliker may have heard of Headen and Petit's experiments while visiting his brother-in-law Walter Bagnall in Thomasville, just sixty miles from Albany. Regardless of how he first made contact, however, Koelliker knew the oil business and quickly discerned the utility of both inventions. He agreed to manufacture the devices when they were ready.[35]

Koelliker's support was critical, especially in view of its timing. On October 29, 1929, only two and a half months after Headen and Petit's August demonstration, the U.S. stock market crashed, sending the American economy into free fall. With economic panic ensuing and the Great Depression on the immediate horizon, Koelliker was an important subscriber and provided the encouragement Headen needed to continue his work. Assured of a solid monetary commitment, he set out to prove his design's utility, initiating extended road trips in a converted six-cylinder Model T Ford. His tests took on greater urgency in December when he faced an attempt by an "unauthorized agent" in Ohio to manufacture a motor fitted with a similar manifold and using an ignition device akin to his and Petit's. In early January 1930, the Associated Press reported that the men intended to confer with the U.S. Patent Office to ask officials to intervene and stop production of the motor. His hand now forced, Headen redoubled his efforts and that spring and summer began making longer trips, using different grades of oil as fuel, including waste oil. Meanwhile, Koelliker, to get ahead of the game, incorporated National Oil Manifolds at the beginning of May. Filing incorporation papers in Delaware, a common practice because of the state's favorable incorporation laws, he located the company in his native Cleveland.[36]

After National Oil Manifolds was created, Headen submitted his initial application for a patent, and to underscore his manifold's readiness drove 200 miles from Albany to Koelliker's home in Tallahassee in a converted Studebaker. Traveling an average of 48 miles on a single gallon of oil, and incurring a total fuel cost of only forty cents, equivalent today to between five and six dollars, he reassured Koelliker of the wisdom of his investment. Soon after, Headen and Petit placed several autos fitted with the spark-ignition and vaporizer devices on display in Albany for public view.[37]

The success of the auto conversions soon attracted an additional backer. George Dickinson Hamilton, president of Hamilton Parking in Cleveland, may have been an associate of Koelliker's. By late summer, he had expressed an interest in helping Headen market his inventions abroad. An English immigrant who had made a tidy sum converting vacant properties in Cleveland into parking lots, or car parks as they would have been called in his native Sunderland, Hamilton was looking to branch out into new profit-making endeavors. By mid-August Headen was on the road north to meet with Hamilton, stopping on the way in Philadelphia to celebrate with Guy and Marie. The following month, on September 15, Hamilton sailed to England to visit his own family and to explore the possibilities of interesting British authorities in Headen's designs.[38]

Koelliker and Hamilton's backing reflected not only Headen's personal creativity in seeking financing, but the niches available to an independent inventor in the period. Historian of technology Eric Hintz has shown that some with an inventive bent worked on their own for long periods, then formed partnerships with corporations. Headen's experience shows other potential paths. One could turn to former corporate leaders such as Koelliker, who speculated in patents, and to individual investors such as Hamilton, who had surplus cash and were eager to add to it by catching "the next big thing."[39]

While Hamilton was abroad hunting markets for the vaporizer he hoped would bring him profits, Headen and Petit learned that the Patent Office had given their ignition device the nod. They assigned three-quarters of the patent rights to Koelliker's new company and one-quarter to white Albany physician Albert S. Bacon, a local ear, nose, and throat specialist who also owned the Tift Silica Brick Company. Headen decided to stay in Cleveland to oversee production of the device.[40]

Headen was likely relieved to depart Albany when he did. Amid worsening economic circumstances, the harmony between the black and white commercial classes in the city, born of the economic boom years of the 1920s, had already begun to crumble. Only months before he left for Cleveland, tensions had erupted into a threatened attack on Joseph Holley. When Holley took out a warrant against the chauffeur of Barrett Waters, a Cincinnati businessman who often visited a plantation he owned near Albany, an angry crowd congregated outside Holley's home, threatening both him and his wife. The chauffeur had evidently driven through the campus of the Georgia Normal and Agricultural College at a reckless speed, endangering students, and was deserving of arrest. But for whites in Albany, a black man taking actions that inconvenienced a wealthy white man (Waters had to pay court costs and a fine for his employee's misbehavior) was intolerable. Unsurprisingly, Headen's move to Cleveland was also his farewell to Albany.[41]

With Hamilton still in England, in January 1931 Headen traveled alone from Cleveland to Chicago to demonstrate his manifold at the National Auto Show, held at the Chicago Coliseum between January 24 and 31. His return to Chicago was bittersweet. While his move to Albany had been a critical turning point in his career, it had cost him his marriage. A year earlier Tena had appeared before a judge in Chicago. In an official deposition dated December 2, 1929, she declared that she had been abandoned. She reported that on October 28, 1924, Headen "just went out to a[n] automobile race and never came back." The race to which she referred was the Election Day event at Ho-Ho-Kus Racetrack. Although she had heard from her husband after his departure, she stated, she had not seen him since that time, and on July 1, 1926, he had cut off all contact. Two days later, Tena's friend Leontina Allimono, wife of Walter Allimono, corroborated Tena's version of events in a separate deposition.[42]

Despite being summoned, Headen did not appear at the hearing scheduled for December 17, 1929. As a result, we do not have his side of the story. Some evidence, however, may contradict Tena's claim that the two had not seen each other since 1924. An item in the "Society" column of the *Chicago Defender* in July 1927 noted that "Mr. and Mrs. L. C. [sic] Headen of 5012 Michigan Ave. entertained at dinner in honor of Mr. and Mrs. W. J. Mear[e]s and their daughters Anita and Marietta of Greensboro, N.C." (After Lucean moved to Albany, Tena had relocated to the Michigan Avenue address.)[43]

Tena Elizabeth Drye Headen Meares. This photo appeared alongside the announcement of Tena's marriage to Norfleet Meares in December 1929. *Chicago Defender*.

The *Defender* item could have two possible explanations. The paper's society editor may have included both Headens as hosts of the dinner as a matter of social protocol. To be abandoned by one's husband was considered shameful, and the editor may have been protecting Tena's reputation. The other possibility is that the couple's break was not as clean or as simple as Tena indicated, and Headen may have spent some time at home in 1927. Regardless, the couple was no doubt at odds over Headen's decision to relocate. Albany offered Headen a community of fellow mechanics and potential investors, but it had little to offer a Chicago socialite. A woman "prominent in the civic and social life of Chicago," Tena had forged strong church and community ties. She had also become accustomed to the relative freedom of the North. Despite spurts of racial violence, Chicago offered a large black community with broader social possibilities than a small Southern city. Having already sacrificed a happy home in Jersey City, and having suffered embarrassment over the failure of the Headen Motor Company in Chicago, Tena had little desire to return to the Jim Crow South to chase her husband's dream.[44]

Thus, even if the two did continue their relationship, they could not reach an agreement about their future, and Tena began considering her options. When William J. Meares (brother of Scotia classmate Lucy Meares and a tailor who likely learned his trade in her father's shop, a few blocks from his childhood home) came to that July dinner, he brought with him a Chicago cousin named Norfleet. Norfleet Meares was a man suited to Tena in temperament and goals. Well known in the city as a good-natured supervising inspector for the Pullman Company, he had thirty years on the job and offered economic and domestic stability. On December 10, 1929, seven days before her divorce was finalized, Tena wed Norfleet Meares in Crown Point, Indiana. Their exchange of vows was registered two weeks later, and the couple left for a honeymoon in New York. After their marriage, Meares began attending Grace Presbyterian Church, embracing the realm in which Tena had always felt most at home. He would be accepted for membership three years later, in January 1933.[45]

Headen's own feelings about his divorce are difficult to plumb. But two actions he took suggest he did not feel entirely comfortable with his decision or at least not with its social consequences. When the census taker arrived at his door three months after the court proceedings, he reported himself as "widowed." Arriving in Chicago less than a year later for the auto show, he chose to check into the McAlpin Hotel rather than stay with friends, as he usually did when traveling. At the McAlpin he could visit with those who did not judge him for his actions without risking unexpected encounters with Tena, Norfleet, or those who blamed him. One man who seems to have had some sympathy for Headen's side of things was Robert Abbott, whose own marriage would end in a bitter divorce four years later. Although Robert and his wife Helen regularly socialized with Tena and Norfleet, and were among those attending their wedding reception, the editor rekindled his friendship with Headen, beginning again to publish stories complimentary of him in the *Defender*.[46]

Whatever his state of mind in the aftermath of his marriage, Headen's trip to Chicago brought home the finality of his decision to leave behind the city that had established him as an inventor and businessman, and the woman he had loved for more than twenty years. But, ambitious and determined, he chose not to dwell on the past. While the door on his life in Chicago had closed, a window was opening almost 4,000 miles away. He was about to leave for London.

CHAPTER NINE

A Dream Crosses the Pond

When Headen returned to Cleveland from Chicago, George Hamilton greeted him with a promising report. Officials in London had agreed to test his manifold. The news was a relief. Despite Koelliker's support, Headen knew that enthusiasm for his invention would never be as great at home as in Britain. While the United States was oil rich, its busy refineries distilling large quantities of gasoline, Britain, as one writer put it, was forced to search "the four corners of the world" for its fuel supplies. In 1930, it purchased a third of its oil from the United States, another quarter from Persia (today Iran) and other Middle Eastern countries, and the remainder from Venezuela, Russia, Romania, Mexico, and the Far East. As a result British consumers paid dearly at the pump. Even after England established the Anglo-Persian Oil Company in Iran to exert greater control over its supply, political exigencies forced costs higher than the British would have liked. In 1931, a newly empowered shah began pushing to retain a larger portion of his country's oil profits. By 1932, he would formally force concessions, and prices increased.[1]

To a driving public already hurting, any means of burning cheaper oils in their automobiles was appealing. The idea of bi-fuel engines was already familiar to many of them, especially those raised on farms. High gasoline (or petrol) prices, combined with the greater availability of other crude oil products relative to petrol, had led many British farmers to adopt petrol-paraffin over petrol-only tractors, and Ford Motor Company had taken note. Although it ceased production of its bi-fuel Fordson for the American market in 1928, Ford continued to manufacture it in Ireland until 1933 and in England from 1933 to 1964. Just prior to Headen's arrival in 1931, such tractors were, according to the *Roadless News*, enjoying an uptick in popularity. Familiar with such machines, and eager to experiment, British motorists represented a promising market for Headen's vaporizing manifold.[2]

Headen's manifold was also the kind of innovation many private and professional groups in Britain hoped to foster. The Royal Automobile Club (RAC), the Royal Agricultural Society of England, and other organizations concerned with road and agricultural vehicles had since the 1910s put their full weight behind the search for alternative fuels, sponsoring open trials of experimental engines, offering prize monies for new designs, and funding research at university and industry laboratories. The RAC took particular notice of Headen's manifold for its potentially broad applications. Suitable for automobiles, tractors, and commercial vehicles, it appealed to the multiple constituencies the club represented. The RAC, despite its name, had since 1903 included a department known as the Commercial Motor Users' Association, which addressed trade and agricultural interests. Although tractors, lorries, and dumpers drew less attention from the public than fashionable automobiles, the RAC encouraged advances in their development. Enthusiastic to see Headen's manifold in action, they invited him to present it before a trial committee in June.[3]

The inventor did not hesitate. The nation that had welcomed him as a young man was again extending opportunity, and Headen, about to turn fifty-two, knew he had an extraordinary chance. Britain held global power, which offered the prospect not only of a British market but of buyers in Europe, the Americas, Asia, Australia, and Africa. With so much at stake, Headen meticulously prepared for the demonstration, making last-minute tweaks to his design and arranging for shipment. He also traveled to Washington, D.C., to meet with his U.S. patent lawyers, afterward signing a power of attorney to allow the Victor Evans firm to communicate on his behalf with Patent Office examiners in his absence. In late May, plans in place, Headen and Hamilton walked up the gangway of the S.S. *Majestic* in New York, excited but nervous.[4]

Upon their arrival in Liverpool on June 4, the pair made a quick trip to see Hamilton's family in Sunderland. They then met with the RAC for an official test. Unfortunately, no record has survived of the June 10 proceedings, but the demonstration likely took place at the Brooklands Racetrack, near Weybridge, Surrey, southwest of London. The club had conducted engine trials there since 1909. We cannot know what ran through the minds of those gathered to see Headen's manifold in operation, but their reaction was undoubtedly positive. Immediately afterward, Headen and Hamilton, who had envisioned only a brief business trip, felt encouraged enough to consider a more permanent stay. Checking into the Strand Palace Hotel off Trafalgar Square in London, Headen took in the familiar surroundings, including his old office at the Admiralty, only a few blocks away. Before the month was over, he and Hamilton had hired a local solicitor, and Headen had submitted a request for a British patent. Soon afterward, the partners settled on a nearby office at 60 The Strand, and they officially founded Headen Hamilton Engineering Limited, registering it as company 257737 with the British Board of Trade.[5]

Headen must have pinched himself over the sudden developments that followed. By August the M.A.P. Trading and Transport Company of London

Headen soon after his arrival in England in 1931. The photo, from his British National Identity Registration Card, clearly shows a facial palsy that developed slowly over his life. Barely visible in 1917, it was noted on his 1917 passport but was easily hidden by his moustache. Its progressive nature suggests Headen may have suffered from Ramsay Hunt syndrome or a similar condition that affected his facial nerve. Courtesy of Lucean Headen Jr.

had fitted two of its Ford petrol lorries with his manifold and started a month-long evaluation under road conditions. The "considerable saving" in fuel costs that resulted stirred interest in various quarters, and it soon caught the attention of *Motor Transport*. In mid-September, a *Transport* writer, curious about the growing buzz, convinced M.A.P. to allow him to accompany the driver of one of the converted lorries on a trip around London. The manifold-fitted engine, he enthused after his ride, had not only used little fuel, it had "behaved admirably," running smoothly, showing acceleration equal to that of a regular petrol motor, and producing no noxious exhaust.[6]

Attention from the RAC and from one of Britain's leading trade publications left Headen encouraged, but he had little opportunity to savor his good fortune. The iron was hot, and he had to strike. He was ready. He had sought a British patent (even though his U.S. application was pending) to advertise the company's intent to produce his manifold in England. He and Hamilton now began the search for suitable factory space.

They would find what they were looking for in Camberley, Surrey, west of Weybridge. The bucolic site of Sandhurst Royal Military College, Camberley was home largely to cadets, faculty, and retired military and foreign service officers. A small but enterprising vanguard in the town, however, was anxious to encourage industry. When Headen surveyed the surroundings, he was attracted not only by the reasonable rents but by the ambitions of two individuals in particular. Local builder James Richard McLean Keil, a former lieutenant in the Royal Air Force, had in 1929 constructed a carpenter's yard off Frimley Road, between Bridge and Krooner Roads at St. Mary's Corner. Keen to develop local businesses, he was making long-range plans to erect factories on the land and rent them to manufacturers. Just across the railway tracks from Keil's St. Mary's Works stood Laurel Works, where William Rowlands had established Rowlands Metal Windows with Keil's help. Business at the company, which produced cast steel windows and door frames, was already bustling.[7]

Other nearby properties were also being exploited by industrial enterprises, including a cluster of buildings off Victoria Avenue, one block south of the main London Road. Within this complex were "workshops and premises" that suited Headen's purposes perfectly. In late January, Headen and Hamilton leased from army captain Arthur B. Thompson a main building and its outdoor lot and sheds, all of which shared a postal address with a house that faced onto 15 Victoria Avenue. To hasten preparations, Headen moved to Camberley, checking into the Duke of York Hotel on the corner of London and Frimley Roads, steps from his new facility.[8]

The next two weeks were a frenzy of activity, as Headen beat a regular path between his Duke of York quarters and his new workplace. He spent daylight hours clearing out rubbish, planning the factory's layout, and installing new machine tools. Evenings, after rubbing elbows in the hotel's lobby with military officers and government officials on business at Sandhurst, he reviewed plans and finances with Hamilton.

By mid-February, with the company on solid ground, and his Cleveland affairs demanding attention, Hamilton returned home, leaving Headen to direct the company. The inventor threw his full energies into the task, excelling at every aspect of the business. Freed from the exhausting affair of selling stock to small investors, he also no longer needed to manage an unwieldy coalition. For the first time in his life he had the latitude to focus principally on creating and selling his designs.[9]

Headen made the most of his new autonomy, embarking on the most productive period in his life. Two weeks after Hamilton departed, he applied for a second British patent, this one for a method to prevent engine damage caused by "pre-ignition." In the vaporization process, air pockets sometimes formed

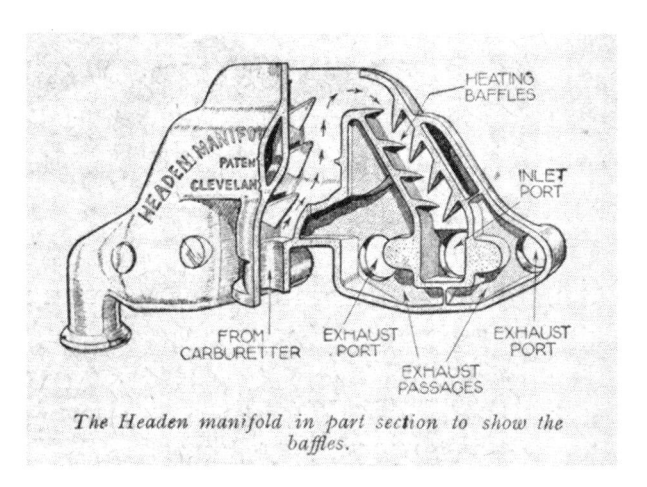

Headen's vaporizing manifold as illustrated in the September 21, 1931, issue of *Motor Transport*.

in an engine's cylinders when oil vapor and air did not mix thoroughly enough. These pockets caused the vapor to explode unexpectedly, making combustion erratic and pitting metal pistons and cylinder walls. To combat the problem, Headen returned to the principle of complete lifecycle heating. Adding to the heat applied near the beginning of the vaporization process, he placed a pipe between the exhaust manifold and the inlet of the carburetor. Directing a portion of the exhaust gases into the inlet, he started the vaporization process earlier, so that by the time the oil-air mixture passed from the carburetor through the vaporizer and entered the cylinders, it did so in a much drier form. The drier the vapor, the more evenly it mixed with air, and the fewer the air pockets that led to pre-ignition.[10]

As he waited for the British Patent Office's approval of his newest idea, Headen went forward with his manufacturing plans. By the end of 1932 he had put into production a converter kit that enabled the owners of Ford automobiles, as well as Chevrolet, Bedford, and Morris commercial vehicles, to switch their engines from petrol to heavier oils. He also offered Fordson tractor owners the option of replacing older vaporizers with his more efficient one. Headen simultaneously turned his attention to sales, demonstrating the promotional finesse he had been building for years. Greeting clients at a new London office at 10 Finsbury Circus, he wooed distributors from across the United Kingdom, who would soon be supplying his kit to a network of agricultural machinery suppliers and garages in England, Scotland, and Northern Ireland. Ranging from lesser known concerns, such as H. R. Evershed in Derby, Derbyshire, to larger, more prominent ones, such as Cuthbert & Son in Dundee, Scotland, these suppliers made Headen's invention widely available.[11]

After displaying his manifold kit at the Commercial Motor Transport Exhibition at Olympia in November 1933, Headen watched it soar in popularity. Once installed, advertisements claimed, his design could cut fuel costs in half. Those who tried it seemed happy with the results. After being on the market for only two years, the manifold was described by the *Commercial Motor* as "One of the first devices for running petrol engines on vaporizing oil to be extensively used in this country." Consumers were particularly pleased that, after Headen had received a patent on his pre-ignition device in 1933, he had incorporated it into his kit. The *Commercial Motor* in 1934 recommended the "Simplicity of Control" of the new assembly, noting that it not only lowered fuel consumption but provided greater engine flexibility. A few months later, in January 1935, Motor Accessments, Ltd., of London, encouraged by sales, signed on as the improved kit's main distributor.[12]

James Keil at St. Mary's Works, witnessing Headen's rise in the motor world, had by 1933 begun to take an interest in the American newcomer. When Headen and Hamilton decided to end their association (perhaps finding it too difficult to coordinate across an ocean), Keil stepped in. Forming Headen Keil Engineering Company Limited, registration number 285739, in early 1934, the new partners decided to maintain production on Victoria Avenue but moved the company's headquarters from London to Keil's offices at St. Mary's Works, where Keil assumed administrative responsibilities.[13]

Keil's contributions were critical. Besides his monetary investment, he possessed considerable wherewithal to further the company's interests. An established contractor of fifteen years, Keil had strong community ties and an inside track to local government. Among his close circle was his mentor and fellow Mason, solicitor Edwyn T. Close, who joined Headen Keil Engineering as its third director. Keil was a member of the Camberley and Frimley Urban Council, and Close was attorney for the Camberley Chamber of Commerce. Their positions gave both men a voice in decisions concerning the town's industries. Not surprisingly, Victoria Avenue was "made up" (paved) in 1937, freeing lorries carrying the company's shipments from having to contend with a muddy, rutted roadway.[14]

With Keil and Close handling logistics, Headen happily returned to his true passion. Just before entering into the partnership with Keil, he had begun working on a means to eliminate the most stubborn impediment remaining to the embrace of bi-fuel engines—the tendency of unburned fuel to dilute crankcase lubricating oil. Even if an engine had excellent vaporization, if its temperatures cooled, the dry vapor that entered the cylinders quickly returned to liquid form, seeping down the cylinders to threaten the engine's crank. As a result, vehicle owners had to replace the thicker crankcase oil with great frequency, adding extra cost, not to mention aggravation. Should they neglect this vital maintenance chore, as many busy motorists and farmers, harried during planting and harvesting season, did, they could face costly repairs.[15]

The journal *Roadless News* lamented that "innumerable efforts" had been made in the 1920s and early 1930s to prevent crankcase oil dilution, but that no one had made any significant progress. That changed with a novel gasket Headen introduced in 1935. Characterized by one trade writer as "a remarkable cure," the nickel-copper alloy device, which fit between the cylinder head and combustion chamber, was cut into a serrated shape and included thin metal projections that reached downward into the combustion chamber. Highly heated, these projections created hot spots that ignited the air-fuel mist as it entered the cylinders. The gasket also formed a flange, or collar, to trap any recondensed vapor. The remaining heat from the chamber explosion burned the trapped condensate prior to the next charge of aerated fuel entering.[16]

Headen's design allowed kerosene, paraffin, TVO, and other fuels to be burned with minimal dilution, even in engines working under very light loads. By mid-1935, he had applied for British, U.S., French, and Canadian patents, and had caught the attention of Roadless Traction Ltd., of Hounslow, Middlesex, publishers of the *Roadless News*. Roadless Traction specialized in fitting tractors, farm machinery, and earth movers with rubber and steel linked tracks, adapted from World War I tank tracks, to make them usable in soft soils. Intrigued by Headen's gasket, the company began examining it in March 1935, running extensive bench analyses, and corresponding with farmers who installed it on their tractors, as well as hauliers who fitted it on their lorries. Witnessing positive outcomes on test beds, and convinced by positive testimonials, in May Roadless praised the gasket's simple, easy-to-install design, and declared itself "so impressed by the results" that it negotiated an arrangement with Headen to become the gasket's sole distributor for Fordson tractors in Britain and in "such foreign countries as their commitments permit."[17]

The deal was significant. American-designed Fordsons were the most widely used tractors in Britain throughout the 1930s and 1940s, and Roadless had a distribution network that stretched across several continents. From May 1935 through 1936, the firm carried out a vigorous campaign to promote Headen's "remarkable invention." The gasket, entered in the Royal Agricultural Society of England's Silver Medal competition for 1937, did not win, but customer enthusiasm for it tempered any disappointment Headen may have felt. In midsummer 1935, Roadless reported that the gasket had received the blessing of the Ford Motor Company, which informed buyers that replacing a factory-installed gasket with Headen's would not invalidate the company's warranty. Receiving requests for the gasket worldwide and watching sales rise, Roadless announced the following spring that increased production would allow them to lower the initial five pound cost, about which some had complained.[18]

Headen's decision to market his gasket primarily to farmers was a considered one. Parliament's Finance Act of 1935 had sharply increased the tax on heavy oils, notably diesel but also paraffin, kerosene, and TVO, if they were used to power road vehicles. Removing some of the cost advantage that heavy oils had represented, the act lessened the incentive for everyday motorists to take a risk on bi-fuel (or on diesel) engines. It also created what one writer to London's *The Motor* described in 1938 as almost "insuperable difficulties" for private individuals to obtain paraffin or kerosene for their cars. The problem was that oil importers, responsible for administering the duty, opted to act as wholesalers for industrial or commercial users rather than support the country's thousands of small fueling stations. Required to calculate and collect the tax for each sale, they found it simply too onerous to sell to individual dealers.[19]

The act had exempted from the higher duty, however, any heavy oil used in farm vehicles, including tractors and the lorries that farmers employed to deliver their products to market. This exclusion was one of many steps taken by the British government to stem a worrisome decline in agricultural cultivation across the United Kingdom. In the years after World War I, and continuing in the economic downturn of the 1930s, a growing number of financially strapped landowners, especially in northern England and Scotland, had begun to abandon fields. Relying increasingly on hand-power and horses to till smaller and smaller plots, they showed ever greater caution toward investing in mechanical means of planting or harvesting. To combat what one agricultural historian has called Britain's "nadir of arable farming," Parliament founded the Agricultural Research Council in 1930 to encourage scientific farming methods, and later provided direct monetary aid to some growers. In 1935, it saw tax relief as another tool to foster the mechanization needed to maintain or boost production.[20]

The act's effect for Headen was that farmers were now his most promising market, and he provided Parliament at least partially what it had hoped. His gasket, according to the *Roadless News*, most benefitted those running older, less efficient tractors, giving reluctant farmers, tempted to abandon machinery altogether, reason to stay engaged with machine production. Unbeknownst to government officials, and to Headen, this fact would prove important in only a few years, with the outbreak of war in Europe.[21]

Headen's new focus on farmers, however, did not stop him from looking in other directions. He knew if his company was to survive, he would have to stay diversified. Fortunately, Parliament, eager to encourage aviation in Britain, had also exempted aeronautical uses of heavy oils from the new duty. In response, while Roadless was advertising his gasket on the agricultural market, Headen began testing it in aircraft engines. During the summer of 1935, he purchased a Hermes 104-horsepower motor. Modifying the gasket for aeronautical use and adding an exhaust-heated fuel-feed boiler and blower driven by a helical gear, he submitted the Hermes to the Air Ministry for trial, hoping to obtain a coveted Certificate of Airworthiness. The engine, according to a representative from *Aeroplane* magazine who witnessed initial tests, ran "perfectly evenly" on heavy oil at all throttle settings, idled well, showed no signs of engine "knock," and demonstrated good horsepower. Encouraged, Headen purchased a Carden-Ford "Flying Flea," a lightweight aircraft whose engine was a modified Ford C Ten auto engine, and converted it to run on heavy oil.[22]

Headen also experimented with using his gasket in stationary engines and in boat motors. Paraffin had long been a popular fuel for both, and the gasket held promise for increasing their efficiency. By the late 1930s, rising sales, stoked by Roadless's steady advertising, the economic benefit his invention provided farmers, demand from commercial users (who a surprised Roadless noted in 1935 had emerged as a good part of its market, despite the new tax on heavy oil for road vehicles), and the gasket's adoption for marine and other purposes, had begun to overwhelm Headen's ability to produce it. In 1937, when granted a U.S. patent, he assigned the overseas production rights to George Koelliker, and by 1942, with copper, a major component of the gasket, being diverted for military use, his company had given up its manufacture in England altogether.[23]

With diesel oil also released from the new duty if used for agriculture, in 1935 Headen began thinking about how to help farmers turn this exemption to their advantage. As always, he had immediate economy in mind. A number of new diesel tractors had recently come on the market (some of the early problems of the diesel engine now having been solved), and these new designs promised both increased power and enviable fuel efficiency. Diesel-engine tractors, however, carried high price tags, and they remained well beyond the means of the average farmer. Recognizing that their high cost often nullified the benefits they provided, Headen approached the problem another way, developing an oil-burning carburetor for tractors designed to run solely on petrol or on petrol and paraffin/TVO.

His configuration, as described by contemporaries, used the tractor's normal carburetor for starting, then switched to an updraft carburetor with dual jets (one for slow running and one for power). The system also included an oil preheater unit, a vaporization chamber surrounding the exhaust manifold, and a "hotbox" to trap impurities. Headen applied for two patents, one for the basic design of his carburetor in 1935 and one for improvements in 1936, and received both in 1937. In July of that year, he placed the carburetor before the public at the Royal Agricultural Show in Wolverhampton. According to the journal *Engineering*, when fitted to a standard Fordson engine, it provided "very considerable economy" and increased performance. Like his gasket, Headen's new design also contended for the Royal Agricultural Society of England's Silver Medal, and though it did not capture the prize, it nonetheless sold well throughout Britain, France, and Australia.[24]

Headen's vaporizing manifold, his popular gasket, and his new carburetor brought him broad recognition in Britain's mechanical engineering community. In January 1937, he was invited to participate in the second annual Oxford Conference on Mechanized Farming at Oxford University. The gathering gave him the opportunity to discuss oil engine mechanics with academic researchers and other manufacturers and to gain immediate feedback on his products from farmers, three hundred of whom attended from across the United Kingdom.[25]

Headen's achievements also led to his emergence as a business leader in Camberley. When the *Camberley News* published a feature in August 1937 on local industrial development, it named the "chief figures" behind it as Keil, Close, Headen, and W. Sturmy Cave, a principal of Rowlands Metal Windows. Headen, in France on business when Keil gave the *News* reporter a tour of their company, did not have a chance to speak for his accomplishments, but the writer went home impressed nonetheless. The company's exports to continental Europe and Australia, the article claimed, were helping carry the name of Camberley "far and wide." The reporter was also struck by Headen's broad-ranging interests, noting that besides gaskets and carburetors, he had spied on the company's premises a "robot control" device that could remotely modulate the speed of a car.[26]

Keil's conversation with the reporter on the future of Camberley industry also reflected Headen's influence. Aware that many local retirees felt upset at "hideous factories" appearing in their "favoured spot," Keil offered an argument that sounded familiar. Industry, he noted, would provide jobs for local youth. Better, though, it would draw a large artisan class to Camberley, which would help "solve for the residential areas the problem of the domestic servant shortage." (The thinking, evidently, was that the artisans' wives would go to work as maids, cooks, and nannies for well-off local residents.) Speaking directly to a major concern of the local social elite, who often complained of their "urgent need for labour," he articulated a plan of mutual cooperation that echoed the legacy of Henry Wood, and of Wood's protégé.[27]

Enjoying steady success, Headen was not content to rest on his inventive laurels or to restrain himself to a single interest. In 1936, with his aviation interests renewed by his experiments with aircraft engines, he set his sights on solving another aeronautical problem, how to combat ice formation on wings, propellers, and aircraft control surfaces, such as the rudder and ailerons. By the time the Air Ministry posted a special notice in November 1937 advertising the critical need for "deicing devices for British aircraft," Headen had already been working on the issue for more than a year. Between 1936 and 1939, the majority of engineers in England who tackled the problem focused on developing alcohol-based sprays to remove ice, or chemical pastes that could be applied to the wings to deter ice buildup. Many designers in the United States touted the adoption of inflatable rubber "boots" (or "overshoes") developed by the B. F. Goodrich Company. Placed over the leading edge of a wing, these boots, when filled with compressed air, expanded and pulsated, cracking any ice that had formed. Still another inventor offered a scheme to place a "metallic matting" on the leading edge of the wing, whose uneven layers, as they moved over each other, broke up ice.[28]

Headen took a different tack. His ice-prevention and deicing designs, patented in Britain, France, and Canada, like his engine modifications, relied on thermal methods. His plan was to employ air heated by exhaust to deter and break up ice on wings and control surfaces. First, he fashioned an outer jacket over the exhaust manifold to trap heat escaping from the engine and use it to warm air. He then added a blower (powered by an external windmill placed in the slipstream of the propeller) to force the heated air into perforated, lightweight metal tubes that ran the length of the wing. He also included branch pipes to the ailerons and tail. Hot air, under pressure in the pipes, shot up in jets through the perforations, warming the leading edge. In the branch pipes, the jets were aimed directly against the ailerons and the elevator and rudder joints and hinges—that is, the surfaces critical to keep clear of ice to maintain control of the aircraft. To avoid any loss of force in the jets along the length of the piping, including the branch pipes, Headen increased the diameter of the perforations in the further reaches of the pipes. This design ensured the jets would release heat with equal force throughout the piping infrastructure. Headen also incorporated valves in the pipes to allow warm air to be routed into the cockpit or exhausted into the outer atmosphere when deicing was not needed.[29]

Headen's "pressure jet system" built on the work of earlier thermal-method pioneers, whose efforts, though they had yielded few marketable products, had greatly advanced his and others' understandings of icing and heat transfer. Key among these individuals were Theodore Theodorsen and William Clay of the National Advisory Committee for Aeronautics (NACA) in the United States. The two had experimented in the late 1920s and early 1930s with steam vapor to prevent ice formation on wings. Heating water, and later an alcohol-water mix, in a small boiler placed within the exhaust pipe, they had funneled the resulting steam through perforated pipes along the wing's leading edge. Although they patented this method, many rejected it because of the weight that the boiler and necessary "sumps" (required to capture water left in the wing when the steam recondensed) added to the plane.[30]

Other experimenters had routed exhaust gases directly into wing structures, or through pipes located throughout the wing. These methods, too, had proved impractical, as the acidic gases corroded and warped the wing materials, and the large number of pipes required added excessive weight. Even those who had early shared Headen's confidence in heated air had encountered difficulties. Employing fans described by Theodorsen and Clay as "clumsy and heavy" to circulate the air within the wings, these early designers also needed extensive piping to guarantee even heating.[31]

Headen's pressure jet design had avoided the problem of a cumbersome boiler and sump by employing heated air rather than steam, had taken measures to solve the problem of heat transfer in piping by incrementing the size of the jet apertures, and had added economy to earlier designs by focusing on providing heat directly where it was most needed.

To deice propellers, Headen applied similar principles. Using the suction created by the propeller's spinning, he pulled hot gases from the engine into the propeller hub. He then constructed flexible, perforated ducts along the leading edge of each propeller blade (covering the ducts with sheet metal to protect them and lessen drag), and funneled either the gases themselves or air heated by them through small exterior pipes that fed into the blade ducts. Finally, he exhausted the gases or hot air through a hole in each blade tip. This system delivered enough heat along the blade edges to break up ice and allow the propellers to fling it off.[32]

It is unknown if Headen worked directly with others in Camberley on his ice prevention and deicing ideas, but he seldom labored in isolation. By the time England entered the European war in 1939, he was already well known locally as a "consulting engineer." He was listed as such in the 1939 National Register, a wartime census undertaken to document all those present in England and

Wales and their war-relevant skills. The *Camberley News*'s observation in September 1937 that Headen was experimenting with a "robot control" device is intriguing because it suggests he may have been working with local military designers. The very month of the reporter's visit to Headen Keil, researchers at the Royal Aircraft Establishment (RAE) in Farnborough, three miles outside Camberley, were preparing to test a radio-controlled plane to be used as a moving target in antiaircraft gunnery training.[33]

Other likely benefactors of Headen's engineering expertise were the wartime businesses that thrived at St. Mary's Works. In 1936, inventor Frank B. Harley had started Aerolex Limited at the works to produce aviation components, and Edwyn Close served as a director. Initially manufacturing parachute connector and release devices, during the war Harley converted his factory to produce full airplane sections, including wings and fuselages. By 1940 St. Mary's had also attracted Vivian Loyd & Company, a maker of small tanks run on Ford truck engines, and Wilkinson Rubber Linatex, the creator of a "self-healing" plastic sealant for airplane petrol tanks that prevented fuel leakage in the event a tank was pierced by machine gun fire. A familiar sight at St. Mary's works, Headen, with valuable aeronautical and engine knowledge to impart, was an integral part of Camberley's engineering community. He likely used this group to vet his deicing methods.[34]

Unfortunately for Headen, any access he may have had to the facilities needed to test his thermal methods disappeared early in the war. The RAE in Farnborough had shown interest in the icing problem, conducting research between 1933 and 1935 on a leather covering for the leading edge of wings that absorbed a water-glycol mixture capable of melting ice, and it later experimented with alcohol-based sprays and chemical pastes in its laboratories. It had also, in 1935, started preliminary wind tunnel tests to calculate the amount of exhaust needed to prevent ice formation. If the RAE's researchers considered his ideas, however, they had little opportunity to give them serious study. A few months after Headen received his propeller deicing patents, the Luftwaffe bombed the RAE grounds, forcing the organization to abandon ice-related research and focus on more immediate demands. The RAE subsequently asked the National Research Council of Canada to take up the work on its behalf. The council obliged, but it directed its energies not to exhaust-based or heated-air methods but to an electrothermal technique in which heat-creating resistors were embedded into wing edges and propeller blades.[35]

Others, though, would pick up on Headen's designs. Among them was British aviation hero Sir Alan Cobham, founder of Flight Refuelling Ltd. It is unclear if Cobham was aware of Headen's patents, but during the war he used

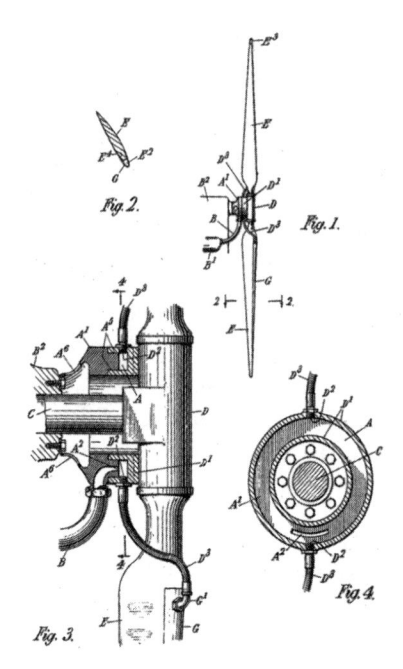

Drawing from GB Patent 506,444, for Headen's propeller deicing system. This patent, along with its corollary GB Patent 505,737, and the corresponding French patents he received for the design were cited by numerous corporate researchers at Curtiss-Wright, Rolls-Royce, and other companies in the 1940s and 1950s, and more recently by designers for Vestas Wind Systems, which operates wind turbines around the world. Image from Google Patents.

his personal influence to convince the Air Ministry to loan his company a Fairey Battle plane to test a system that closely resembled Headen's. Like Headen, Cobham conducted exhaust-heated air through to the leading edge of the wing. However, according to his chief engineer at the time, he was unable to make his system work, encountering issues with weight and problems with wing distortion.[36]

Efforts in the United States proved more successful. Taking over from Theodorsen and Clay, in 1936 Lewis Rodert revived NACA's interest in icing, initiating experiments in 1937 in which he pumped hot exhaust gases directly through pipes along the wing's leading edge. He continued work on this method until 1941, when he met resistance from military observers, who pointed out the dangers of gas-filled pipes being punctured by a bullet and exploding. At this point, Rodert began to experiment with using heated air instead, building over the next four years an effective "hot wing" that pumped air, warmed by exhaust, through an enclosed chamber along the leading edge. Many have credited Rodert's work with laying the foundation for current-day anti-icing systems, and he received the Collier Trophy in 1946 for his contributions.[37]

Working outside the military-industrial laboratories of Flight Refuelling Ltd., the Air Ministry, the National Research Council of Canada, and NACA,

Headen could only watch as others built the wind and icing tunnels needed to test his principles, enjoyed the support of academic and military mathematicians and physicists to help develop critical calculations, and garnered access to military test planes. The one man with whom Headen might have had his best chance to develop his ideas, Lieutenant John King Hardy of the RAE in Farnborough, was by the early 1940s on his way to California, transferred there to work with Rodert and his team at the Ames Research Center. A mathematician of note, and possessing significant aeronautical experience, Hardy provided Rodert with the calculations on heat dissipation under icing conditions that were critical to making his "hot wing" work.[38]

Despite the languishing of his anti-icing work, Headen could take satisfaction in the fact that his earlier inventions assumed greater importance in the crisis of war. With able-bodied men leaving the fields to fight, mechanized agriculture in Britain was no longer a choice, it was a necessity, and every machine, no matter how old, had either to be scrapped for its metal or made serviceable for the national emergency. Headen's gasket and his improved converter kit (popularly known as the Headen Heat Unit), by increasing the fuel efficiency of aged tractors, extended their working lives. Allowing farmers to save precious paraffin, kerosene, and TVO, now all rationed commodities, they became part of what one writer in 1942 called "The Offensive on the Farm."[39]

Commercial vehicle makers and the military also turned to Headen's technology. Just as Britain entered the conflict in 1939, Aveling-Barford Ltd. of Grantham, Lincolnshire, began offering his converter kit for its "dumpers," which included small earth movers frequently employed on military bases. The *Commercial Motor* noted that the kit combined Headen's antidilution gasket, a hot box (attached to the exhaust manifold), a radiator thermostat to maintain the engine at the correct temperature, and an auxiliary petrol tank for the carburetor. In addition, the Air Ministry in April 1936 had purchased a batch of Fordson Model N tractors from Roadless Traction, just as Roadless was enthusiastically promoting Headen's gasket. Roadless had refitted the Fordsons with its signature steel and rubber linked tracks to make them suitable for mowing airstrips. When war broke out, the Royal Air Force pressed this lot of Fordson Ns into service at its air bases. Although the RAF also purchased powerful, quick-starting petrol tractors to haul bombs and aircraft, the 1936 Fordsons fit the bill for mowing, snow removal, earth moving, and other tasks around the airstrip. In addition, according to the *West Sussex News*, the military was converting some tanks and planes to burn paraffin, although it is not known if they used Headen's gasket on these.[40]

Finally, Headen may also have enjoyed additional income from sales of his converter kit resulting from its clandestine use by motorists. Stephen Corsi, a young man who lived in the countryside outside London, later noted that during the war "only essential vehicles were allowed to have petrol." Thus, some desperate farmers secretly adapted their cars to make local trips running on the paraffin they received for agricultural purposes.[41]

Sales of the Headen Heat Unit remained strong among farmers, even after mid-1942, when fuel rationing eased with the arrival of new American oil supplies. In November 1942, Headen remarked, in response to an inquiry from the National Institute of Agricultural Engineering (later the Silsoe Institute), that his kit was selling briskly. As evidence, he referred the institute to several long-established Ford distributors, including the County Garage Company of Carlisle, Cumbria, and Reginald Tildesley Ltd., Willenhall, South Staffordshire. Tildesley alone, he told the institute, had recently sold a thousand units "without complaints." Heavy advertisement of the kit across the United Kingdom throughout the war indicates sales did not slow after that year. Offering economy and flexibility to the owners of the 137,000 Fordsons in use during the war years, his invention was the perfect answer to immediate needs.[42]

While Headen's business advanced, his personal life holds more mystery. All evidence indicates he was happy in Camberley, where he relished the independence he achieved through his ideas. "I have made my living out of inventions," he told a U.S. Embassy employee on a visit to London in 1955. "My method is to develop them, get a sale by putting them on the market and then sell the patent rights." Maintaining the confidence he had first asserted in letters to Josephus Daniels in 1917, he had proved the mettle behind the moxie, and the coveted title of inventor was undisputedly his.[43]

Headen's success also provided material comfort. In Camberley he inhabited the best-appointed hotels, dining in or out as he pleased. Registered between 1932 and 1937 at the Duke of York, with a short stint at the Alverstone Hotel in Bagshot, he relocated in September 1938 to the Camberley Court Hotel at the corner of Park Road and Firlands Avenue. The move reflected his rising fortunes. Described as "the finest residential hotel in the district," Camberley Court was equipped with rare amenities, including central heating and running water in its rooms, and it offered its residents gardens, tennis courts, greens for putting, bowling, and croquet, and private garages. The latter were especially convenient for storing the two cars Headen then owned, a Ford and a Hudson. The hotel, home to Camberley's elite, in 1939 housed in immediate proximity to Headen a retired general, a bank manager, the director of a tin and steel company, and a woman "of private means."[44]

Headen also gained in England a level of public respect he never could have imagined at home, escaping segregation and the assault of daily indignities he had endured throughout his life. The *Afro-American*'s William N. Jones remarked in November 1933 that many hotels and restaurants in London practiced "no discrimination of any kind," and historian Joel A. Rogers added six months later that those with light complexions enjoyed remarkable freedom. Headen's experience confirmed both observations. He was "medium light," a skin tone he shared with Nannie, and his presence sparked no protests. In London he had resided at the Strand Palace Hotel, the city's art deco showpiece, without difficulty, and in Camberley those at the Duke of York and Camberley Court welcomed him as a neighbor. The same was true as he traveled across Britain. On business trips, he lodged at some of the country's best accommodations, including Bristol's exclusive Grand Hotel and the Queens Hotel in Leeds.[45]

Headen's role in the British engineering community and the Camberley commercial class similarly raised no consternation. Trade journals and scientific proceedings discussed his inventions and actions without mentioning his race, and the *Camberley News* portrayed him as a leader in local industry, rather than creating the narrative of an African American descendant of slaves in their midst. To James Keil's son Alan, Headen was simply the "American who had a great big car," and who thrilled the Keil children with a ride in it in the 1930s, when few citizens owned powerful automobiles. In Britain, Headen was free of the American tunnel vision that often saw him only as "L. A. Headen, a negro." He became instead, as his 1957 obituary called him, "An American Who Settled in Frimley Green," the village where he would spend many of his later years.[46]

Despite his success and the welcome given him, however, starting over in a new country was difficult. For a man already in his fifties, homesickness and loneliness were inevitable. The sense of belonging Headen had felt in the pews of John Hall Chapel, the desks of Dayton and Albion Academies, the Erie's dining cars, the grease pits of Wabash Avenue, the chairs of State Street's barber shops, and the worn seat of his Headen Special as he flew around a track to cheering crowds was not easily recreated in England. In the mid-1930s he was one of only an estimated ten to fifteen thousand people of African descent living in Britain. And few, with the exception of black Londoners, lived in the south of England, residing instead where they could find work on the docks, in industries, or in the coal mines of Liverpool, Cardiff, Swansea, and Hull, all far from Surrey. In an almost entirely white European environment, locating others who understood or shared his history and perspective required effort.[47]

Headen found one important, if limited, source of affiliation with the small black population that flourished in London. He shared their excitement when, in the spring of 1935, British moviemakers announced that famed American singer and actor Paul Robeson and silent film star Nina Mae McKinney would appear together in a feature film titled *Sanders of the River*. On April 1, 1935, Headen wrote his friend Robert Abbott about the film, enclosing press clippings on the upcoming premier at the Leicester Square Theatre. He stated that he planned to attend, despite the $52.50 admission fee (equivalent today to almost £780, or $1,000). In his understated way, he commented only that, "That is a very high price but I am planning on seeing same tomorrow." His lack of concern over the cost speaks not only to the health of his business but to his desire to maintain an identification with a larger black community and its interests.[48]

Headen's connection to those in London, however, yielded only partial satisfaction. As an engineer, he had little beyond his race in common with the students, intellectuals, political activists, artists, and athletes living in the city. Most were much younger than he and hailed from the far corners of Britain's empire, representing the divergent cultures of the West Indies and Africa. Most black Americans who came to the city were musicians and entertainers appearing in local theaters, and unlike Robeson they rarely stayed longer than a few months. As Headen struggled to find common ground with black Londoners, they likewise seem to have taken little interest in him. Popular journals published in the city, such as *The Keys*, edited by the city's League of Coloured Peoples, never mentioned Headen or his achievements, and his name does not appear on any membership or contribution lists the journal published.[49]

Headen would at times succumb to nostalgia for his old life. Writing to congratulate Abbott on the thirtieth anniversary of the founding of the *Chicago Defender*, he remarked wistfully that the event had prompted him to "go back into the annals of my life for 30 years and recall the little one room that afforded the birthplace of such an enormous institution." He knew when he wrote those words that he would likely never see that little room, the bustling press building that had replaced it, or the man who had started the *Defender*, again. Despite their separation, however, Abbott remained important to Headen. Only a few of the letters they exchanged have survived, but their contents indicate that he found in Abbott, and in his newspaper, a lifeline to home.[50]

Headen relished the viewpoint, absent in the English press, he found in the *Defender*. The paper, he wrote Abbott, gave him "the true reflection of things in America." The two also discussed the "true reflection of things" in England.

Despite his greater freedom, Headen had no illusions that his adopted country was free of racism. Like Paul Robeson's wife, Eslanda, he found England "warm and friendly and unprejudiced," but he was aware of dangers beneath the surface. Abbott, whose skin was considerably darker than his own, had been asked to leave several London hotels in 1929 after white American tourists recoiled at his presence. Other dark-skinned men such as Universal Negro Improvement Association founder Marcus Garvey, and even on occasion Robeson himself, had experienced similar insults. As the *Afro*'s William Jones put it, despite fundamentally better race relations in England, a stranger nonetheless was at some point "bound to run into Old Man Prejudice." If intermittent segregation went unchecked, Headen knew, the color line could tighten around him.[51]

As he thought of his new home, Headen seems to have viewed it much as he had France in his youth, as a racial haven imperiled by American racism. Many shared his viewpoint. In response to Abbott's experience, the *Pittsburgh Courier* had lamented "The Americanization of London" and a *Defender* writer had claimed "London Hotels Bow to American Prejudice." NAACP head William Pickens warned of "American color poison" being allowed to enter the country. Hotelkeepers and restaurant owners, they reasoned, were not motivated by deep-seated prejudice but by economic necessity. They turned blacks away because they feared losing the white American travelers whose patronage kept them afloat. As the *Defender* put it, "Money talks." Abbott initially took a dimmer view, publishing an article upon his return to the United States that documented a long history of racial prejudice in England. Once the sting of rejection faded, though, he too was increasingly drawn to the idea of white American influence abroad.[52]

Keen to defend England against the menace of color prejudice, Headen, like many writers in London, began providing Abbott fodder for stories on American racism abroad. Becoming the publisher's eyes and ears in the southern countryside, he regularly collected information on white tourists' misconduct observed in Camberley and elsewhere during his travels. "I am more than pleased that the information I gather here is ammunition," he wrote in 1934. He also sought to soften Abbott's view of the English, insisting that the actions of those in the tourist industry did not reflect the nation's true feelings and did not fit the sentiments of England's civil authorities. Government officials showed no fear in confronting American haughtiness, he told Abbott, citing as proof an incident in which the passport of a white American woman was revoked after she argued with a town constable over an accident she caused near his factory. Although alert to danger, Headen appreciated the rule of law in England, and he hoped that by shining a light on the Americans who threatened it, he could help preserve it.[53]

In early 1940, after a year's illness, Robert Abbott died from kidney failure. Headen grieved for his confidant. He also mourned an important tether to his past. He still had family ties, but it is unclear how closely he stayed in touch during the busy 1930s or in the war years, when travel home became impossible. Evidence indicates that he and Nannie were still in close contact when he lived in Albany. She proudly passed on information about his efforts to rebuild his factory to the *Winston-Salem Journal*, which published an article on his work in 1926. In 1930, before leaving for England, he made a trip through Philadelphia to visit with Guy and Marie. Family stories also note that he corresponded with Nannie in the postwar years. Given their bond, it is reasonable to assume that she wrote Headen with news of home during his early years in England.[54]

Separation from friends and from his father and sisters was undoubtedly difficult for Headen. Yet he seems to have had few regrets over his decision to become an expatriate. Throughout his life he saw himself as an American, never applying for British citizenship. As war clouds gathered, however, it became clear just how fully he had accepted England as his home and how much loyalty he felt for his new country. While many resident aliens fled, Headen chose to stay, even as he faced mortal danger. In late 1938, in his last surviving letter to Abbott, Headen explained that, "we are always expecting a fight." Noting that the government had supplied a gas mask to every individual in the country, he remarked that local residents were digging pits and cellars for shelter during air raids. Thirty miles from London and close to military facilities, Camberley's residents were intensely aware that they would be a direct target for the Luftwaffe, which after 1940 had airfields just across the English Channel. They were right. Though escaping the devastation dealt London in the course of the war, the Frimley and Camberley District suffered the dropping of 300 bombs, ranging from explosive and incendiary devices delivered from the air to cruise missile "doodlebugs" launched from the French coast.[55]

Running a factory in an industrial area near the railroad and located just across London Road from Sandhurst Royal Military Academy, Headen knew he was in particular danger. Bomb strikes, such as the one on the RAE in August 1940, which left two dead; another that hit Frimley Road in 1941, killing one; and a December 1941 blast at Sandhurst, in which four cadets perished and eleven others were injured, quickly brought home the threat. The Frimley Road and Sandhurst bombs had fallen less than a mile from 15 Victoria Avenue.[56]

Headen proudly wore the uniform of the Home Guard during World War II. His arm patch carries the designation "U.S.A.," capturing his dual allegiance to his native country and to the one he adopted. Courtesy of Lucean Headen Jr.

Headen, nonetheless, committed himself fully to the war effort. In February 1940, he left the comforts of the Camberley Court Hotel to live at 11 Edward Avenue, a block south of his factory. Being only a minute away allowed him to keep watch for saboteurs, a nagging concern of wartime manufacturers, and to devote longer hours to production. Headen also joined the first wave of enlistees in the Local Defence Volunteers. Soon to be known as the Home Guard, the organization relied on men too old or too young for His Majesty's forces. Among the excited crowd that thronged the local Police Station to register in May 1940, Headen enlisted in the Camberley Regiment of the Surrey 1st Battalion. In the coming months he trained alongside his fellow volunteers in drilling, first aid, rifle fire, and grenade launching. In November, he traveled to Builth Wells, Breconshire, Wales, possibly for further training at the newly established Sennybridge Training Area located just north of the village.[57]

In addition to working long hours at the factory and contributing to guard duty, roadblocks, and defense measures, Headen purchased war bonds and, according to family lore, lent his personal boat (likely the one he had used in his 1936 gasket experiments) to help evacuate soldiers from Dunkirk. His generosity and willingness to put himself in harm's way endeared him to many in Camberley, who looked past a general suspicion of aliens to embrace him. Fears of foreign spies were rife during the war and led to strict regulations. Although Headen had always been required to register address changes with the local constabulary, he now had to report out-of-town trips and faced a curfew whenever he traveled. On a trip to Leeds in 1940, for instance, he was required to remain inside his hotel between 10:30 P.M. and 6:00 A.M. The consequences of breaking the rules included fines or imprisonment, as a rueful Belgian businessman in nearby Aldershot, a twenty-year resident of England, learned in 1940. Tried after failing to report a two-week absence from his home, he faced a stern warning and a monetary fine. Headen suffered the expanded restrictions on his movements without complaint, and this seems only to have further cemented the goodwill of those in Camberley.[58]

World War II allowed Headen to share in a bonding experience essential to British identity, and working shoulder to shoulder with his townsmen and fellow engineers at St. Mary's Works was an effective antidote to any loneliness he still felt. His isolation would further dissipate when, after almost seventeen years as a bachelor, he again found love. The recipient of his affections was Frimley Green resident Gladys Hollamby. Where Lucean and Gladys met is unclear, but at the time of their marriage the twenty-six-year-old was working as a secretary and typist for the Aircraft Inspection Department of a local company. That company was possibly Aerolex, which hired a large female workforce. The couple married in a civil ceremony at the Surrey Register Office on November 3, 1945, with Gladys's older brother William Hollamby Jr., a local businessman, as a witness.[59]

As he had with Tena, Headen shared with his new wife the experience of a parent's early passing. Gladys's father, William Hollamby Sr., an Aldershot assurance agent and photographer, had died in 1936, just before his daughter's seventeenth birthday. Soon afterward, Gladys's mother Mary relocated the family to Frimley Green, south of Camberley, where they moved into Holmwood, a small home on Beech Road near the village's green. Mary Hollamby passed away only five years later, leaving Gladys, the youngest of the couple's thirteen children, an orphan at twenty-two. She and several of her siblings pooled their resources to remain at Holmwood after their mother's death.[60]

Attentive to his new wife's wish to stay close to her family, Headen moved with her to Orchardleigh, next door to Holmwood. Despite the thirty-five-year difference in their ages, the couple had a compatible, affectionate relationship.

Gladys Hollamby, whom Headen married in 1945. This photo was taken not long before the couple wed in November 1945. Courtesy of Lucean Headen Jr.

After a three-day honeymoon at the Ritz Hotel in London, a luxury spot that had survived Germany's bombs, they settled into domestic life, and Headen once again had family to moor him.[61]

Marriage would not be the only transition Headen experienced in the postwar years. At the conflict's end, James Keil became increasingly occupied with a new company, Ancillary Developments Ltd. Based at Blackbushe Aerodrome, the firm produced camera equipment for the RAF and, later, electronic sensors and aircraft instruments. He shifted the remainder of his focus to his expanding real estate and commercial interests in Camberley and Farnborough. In 1946, Keil left the chairmanship of Rowlands Metal Windows, and he withdrew from Headen Keil Engineering a year later. Keil's departure was a blow to Headen, although he must have known it was inevitable. The heyday of bi-fuel engines was rapidly passing.[62]

As early as 1938, an article in *The Science of Petroleum* had predicted that, despite impressive improvements "in the design and flexibility of spark-ignited kerosine engines," the diesel engine would inevitably replace them. The prediction would prove true. By the end of the war, diesel engine designers had fully mastered the creation of high compression without adding excessive weight to a vehicle, and they had virtually eliminated crankcase dilution problems. The new designs they offered possessed significant advantages over spark engines that burned oil, including the fact that they did not require separate fuel mechanisms, a vaporizer, or special gaskets. More powerful petrol engines, too, had achieved higher compression, dramatically improving fuel efficiencies, and outstripping what bi-fuel motors could offer. Moreover, octane additives had addressed the issue of "knock," and petrol prices had dropped in relation to heavy oils after new catalysts were introduced into the crude oil distillation process, yielding a much higher proportion of petrol during distillation.[63]

Although tractors burning kerosene, paraffin, and TVO continued to be produced by Ford, Harry Ferguson, and others after the war, the market increasingly belonged to diesel and petrol vehicles. Even Vivian Loyd & Company at St. Mary's Works, which converted its factory to build tractors after the war, took up the trend, rolling out the diesel "Red Dragon" in 1950. Headen's advances had helped sustain interest in mechanics on farms during the years of agricultural depression, and they had helped support the war effort, but the future of engine technology belonged to a new generation of engineers. Headen, now sixty-six, no longer possessed the means to compete in a rapidly changing motor industry.[64]

With capital limited and his expertise supplanted, Headen looked to innovate in a more affordable direction. Forever adaptable and perceptive, he recognized that even as manufacturers were moving toward new technologies, a war-devastated Europe had little money to invest in them. Thus, he focused on filling a temporary niche in the agricultural economy. With metal supplies depleted by the conflict, he designed a simple, inexpensive replacement tip for plowshares that would appeal to cash-poor farmers. Cast from chilled iron, the "Headen Cap," when attached to an existing share, could extend its life, saving precious metal and expense.[65]

In 1947, Headen founded the Headen Novelty Company to produce the cap, retooling his Victoria Avenue factory for the purpose. The product hit a nerve. By February 1948 he had sold over 200,000 of the tips in England, France, Belgium, and Holland, and he was looking to expand its export possibilities. He approached the U.S. Embassy in London to request a European Recovery Program contract to supply the Headen Cap for use in the revival of agriculture in Germany. The Embassy official who received him informed his superiors at the State Department that Headen impressed him as "a very serious-minded and patriotic citizen of the United States." We do not know if the good impression succeeded in winning orders under the program as State Department files were heavily culled when archived, destroying most of the record.[66]

A month after his visit to the Embassy, however, Headen advertised the share tip's availability for worldwide export in *Foreign Commerce Weekly*, and he soon expanded its sales to India, where the Indian Agricultural Research Institute in Calcutta tested the cap in 1949, noting that it could increase the life of a steel share from twenty to sixty hours of plowing time. Headen continued to manufacture his share tip in Camberley until May 1951, when he moved production to Bedford Lane in Frimley Green, a short walk across the green from his new home. Receiving a British patent in 1952, he was still advertising his product as late as 1954, although by that time sales had slowed.[67]

In the years he operated Headen Novelty Company, Headen also made another life-changing transition. In early November 1948, after three years of marriage, he and Gladys adopted a child. Neither Headen nor his sister Nannie seem to have been able to have children. Both remained childless despite long marriages. Headen welcomed the opportunity now, proudly naming his new son, just six weeks old, Lucean Arthur Headen Jr.[68]

Having a child brought new priorities to the fore for Headen, including religious life. With no Presbyterian churches close by, he and Gladys chose Camberley Methodist Church for Lucean Jr.'s baptism. A few years later they would enter him in Sunday School at Frimley Green Methodist Church. Embracing the spirit of evangelism, Lucean and Gladys also attended revivals conducted by American preacher Billy Graham during his Greater London Crusade in 1954, and Headen for the first time in his life embraced service to a congregation. Lucean Jr. remembers that as a child he believed that his father had a hand in installing electric speaker tubes at the church that provided amplification of sermons for those hard of hearing. Neither Lucean nor Gladys (whose family was affiliated with the Church of England) ever became members at Frimley Green, but they remained devoted churchgoers.[69]

When Lucean Jr., called Junior at home, reached school age, Headen also worked to pass on to his son the benefit of a solid education. In the early 1950s, this was not a simple task. The war had left English education in shambles, destroying many school buildings and overcrowding others. Camberley, one of the sites to which children had been relocated from bomb-ravaged London, suffered greatly from the war's effects. Parents endured long waiting lists for school placements, and competed fiercely for access to academic training. English schools of the time consisted of primary schools for the young, and grammar and trade schools for older children. An examination known as the 11+ determined which pupils entered an academic track at a grammar school and which would have only the trade school option.

By the mid-1950s Headen's income was diminishing, making the alternative of private education a stretch. With plowshare tip sales dropping, he had to seek a new source of income. Founding the Junior Specialty Company (its name an affectionate nod to his son) in 1954, he was solvent but short funded. By this year the Headen family had moved into newly constructed council housing, reserved for those with modest incomes, in Frimley, a small village between Frimley Green and Camberley. While Headen continued to support the family with his inventions, he would never again enjoy financial ease.[70]

Despite the difficulties, however, he was determined to ensure his son's future. In 1954, he enrolled Lucean Jr. in the well-regarded Lyndhurst preparatory school in Camberley and redoubled his efforts to bring in greater earnings. His most lucrative prospect came the following year, when he began investigating the possibilities of selling the "Headen Hydraulic Lift," designed to propel large troop and tank carriers back into the water after they had come aground. He told an American Embassy official that his idea was "quite four years old," but "due to my financial position, I have not gone forward with it in the right way." He added, though, that he had recently located a buyer who had offered him an "amount that is extremely interesting." The rub was that the buyer represented the mainland Chinese government, with which the United States had strained relations, and he needed to know if that would prohibit the sale.[71]

In his interactions with the embassy, Headen revealed that one trait, impatience, had never left him. In a letter to the embassy, Headen did not equivocate, taking the same tone he had assumed almost four decades before with the Naval Consulting Board. He wished first to offer his device to his own country, he stated, but reserved the right to sell it to the Chinese if the United States had no interest. He insisted that the embassy respond to his inquiry "within the next ten days," or he would "assume that it is all right for me to go ahead with the other party." When he had received no reply within eight days, Headen made a personal visit to London.[72]

Headen's haste rubbed at least one embassy worker, Second Secretary Dwight Scarborough, the wrong way. Scarborough had forwarded Headen's letter to the embassy's naval attaché as soon as it had been received, and the specified ten days had not yet passed. Scarborough complained to the State

Department that this was not the first time Headen had imposed such a deadline, noting that he had earlier threatened to sell his plowshare tip to the Russians if he did not receive a prompt, satisfactory answer concerning it. In both cases, Headen, clearly fearing his ideas might be appropriated, also had to be cajoled to submit enough technical detail for officials to make a decision.[73]

Ultimately, once full specifications for the lift were in hand, the embassy sent Headen's request to its British legal attaché for clearance. By the ninth of February, Headen had his answer. The attaché reported the British Admiralty's ruling that under British law it would be illegal to sell his device to the Chinese. With the sale thwarted, Headen decided to appeal to other authorities. He immediately wrote the White House, and in his letter informed the president's personal secretary that he had met Eisenhower during the war (Eisenhower spoke at Sandhurst in 1944), and that he believed the former general would have a full appreciation of his invention's contribution to the navy. He requested that the secretary show his letter directly to the president for consideration, and he informed him that he could outfit fifty surplus sea transports left over from the war with the device and have them ready for use within ninety days.[74]

Headen's boldness in addressing the White House was not out of character. He was accustomed to dealing with highly placed government officials. He had also early observed his uncle Henry enjoy access to American presidents. In this context, writing the chief executive did not seem such a leap. Moreover, Headen, with complete faith in his creations, saw no reason that others, regardless of station, should not share his assessment. And, perhaps, although we cannot know, by dictating the terms of the interaction from the start, he hoped to stave off the possibility of being dismissed entirely or of being ridiculed, as he had been as a young man. Whatever the origin of Headen's agitation, with his son's future at stake, he had far more invested in the sale of his hydraulic lift than ego.

No evidence indicates Headen ever successfully convinced the U.S. Navy or others to buy his invention. After he received the embassy's reply, he may have tried to sell it to an unknown party in Italy. Lucean Jr. recalls that his parents traveled there in the mid-1950s (bringing him back, to his delight, a boy's suit of armor). However, the effort does not seem to have borne fruit. It would not be long before Headen shifted his energies to another more affordable project. In 1953, he had applied for a patent on a "bicycle protective device." The invention consisted of a rainproof hood and cape attached to canvas leg flaps that extended downward from the handlebars to protect a cyclist from water splashed up by the front wheel. Headen's recent trade of a green V-8 Ford for a cycle, which he motorized, and inevitable subsequent soakings on the road, may have given him the idea. By 1956 he had already begun testing his new gear around Frimley and Frimley Green, where Jack Day, then a teenager, remembers being intrigued by both the two-stroke engine Headen had mounted on the front wheel of the cycle and by the rain outfit. Putting his new invention into production, Headen was able to support his family, if not in the fashion he desired.[75]

Ironically, as Headen struggled to fund his newest ideas, others were just beginning to acknowledge his earlier work, especially that on icing. After the war, several leading American and British engineers working on anti-icing methods for propeller-driven and rotor aircraft turned to his earlier patents. Researchers for Curtiss-Wright Corporation of New York led the way. A pioneer in the 1930s in the development of hollow steel, variable-pitch propellers, Curtiss-Wright had also led advancements in the design of "cuffs," placed on propeller hubs for engine-cooling purposes. During the war years, it provided a considerable proportion of propellers used on U.S. aircraft.[76]

The company, however, despite research it conducted during the war, had never found a satisfactory method of keeping its propellers clear of ice. This failure took on new importance as military funding dried up, leaving Curtiss-Wright in fierce competition with others for commercial business. Much of that business would come, it knew, from airline companies that hoped to open new routes over the North Atlantic. Temperatures in this region could dip as low as −70 degrees Fahrenheit (−57 Celsius) in winter. If the company hoped to "pave the way for year-round inter-continental operations over the far northern great circle routes," as it noted in a 1944 market analysis, it would have to design propellers and engines that worked safely in the extreme cold.[77]

The team it hoped could achieve this goal included Louis Enos, assistant chief engineer of the Propeller Division during the war, George A. Dean, who had headed the cuff design department, and Everett P. Palmatier, an engineer in the Propeller Division who had left to become director of research for the Carrier Corporation. The designs all three men created would rely in part on basic principles Headen had set out in his patent specifications.

Of the team, Enos favored chemical methods of deicing. Receiving U.S. Patent 2,619,305, "Deicing Means for Propellers," in 1952, he cited a number of his predecessors in propeller design and antifreeze spraying methods, but it was Headen he acknowledged for his delivery system. In his design, he routed antifreeze solution from the propeller hub out through a tubular conduit built into each leading blade edge, then discharged the fluid through the propeller tip. Although he had not used heated air as Headen had proposed, he dispersed his solution in an identical method.[78]

A proponent of exhaust gases, Dean rejected Enos's solutions, as well as the electrothermal methods developed by the National Research Council of Canada, as impractical for hollow blades. Developing his own approach, he earned U.S. Patent 2,449,457, "Deicing System for Propeller Blades," in September 1948. The patent cited only two precedents: Headen's GB Patent 506,444, "Improvements in or Connected with Means for De-icing Aircraft Propellers," and George Houston's U.S. Patent 1,899,689, "Propeller." Houston, a designer for Bendix, had in 1933 proposed a means to expel engine exhaust through hollow propeller blades rather than exhaust pipes to improve engine performance and lessen the drag created by the extruding pipes. While Houston had introduced the idea of exhausting gases through the propeller, Headen had worked out the means to capture those gases for deicing purposes. Now Dean adapted both men's ideas as the basis for the system he designed for multiblade controllable pitch propellers. His system refined Headen's ducting method. Instead of routing the gases from the hub into external pipes that led them into the leading-edge ducts, he constructed a rotating chamber inside the hub that fed the gases directly into the ducts.[79]

Palmatier, who had begun research related to anti-icing designs at Curtiss-Wright as early as 1942, assigned several deicing and ice prevention methods to the company in the postwar period. Palmatier received three patents between 1948 and 1950, each based in part on Headen's ideas. His designs proposed techniques to deice wings, propellers, ailerons, and tail sections that adapted Headen's basic delivery system to modern aircraft. For propellers, he (like Dean) modified the hub to build a gas-dispersal system in the hub interior. His system allowed gases to be directed through tubes to both the blades and cuffs, and was well adapted to multipropeller craft. For wings and control surfaces, Palmatier modified Headen's heated-air system to make it suitable for more powerful engines and borrowed both his pressurized jet idea and that of directing the air directly onto targeted areas.[80]

Researchers at other aircraft companies in competition with Curtiss-Wright were also cognizant of Headen. Among those listing his work as a precedent were Joseph Stuart III and Warren Berkley of General Motors Corporation in Detroit, who received a patent in 1951 for a hot-air heating system to prevent ice formation on hollow pitch-shiftable propellers, and Erle Martin, also of General Motors, who received U.S. Patent 2,522,955, "Means for Heating Hollow Propeller Blades," in 1950. Erle's invention closely resembled Headen's, creating a channel along the leading edge of propellers through which to route heated air sucked from the engine, then exhausting it through the propeller tip. In 1950, Wilfred Thomas of Grumman Aerospace Corporation received

U.S. Patent 2,514,105 for a laminated encasement that also echoed Headen's design, providing an outer sheathing through which exhaust-heated air was forced using a blower.[81]

Those interested in rotor craft also found Headen's ideas useful. No less a designer than Igor Sikorsky cited Headen's work in a 1952 U.S. patent for a helicopter blade, as did Robert Mayne of the Goodyear Aircraft Corporation. Those working on gas turbine engines, too, acknowledged him. Albert George Elliott, key designer of automotive and aircraft engines for Rolls-Royce, listed Headen's propeller deicing patent, along with George Houston's propeller exhaust means, as the two earliest precedents for patents he took out in the early 1950s for a method to direct heated air to turbine blades and guide vanes in the air intake assemblies of jet engines. Headen's designs still hold relevance for jet engines, being applied in 1995 by Grumman researcher Vincent T. Padden in his development of a "Strain Isolator Assembly," which supported a hot-air blower tube inside the cowling of a jet engine unit, and being acknowledged in 2017 by assignees to the Boeing Company and to Mitsubishi Aircraft for heated-air tube systems.[82]

Headen's methods have implications today for keeping wind turbine blades free of ice. His work anticipated the modern-day ice removal system currently operated in locations around the world by Vestas Wind Systems of Denmark. The Vestas design is based on Headen's main principle of forcing heated air through flexible tubes with perforations that direct jets of hot air to the leading edges of the blades and to targeted areas such as the root of the blades in the rotor hub.[83]

Thus, although Headen never had the opportunity to step into an aeronautical research laboratory, his ideas became part of the body of knowledge on which industrial aeronautical engineers relied. "While the first schemes proposed may not be the most suitable or most economical in the long run," Albert Elliott noted in 1947, "their investigation . . . provide[s] data for defining the policy of future development." His words would prove true for Headen's contributions not only to deicing but also to engines. Although the use of oils in spark-ignition internal combustion engines eventually became obsolete, the ideas Headen offered on vaporization and fuel induction systems subsequently informed the work of engineers for Briggs and Stratton, Toyota, and Volkswagenwerk, among others, and his spark-ignition device, patented in 1930, provided a template for an electric spark ignition system designed for an electric hybrid vehicle in 1991.[84]

Headen's story illustrates that while historians of technology often focus on "breakthrough" inventors, whose creations revolutionize how we live and ex-

Nannie Headen Jones as she appeared in the faculty and staff section of North Carolina College's *The Maroon and Gray* in 1946. After a long career of teaching and community activism, Nannie served as house directress at the school (today North Carolina Central University) from 1940 to 1950. Courtesy of NCCU Digital Yearbook Collection, J. E. Shepard Memorial Library University Archives, Records and History Center, North Carolina Central University.

pend our labor, the endeavors of others can also be of importance. Headen's creativity, despite his limited opportunities to develop it, influenced both his contemporaries and industrial engineers for decades afterward.

We do not know if Headen was aware of the researchers considering his designs in the late 1940s and early 1950s. We do know that, sadly, he would not live to see his ideas reflected in the many engine, rotor deicing, and wind power technologies developed in the latter part of the twentieth century and the beginning of the next. On the cool, cloudy day of September 18, 1957, Headen reached the end of his remarkable journey when he suffered a sudden heart attack. The details of his death have been lost, but his funeral was held several days later at Frimley Green Methodist Church, presided over by its pastor, Reverend William Briggs. Gladys, her family, and the other mourners then followed his coffin as it was transported to St. Peter's Churchyard in Frimley, where it finally came to rest at grave site 414.[85]

As Headen's story had not begun with him, however, it also did not end with his death. Not only would his ideas continue to live, but he passed on the legacy of education and entrepreneurship his family and community had provided him so many years earlier. Lucean Jr. would benefit greatly from his father's insistence on his receiving the best possible academic training and from his mother's determination to carry through on that promise. Thriving at the Lyndhurst School, he went on to graduate from Woking Grammar School for Boys, with his mother working as an electronics inspector and later as forewoman in a hospital laundry to help pay for her son's schooling. Nannie Jones, too, contributed, sending her nephew U.S. savings bonds. After earning a degree in occupational psychology from Cardiff University and conducting postgraduate research to improve the interpretation of psychometric tests, Lucean Jr., like his father, became a businessman. Together with his wife, Cherryl, he founded a successful management consulting firm in Wales.

Epilogue

I have often wondered how Lucean Headen might have told his own story. Central to his narrative, I am certain, would have been invention. His words clearly evince the deep pride he felt in being an inventor. The intellectual swagger he displayed as he presented his "mechanical ingenuity" for scrutiny by the navy in 1917 was still there in 1955, if a bit more understated, when he declared with satisfaction to a U.S. Embassy representative that he had made his living "out of inventions." Turning talent and experience into practical, marketable products, Headen saw himself as the embodiment of American ingenuity.

Headen came of age when the United States was rising as an industrial power, and the inventor was becoming a national hero. He first encountered the adulation the innovator could evoke in the *Carthage Blade* and the *Jonesboro Leader*. He also saw the appreciation of Carthage's residents for the mechanical creativity demonstrated at the Tyson & Jones Buggy Company and for his own forebearers' mastery at the wheelwright's bench, the forge, and the sawmill. Spurred by the achievements of those around him, he came to love practical problem-solving, and he found in inventive activity the joy that only an authentic passion can bring.

Invention also gave Headen a benchmark by which to measure himself in a Jim Crow society. Making him a "man of importance" in numerous communities, it earned him respect from coworkers, journalists, and fellow engineers. Those who labored alongside him in the Erie Railroad's dining cars deemed him an "inventive genius," and contemporary William Polite in 1917 proudly carried a copy of the *Chicago Tribune*'s article on Headen's camouflage device to the *Wilmington Star*. Polite asked that the white newspaper reprint it and was delighted when it did. Throughout the 1920s, writers for the black press enthusiastically promoted Headen's automotive designs and business ventures, and even some southern white writers admired his "remarkable mechanical genius."[1]

Bolstered by personal acknowledgment, Headen gained broader validation from the U.S. and British Patent Offices. Examiners did not ask an applicant's race, and their stamp of approval granted an inventor unassailable proof of ability. Eagerly pursuing the patent process, Headen used it to stake his claim to mechanical expertise and to being fully American, despite many whites' insistence that blacks could achieve neither. He would never waver in his national allegiance. Even as he chose to reside in England for the last three decades of his life, both invention and America remained at the core of how he viewed himself.

With invention as his polestar, Headen strove all his life to find ways to develop his ideas. He judged his progress not only by his ability to secure patents but in relation to a success myth that posited anyone could rise in the "land of opportunity." This myth appealed strongly to members of the southern black artisanal and commercial class from which he came. In 1895, when Headen was sixteen, his great-uncle Joseph Tyson attended the Cotton States Exposition in Atlanta, where he heard Tuskegee University president Booker T. Washington tell black Americans to "cast down your buckets where you are." Washington touted self-help through capitalism as the way forward for black Americans, and he encouraged them to build farms, businesses, and professional enterprises in the South.[2]

Headen's family had embraced the philosophy that Washington articulated long before the famed orator mounted the podium in Atlanta. Through practical education and business initiative, they had sought in seamless fashion to achieve personal success and to advance their larger community's fortunes. Their faith in capitalism proved resilient. Not even the worst of Jim Crow, with its violence and political oppression, dampened their enthusiasm. When the Headen & Tyson Saw and Shingle Mill burned, Guy Tyson became a sales agent for a black-run silk mill in Fayetteville, traveling as far as Washington, D.C., to promote its products. Jerry Headen started over in Aberdeen, gradually rebuilding his lumber business and establishing himself as a prosperous fruit grower.[3]

Although Lucean chose to leave North Carolina, the seed had been sown. As the younger man joined the migrant stream, he carried with him the values and strategies he had imbibed on his grandfather's farm, in his father's mill, in his great-uncle's shop, and at Dayton and Albion Academies. He also brought with him the imperative to succeed. Had he been inclined toward autobiography, my hunch is Headen would have crafted his life as a success narrative.

While we cannot know the full contours of that narrative, it is doubtful that Headen would have hewed too closely to the popular works of his youth. When Headen was twelve, writer Horatio Alger, literary popularizer of the American success myth, published a novel titled *The Erie Train Boy*. Reprinted well into the twentieth century, the book told the tale of a lowly white worker in the Erie's dining car department who, after displaying honesty and initiative in his difficult circumstances, was rewarded with opportunity by wealthy riders. Headen would have been intimately familiar with Alger's best-selling "rags to riches" stories and the parade of young sidewalk vendors, bootblacks, and street urchins in their pages lifted from obscurity to prosperity by personal earnestness and the intervention of well-heeled, noble-hearted businessmen. But his own experience would have exposed their fictions. In the decade he hoisted the trunks, tucked the bed linens, poured the coffee, and shined the shoes of affluent passengers, none ever took an interest in his future. When he did enjoy the patronage of a wealthy white family, it would not be through a serendipitous encounter on a train, but through religious and educational connections built by the Reverend Henry Wood.[4]

Had Headen put pen to paper, he would have been far more inclined, I believe, to cast himself in a role closer to that he enjoyed in the newspapers of his day—the "race man." This characterization began as early as 1912, when the *New York Age* claimed Headen's skill at flying had proven it was "impossible to keep the Negro down." Throughout his career, writers and editors touted his innovations as proof of more general black capacity. When the *California Eagle* asserted in 1917, after learning of Headen's anti-submarine device, that "The Caucasian has not after all outdistanced the Negro," and the *Defender* observed that the Headen Special had "caused stock in the race to jump 50 per cent," they offered Headen's creations as direct counter evidence to the vicious caricatures then prevalent of blacks as unintelligent, cowardly, and mechanically inept. Others, including sociologist Monroe Work and historian Benjamin Harrison, ensconced Headen in a national pantheon of black heroes, including his achievements in popular works such as the annual *Negro Year Book* and the *Colored Girls' and Boys' Inspiring United States History*.[5]

Being a race man demanded more than achievement. It called for loyalty to the goal of black advancement. Headen willingly addressed this expectation. While he displayed limited affinity for uplift efforts that emphasized social respectability or enforced moral judgments, he enthusiastically embraced attempts to improve the social and economic prospects of African Americans. He first publicly criticized the color line in 1912 when promoting his St. Louis flying exhibition, and his Headen Motor Company brochure repeated the criticism a decade later. Calling his company a "Pioneer in The Automobile Industry Among Our People," he encouraged black enterprise among men and women. Through the automobile, he proclaimed, blacks could create monetary opportunities and free themselves from the restrictions of Jim Crow. He took on the role of racial advocate in England as well, working to help Robert Abbott combat the threat to black freedom posed by white American tourists.[6]

Comfortable in the roles of representative and spokesman, Headen only briefly flirted with the oppositional image Robert Abbott was famous for creating. Abbott regularly infused heroes in the *Defender* with a defiant spirit. In 1911, he described aerial pioneer Ulysses Scott as a man who "forced himself to the front," and who "Tho Black He Rose." He invoked strikingly similar language to describe Headen. In 1917, the *Defender* declared that when Headen arrived in Washington to present his cloaking device to the U.S. Navy, those gathered initially refused "to take the matter seriously," doubtful that he had any real knowledge of submarines. But, "Denied every chance because he was of African descent, he rose," the paper declared, and his demonstration "dumbfounded" the skeptical white officials.[7]

Headen did not balk at such portrayals of himself, and he refused to bow to men such as Josephus Daniels. Pugnacity, however, did not suit his introverted character. It also did not suit his purpose. More pragmatist than crusader, Headen hoped to pursue his goals by building economic alliances that reached across traditional lines of race, class, and gender. Appealing to a broad range of investors, he drew on the strength of the networks that diverse groups brought to the table. Like his mentors, Headen saw economic success as a means to both personal goals and to racial prosperity, and he was willing to take all roads leading in that direction.

Historian Rayvon Fouché, in a 2003 study of black inventors, warned historians not to reduce black patent holders to one-dimensional heroes. Describing what he called the black inventor myth, he argued that among its key tenets has been the historical notion that black innovators undertook their pursuits on behalf of their race. Fouché contended that none of the three inventors whose lives he examined in *Black Inventors in the Age of Segregation* held such altruistic goals, and he called for biographers to think more deeply about the lives and motivations of inventive black Americans.[8]

Headen's story offers a new dimension to consider. Although he would not have seen himself as inventing solely "for his race," race was an inextricable part of his vision for technology and for business. The portion of his narrative that has survived portrays the automobile as socially transformative, capable of bypassing Jim Crow and of building economic power. Many of Headen's peers shared this view, finding the economic promise the auto industry represented especially attractive. A Chicago writer in 1925, after hearing that 7,000 African Americans were employed at a Ford plant in Del Ray, Michigan, predicted that the industry could provide black workers a permanent way out of menial work. Benjamin F. Thomas wholeheartedly agreed, arguing in 1929 that "The Negro has been especially blessed by the automobile, for it gives him better wages and more jobs than any other industry."[9]

Historians Kathleen Franz and Cotten Seiler have described the myriad other reasons black Americans seized the agency of the automobile: to avoid the dirty, cramped, cinder-sprayed quarters of segregated train travel, to gain a sense of control and independence on the road and in the yard "tinkering," and, as Seiler argues, to assert a sense of American citizenship by participating in the country's burgeoning driving culture. Examining the motives of black participants in Headen's early automotive coalitions illuminates other motivations that a nascent black middle class in the 1910s and 1920s had for tying its fortunes to the new technology.[10]

Automobiles promised a highly mobile group a means to overcome the separations created by migration. Cars not only made it possible to maintain and renew relationships with family members and friends scattered across the country, they allowed drivers to build new connections as they traveled, often staying with family or with friends of friends. The automobile thus became an important factor in keeping alive and extending critical networks. It, as sociologist John Urry has argued regarding many groups, helped preserve and build "social capital." And, even as the auto could separate individuals, such as when Headen left Tena to pursue his racing career, it could also lead to new relationships. Tena had met her second husband when her childhood friend William J. Meares drove his family from Greensboro to Chicago. When Meares pulled up in front of Tena's Michigan Avenue apartment, his car held not only his wife and daughters but his cousin Norfleet.[11]

The automobile also offered much of practical value. Black women such as Emma Wynn found it fitted their needs perfectly. A recent study of black beauticians by Tiffany Gill has revealed the pivotal role such women played in social organizing and civil rights work in their communities. Like other salon owners, Wynn made her beauty shop a gathering place. The City Federation of Colored Women's Clubs, for which she traveled as a state organizer, sponsored educational and charity work and lobbied local governments to improve black lives. It would be the automobile that empowered Wynn to expand her efforts across Georgia, penetrating rural areas not served by trains. It also expanded her economic reach.[12]

Wynn's participation in the Headen Motor Company indicates that some early beauty entrepreneurs were moving beyond being car owners to provide startup capital or other support for transportation businesses. This pattern is intriguing. Aviator Bessie Coleman had worked as a manicurist before she learned to fly. By 1926, a few months prior to her death, she had initiated plans to start a hair salon to earn the money needed to fund a flying school. A decade later, beauty pioneer Annie Malone, head of Poro Beauty College, helped underwrite the efforts of aviator John Robinson. Robinson, after starting a flying club in Chicago had led Haile Selassie's fledgling air force during the Italo-Ethiopian War. Upon his return home in 1936, he hoped to start a school of his own but was unable to find a business location he could afford. Malone stepped in, offering Robinson free space on her South Side campus. That fall he founded the John Robinson Air College and Automotive Engineering School. In appreciation, the following summer he treated Malone and her employees to their first airplane rides.[13]

Underpinning this enthusiasm for invention, and for the automobile and the airplane, was often the influence of artisans. The inventors and entrepreneurs who pioneered in transportation technologies were frequently men and women who had been raised by artisans, had themselves trained in craft trades, or had been educated in schools that artisans founded. For such individuals, specialized skills, self-employment, and hustle were a way of life. From a tradition that merged innovation, entrepreneurship, and the common good, they infused the technologies they embraced with these values. Thus although Fouché is correct that not every inventor relished the goal of racial advancement, those such as Headen, George Washington Murray, Charles Chappelle, Benjamin Thomas, and many of their contemporaries did.[14]

This group's devotion to the new machines of the twentieth century and to entrepreneurship should not surprise us. It was a logical extension of their past. For Headen and his peers, creativity, enterprise, and industry were their birthright. As Juliet E. K. Walker's work on slave enterprise makes clear, the entrepreneurial impetus had deep roots in many slave communities. Some, like Adam Tyson, had managed their owners' plantations. Others had tended businesses on behalf of their owners, started small stores of their own on plantations, or used their free time to gather produce, fish, eggs, and berries to sell to residents of nearby towns. Walker's great-great grandfather, Frank McWorter, purchased his family's freedom by mining and selling saltpeter for gunpowder in his time free from the fields. In the 1910s, his grandson, postman John E. McWorter, spent his evenings patenting helicopter designs, which he demonstrated to the U.S. Army Signal Corps and assigned to a private company.[15]

Opportunities to gain business experience were especially open to artisans, whose work was often "hired out" to those needing temporary assistance, and who could at times negotiate their own contracts and keep a portion of their wages. In the postwar years, as Catherine Bishir's recent study of former slave craftsmen in New Bern, North Carolina, reveals, their experience paid off as skilled freedmen applied the profits of their trades to building the city's first black churches and schools. The same pattern had unfolded 130 miles to the west in small-town Carthage.[16]

As they carried the values of their families north and west, Headen's generation showed great creativity in devising the means to finance their careers. Relocating frequently between cities, or moving back and forth between their new homes and their native South, they took their fates into their own hands, retooling their parents' and grandparents' legacies to prepare for an increasingly technological future.

As Headen confronted Jim Crow and the challenges of the independent inventor, he experimented widely to identify a financial formula that worked for him. His approach became part of his personal legacy. Adapting Henry Wood's methods to a modern world, he started sometimes with black partners, sometimes with white, depending on the opportunities that presented themselves, then gradually expanded his efforts to build multiracial, cross-gender, geographically and socially diverse coalitions. This model gave him a route past the shrinking opportunities for those working independently, and his exclusion from the advanced technical schools and jobs needed to develop his ideas. Eventually it brought him to the point where he could attract the interest of those with deeper pockets, who helped establish him on firm ground.

His "coalition economics" also had a direct impact on other transportation pioneers, as seen in the examples of Bessie Coleman and William Powell, who watched him build the Headen Motor Company. Coleman, the daughter of a farmer, did not share Headen's artisanal background, but her admiration for his ideas and approach can be seen in her actions. As she conducted flights across the country, she skillfully built her own coalitions. Coleman started with backing from Robert Abbott, banker Jesse Binga, and a handful of black entertainment promoters, but she soon added an eclectic corps of supporters that rivaled Headen's in its variety. Among her supporters were black workers in the YWCA and the Negro Welfare League; white pilots Anthony Fokker (from whom she had learned stunt flying in Holland) and David Benchke (whose Chicago flying troop she joined); white California tire executive Paul Sachs (who hired her to promote his products, and whom she taught to fly); black editors Joseph and Charlotta Bass of the *California Eagle* and O. P. DeWalt of the *Houston Informer*; white filmmaker Richard Norman; several black entertainment figures; white chewing gum heir Edwin Beeman; and a black Baptist evangelical community in Orlando.[17]

William Powell, too, turned to the approach, building a coalition to fund the Bessie Coleman Aero Club, and later the Craftsmen of Black Wings, a flight school and aircraft manufactory he started in Los Angeles. Allying with journalists from the *California Eagle* and *Los Angeles News* and white filmmakers in Los Angeles, he solicited help as well from black and white philanthropists, black businessmen, New Deal government program administrators, representatives of a growing number of black flying clubs that were being established across the country, and members of his Baptist church community.[18]

Enthusiasm for Headen's business model suggests the various forms that black business could take in the first decades of the twentieth century. Historians have widely studied Booker T. Washington and the influence of his NNBL, documented the rise of the black banking and insurance industries, and explored the economic thrust of mutual aid societies and organizations such as the UNIA. But the experience of Headen and those who followed his lead suggest a greater range of strategies was in play. One must wonder whether the micro-level work needed to uncover the officers, board members, and financiers of small black enterprises across the country in the 1920s and 1930s might reveal that economic cooperation between the races and between men and women was more common than expected. Whether this is so (or the approach was more particularly suited to transportation technologies because of their broad appeal) calls for further research.

Besides his legacy as a businessman, Headen, as his Erie coworkers predicted, also made his mark as an inventor. His patents have shown unusual staying power. We do not have a statistical breakdown of patent longevity for the years after 1930, when Headen received his patents, but figures for 1928–29 are illuminating. According to one study, only a quarter of U.S. patents assigned at their issue in this period to large R&D firms, and less than a third of those assigned to small to medium-sized firms, were later cited in patents granted between 1975 and 2002. Headen's patents, in contrast, informed the work of corporate researchers from the 1940s through the early 1970s, enjoyed frequent citation in the 1975–2002 period, and are still cited today.[19]

Headen's inventions ultimately did not transform an industry or dramatically change the way we live. He provided practical, streamlined designs for ideas already under study, and he never enjoyed sufficient resources to fully develop his ideas. That would be the privilege of the better situated industrial scientists. Yet his achievements are instructive. They shift our focus from the question so frequently asked by historians of technology, concerning who has most driven critical innovation, to another: What role do less transformative technologies play in our lives?

Most of Headen's inventions were directed at those with limited means, who could not afford the expense or trouble of experimenting with the "latest thing" and needed immediate solutions to immediate problems. His products had helped keep farmers engaged with machines in a time of agricultural depression, encouraging them to maintain mechanical skills that became important as Britain entered the world war. In that national crisis, he offered on-the-shelf options for fuel conservation, while more radical inventions sat unfinished on the drawing board. After the war, he again helped farmers, offering them a way to save money by extending the life of expensive plowshares. Simple, practical, and accessible, his technologies served the needs of everyday people, and as a result, made a valuable contribution to home-front and postwar needs.

Despite Headen's accomplishments as a businessman and an inventor, the approach he adopted had clear limits. It did not gain him entry into the inventive elite, earn him a fortune, or defeat Jim Crow. It also never offered a widely shared economic benefit for black Americans. Its track record on women, too, was mixed. Headen recruited women as investors and customers, and they played an important part in his early coalitions. On the racetrack, however, he relegated them to a secondary status. And, it seems unlikely that, were this an autobiography, he would have acknowledged his aunts' or his first wife's contributions to his career.

Still, I believe Headen would find puzzling the negative assessments modern-day historians have made of the race man and of the black middle class more generally. Many have argued that educated black Americans believed that the role of the racial representative was to provide an example that would raise the less fortunate to a more "civilized" level. While some members of the black middle class succumbed to the trappings of social snobbery, and some internalized negative beliefs, Headen never warmed to elitism. He was more comfortable on the racetrack than in a church pew or a ballroom, and he gladly rubbed elbows with "greasy, rough talking men." His automotive appeals reached out to people of all economic strata, in part to further his own aims, but also because he believed technology offered a future to those who, like himself, were excluded from almost every other avenue for advancement. No mention of civilization ever entered his arguments. Raised in a proud tradition, he was eager to prove his *worth*, but he never questioned his own or others' *worthiness*.[20]

And, to be fair to Headen, no strategy in his time survived the ravages of white's pervasive efforts to deny blacks opportunity—not his coalition approach, not Pan-Africanism, not Garveyism, not efforts to build black farm cooperatives or black-white Communist alliances. American racial hatred was simply too potent a force, and black numbers too small, to defeat it. But Headen's striving, as that of others, did make a difference. Given the enormous popularity of papers like the *Defender*, especially in the South, it is hard to discount the psychological importance of having heroes like Headen. He offered black youth a clear reflection of themselves that counteracted the distorted funhouse images of blackface minstrelsy and the disdain they regularly spied in white countenances. Challenging this scorn, Headen and other figures in the press offered proof that one could aspire to and achieve important goals.

Moreover, Headen's family and the families of other artisans produced many of the teachers and doctors who served black communities when whites refused to. They also nurtured civic and political leaders such as Henry and Guy Tyson and social activists such as Marie Tyson and Nannie Headen Jones. After leaving Carthage, Marie Tyson emerged as a leader in West Philadelphia's black community, leading efforts to fund Berean Manual and Training School, Lombard Central Presbyterian Church, Mercy Hospital, the Independent Women's Welfare Council, and the city's Lyceum. She also joined the fight for women's suffrage. Nannie helped lead the Phillis Wheatley branch of the YWCA in Winston-Salem, including overseeing its basketball program, for over twenty years, before leaving to teach sewing at Philadelphia's Sleighton Farm School for "delinquent girls." Passing on the skills she had learned at Dayton Academy, she hoped to give her students a means of economic support that would allow them to escape crime. In the 1940s, she mentored another generation of black college women at North Carolina College (today North Carolina Central University).[21]

Louise Headen Ables taught school in Greensboro and Statesville before relocating to Pittsburgh, where her husband, Fred Ables, provided insurance services to black subscribers. Their daughter, Jane Ables Greenwood, for many years dean at the Homewood-Brushton campus of the Community College of Allegheny County in Pittsburgh, is today director of student life at the college's Allegheny campus. She has led numerous efforts in the city to advance civil rights, support low-income residents, and ensure the well-being of her students. Although such individuals did not succeed in singlehandedly dismantling the pernicious laws and mores of their country, they have bequeathed us stories of hope, the remnants of networks, and the example to build new ones.[22]

Historical perspective gives us the opportunity to see in Headen's story what he perhaps could not—the critical importance of networks. The social infrastructure from which he benefitted gave him the knowledge and tools to compete, offered him social standing central to his self-esteem, gave him comfort and encouragement in trying times, and provided him with a pool of investors. Perhaps most important, it afforded him the opportunity to fail. As current-day inventor Kevin Ashton has pointed out, invention rarely comes in bursts of inspiration. Rather it emerges out of trial, error, and accrued experience. For each failed attempt and experiment gone wrong, we learn things necessary to our future success.[23]

In a period when the bar for succeeding as an inventor was rising, support from his first wife and family bought Headen time to build knowledge and experiment, and it gave him a safety net. When his hopes of profiting as an exhibition pilot did not pan out, he had the Reverend Henry Wood's contacts with the McCormick family to turn to for employment. When he needed investors for his ship-cloaking device and his car company, he had Tena's church friends, as well as the fraternal connections of his brother-in-law and others, to help. While he would eventually leave family and community networks behind, crossing an ocean to pursue new opportunities, without them he would never have been positioned to take advantage of the possibilities England offered.

This aspect of Headen's story has implications for how we look to the future. Often our discussions of success become a treatise on "genius" and the ability of any individual with enough talent and gumption to reach the apex of the American Dream. This view has focused our attention on the highest achievers, men such as Edison, who rose from obscure origins to become a technological superstar. It has ignored that most success occurs in far less lofty arenas. A vast network of engineers, electricians, business operators, bankers, doctors, nurses, scholars, administrators, librarians, insurance agents, lawyers, computer programmers, writers, and schoolteachers make up our professional workforce. For those who aspire to become part of that economy, ability and determination do not always suffice. For every individual who succeeds spectacularly with limited resources, many others rely on family, friends, social ties, and institutions to help realize their ambitions.

Headen's story also shows us that attempts to expand opportunity cannot be limited to a narrow concentration on the individual. We enter the competitive arena not alone but as members of communities. Thus, we need to think as much on the communal as the individual plane. Public policies such as affirmative action and equal employment opportunity can only succeed if supplemented with community advocacy, and efforts directed at individual advancement can do little good if highway construction and gentrification projects destroy black neighborhoods and their institutions. The businesses, churches, schools, hospitals, and cultural organizations that buffer and support individuals must always be central in our awareness.

Networks may not automatically solve systemic problems, but they give us a way to move forward and to develop the supports necessary for building a better future. Although not everyone with resources will succeed, and not everyone without them will fail, networks greatly increase our chances. And the greater their diversity, the better our odds. Thus, even as we recognize their inevitable fault lines, and even as we strive to create greater equality within them, we need to keep at the work of creating them.

As we take our turn behind the wheel, we, like Headen, must look for all roads to our destination.

Acknowledgments

Many people have had a hand in creating this book. I owe each of them more than I can ever repay.

My largest debt is to fellow historians Pam Grundy and Jerma Jackson, who fifteen years ago invited me to join their writing group. Pam and Jerma have been in my corner ever since, reading innumerable drafts of this and other manuscripts and both encouraging and challenging me. Their honest (and always respectful) criticism, passion for history, clear-eyed analysis, editorial guidance (thank you especially, Pam), and steady advocacy have made them the "smiths who allowed me to put my ideas to work." I am grateful for the commitment they have made to me professionally, and I cherish our enduring friendship.

Several other long-time friends have been critical to this book's completion. Slate Raymond and Gary Chappell generously opened their homes to me during numerous research trips back and forth between Chapel Hill and Washington, D.C. Slate, along with Anne Lutes, was among the first to read the initial sketch I wrote of Headen, which eventually became this biography.

Besides these personal supports, I have had the privilege to learn from a number of remarkable people, in the United States and in England. Carthage natives Harriet Hayes Warrington, Headen's cousin, and Gussie Brown McNair spent hours talking with me (and thankfully still do) about their hometown, John Hall Presbyterian and Shady Grove Presbyterian Churches, and their families. John Hall elder Pat Brown helped me make many local contacts in Carthage, among them George Wilson and Barbara Gomez, the grandchildren of the Rev. Henry Wood. Barbara, stated clerk of the John Hall session, opened the church's records to me and she and George shared their own family stories.

When I visited England in 2016, Lucean Arthur Headen Jr. embraced this project. He first met me in London, then invited me to spend time at his home in Wales. The two days there were the most valuable of my trip, yielding insights into his father's life that I could have gained nowhere else. I thank Lucean for his kindness and for his patience with my questions, and his wife Cherryl for her gracious welcome of a stranger. I could not have dreamed of meeting better people.

Others who ensured my trip's success were Malcolm MacAdam and his wife, Wendy, of Camberley, Ann Taylor and Michael Giles of Frimely Green Methodist Church, Clare Peel of St. Peter's in Frimley, and Fred Penhallow and Jack Day. Malcolm, the grandson of James Keil, gave me a good sense of his grandfather, and both he and Wendy took time from hectic schedules to help me get my bearings in Camberley. Their daughters Rebecca and Grace also helped feed and entertain a traveler. Michael Giles gave me an impromptu tour of the church that Headen made his home in the last decade of his life, and Ann Taylor provided important information on its history. Memories that Fred Penhallow and Jack Day shared provided me a picture of Camberley at the time Headen lived there. Clare Peel helped me locate Headen's grave in St. Peter's Churchyard, and provided good conversation on my visit to the church. I sincerely thank all those in Camberley, Frimley, and Frimley Green for their help.

Equally indispensable to this book have been the many talented archivists, librarians, and other professionals, here and abroad, who facilitated my research. Chief among them are researcher Don Evans, an expert in the collections of the Georgia Archives, and reference librarian Arlene Balkansky of the Library of Congress. Don helped me explore Headen's business activities in Albany by examining tax, incorporation, and other records and conducted research in the *Albany Herald* on my behalf. His skills are unsurpassed, and I am lucky to have found him. Arlene has over many years helped me identify scattered U.S. newspaper collections, from rare hard copies to those on microfilm, and more recently in digital formats. Her breadth of knowledge and bibliographic skills helped me uncover a myriad of sources used in this book. Similarly, Stephanie Masten Marcus of the Library of Congress's Science and Technology Reading Room assisted me in tracking down many of the British trade journals in the library's collections, and Kimberly Winfrey helped make sure I received requested materials as quickly as possible. Her attention to detail and friendly disposition made late nights in the reading room much more enjoyable than they otherwise would have been.

Everywhere I have traveled, I have found such professionals on whom to rely. In Headen's hometown of Carthage, Martha Ferguson, Alice Thomas, and Kaye Brown of the Moore County Library and Lillie Barrett of the Moore County Register of Deeds Office expended many hours on my behalf. The Reverend Rick Martindale of First Presbyterian Church also opened his church's historical records, through which I learned of Adam and Ann Tyson's membership at the original Carthage Presbyterian Church.

In Chicago, Jo Ellen McKillop Dickie of the Newberry Library led me through the complex records of the Pullman Company. Eric Gillespie of the Cantigny Foundation helped me navigate the Robert R. McCormick papers. Andy Huse, Jonathan Rodriguez-Perez, and Sydney Jordan of the University of South Florida's Special Collections Library assisted me in my exploration of the Armwood family papers. They also suggested many helpful additional sources. In Philadelphia, Lisa Jacobson and Nancy J. Taylor of the Presbyterian Historical Society provided much appreciated help with the society's extensive records.

Archivists in England proved equally valuable to my pursuits. Mary Ann Bennett, retired assistant curator of the Surrey Heath Museum, was key to what I was able to learn about Headen Keil Engineering Company Ltd. Author of the comprehensive *Camberley: A History*, she provided indispensable background on industries in the town, and she took time from her own projects to direct me through the museum's collections. I would have been lost without her help. Thank you is also due to Gillian Barnes-Riding and Verity Kerins of the museum for their daily assistance and the enthusiasm they expressed for my project.

In Woking, the staff of the Surrey History Centre, especially Di Stiff, Jane Lewis, and Duncan Mirylees, made my trip there as much pleasure as work. Besides welcoming me warmly, they helped me identify and scan through numerous Home Guard and parish records and to interpret an extensive map collection. Many kind librarians at the British Library and the National Archive in Kew, whom I do not know by name, did the same in opening their records.

Archivists and others I have never met have also contributed to this work. Responding to email and phone requests, they gave me access to materials housed in institutions I could not visit. These include Robert Beebe of the National Archives in Kansas City, Missouri, Krista Sorenson of the Government and Heritage Library of North Carolina, Anne Thomason, Elizabeth Ludowise, and Lillie Therieau of the Special Collections Library of Lake Forest College, Ralph Scott of East Carolina University's Joyner Library, Wayne Sparkman of the PCA Historical Center in St. Louis, and Lori B. Besler of the Wisconsin Historical Society. I also want to acknowledge James Sponholz of Milwaukee, who indexed the *Erie Railroad Employes' Magazine* and placed the index on RootsWeb, allowing me to discover Headen's position on the Erie and his plans for his barnstorming tour.

Many mentors and colleagues have shaped this work. Long before it was created, its foundation was laid at the University of North Carolina and the Smithsonian Institution. At UNC I had the privilege to work with two enormously talented people, John Kasson and Nell Irvin Painter Schafer. Nell and John directed my dissertation on black visions of aviation; work that directly informed this biography. Both pushed me to examine complexity and never accept the simple answer. I am grateful, too, to the late Roslyn (Lynn) Holdzkom of The Wilson Library Manuscripts Department, who taught me the intricacies of library systems and archival records, giving me the tools to probe the complexity on which Nell and John insisted.

At the Smithsonian's National Air and Space Museum, where I was a fellow in the late 1980s and again in the mid-1990s, curators Dominick Pisano, Von Hardesty, and Cathleen Lewis forged the way for the study of black American aviators. They gave me critical encouragement and provided me with important mentorship in my years there. As this book reached its final stages, Bob Van der Linden, Roger Connor, and Alex Spencer of the museum directly aided my progress, helping me vet my ideas on icing technologies and, in Roger's case, digging into a number of archival resources on my behalf. Roger also offered information on the development of remote control technologies by the Royal Air Force and the British Navy, and Alex shared insights from his work on British aviation. He also fortuitously steered me to Peter Liebhold of the National Museum of American History. Peter pushed me to consider more carefully the history of oil supplies in Britain in the 1930s and how that affected Headen's inventions.

Funding for my early research came from the Smithsonian's Predoctoral Fellows program, the National Air & Space Museum's Alfred Verville Fellowship, and the American Historical Association / National Aeronautics & Space Administration's joint fellowship in Aerospace History. Without the research they financed, I could not have placed Headen into a larger context of transportation pioneers.

There are many others who deserve thanks. Dr. Lisa Soule of Rockville, Maryland, helped me understand the possible causes of Headen's facial palsy. Mark Simpson-Vos, Jessica Newman, and Iris Levesque of UNC Press expertly guided this manuscript through the many-faceted publication process. I am forever indebted to Iris and Kate Gibson of Westchester Publishing Services for bringing order to my often complicated and sometimes impenetrable endnotes. Kathleen Mohar, Christine Krahulec, and Alicia Green, my workplace managers, patiently tolerated my taking time away from the job over the years to conduct research. Friends, especially Gary Chappell, Marian Brady, Sharon Chappell, Julie Haidemenos, Steve Tobey, Clark May, Sera Morgan, and Cayo Gamber kept my spirits up with their interest in my work. In addition, two young men, Thomas and Jose, of the K & 17th Street Pret a Manger watched me write most of this manuscript and good naturedly allowed me on many occasions to stay past closing time to finish "that last paragraph." Their generosity, youthful energy, and passion for their own dreams kept me inspired.

Finally, and most important, I must acknowledge my family, especially my mother, to whom this book is dedicated. Despite her own lack of opportunities, she always took joy in mine, and she modeled for me hard work, loyalty, and sacrifice. My sister Vickie, who helped raise me, taught me determination, honesty, and enterprise, as did my brother Kent. I have always known that both would be there for me, no matter what, and that has meant the world. I am also indebted to my brothers Harold, Tim, and Jon, to my late brother Mark, to my brother-in-law Archie, to my sisters-in-law Julie, Frankie, Diane, and Kathy, and to my many nieces and nephews for all they have taught me, and for the love and support they have given an often absent family member.

I am immensely grateful, too, to Mary O'Melia and Mary Jo Festle, who shared a large portion of my life. Both shaped me in more ways than I can imagine, and their love, perspectives on the world, belief in me, and steadfast commitments to the values we shared will forever be a part of who I am.

Notes

Abbreviations in Notes

AH	*Albany Herald*
AIAA	American Institute of Aeronautics and Astronautics
AHMcNP	Alexander Hamilton McNeill Papers
BAA	*Baltimore Afro-American*
CB	*Carthage Blade*
CHS	Chicago Historical Society
CM	*The Commercial Motor*
CN	*Camberley News*
CPL	Chicago Public Library
CRRMcCRC	Colonel Robert R. McCormick Research Center
CT	*Chicago Tribune*
ECU	East Carolina University
EREM	*Erie Railroad Employes' Magazine*
FT	*Franklin Times*
GA	Georgia Archives
GAMPCUSA	Minutes of the General Assembly of the Presbyterian Church in the United States of America
HMM	*Home Mission Monthly*
IASA	Institute of the Aerospace Sciences Archives
JL	*Jonesboro Leader*
LC	Library of Congress
MCNY	Museum of the City of New York
MG	*Moore Gazette*
MI	*Moore Index*
MCLHC	Moore County Library Historical Collection
MERL	Museum of English Rural Life
MT	*Macon Telegraph*
MYP	Minutes, Yadkin Presbytery, vol. 2, 2nd series, Presbyterian Historical Society
N&O	*News & Observer*
NA, Kew	National Archive, Kew, Richmond, Surrey
NARA, College Park	National Archives and Records Administration, College Park, Md.
NARA, Kansas City	National Archives and Records Administration, Kansas City, Mo.
NARA, Washington	National Archives and Records Administration, Washington, D.C.
NASM	National Air & Space Museum
NCCU	North Carolina Central University
NCIA	North Carolina Industrial Association

NCSA	North Carolina State Archives
NL	Newberry Library
NYA	*New York Age*
NYAR	National Youth Administration Records
NYT	*New York Times*
OEO FOIA	Office of Enforcement Operations Freedom of Information Act
PA	*People's Advocate*
PC	*Pittsburgh Courier*
PCAHC	Presbyterian Church in America Historical Center
PCR	Pullman Company Records
PCUS	Presbyterian Church in the United States
PCUSA	Presbyterian Church in the United States of America
PHS	Presbyterian Historical Society
PMR	*Presbyterian Monthly Record*
PT	*Philadelphia Tribune*
RG	Record Group
RN	*The Roadless News*
RP	*Richmond Planet*
SC	*State Chronicle*
SAE	Society of Automotive Engineers
SHC	Surrey Heath Centre
SHM	Surrey Heath Museum
UHRC	Udvar-Hazy Research Center
UNIA	Universal Negro Improvement Association
USAFA	U.S. Air Force Academy
USAFAL	U.S. Air Force Academy Library
UNCCH	University of North Carolina at Chapel Hill
VPNL	*Virginian-Pilot and Norfolk Landmark*
WB	*Washington Bee*
WM	*Wilmington Messenger*
WMS	*Wilmington Morning Star*

Introduction

1. Thomas P. Hughes argued in 1989 that the transition from the independent "heroic" inventor to the industrial scientist was by the end of World War I well on its way to being established (Hughes, *American Genesis*). Many scholars have since ably questioned this thesis, arguing for a less dramatic shift than Hughes proposed, uncovering differences across geographic regions and markets, and documenting the role that independent inventors continued to play. The very vigor of the debate that Hughes sparked, however, is a testament to the import of the change he described, and recent historians have recognized the difficulties this shift created for inventors working outside the industrial research environment. For the best discussion of obstacles that the new inventive landscape posed, see Lamoreaux and Sokoloff, "The Rise and Decline of the Independent Inventor," 43–78. For arguments concerning the continuing importance of independent inventors, see especially Hintz, "The

Post-Heroic Generation: American Independent Inventors, 1900–1950," and Nicholas, "The Role of Independent Invention in U.S. Technological Development, 1880–1930."

Chapter One

1. A handful of candidates besides Headen could contend for the honor of being the first black American pilot. Among them are Charles Wesley Peters of Pittsburgh, Ulysses Grant Scott of New York, Emory Malick of Philadelphia, Fred Bradford of Chicago, Artis Ward and Joel Foreman of Los Angeles, and James Marshall of Macon, Georgia. See Snider dissertation, "Flying to Freedom," 8–48; Barbour, "Early Black Flyers of Western Pennsylvania," 95–97; Rebecca Maskell, "The Unrecognized First," *Air & Space* magazine, March 2011, 14. The author currently has work in progress on this question. For coverage of Headen's flights at Mineola, see "Negro Aviator Gets Medal, Lucian Headin, Honored by Aeronautical Society," *New York Age* (hereafter *NYA*), January 18, 1912, 1; untitled editorial, *NYA*, January 25, 1912, 4. For reprintings, see, for example, "Negro Aviator Wins a Medal; Is an Inventor," *Pittsburgh Courier* (hereafter *PC*), February 10, 1912, 1; "Negro Aviator Gets Medal," *Cleveland Gazette*, February 17, 1912, 1; "Negro Aviator Gets Medal," *Colorado Statesman*, February 17, 1912, [6]; "Along the Color Line," *The Crisis*, March 1912, 187.

2. "Sole Negro Aviator Due, Only Licensed Member of Race in World to Fly at Emancipation Event," *Globe-Democrat*, September 20, 1912, 7.

3. Ann Tyson's maiden name, Person, is listed in the death record of her son Henry. See Henry Clay Lyson [Tyson], death certificate, July 3, 1926, Charlotte, Mecklenburg Co., N.C., Ancestry.com, *North Carolina, Death Certificates*. Note: A transcription error in the Ancestry index lists Henry's name as Lyson; however, the original record shows it to be spelled Tyson. Carthage population counts from "Table III, Population of Civil Divisions Less than Counties, in the Aggregate, at the Censuses of 1880 and 1870, North Carolina," in U.S. Bureau of the Census, *Statistics of the Population of the United States at the Tenth Census*, 282. Information on Tyson & Jones is from "Products of Industry in the County of Moore, in the State of North Carolina, Carthage Township, Carriage and Wagon Manufacturers, May 31, 1880," *North Carolina Manufacturing Census: 1880*, ED 132, Schedule 3. Jones quote from W. H. P., "A New Year's Story that Illustrates the Doctrine of Self-Help," *State Chronicle* (hereafter *SC*), January 5, 1884, 1.

4. For discussion of the Blue family's ordeal and violence in and near Jonesboro, see Testimony of Joseph G. Hester, in U.S. Congress, *Testimony Taken by the Joint Select Committee to Inquire into the Condition of Affairs in the Late Insurrectionary States*, vol. 2, *North Carolina*, 13–19; Testimony of Webster Shaffer, in U.S. Congress, *Testimony Taken by the Joint Select Committee to Inquire into the Condition of Affairs in the Late Insurrectionary States*, vol. 2, *North Carolina*, 36–37; Testimony of Daniel A. Graham, attachment, letter, John A. Barrett to Gov. William H. Holden, May 31, 1870, box G. P. 223, folder (Correspondence, May 17, 1870–May 31, 1870), Governor's Papers, NCSA; "Brutal Whipping of Women," and "Shocking Fate of a Quadroon Family," in Ireland, *The Nation's Peril*, 80–84, 110–14; Bradley, *Bluecoats and Tar Heels*, 207, 227. Note: Blue's Crossing officially became Aberdeen in October 1887, when Neill A. McKeithan was appointed its first postmaster. See U.S. Post Office Department, *Record of Appointment of U.S. Postmasters, 1832–Sept. 30, 1971*, Archive Publ. M841 (microfilm), Moore Co., N.C., vol. 49, roll #94, 418, NARA, Washington, D.C.

5. See *Ninth Census of the United States: 1870*, Household of Mariah Street, Sloan's Township No. 6, Jonesboro, Moore Co., N.C., 4; Household of D. J. Shields, Sloan's Township No. 6, Jonesboro, Moore Co., N.C., 16; and Household of Matilda Cheek, Ritter's Township No. 4, Prosperity, Moore Co., N.C., 32.

6. Nannie's full name comes from the Social Security registration card she completed in 1951. See "Application for a Social Security Account Number, Nan H. Jones, June 25, 1951, Philadelphia, Pa.," available from OEO FOIA Workgroup, Social Security Administration, Baltimore, Md. (hereafter Nan H. Jones Social Security application). For election results and Moore's representatives, see Connor, *The North Carolina Manual*, 713, 771; and "Officers," *Moore Index* (hereafter *MI*), February 12, 1880, 1. Republicans would make small gains in the election of 1878, when William M. Black replaced Marmaduke Robins, a conscription agent during the war, in the state senate, and Moore's Republicans won the seats for register of deeds and sheriff. For information on McIver and Robins in the Civil War, see "Captain James D. McIver, Co. H, 26th Regiment," in Jordan and Manarin, *North Carolina Troops, 1861–1865*, vol. 7, 561; "Marmaduke Swaim Robins, Outspoken Critic of Times," in *Randolph Guide, The Bicentennial Report, 1776–1976*, Asheboro, N.C., July 21, 1976; untitled editorial, *Asheboro Courier*, October 15, 1884, 2. For discussion of Robins's founding of the newspaper that is today the *Asheboro Courier*, see *Randolph County, N.C., 1779–1979* (Asheboro, N.C.: Randolph County Historical Society and Randolph Arts Guild, 1980), 124.

7. "New Enterprise, Millstones from Moore," *Charlotte Observer*, October 1, 1879, 3; "North Carolina Mill-Stone Company," *Moore Gazette* (hereafter *MG*), February 17, 1881, 3.

8. Opening of the telegraph office is noted in "Carthage," *Jonesboro Leader* (hereafter *JL*), September 5, 1888, 5. The Main Street location of the depot appears in an advertisement for the Tyson House Hotel, which described it as on "Main Street between Depot and Court House." See "Tyson House Hotel," advertisement, *Carthage Blade* (hereafter *CB*), November 8, 1905, 3. For opening of the railroad spur, see Johnson, *Through the Heart of the South*, 21; and Carriker, *Railroading in the Carolina Sandhills*, 64. Comment on the railroad's effect is from "Localets," *CB*, September 13, 1888, 3. Jones's method of delivering buggies is noted in W. H. P., "A New Year's Story," *SC*, January 5, 1884, 1; and "The Tyson Family," in Hamilton, Boyd, and Connor, *History of North Carolina*, vol. 6, 206–7.

9. "Bustle" quote is from "Carthage's Growth," *CB*, March 20, 1890, 2. William Jones and Lucien Person Tyson (Thomas B. Tyson's son) were two of the seven incorporators of the Carthage Railroad (chartered March 11, 1885). See North Carolina General Assembly, "An Act to Incorporate the Carthage Railroad," 398. Tyson & Jones's plan to double capacity is noted in "Carthage, Carriage Factory," *The South, An Immigration Journal*, March 1889, 11. Several writers have reported that Tyson & Jones installed their first steam engine in the 1870s. Unfortunately, a specific date is difficult to confirm. The Manufacturing Census of May 1880 did not record the motive power used by the company. However, according to a 1919 history of the Tyson family, Tyson & Jones installed a steam engine in a separate machine shop early in William T. Jones's tenure as a full partner, which began in 1873. Its arrival, the author of the history claimed, "attracted more attention from the natives than would the unloading of a circus today." A steam-driven machine shop was definitely in place at Tyson & Jones by January 1884, when W. T. Jones described it in an interview with the *State Chronicle*. See "Products of Industry in the County of Moore, in the State of North Carolina, Carthage Township, Carriage and Wagon Manufacturers, May 31, 1880," *North Carolina Manufactur-*

ing Census: 1880, ED 132, Schedule 3; "The Tyson Family," in Hamilton, Boyd, and Connor, *History of North Carolina*, vol. 6, 206–7; W. H. P., "A New Year's Story," *SC*, January 5, 1884, 1. Other businesses Tyson & Jones operated in 1880 still used a mix of power sources, with the firm's flour and grist mill operating that year on water and its lumber mill on steam. See "Special Schedule of Manufactures—Nos. 7 and 8, Flouring and Grist Mills, Carthage Township, Moore Co., N.C.," and "Special Schedules of Manufactures—Nos. 5 and 6, Lumber Mills and Saw-Mills—Brick Yards and Tile Works, Products of Industry in Carthage Township, in the County of Moore, State of North Carolina, During the Months Beginning June 1, 1879, and Ending May 31, 1880," *North Carolina Manufacturing Census*, ED 132. For documentation of the later purchase of boilers by the company, see *Wade's Fibre & Fabric*, advertisement, September 8, 1888, 219; and "Local Briefs," *CB*, May 8, 1890, 3. The *Blade* noted the construction of the new blacksmith shop in "Localets," *CB*, August 30, 1888, 3. The construction of the water tower is noted in Reilly, "Tyson & Jones Buggy Company," 204–5. For a detailed description of the three-story brick building built circa 1896, see "A Growing Industry, an Example of What Energy and Perseverance Can Accomplish, Backed by Sound Business Ideas, the Marvelous Success of a Home Industry—Sketch of the T.&J. Buggy Company," *CB*, October 6, 1897, 3. The company would add other large brick structures in 1905 (see "The Fayetteville District Conference," *Raleigh Christian Advocate*, March 29, 1905, 1) and in 1907 (see "Carthage Buggy Company," *CB*, August 1, 1907, 5). The "largest and best equipped" quote is from "State News," *The Hub*, January 1896, 756. See also "Carthage, Its Remarkable Growth in a Decade," *CB*, January 28, 1896, 2. Plans for a new hotel are noted in "New Hotel at Carthage," *S.A.L.magundi*, May 1897, 3. Although his name, Thomas B. Tyson II, suggests the younger Thomas was the son of Thomas B. Tyson, he was actually the child of Thomas's son, Lucien Person Tyson, with his first wife, Nannie Marsh Tyson. Thomas Tyson II was raised by his grandparents after his mother died when he was a toddler. See "The Tyson Family," in Hamilton, Boyd, and Connor, *History of North Carolina*, vol. 6, 206–7.

10. A recent history of Tyson & Jones identified eleven African Americans who worked at the company: laborer Eugene Barrett; janitor Thomas W. Buckner; wheelwright Adam Tyson; blacksmiths Noah Jackson, Joseph Tyson, Joseph's sons Frank Tyson and Willie Tyson, and Edinboro Kelly; trim painter Sandy A. Jackson; trim shop worker Morris Tyson; and fireman Will Robertson. See Koster, *The Story of the Tyson & Jones Buggy Company*, 49–53. Six additional black workers identified in census records and newspaper articles are John Jackson, Calvin Peace, Tom Clegg, King Goins, A. Thomas Person, and Floyd J. Brower. Mention of Jackson's employment appears in an 1884 notice of his death (his occupation was not recorded). See "Local Briefs," *CB*, February 8, 1888, 4. Peace was listed as a Blacksmith (Buggy) and Blacksmith (Carriage Factory) in the 1900 and 1910 censuses, respectively. See *Twelfth Census of the United States: 1900*, Household of Calvin Peace, East Carthage Precinct, Moore Co., N.C., ED 68, sheet B9; and *Thirteenth Census of the United States: 1910*, Household of Calvin Peace, Carthage Township, Moore Co., N.C., ED 66, sheet 3A. Clegg was listed as a Laborer (Buggy Factory) in 1910. See *Thirteenth Census of the United States: 1910*, Household of Tom Clegg, Carthage Township, Moore Co., N.C., ED 67, sheet 17B. Person was listed as a Painter (Buggy Factory) in *Thirteenth Census of the United States: 1910*, Household of A. Thomas Person, Southwest Carthage Township, Moore Co., N.C., ED 67, sheet 7B; and *Fourteenth United States Census: 1920*, Household of Thomas Person, Carthage

Township, Moore Co., N.C., ED 83, sheet 5B. Goins was listed as a Laborer (Buggy Factory) in *Thirteenth Census of the United States: 1910*, Household of King Goins, Southwest Carthage Township, Moore Co., N.C., ED 67, sheet 16A. Brower was employed as a truck driver by the company in 1920. See *Fourteenth United States Census: 1920*, Household of Floid J. Brower, Carthage Township, Moore Co., N.C., ED 83, sheet 11A.

11. When Elizabeth married James McGilvary in 1840, Jenny Tyson went to live with the newlyweds in Fayetteville, likely as a wedding present. See death notice (Jenny Tyson), in "Local Paragraphs," *CB*, August 28, 1894, 3. A *Fayetteville Observer* notice of Jenny's death states that she also nursed James and Elizabeth's son, James Jr., as well as the children James McGilvary had with his second wife, Hannah. See "Died at 106," *Fayetteville Weekly Observer*, September 6, 1894, 3. John Tyson will, filed October 13, 1851, Moore County Wills, Will Book B, 234–36, *Records of Wills, 1783–1965* (microfilm), NCSA. Joseph Tyson was born on John Tyson's plantation in 1842. His death certificate lists Jenny Tyson as his mother but does not list a father. A *Carthage Blade* notice of Jenny's death in 1894 states that Adam and Joe were brothers. See Joseph Tyson, death certificate, April 26, 1927, Moore Co., N.C., Ancestry.com, *North Carolina, Death Certificates*; "Local Paragraphs," *CB*, August 28, 1894, 3; [Slave] Bill of Sale, May 31, 1852, Thomas B. Tyson, executor for John Tyson, to Alexander Kelly, for slaves Amy, Fanny, and Joe, registered October 1852, Moore County, N.C., Book A.M., 253, http://files.usgwarchives.net/nc/moore/court/tysondec2399gwl.txt.

12. Quote concerning Seawell, the company's former owner, is from Tyson, "Tyson and Jones Buggies Kept Rolling On and On," reprinted in Paschal and Old, *The Methodists of Carthage*, 99. The eight-man workforce is noted in Wellman, *The Story of Moore County*, 78; and Paschal and Old, *The Methodists of Carthage*, 99. Adam Tyson's injury is noted in "Local Items," *CB*, November 12, 1895, 4.

13. Tyson & Jones's gold medal is noted in "Local News Items," *CB*, December 3, 1895, 4; and Reilly, "Tyson & Jones Buggy Company," 206–7. An *Atlanta Constitution* reporter, after viewing the Tyson & Jones exhibit, praised the company's products as "magnificent" in style, finish, and durability. See "The Tyson & Jones Buggy Co.," *Atlanta Constitution*, November 29, 1895, 12. The timing of Joseph Tyson and Kade Kelly's attendance at the fair is noted in "Local Items," *CB*, November 19, 1895, 4; and "Local Items," *CB*, December 3, 1895, 4. Sympathy for Adam Tyson was expressed in "Local Items," *CB*, November 12, 1895, 4. Duncan McRae owned a barbershop just off the town square, and he built furniture in a cabinet-making shop located in its rear. See "The Carthage Barber," *CB*, July 20, 1897, 3. McRae also frequently made repairs to public buildings such as the courthouse for the town. See, for example, "Commissioner's Proceedings," *CB*, February 7, 1894, 3.

14. A county courthouse fire in September 1889 destroyed the deed for the land on which Adam Tyson lived in 1870, and it was never rerecorded. However, Adam was listed as its owner in both the Population and the Agricultural Census Schedules for 1870. See *Ninth United States Census: 1870*, Household of Adam Tyson, Carthage Township, Moore Co., N.C., 5; and *North Carolina Agricultural Census: 1870*, Farm of Adam Tyson, "Productions of Agriculture in Township No. 1, in the County of Moore, in the State of North Carolina, Post Office: Carthage," June 20, 1870, Schedule 3, 1. Tyson's second land purchase, for $1,000, is recorded in "Thomas B. and Mary P. Tyson to Adam Tyson," originally recorded April 6, 1876, rerecorded February 21, 1891 (Deed Book 3, 501–3), Moore County, N.C., in *Record of Deeds, 1888–1961* (microfilm), NCSA. He is also listed as the owner in *North Carolina Agri-*

cultural Census: 1880, Farm of Adam Tyson, "Productions of Agriculture in Carthage Township in the County of Moore, State of North Carolina," June 14, 1880, ED 132, Schedule 2, 8. The presence of a farm hand and housekeeper in the Tyson household in 1880 is noted in *Tenth United States Census: 1880*, Household of Adam Tyson, Carthage Township, Moore Co., N.C., ED 132, 12. James and Adam Tyson opened their store in 1884. See "James A. & Adam Tyson," advertisement, *MG*, July 31, 1884, 3; "To Violinists and Other Musicians," advertisement, *MG*, September 11, 1884, 3; "Notice," *MG*, December 18, 1884, 3; and "James A. & Adam Tyson," advertisement, *MG*, December 25, 1884, 3. It is unclear how long the store operated, but by the early 1890s James was working as a clerk in the T. B. Tyson & Son general store, managed by Lucien Person Tyson. James left this position in January 1896 to again start his own business, opening a grocery and confectionery shop near the town square. See "Local News Items," *CB*, January 21, 1896, 3. James (full name James Andrew Tyson) was the son of Andrew Williams and Mary Tyson. Williams, along with his brothers Sandy and Isham Person, was a slave of Presbyterian minister Neill McKay of nearby Harnett County. When McKay moved to Pine Bluff, Arkansas, in the late 1850s, he took Williams with him. James, his brother Morris, and sister Lizzie, also Williams's children, remained with their mother Mary in Carthage and retained the Tyson name. After the Civil War, Morris and Lizzie lived with their mother and stepfather, Shephard Barrett, while James became a live-in servant in Thomas B. Tyson's home. Morris later worked as a buggy crater in the Tyson & Jones trim shop. Lizzie married John Harvey, a local beef market owner (see "Local News Items," *CB*, February 16, 1897, 3). For the family relationships of Andrew Williams, see "Returned to the Scenes of his Childhood," *CB*, May 28, 1895, 1. For the residence of Mary Tyson Barrett, Morris and Lizzie, and Mary and Shephard Barrett's son Walter Barrett, see *Ninth United States Census: 1870*, Household of Shephard Barrett, Carthage Township, Carthage Post Office, Moore Co., N.C., 4. For James's residence with Thomas Tyson, see *Ninth United States Census: 1870*, Household of Thomas B. Tyson, Carthage Township No. 1, Carthage Post Office, Moore Co., N.C., 1. When Andrew Williams returned to Carthage in 1895, he brought with him two-and-a-half-year-old Hessie A. Williams, born in Arkansas. Hessie may also have been his child or grandchild. James A. Tyson and his wife, Harriett Worthy Tyson, raised Hessie in their home. *Twelfth United States Census: 1900*, Household of James A. Tyson, West Carthage Precinct, Moore Co., N.C., ED 59, sheet 12A; Hattie Hayes Warrington, telephone conversation with the author, December 8, 2014.

15. *Tenth United States Census: 1880*, Household of Jerry M. Hedden [Headen], Jonesboro, Moore Co., N.C., ED 134, 6; Jerry M. Headen will, filed September 22, 1947, Moore Co., N.C., in *Record of Wills, 1946–1949*, vol. P, 118–20, NCSA. Nannie, born February 14, 1877, was two-and-a-half years older than Lucean. The year of her birth is documented in the 1880 census, and the month and day in her Social Security application (which incorrectly listed her birth year as 1889). See Nan H. Jones Social Security application.

16. Henry's delivery of the valedictory address in 1879 is noted in Harris, "Report of the Principal," Document No. 5, 40. In 1875, John and Henry published their thoughts on education and temperance in *The Educator*, a Fayetteville publication. See John Tyson, "Education," *The Educator*, February 6, 1875, 2; and Henry Tyson, "Whiskey," *The Educator*, February 6, 1875, 2. John and Henry graduated in 1879 and William Thomas (who usually went by W. T.) in 1882. See "List of Graduates of the School and Their Occupations," Fayetteville State Normal School catalogue, 1908–9, 30–31. Lucy Tyson's attendance at the State

Colored Normal School between 1879 and 1880 is noted in North Carolina Department of Public Instruction, *Annual Report of the Superintendent of Public Instruction*, 1880, 44; and "Catalogue of Students Attending Colored Normal School at Fayetteville, Session of 1880–'81," in "Annual Report of the Superintendent of Public Instruction, Scholastic Years 1881–'82," in North Carolina Department of Public Instruction, *Biennial Report of the Superintendent of Public Instruction*, 1881–82, 101. Her attendance at Scotia Seminary is noted in "Middle Class," in Scotia Seminary catalogue, 1881–82, 13. Mention of Guy Tyson's graduation from Bennett Seminary appears in "Greensboro, N.C.," *NYA*, July 14, 1923, 5; and "Pennsylvania, Philadelphia News," *Chicago Defender* (hereafter *CD*), June 7, 1924, 22. Bennett Seminary was founded in 1873 by the Freedmen's Aid Society of the American Missionary Association. It was designated a four-year college in 1889, the year Guy Tyson matriculated. The school was largely funded by the Methodist Episcopal Church. "History and Status of Education Among the Colored People," in Smith, *The History of Education in North Carolina*, 159; and "Bennett College," in Brooks and Starks, *Historically Black Colleges and Universities*, 60. Laura and Elizabeth Tyson's literacy is noted in *Ninth United States Census: 1870*, Household of Adam Tyson, Carthage Township, Moore Co., N.C., 5.

17. The diphtheria outbreak of 1875 and its devastating effect were noted over seventy years later in "Salmon Child Dies of Diphtheria in Moore Co. Hospital," *The Pilot*, November 15, 1946, 1. Lucean Tyson was listed with the family in 1870. However, after that date he disappears from the record. Lucean Headen's name was reported as Arthur rather than Lucean in the 1880 and 1900 censuses and in an early employment record with the Pullman Company. He also entered Arthur instead of Lucean on his application for a passport in 1915. See *Tenth United States Census: 1880*, Household of Jerry M. Hedden [Headen], Jonesboro, Moore Co., N.C., ED 134, 6; *Twelfth United States Census: 1900*, Household of Adam Tyson, Carthage, Moore Co., N.C., ED 69, sheet 11; entry for Arthur Headden [sic], Vol. 1, Jan. 1, 1900–Dec. 31, 1906, Alphabetical Sect. H, 1, in 06/02/06, Employee and Labor Relations, Personnel Administration Department, Discharge and Release Records, 1880–1957, Porter Discharge Registers, Pullman Company Records, NL; [Lucean] Arthur Headen, U.S. passport certificate no. 51370, February 16, 1915, Ancestry.com, *U.S. Passport Applications*.

18. Adam Tyson's postwar membership at Carthage Presbyterian is documented in "A List of Members of Carthage Church Assessed and Given to A. H. McNeill to Collect for Pay of the Rev. M. McQueen for 1866," box PC 1761.16, Miscellaneous, Personal Miscellanea, 1792–1920, folder (Presbyterian Church, Carthage, N.C.), AHMcNP, NCSA. Ann Tyson, along with three other black women, joined Carthage Presbyterian following a revival at the church in October 1874. See Carthage Presbyterian Church (today First Presbyterian Church), *Session Book, Carthage Church, September 1, 1850 to April 26, 1906* (housed in the church office of First Presbyterian, Carthage, N.C.), 63–64 (hereafter referred to as Carthage Presbyterian, *Session Book*). Carthage Church, started by black residents, organized under the auspices of the Presbyterian Church North (officially the Presbyterian Church in the United States of America, or PCUSA). Carthage Church first appears in PCUSA records in December 1876. See "General Assembly's Committee on Freedmen, Money Received and Expended on the Field During the Quarter Ending December 31st, 1876," *Presbyterian Monthly Record* (hereafter *PMR*), April 1877, 128. The deed for the original land granted Carthage Church in 1876 was destroyed in the 1889 courthouse fire and was never rerecorded. This tract, however, is mentioned in the deed for adjacent land that Thomas B. Tyson granted

the church in 1879. The deed for the 1879 parcel (rerecorded in 1891) describes it as "Beginning at a large pine stump *near the Church at Sassafras Spring*" (emphasis mine), documenting that a church structure had already been built on the first parcel. See "Thomas B. and Mary P. Tyson to Trustees of the Presbyterian Church & their successors for the Presbyterian Church North," originally recorded February 4, 1879 (Deed Book 46, 87), rerecorded July 24, 1891 (Deed Book, vol. 6, 95–97), Moore County, N.C., in *Record of Deeds, 1888–1961* (microfilm), NCSA. The northern church, unlike its southern counterpart, afforded black members voting rights, ordained them as ministers, and encouraged their service as deacons, elders, and trustees, and it offered hope for an integrated church. In 1874, its Atlantic Synod, comprising presbyteries in North and South Carolina, Georgia, and Florida, had twenty black and fourteen white ministers working side by side. See Heckman, "The Presbyterian Church," 229. Prior to joining the PCUSA, those in Carthage had earlier attempted to join the Presbyterian Church South (known as the Presbyterian Church in the United States, or PCUS), which split from the PCUSA in the Civil War. However, they abandoned their attempts after it became clear the PCUS intended to maintain segregation and limit the role of blacks. See note of Session Clerk Daniel P. Shields ("Collered Members of this Church to join a black Church in the bounds of Union Church") in entry for June 16, 1872, Carthage Presbyterian, *Session Book*, 54. The southern church established the Colored Evangelistic Fund in May 1874 to train black ministers. See "Saturday Morning, May 30, 1874, 9 o'clock," *Minutes of the General Assembly of the Presbyterian Church in the United States* [PCUS], 1874, 516–18. By 1876, however, the PCUS could show for its efforts only three black ministers, three licentiates, and one ministerial candidate. In addition, forty-four of fifty-seven presbyteries reported that year that they had taken *no* steps toward further evangelization of the freedmen. See Thompson, "Black Presbyterians," 57.

19. For John Tyson's role in the Independent Order of Good Templars, see "Good Templars," *MG*, June 16, 1881, 3. For a history of the organization's establishment in North Carolina, see Haley, *Charles N. Hunter*, 28–30. McRae was long active in Republican politics. In 1888, he served as one of the county party's three representatives for Carthage Township. Four years later, in 1892, he was named an alternate delegate to the Republican National Convention in Minneapolis, representing the 3rd Congressional District. In 1896, he was Republican poll holder for East Carthage. See John B. Campbell, "Localets," *CB*, October 4, 1888, 3; Rose and Burke, *Proceedings of the Tenth Republican National Convention*, 105; and "Poll Holders for Moore County," *CB*, October 6, 1896, 3. Prior to leaving for school, William Thomas Tyson was elected assistant secretary for the county Republican convention and was asked, along with McRae, to speak at the meeting, held at the county courthouse. The role Tyson and McRae played in the convention is discussed in D. C. Evans, letter to the editor, "Convention!" *Wilmington Post*, September 24, 1882, 2. Tyson and McRae worked closely in their political efforts with Evans, a former classmate of Tyson's at the Fayetteville Colored Normal School, as well as with another classmate, William Thomas Chalmers (called Thomas). Tyson and Chalmers entered Lincoln University together in the fall of 1882. See H. C. Tyson, "The Fayetteville Normal School," *The Carthaginian*, March 21, 1878, 2; Fayetteville State Normal School catalogue, 1881–82, 44; "Preparatory Department, Students," Lincoln University catalogue, 1882–83, 19.

20. Dedication description and Wood quote from "Church Dedicated," *PMR*, June 1885, 245–46. Church membership and Sunday school enrollment figures for 1885 through 1892

reported in the *Minutes of the General Assembly of the Presbyterian Church in the United States of America* [PCUSA], New Series (hereafter *GAMPCUSA*), 1885, 1117; 1886, 269; 1887, 299; 1888, 314; 1889, 316; 1890, 316; 1891, 316; and 1892, 426.

21. Henry Wood and Anna Riter married in Trenton, New Jersey, in 1866. See Henry D. Wood and Annie Riter, marriage certificate, August 19, 1866, Trenton, N.J., in Henry D. Wood Pension File, XC No. 962,110, Certificate 914,342, Held by the Department of Veterans Affairs, Baltimore Regional Office, Baltimore, Md. (hereafter Wood pension file). Wood was appointed a licentiate for Moore County in 1879. See "Licentiates," in "Statistical Reports, Synod of Atlantic, Presbytery of Yadkin," *GAMPCUSA*, 1880, 207. The school, initially conducted by the Woods in their home, later moved to Sassafras Springs, then to John Hall Chapel upon the church building's completion. See "Freedmen, From the Field," *PMR*, July 1883, 254–55. Jane Beze Perry graduated from the Fayetteville State Colored Normal School in 1878. See "List of Graduates of the School and Their Occupations," Fayetteville State Normal School catalogue, 1908–9, 30. She married Henry Tyson in 1879. See Henry C. Tyson and Jane B. Perry, marriage record, July 2, 1879, Cumberland Co., N.C., Ancestry.com, *North Carolina, Marriage Records*. Jane Tyson's commission to teach at John Hall's parochial school is noted in "Missions and Missionaries in the Year Ending March 31, 1889," in Board of Missions for Freedmen, *Twenty-Fourth Annual Report*, 1889, 39. While Henry lived in Washington year round, Jane remained in North Carolina during the school months to teach, before joining him permanently in 1885. Henry made frequent visits. See, for example, "Local," *People's Advocate* (hereafter *PA*), March 8, 1884, 3, and March 15, 1884, 3.

22. In 1883, Henry Wood commented on the emotion it stirred in him "to see the aged man and the young child learning the alphabet together." See Henry D. Wood, letter to the Board of Missions for Freedmen, *PMR*, July 1883, 255. Jerry Headen's literacy status is noted in *Tenth United States Census: 1880*, Household of Jerry M. Hedden [Headen], Jonesboro, Moore Co., N.C., ED 134, 6; and *Twelfth United States Census: 1900*, Household of Jerry M. Haden [Headen], Mineral Springs Township, Moore Co., N.C., ED 79, sheet 10B.

23. For Dayton Academy's founding, see Henry D. Wood, "A Correction," letter to the editor, *CB*, March 30, 1897, 3; and Richings, *Evidences of Progress*, 175–76. The opening date is mentioned in Board of Missions for Freedmen, *Twenty-Fifth Annual Report*, 1890, 7. The number of students is from "List of Private Schools, &c.," in North Carolina Department of Public Instruction, *Biennial Report of the Superintendent of Public Instruction*, 1889–90, 100. Marie Walker graduated from Claflin University in 1888. Prior to joining Dayton Academy, she taught at Claflin and at Bennett Seminary, where she met Guy Tyson. The couple married in April 1892. See Claflin University catalogue, 1889–1890, 8, 12, 37; and "Graduates," in Claflin University catalogue, 1890–1891, 33; Adam G. Tyson and Marie L. Walker, marriage certificate, April 28, 1892, Guilford Co., N.C., Ancestry.com, *North Carolina, Marriage Records*. Marie was commissioned to teach at Dayton in July 1892. See Records of the Presbyterian Committee for Freedmen, vol. 4, July 25, 1892, 143, in box 3, folder 2 (Minute Book, April 1891–May 1893), RG 376, Board of Missions for Freedmen Records, PHS. For information on Susie McRae, see D. J. McRae, "Grand Rallying Day at John Hall Chapel," *CB*, October 17, 1893, 3. According to Deanna McRae King, the McRaes' great-great-granddaughter Susan ("Susie") Nichols McRae was a classically trained pianist. See King quoted in Martha J. Henderson, "Tyson Descendents [sic] to Visit Carthage, Attend 25th Annual Buggy Festival," *The Pilot*, May 5, 2013, http://www.thepilot.com/news-tyson-descendents-to-visit

-carthage-attend-th-annual-buggy-festival/article_83cacfof-7c10-54a2-815a-2ba0db852130
.html?mode=jqm. The best candidate for Lucean's other teacher was Isabella Kelly. A graduate of Scotia Seminary and the daughter of John Hall trustee Edinboro Kelly, "Belle" was listed as a teacher in Carthage as early as 1890 in *Branson's North Carolina Business Directory*, 1890, vol. 7, 465. Guy Tyson also joined the school's staff in the late 1890s. See *Branson's Moore County Business Directory*, 1898, 122. Annie Wood's appointment for the 1891–92 school year shows the board commissioned her for five months. However, when it commissioned Marie Tyson for the 1892–93 school year, it did so for six months. See Records of the Presbyterian Committee for Freedmen, vol. 4, May 4, 1891, 10, and vol. 4, July 25, 1892, 143, in box 3, folder 2 (Minute Book, April 1891–May 1893), Board of Missions for Freedmen Records, PHS.

24. "Universal training program" description from Parker, *The Rise and Decline of the Program of Education for Black Presbyterians*, 29. Wood quote from Henry D. Wood, "Report of Committee on Freedmen, [Annual Meeting], April 15, 1896," minutes, Yadkin Presbytery, vol. 2, 2nd series (hereafter MYP), 9, PHS. The Yadkin Presbytery, to which John Hall Chapel belonged, noted the use by its churches of the *Westminster Lesson Leaf* in April 1888. See "Twenty-Eighth Annual Meeting, April 19th 1888," MYP, 184–85. The description given here is based on issues of the *Westminster Lesson Leaf* dated October 7, 14, 21, and 28, 1888, box 333, file 76, Steele Papers, PCAHC, St. Louis, Mo. The presbytery noted the adoption of the other texts in "29th Annual Meeting, April 1889," MYP, 198. For general descriptions of materials used in Presbyterian Sunday schools in the 1880s, see "What the Board Is Doing in Its Periodical Work," *PMR*, December 1886, 471–74. For incorporation of the *Africo-American Presbyterian*, see North Carolina General Assembly, "An Act to Incorporate the Africo-American Presbyterian Publishing Company," 936–37. The paper's founder and editor, Rev. Daniel J. Sanders, moved the paper from Wilmington to Charlotte in 1891, when he became the first black president of Biddle University (today Johnson C. Smith University).

25. Meade Seawell noted Marie Tyson's "artistic handwriting" in her memoir, *Edgehill Entry*, 119.

26. Mrs. C. E. Coulter noted the transition of Dayton Industrial and Normal School from a parochial to a boarding school in her 1894 report to the General Assembly. According to Coulter, the school at that time had 189 students. See Mrs. C. E. Coulter, "Report of Freedmen's Department, The Field," *Home Mission Monthly* (hereafter *HMM*), July 1895, 202. The school's name change is recorded in "Annual Meeting of Yadkin Presbytery," April 20, 1894, MYP, 297. Dayton Academy in 1897 became affiliated with Charlotte's Biddle University. See Presbyterian Church in the U.S.A., "Freedmen, Affiliated Schools," *The Church at Home and Abroad*, August 1897, 105; and "Theological Seminaries, XIII. Biddle University," in *GAMPCUSA*, 1898, 220.

27. For Henry Wood's perspective on the cause of the split, see letter, Henry D. Wood to A. H. McNeill, June 11, 1890, box 1761.3, Personal Correspondence, folder (1890), AHMcNP, NCSA. For the Yadkin Presbytery's actions concerning the split, see untitled entry [33rd Annual Meeting, April 1893], MYP, vol. 2, 267–68, PHS. For information on the construction of the new church at Sassafras Springs, see "Appendix, Appropriations for Churches and Manses," in Board of Missions for Freedmen, *Twenty-Eighth Annual Report*, 29, 36. The congregation that moved to Sassafras Springs built a less commanding structure than John Hall Chapel. Gussie Brown McNair, now 95, whose grandfather Nathan Brown helped found the

original Carthage Church and who was one of those who left John Hall, remembers attending church at Sassafras Springs as a child. She recalls the 1892 church building, located in the upper reach of the Sassafras Spring Cemetery, as smaller than John Hall Chapel. She also remembers playing in the original 1870s structure, located on the bank of the spring in the cemetery's lower reach. She describes this original building as having a packed dirt floor and rough pinewood benches. When the congregation ultimately decided to leave the Sassafras Springs location and move a half-mile away, where they built Shady Grove Church in 1912, the 1870s and 1892 buildings fell from use and were later torn down. McNair, conversation with the author, November 24, 2014, Carthage, N.C.

28. Ann Person Tyson's death is noted in "Town and County News," *CB*, January 19, 1892, 4. John Tyson's death from tuberculosis is noted in "Local Paragraphs," *CB*, June 5, 1894, 3. William Worthy's death, also from tuberculosis, is noted in "Local Paragraphs," *CB*, July 10, 1894, 3. William's mother, Caroline Worthy, fell victim to the disease in January 1895. See "Local Paragraphs," *CB*, January 15, 1895, 4. For coverage of Jenny Tyson's death, see "Local Paragraphs," *CB*, July 10, 1894, 3; "Local Paragraphs," *CB*, August 28, 1894, 3; and "Died at 106," *Fayetteville Weekly Observer*, September 6, 1894, 3. For Nannie's enrollment at Scotia, see "Preparatory Department, First Grade," in Scotia Seminary catalogue, 1894–95, 9.

29. For the fire, see "Local Paragraphs," *CB*, January 15, 1895, 4. For the flooding, see "Local Paragraphs," *CB*, April 9, 1895, 4. For Tyson's accident, see "Local Items," *CB*, November 12, 1895, 4.

30. Annie's parents, Edward and Lydia Riter, had died by the time she was four. Their names are taken from Annie's marriage certificate. In 1850, Annie was being raised by Peter and Hannah Logan in New Castle, Pennsylvania. See Henry D. Wood and Annie Riter, marriage certificate, August 19, 1866, in Wood pension file; and *Seventh United States Census: 1850*, Annie Riter in the Household of Peter Logan, "Schedule I, Free Inhabitants in the Borough of New Castle in the County of Laurence, State of Penna., Dwelling No. 38," September 3, 1850. For a description of the Fourth of July picnic, see "Local Paragraphs," *CB*, July 3, 1894, 3.

31. Quote on Tyson's shop is from Seawell, *Edgehill Entry*, 61. Praise of Tyson's razor appears in untitled item, *MG*, reprinted in *Chatham Record*, July 24, 1884, 3. His razor's display at the North Carolina State Fair is noted in untitled item, *MG*, reprinted in *Chatham Record*, August 21, 1884, 2.

32. "Fruit Pruner," *MG*, February 17, 1881, 3; clipping, "'Uncle Joe' Was Gifted Person," *Moore County News*, February 19, 1975, MCLHC. In 1903, a local man stole a letter addressed to Tyson from a Georgia customer and, posing as him, falsely received payment. See "Case in the Federal Court," *Wilmington Messenger*, December 2, 1903, 3.

33. For local papers' enthusiasm for invention, see, for example, "An Inventor's Advice," *MG*, September 3, 1885, 4; "The Electric Light," *JL*, February 13, 1889, 8; "Wizard Edison, He Talks of Inventions He Will Some Day Bring Out," *JL*, October 2, 1889, 7; "A Wonderful Invention," *CB*, June 19, 1890, 2; "Invention of the Compass," *CB*, July 24, 1890, 4; "'Marvelous Machine,' Wonders Expected of Edison's New Phonograph," *CB*, January 25, 1888, 1. Quote from "Tesla's Triumph," *CB*, June 22, 1897, 1. For Cole's patent, see Cole, "Seed-Planter," US Patent 439,773. Cole, who grew up on a farm near Union Presbyterian Church, was later a teacher in Cool Springs. See "Local Items," *CB*, August 27, 1895, 4.

34. Edison's gold extraction method is discussed in "Edison the Wizard: The Great Electrician and His Wonderful Discoveries," *Lincoln Courier*, March 28, 1890, 2; and "Edison's Dis-

covery in Gold Mining," *Macon Telegraph*, April 2, 1880, 2. Platinum, too, was of interest to Edison because of its use in the filaments of his incandescent light bulb. His interest in North Carolina, in fact, had started with the search for platinum. In 1880, he had commissioned William Earl Hidden of New York to travel to the state to seek out mines that might provide it. See Hidden, "Addendum to the Minerals and Mineral Localities of North Carolina," 45. The search by those for gold and other minerals on their land is noted in "Local Briefs," *CB*, March 6, 1890, 3; and untitled item, *Chatham Record*, April 17, 1890, 3 (reprinted from *Carthage Blade*).

35. For the *Blade*'s early coverage of Edison's trip, see "News Summary from All Over the Southland: Accidents, Calamities, Pleasant News and Notes of Industry, North Carolina," *CB*, February 20, 1890, 1; "Mr. Edison Likes the Country," *CB*, March 20, 1890, 1; and "The Wizard of Menlo Park Again," *CB*, April 10, 1890, 1. Edison's scheduled arrival was noted in untitled item, "Local Briefs," *CB*, May 8, 1890, 3 (reprinted from *Sanford Express*) and "Local Briefs," *CB*, May 15, 1890, 3. The *News & Observer* (hereafter *N&O*) in its June 24, 1890 issue, reported that Edison had been in Moore County two weeks earlier. See "Edison Was in Moore County," *N&O*, June 24, 1890, 2. Edison's trip is also mentioned in "Edison's Work in North Carolina," *New York Times* (hereafter *NYT*), July 5, 1890, 1. Although not all the mines Edison visited are known, his personal notebooks mention Moore County's Grampers, Bell, Brown, Shields, Bat Roost, Cagle, Clegg, and Burns Mines. See Edison, "Notebook, Jan. 1, 1890–Dec. 31, 1890, No. N-90-01-04.2," 26–27, folder (003508-100-0001), Notebook Series—Notebooks by Thomas Edison, Part III, 1887–1898, Thomas Alva Edison Papers, available through ProQuest History Vault.

36. "Invention by Albany Men Makes Use of Crude Oil in Motors Possible, Patent Is Issued for Vaporizer that Is Expected to Revolutionize Automotive Industry—Slight Change in Ordinary Gasoline Motor Transforms It into One Using Either Gasoline or Crude Oil," *Albany Herald*, August 21, 1929, 1–2. The 1895 Paris-to-Bordeaux race is described in H. M. Holleman, "Horseless Carriages," *CB*, September 10, 1895, 3.

37. The Robinson and Franklin Brothers' purchase and display of automobiles is described in "The Famous Rose Dockrill, One of the Features of the Great John Robinson and Franklin Bros.' Combined Shows," *Durham Sun*, September 23, 1896, 4; "Today's Great Event, the Great John Robinson and Franklin Circus Is Here and the Children Are Happy," *N&O*, October 19, 1897, 3; "A Show Truly Moral," *Raleigh Times*, October 12, 1897, 1; and "Entries at State Fair," *N&O*, September 30, 1900, 10. Although a separate "colored day" was designated as part of the North Carolina State Fair beginning in 1891, blacks did not confine their attendance to that day, and the fair remained a biracial event. See McLaurin, "The Nineteenth-Century North Carolina State Fair," 221. In addition to attending the main fair, many blacks between 1879 and 1924 also attended an entirely separate black fair, sponsored by the North Carolina Industrial Association (NCIA). For historical background on the North Carolina Negro State Fair, see Haley, *Charles N. Hunter*, 46–56, 65, 85, 96–97, 116, 150, 154–55, 165, 247, 280–82.

38. William Darnell Polite, quoted in Reaves, *Strength Through Struggle*, 449 (original quote from David Brinkley, *Wilmington Star*, 1939). For examples of patent agent advertisements, see "Patents, J. R. Little" and "Munn & Co. Patents," *CB*, February 15, 1888, 3; "Patents, C. A. Snow & Co.," *CB*, October 15, 1895, 3, June 16, 1896, 4, and April 27, 1897, 4; "Patents, C. A. Snow & Co.," *JL*, June 18, 1890, 1; "Patents, Muse & Co., Patent Solicitors," *Africo-American Presbyterian*, September 5, 1889, 3.

39. The Carthage Railroad expansion, completed in early 1893, extended the Carthage spur south of Curriesville in Mineral Springs Township. See "Town and County News," *CB*, January 31, 1893, 3. Several lumber mills sprang up along the extended line to process trees damaged by the fire. See "A Pleasant Junket to Curriesville," *CB*, May 2, 1893, 3. The early success of the mill and its burning are noted in "Saw and Shingle Mills of Headen & Tyson Burned Near Carthage," *Charlotte Daily Observer*, December 14, 1900, 2. Already by 1888, business at Tyson & Jones was booming, and workers struggled to keep up with orders, some even striking when the company instituted a ten-and-a-half-hour workday to meet demand. See "The Strike," *CB*, April 4, 1888, 4; and "Carthage," *JL*, February 27, 1889, 4.

40. Documentation that Jerry Headen was James Street's father appears in Street's death record. See James L. Street, death certificate, March 30, 1924, Tampa, Hillsborough Co., Fla., FamilySearch.com, *Florida, Deaths*. (Note: FamilySearch.com contains a transcription error that lists Street's name as W. S. Street. However, viewing the original record confirms the name as Jas. L. Street.) See also entry for James L. Street in Tampa city directory, 1899, 368. The Jacksonville, Tampa and Key West Railway was at the time part of the "Plant System." On April 4, 1899, the Plant Investment Co., operated by Harry B. Plant, bought the railroad and incorporated it into its larger network of railroads and steamship lines. See "Jacksonville, Tampa & Key West Ry.," *The Investor's Supplement of the Commercial & Financial Chronicle*, July 29, 1899, 72. The description of the car inspector's job is taken from two court cases based on the failure of inspectors to carry out their duties. See "*McDonald v. Mich. Cent. R. Co.*," in Michie, *Railroad Reports*, vol. 7, 290, 295; and "*Northern Pacific Railroad v. Everett*, Statement of the Case," in Chandler et al., *United States Reports*, vol. 152, 111.

41. Henry Wood was the son of Albert and Lucy Ann Wood of Trenton. See *Seventh United States Census: 1850*, Household of Albert Wood, West Ward, City of Trenton, Mercer Co., N.J., July 20, 1850, line 90; and letter, Mary L. Wood, Carthage, N.C., to Winslow H. Randolph, Jr., Veterans Administration, Washington, D.C., [September] 1961, in Wood pension file. Wood's graduation from Lincoln University is noted in "Theological Department of Lincoln University, Annual Report of the Faculty," *GAMPCUSA*, 1878, 162. His residences prior to and after his graduation are documented in: Adjutant General, *Massachusetts Soldiers, Sailors, and Marines in the Civil War*, vol. 4, 700; "Roll of Members Since 1860" and "List of Officers from the Organization to Date, Ruling Elders," in Siloam Presbyterian Church, *Siloam Presbyterian Church*, 31, 36; and entry for Henry D. Wood in Newport city directory, 1879, 141. Wood's enlistment and service are documented in Adjutant General, *Massachusetts Soldiers, Sailors, and Marines in the Civil War*, vol. 4, 700. Upon coming south, Wood first lived in Cameron, North Carolina. He moved permanently to Carthage in late 1880. See "Freedmen, Committee on Freedmen," *PMR*, December 1880, 426. The location on his residence near Adam Tyson is documented in *Twelfth United States Census: 1900*, Household of Henry Wood, Carthage, Moore Co., N.C., ED 69, sheet 11.

42. McNeill's membership in the Klan is noted in Testimony of Daniel A. Graham, attachment, letter, John A. Barrett, Carthage, N.C., to Gov. William H. Holden, May 31, 1870, box G. P. 223, folder (Correspondence, May 17, 1870–May 31, 1870), Governor's Papers, NCSA. Wood's participation in the assault on Fort Wagner is documented in Affidavit, L. A. Finney, Special Examiner, November 4, 1911, Wood pension file. The sale of the land by McNeill to the church (for the nominal fee of $1) "for the purpose of building and erecting a Church" is documented in "Deed, A. H. McNeill and wife Margaret McNeill to Joseph Cad-

dell, Sam Currie, Kade Kelly, and Stephen Currie and their Successors as Trustees," originally recorded July 14, 1884 (Deed Book 54, 292), rerecorded September 24, 1891 (Deed Book 5, 200–201), Moore County, N.C., in *Record of Deeds, 1888–1961* (microfilm), NCSA. The role of First Presbyterian of Trenton in helping fund the church is discussed in Rev. John Hall's history of First Presbyterian. See Hall, *History of the Presbyterian Church in Trenton*, 268–69, 276. The Yadkin Presbytery at its 1884 annual meeting recommended $250 be granted Carthage Church by the Board of Church Erection. See "Twenty Third Annual Meeting [April 23–29, 1884]," MYP, 61–62. The actual amount loaned on July 1, 1884, was $300. See "Grant Mortgage, Yadkin Presbytery," in box 2, folder 8 (Yadkin Presbytery, Mortgage Loan Records–Date Unknown, Pamphlet–1928–1929), RG 395, African American Synods and Presbyteries Collection, PHS. Three-quarters of those in the Yadkin Presbytery were fellow Lincoln alumni. See *GAMPCUSA*, 1881, 576. Prior to winning over McNeill, Wood had proved an able mediator in 1882, when an "opposing and disturbing element" threatened Faith Chapel in Blue's Crossing. Wood met the challenge by preaching revivals to blacks and whites, quelling the opposition. The church opened later that year unmolested. See "Freedmen," *PMR*, November 1882, 398–99; "Freedmen, From the Field," *PMR*, November 1883, 403; and "Freedmen, From the Field," *PMR*, March 1884, 112–13. The attendance of local white leaders at the church's dedication is discussed in "Freedmen," *PMR*, October 1885, 401.

43. "Christian life" story from "Church Dedicated," in "Freedmen, Board of Missions for Freedmen," *PMR*, June 1885, 245–46. A joint program between John Hall and St. Augustine in 1893 illustrates Wood's emphasis on shared values of family, education, and community. At the service, St. Augustine's Rev. George H. Miles said the opening prayer. The combined congregations then listened to Guy Tyson expound on "The Significance of Home," Duncan McRae speak on "The Duty of Parents," Sherman Henry Kidd (superintendent of John Hall's Sunday school) lecture on "The Duty of the Teachers," and visiting AMEZ minister Rev. C. W. Simmons address "What We Need." See "Union Pic-Nic," *CB*, May 23, 1893, 3. See also "Freedmen, From the Field," *PMR*, November 1893, 403; and D. J. McRae, "Grand Rallying Day at John Hall Chapel," *CB*, October 17, 1893, 3. Rev. Wood was so successful at bringing Methodists and Presbyterians together that some families began attending the two churches on alternate Sundays when Wood was across town preaching to the splinter congregation at Sassafras Springs. Hattie Hayes Warrington recalls that her grandparents, James A. and Harriet "Hattie" Worthy Tyson, and her own parents, George and Mary Elizabeth "Betsy" Tyson Hayes, attended both John Hall and St. Augustine. She also notes that many families did the same. Warrington, conversation with the author, November 24, 2014, Carthage, N.C.

44. The role of Margaret (Mrs. William L.) Dayton in raising money for the Woods' school, and the naming of the school for her, is noted in Hall, *History of the Presbyterian Church in Trenton*, 276. McNeill sold the Board of Missions for Freedmen an almost two-acre tract adjacent to John Hall Chapel for the low price of $75, equal today to about $1,800. See "Deed, Alexander H. McNeill to Board of Missions for Freedmen, Presbyterian Church in the United States of America," originally recorded September 10, 1888 (Deed Book 68, 207–8), rerecorded September 22, 1891 (Deed Book 5, 198–99), Moore Co., N.C., in *Record of Deeds, 1888–1961*, NCSA. Meade Seawell notes that McNeill (her grandfather) gave the timber for the building. See Seawell, *Edgehill Entry*, 276.

45. Opportunity quote from Henry D. Wood, letter to the editor, *Carthage Vindicator*, reprinted as "Conditions of the Negro Race," *CB*, June 16, 1896, 4. Wood's tone in relation to

Northern supporters can be seen, for example, in his comments in "Freedmen, From the Field," *PMR*, November 1883, 403–4; and in H. D. Wood, letter, January 3, 1884, "Freedmen, From the Field," *PMR*, March 1884, 113–14. "I am not a politician," Wood told the *Vindicator*, "for I am not one of those who believe our salvation in this life or the world to come, is a question of politics." Henry D. Wood, quoted from the *Carthage Vindicator* in "Conditions of the Negro Race," *CB*, June 16, 1896, 4. (The *Vindicator*, a short-lived paper edited by Edwin Long, ceased publication in September 1896. See "Local News Items," *CB*, September 8, 1896, 3.)

46. Wood served as stated clerk of Yadkin Presbytery from 1886 to 1892 and again from 1899 to 1906. For documentation of the protests by the committees he led, see "Twenty-Fifth Annual Meeting [April 28–May 3, 1886]," 140; "31st Annual Meeting, 1891," [April 15–18, 1891], 237; and "Annual Meeting of Yadkin Presbytery," [April 18–21, 1894], 288–89, MYP. For incorporation of the *Africo-American Presbyterian*, see North Carolina General Assembly, "An Act to Incorporate the Africo-American Presbyterian Publishing Company," 936–37.

47. For Guy Tyson's political activities in 1894, see "Republican Convention," *CB*, August 14, 1894, 3; and "Local Paragraphs," *CB*, September 18, 1894, 3. Tyson served as secretary of the Moore County Republican Convention in 1896. See "A Skeleton Ticket Nominated," *CB*, September 1, 1896, 3. In July 1897, he was appointed a poll holder for the election in West Carthage to select school committeemen. See "Poll Holders for School Election," *CB*, July 13, 1897, 3. In 1896, Charles Foushee was nominated, though not chosen, as the candidate for register of deeds at the Moore County Republican Convention. See "Glendon Notes," *CB*, September 1, 1896, 3. Among Tyson, Duncan McRae, and Charles Foushee's chief white allies were *Southern Protectionist* editor Alfred V. Dockery (son of former U.S. Congressman Oliver Dockery), Republican firebrand John Andrew Barrett, who farmed near Adam Tyson, Thomas W. Ritter, who later served as register of deeds, G. Henry Makepeace of Sanford, and Jonesboro banker Sion H. Buchanan. (The *Carthage Blade* noted the release of the first issue of the *Protectionist* in "Local Briefs," *CB*, February 8, 1888, 4.) Key black activists with whom they worked included Noah Jackson, a blacksmith at Tyson & Jones, Sandy and N. A. McLeod, both carpenters from Aberdeen, and D. C. Evans and John Evans (a skilled cooper) of Manly Station. For a negatively biased description of their political activities, see "'The Great Harrison-Weaver Combination Circus and Animal Show,' A Mixed Crowd," *CB*, August 9, 1892, 1. For the 1896 election results in Moore County, see "Official Vote of Moore County, as Cast November 3rd, 1896," and "Official Vote of Moore County, 1896, County Offices, &c.," *CB*, November 10, 1896, 3. Fusionists also took an open spot on the board of county commissioners that year.

48. U.S. Post Office Department, *Record of Appointment of Postmasters*, M841, Moore Co., N.C., roll #94, 403, NARA, Washington, D.C.

49. Henry's position on the faculty is noted in "Annual Report of the Superintendent of Public Instruction, Scholastic Years 1881–'82," in North Carolina Department of Public Instruction, *Biennial Report of the Superintendent of Public Instruction*, 1881–82, 99–100. His identification as Chesnutt's assistant appears in "State Colored Normal School," *MG*, June 16, 1881, 3; and "Report of Fayetteville Normal School, 1882," in North Carolina Department of Public Instruction, *Biennial Report of the Superintendent of Public Instruction*, 1881–82, 147. Charles Chesnutt married Susan Perry in June 1878, and Henry Tyson married Susan's sister Jane a year later. Both were the daughters of Edwin and Catherine Perry of Fayetteville. See

Chas. W. Chesnutt and Susan U. Perry, marriage certificate, June 6, 1878, Cumberland Co., N.C., and Henry C. Tyson and Jane B[eze] Perry, marriage record, July 2, 1879, Cumberland Co., N.C., Ancestry.com, *North Carolina, Marriage Records*. Henry's employment by the Treasury Department is noted in entry for Henry C. Tyson, "Office of Sixth Auditor, for Post-Office Department," in U.S. Civil Service Commission, *Official Register of the United States*, vol. 2, 1884, 15. "Tarheel bunch" and "Tar heel boys" were terms educator Roscoe Conklin Bruce (writing under the pseudonym "Sage of the Potomac") often applied in the *Washington Bee* to Henry Tyson, John Dancy, John Goins, Armond Scott, John Howe, Doc Norwood, Chord McCullen, and other prominent figures in Washington who hailed from North Carolina. See, for example, Sage of the Potomac [Roscoe Conklin Bruce], "Public Men and Things," *Washington Bee* (hereafter *WB*), August 12, 1911, [4]; September 21, 1912, [4]; October 28, 1911, [4]; June 8, 1912, [4]; and October 18, 1913, [4]. In 1975, the *Moore County News* reported that Joseph Tyson's razors were presented to three presidents by Henry Clay Tyson. However, the paper misidentified Henry as Joseph Tyson's (rather than Adam Tyson's) son. Joseph, like Adam, did have a son named Henry Clay Tyson, but his son Henry was not born until 1886. See "'Uncle Joe' Was Gifted Person," MCLHC.

50. Henry Tyson was identified as Cheatham's private secretary in Sage of the Potomac [Roscoe Conkling Bruce], "Public Men and Things," *WB*, October 18, 1913, [4]; and "Some Race Doings," *Cleveland Gazette*, August 22, 1891, 1. Henry's early visits to North Carolina are mentioned in "Local," *PA*, March 8, 1884, 3; "Local," *PA*, March 15, 1884, 3; "Personal," *CB*, July 19, 1888, 4; and "Town and County News," *CB*, April 4, 1893, 3. Although Henry was not a member of the original board of trustees for A&M (established in 1891), he served on the board from 1893 through at least 1906, and established the Tyson scholarship for the school in 1902. See "The General Assembly; Report of the Proceedings of the Fifty-First Day," *SC*, March 5, 1893, 4; "Trustees, A.&M. College at Greensboro for the Colored Race," in *News & Observer*, *The North Carolina Year Book*, 1906, 8; Gibbs, *History of the North Carolina Agricultural and Technical College*, 6; and "Medals and Scholarships," in Greensboro A&M College catalogue, 1903–4, 53, 63. In 1900 Henry made at least three trips to North Carolina, one to attend A&M's commencement, one specifically to visit family, and one (for a duration of three weeks) to campaign against the proposed amendment to the state's constitution to limit black suffrage. See "City Paragraphs," *Colored American* (hereafter *CA*), January 13, 1900, 6; "'The Bright Side,'" *CA*, June 2, 1900, [6]; and untitled item, *CA*, August 18, 1900, 2. Henry's extended time away from North Carolina even led the *Washington Bee* to complain that "Mr. Tyson's interest[s] are in North Carolina and not in the District of Columbia." See "Trustee Wright to Remain," *WB*, October 14, 1899, [3]. Cheatham's speech at the Moore County Courthouse in Carthage is described in "Congressman Cheatham," *CB*, January 5, 1892, 4.

51. H. C. Tyson, "North Carolina Industrial Fair," *MI*, November 27, 1879, 2. Quote from H. C. Tyson, "Education," in "J. E. O'Hara, Our Sole Representative: The North Carolinians in Washington Honor Him," *PA*, January 26, 1884, 1. Tyson was a voting member of the Bethel Society and served on the association's board of managers. See Cromwell, *History of the Bethel Literary and Historical Association*, 23; and Fouché, *Black Inventors in the Age of Segregation*, 146, 203 (34n). For documentation of Tyson's social relationship with black inventors in Washington, see "Colored Odd Fellows," *Evening Star*, February 19, 1896, 12; "Coming Elections," *CA*, May 5, 1900, [7]; "Arundel on the Bay—Notes," *CA*, July 27, 1901, 4; "Literary

194 Notes to Chapter Two

Society Elects Officers," *Evening Star*, May 20, 1902, 3; "Pen and Pencil Banquet," *CA*, February 21, 1903, 4–5; "Mrs. M. C. Terrell Honored," *CA*, August 20, 1904, 5; and "He Is Honored, Commissioner Scott Banqueted," *WB*, July 24, 1909, 1.

Chapter Two

1. The title of Lucean's essay is from "Decision of Judges, Awarding of Prizes," Albion Academy catalogue (1901–2), 21.

2. For a comprehensive discussion of events leading up to the riot, the riot's unfolding, and its aftermath, see Prather, *We Have Taken a City*; Wilmington Race Riot Commission, *1898 Wilmington Race Riot Report*; and Reaves, *Strength Through Struggle*, 244–71. Wilmington's population near the time of the riot was approximately 57 percent black, but in the riot's aftermath, the city's more than 8,000 black citizens lost any say in local governance. By 1900, whites outnumbered them, and a large proportion of successful black artisans and entrepreneurs had either lost their businesses or decided to leave Wilmington. For 1890 population figures, see "Table 34. North Carolina—Race and Hispanic Origin for Selected Large Cities and Other Places: Earliest Census to 1990," in Gibson and Jung, *Historical Census Statistics on Population Totals by Race, 1790 to 1990*, 85. For discussion of the damage done to black entrepreneurs, see Prather, *We Have Taken a City*, 148–49.

3. Quote from James Walker Hood, "Race Disturbance, Bad Leadership the Cause of It in North Carolina, Political Extract from Bishop J. W. Hood's Annual Address Delivered Before the Central North Carolina Conference in Carthage, N.C., Two Weeks Ago," *Star of Zion*, December 15, 1898, 4. Tyson and White's representation of their respective North Carolina presbyteries at the General Assembly appears in "Roll of the Assembly," *GAMPCUSA*, 1899, 4. Nannie's Wilmington classmates at Scotia included Tena Elizabeth Drye (whom Lucean later married), sisters Carrie K. and Addie B. Whiteman, Mary B. Womble, Lula A. Murray, Sarah C. Hill, Cammie E. Davis, Annie J. Austin, and Leonora Hargraves. See Scotia catalogues, 1894–95, 1895–96, and 1896–97.

4. North Carolina General Assembly, "An Act to Promote the Comfort of Travellers on Railroad Trains, and for Other Purposes," 539–40. For examples of Susie McRae's visits to see Tena Nichols and other family members in Raleigh, see "About People You Know," *The Gazette*, September 18, 1897, 2; and "After Many Years," *The Gazette*, October 9, 1897, 3.

5. Dr. Gilbert McLeod's remarks on Ritter are recorded in "A Murder Near Carthage, George Ritter, Colored, Shot to Death Then Swung to a Tree," *Sanford Express*, reprinted in *N&O*, March 24, 1900, 4. Ritter had married Sarah Jane Martin Clark only a year earlier and settled near his parents, Jerry and Bethany Ritter, in West Carthage. See George Ritter and Sarah Martin Clark, marriage certificate, March 2, 1899, Moore Co., N.C., Ancestry.com, *North Carolina, Marriage Records*; and *Twelfth United States Census: 1900*, Household of Sarah Ritter (widow), and Household of Jerry Ritter, West Carthage Precinct, Carthage, Moore Co., N.C., ED 69, sheet 14A. After their son's death, Jerry and Bethany moved to northern Moore County. See *Thirteenth United States Census: 1910*, Household of Jerry Ritter, Ritter's Township, Moore Co., N.C., ED 72, sheet 3A. Sarah remarried in December 1903 to John Walden in Pinehurst, and the couple moved to Cumberland County. See John Walden and Sarah Jane Ritter, marriage record, April 8, 1904, Moore Co., N.C., Ancestry.com, *North Carolina, Marriage Records*; and *Thirteenth United States Census: 1910*, Household of John

Walden, Pearces Mill Township, Cumberland Co., N.C., ED 7, sheet 18A. The farmer mentioned was Samuel McIntosh and the local merchant Charles J. Jones. Reports of barn burnings, including that of McIntosh's barn, appear in "Wanted Blood-Hounds to Chase Barn-Burners," *North Carolinian*, January 26, 1899, 8; and "Incendiary Fire, Wild Reports That Carthage Was Burning Up Unfounded," *Times-Visitor*, January 23, 1899, 1. Key reports of Jones and McIntosh's indictment and trial appear in "Sensation in Moore County," *Progressive Farmer*, August 20, 1901, 3; "Habeas Corpus in North Carolina, Bail Granted to Two Men Charged with Murder," *The Times*, August 21, 1901, 6; "Charged with Murder, C. J. Jones and Samuel M'Intosh of Pee Dee Village, True Bill Found Against Them in Moore County—Released on Habeas Corpus Proceedings—They Are Men of Good Character and Claim the Prosecution Is Entirely Malicious," *The Anglo-Saxon*, August 22, 1901, 2; "Unusual Charge," *Charlotte News*, April 26, 1902, 1; and "State News," *Washington Progress*, May 8, 1902, 2.

6. Spruill, a Franklin County lawyer, was a prominent Democratic organizer and joined Aycock's campaign in mid-1900. See "Frank Shepherd Spruill," in Hamilton, Boyd, and Connor, *History of North Carolina*, vol. 5, 217–18. Description of the procession is from "Aycock and Spruill," *N&O*, July 18, 1900, 4. Background on the Red Shirts is from Prather, "The Red Shirt Movement in North Carolina," 181.

7. Adam Tyson's voter registration is documented in "List of Carthage West Precinct, Cold. Voters," October 18, 1878, folder (Political—Miscellaneous 1878); and "Col'd. [Voters]," folder (Political—Elections [polls]), box PC1761.16, AHMcNP, NCSA. The literacy requirement and its associated "grandfather clause" became part of the North Carolina constitution in 1900. See North Carolina General Assembly, "Suffrage and Eligibility to Office," 55. Passed by popular vote on August 2, 1900, it went into effect on July 1, 1902. It left implementation of the law to the state legislature. See Mordecai, *Law Lectures*, 40.

8. Notices of the mill's burning appeared in "Saw and Shingle Mills of Headen & Tyson Burned Near Carthage," *Charlotte Daily Observer*, December 14, 1900, 2; "State News," *N&O*, December 15, 1900, 3; "North Carolina," *Wilmington Messenger* (hereafter *WM*), December 19, 1900, 2; "Burned," *The Wood-Worker*, January 1901, 43. In November 1901, state officials convinced the U.S. Postal Service to discontinue the Flynn post office, effectively eliminating Tyson's position. See Koster, *The Post Offices of Moore County*, 31. The last of the black postmasters was Samuel H. Vick of Wilson. Theodore Roosevelt, under pressure from southern Democrats, replaced Vick in 1903 with a white bartender. See "Vick Loses His Job," *CB*, April 2, 1903, 1.

9. The mill's value is from "Saw and Shingle Mills of Headen & Tyson Burned Near Carthage," *Charlotte Daily Observer*, December 14, 1900, 2. The fire created hardship for Jerry Headen. Soon after, a lot he still owned in Jonesboro was sold at a sheriff's sale to pay his taxes. See "Notice, to Jerry Headen," *CB*, January 8, 1903, 2. In October 1901, Jerry Headen married Rockingham schoolteacher Nettie Jackson. See Jerry Headen and Nettie B. Jackson, marriage record, October 6, 1901, Moore Co., N.C., Ancestry.com, *North Carolina, Marriage Records*. Nettie was born in Rockingham, North Carolina, and prior to coming to Carthage taught in that city's Hookerton School, operated by the Presbyterian Church North. See Records of the Presbyterian Committee for Freedmen, vol. 4, July 25, 1892, 144, box 3, folder 2 (Minute Book, April 1891–May 1893), RG 376, Board of Missions for Freedmen Records, PHS. See also "Funeral Rites Held for Mrs. Nettie Headen," *PC*, September 19, 1959, 32. By 1910, Headen was again listed in the census as a lumberman. See *Thirteenth United*

States Census: 1910, Household of Jerry Headen, Sand Hill Township, Moore Co., N.C., ED 73, sheet 18A. Jerry Headen's farming activities in Aberdeen are described in H. A. Wiseman, "News of Colored People in the City and County, Mrs. W. A. Jones Returns to City," *Winston-Salem Journal*, July 2, 1925, 11. Wiseman described Jerry as "one of the wealthiest farmers in that section" (i.e., southern Moore County). In 1902 Guy Tyson was a sales representative for the Ashley & Bailey Co. silk mill in Fayetteville. That year, he made a sales trip to Washington, D.C., for the firm, staying with his older brother Henry while in the city. See "City Paragraphs," *CA*, June 14, 1902, 16. For more information on the Ashley & Bailey Co. (white owned but managed and operated by black labor) and ties it forged with the Fayetteville State Normal School, see "Manned and Managed by Negroes," *Roanoke Beacon*, April 5, 1901, 1; and "From the Ranks to Captain, Dwight" and "Special Meeting of Board of Aldermen," *Fayetteville Weekly Observer*, June 4, 1903, 3. Documentation of Guy's children in 1900 is from *Twelfth United States Census: 1900*, Household of Adam Tyson, Carthage, Moore Co., N.C., ED 69, sheet 11.

10. For a discussion of the relationship between slaveholders and slave artisans in the antebellum period, their relationship after the war, and the political actions taken by white artisans in response, see "The Negro Skilled Worker, an Inquiry Conducted by THE TRADESMAN (Chattanooga, Tenn.) in Conjunction with the Sociological Department of Atlanta University," in Du Bois, *The Negro Artisan*, 12–23. See also Takaki, *A Pro-Slavery Crusade*, 44–50. The role of white artisans' anger in the Wilmington Riot of 1898 is discussed in Suggs, "Romanticism, Labor, and the Suppression of African-American Citizenship," 71–72. For the seeking of a white monopoly, see, for example, letter, S. S. Toler, Tarboro, N.C., to B. R. Lacy, Labor Commissioner, Raleigh, N.C. [1899], reprinted in "Condition of the Trades," in North Carolina Department of Labor and Printing, *Annual Report of the Bureau of Labor Statistics* (1899), 147. For the claim that "negro mechanics" suppressed white wages, see "Greatest Hindrance to Better Wages," column in "Table 2, Financial, Social and Moral Condition of the Trades," chap. 2, "Trades," in Department of Labor and Printing, *Annual Report of the Bureau of Labor Statistics* (1899), 84.

11. Edinboro Kelly, along with Adam Tyson, had been one of the firm's original employees, and Calvin Peace was already at Tyson & Jones by at least 1900. See *Twelfth United States Census: 1900*, Household of Calvin Peace, East Carthage Precinct, Moore Co., N.C., ED 68, sheet B9. Jackson at his death in 1926 was noted as having worked for Tyson & Jones for thirty-two years, having thus joined Tyson & Jones in 1894. See Koster, *The Story of the Tyson & Jones Buggy Company*, 49; and Sandy Jackson, death certificate, September 13, 1926, Moore Co., N.C., Ancestry.com, *North Carolina, Death Certificates*. Buckner was described as a forty-year employee in his 1922 obituary, meaning he began work at the firm in 1882. See "Well-Known Colored Man Passes Away," *Moore County News*, July 6, 1922, 8.

12. Lucean's employment as a porter is documented in *Twelfth United States Census: 1900*, Household of Adam Tyson, Carthage, Moore Co., N.C., ED 69, sheet 11. The track of the Carthage Railroad between Carthage and Curriesville was torn up in 1898. See Coleman, *Railroads of North Carolina*, 36; and Brown, *Railroad Map of North Carolina, 1900*, Map Collection, Wilson Library, UNCCH. An 1899–1900 schedule shows that one engine traveled from Cameron to Hallison in the morning and returned to Cameron in the evening, and that another ran from Cameron to Carthage each morning and returned to Cameron each evening. See "Carthage Railroad Time Table, in Effect October 1, 1899," *Pinehurst Outlook*,

April 20, 1900, 7. The expansion of the SAL and its acquisition of the Raleigh & Augusta Air Line is described in Carriker, *Railroading in the Carolina Sandhills*, 64, 151–65; and Johnson, *Through the Heart of the South*, 21.

13. The railroad porter's job is described in Thorne, *Recollections of a Sleeping Car Porter*, 12. A sketch of Douglass appears in Richardson, *The National Cyclopedia of the Colored Race*, vol. 1, 118–19 (quote on 119). By 1919, Douglass owned the Douglass Theatre and the Colonial House Hotel and had extensive real estate holdings in Macon. For an excellent map of the SAL main lines and connecting railroads in 1896, see "Map of the Seaboard Airline Railroad and Its Principal Connections, North, South, East, and West, 1896," *S.A.L.magundi*, February 1897, 3.

14. Tye, *Rising from the Rails*, 94–95.

15. Lucean's firing is noted in entry for Arthur Headden [*sic*], Discharge Register, *Vol. 1, Jan. 1, 1900—Dec. 31, 1906*, Alphabetical Sect. H, 1, 06/02/06, Employee and Labor Relations, Personnel Administration Department, Discharge and Release Records, 1880–1957, Porter Discharge Registers, Pullman Company Records, NL. Thomas Tyson's death is noted in "Thomas B. Tyson, Sr.," obituary, *CB*, April 4, 1893, 2. Susie McRae being his daughter is noted in Martha J. Henderson, "Tyson Descendants to Visit Carthage, Attend 25th Annual Buggy Festival," *The Pilot*, May 5, 2013, http://www.thepilot.com/news/tyson-descendents-to-visit-carthage-attend-th-annual-buggy-festival/article_83cacf0f-7c10-54a2-815a-2ba0db852130.html. McNeill's death on November 6, 1906, is noted by his granddaughter Meade Seawell in *Edgehill Entry*, 118.

16. Lucien P. Tyson, although he never sought office, was a Democratic leader in Carthage, helping found the Carthage Cleveland-Carr Club (or the "4 Cs"), which grew out of a statewide movement to curb Republican and Populist gains. George W. McNeill, a lawyer, took an early interest in politics and had by 1910 risen to be chairman of the Democratic Executive Committee of Moore County. He, like his father, also served as clerk of the Moore County Superior Court. See "'4 C's'—Carthage Cleveland-Carr Club," *CB*, July 12, 1892, 4; "Death of Mr. L. P. Tyson," *CB*, October 10, 1907, 5; and George Stevenson, untitled biographical sketch of George W. McNeill, in "Inventory of George W. McNeill Papers, 1931–1946," http://digital.lib.ecu.edu/special/ead/findingaids/0492/. Alexander McNeill had his corn ground at Tyson's mill until his death in 1906. See "Memorandum Book [1906–1907]," 2, box PC 1761.16, folder (Memorandum Books, 1884–1906), AHMcNP, NCSA. The suit threatened by George McNeill is documented in George W. McNeill to Adam Tyson, letter, July 18, 1904, box 12, folder (zze), GWMcNP, Joyner Library, ECU.

17. Nannie's training and early teaching career are documented in Scotia Seminary catalogue, 1896–97, 9; "Moore County, Teachers," in *Branson's Moore County Business Directory*, 1898, 29; "Negro Must Face the Inevitable, Movement in the South for Disfranchisement, Meserve's Sage Advice, Let Politics Alone and Foster Your Schools, Make Friends with the White People, Commencement Exercises at Shaw University, Seventeen Graduates, Annual Address by Mr. Brown, Speech by Gov. Jarvis," *N&O*, May 11, 1900, 3.

18. For information on Albion's history, see Parker, "Albion Academy, Franklinton," data file, n.d., PHS. Albion's name was changed to the Franklin Colored Normal School in 1881 when it became part of the state's educational system. Despite the school's affiliation with the state, however, the Presbyterian Church North continued to provide the salaries of some faculty, and in 1905 Albion reverted back to the church. Wood served as vice president of

Albion Academy's board of trustees during the 1884–85 school year. See Albion Academy catalogue, 1884–85, 1. Catalogues are not extant for the period 1885–91, so it is unclear how long he remained on the board. He is not listed on the board in the 1892 catalogue. For Savage's overlapping at Lincoln University with Wood, see "Rev. John A. Savage, D.D.," in Richings, *An Album of Negro Educators*, 32.

19. Charles E. Tucker earned undergraduate (1892) and doctoral (1895) degrees from Lincoln University. See entry for Charles E. Tucker, D. D., in "Class of 1892," and "Alphabetical List of Alumni," in *The Alumni Directory of Lincoln University*, 1954, 6, 150. Louis Napoleon Neal was an 1894 graduate of Shaw University. See sketch of Neal in Caldwell, *History of the American Negro*, vol. 4, 553–54. Benjamin Franklin Person, after attending St. Augustine's College, graduated from Shaw University in 1884. Besides his teaching duties, he was active in the State Teachers Association and the Franklin County School Board. He also founded the Colored Musical Association. Franklinton's Benjamin F. Person High School was named for him. See sketch of Person in Caldwell, *History of the American Negro*, vol. 4, 28–29. See also, "A Comparison," *Franklin Times* (hereafter *FT*), October 10, 1902, 2; and "Locals," *FT*, August 13, 1909, 2. Rounding out the faculty were Joel S. Fuller, an 1891 Lincoln University graduate, and Mary L. Wilson. Fuller's graduation from Lincoln is noted in "Visit to Greensboro, N.C.," *Lincoln University Herald*, December 1912, 3. Albion's catalogue notes that Wilson held a college degree but does not specify her alma mater. The catalogue also documents the subjects Lucean studied and his selection to participate in the spring debating contest in 1902 based on his class ranking. See "Faculty of Instruction and Government," 4; "Course of Study," 13; and "Decision of Judges, Awarding of Prizes," 21 in Albion Academy catalogue, 1901–2.

20. Essay topics are listed in "Honors for the Year 1902," Albion Academy catalogue 1901–2, 21–22. Henry Fuller was already established as a carpenter in 1870 and likely learned his trade as a slave. See *Ninth United States Census: 1870*, Household of Henry W. Fuller, Louisburg, Franklin Co., N.C., 3. "Three students in one bed" quote from John A. Savage, "Albion Academy, Franklinton, N.C.," in "Two North Carolina Schools," *HMM*, April 1901, 135. For building of the barracks, see John A. Savage, "Franklinton Normal School" (Report to the Superintendent of Public Instruction dated July 9, 1902), in North Carolina Department of Public Instruction, *Biennial Report of the Superintendent of Public Instruction*, 1900–1901 and 1901–2, 351.

21. Hawkins, "A Brief History of Albion Academy." Although Hawkins remembered the ram system as being installed sometime prior to 1900, none of the yearly reports the school submitted to the superintendent of public instruction mention it, although they consistently describe other improvement projects. The school, however, reported to the state treasurer that it had in October 1902 expended $10.65 for "54 joints of pipe." This amount of piping is consistent with a ram project. No other year's report to the treasurer mentions the purchase of pipe. See "Franklinton Colored Normal School, in Account with B. W. Ballard, Treasurer," North Carolina Department of Public Instruction, *Biennial Report and Recommendations of the Superintendent of Public Instruction*, 1904, 558. The continued use of the ram pump is noted in "The Lay of the Pump," *HMM*, April 1916, 140.

22. The press and blacksmith shop are noted in "Third Year Normal," Albion Academy catalogue, 1901–2, 7.

23. Perman, *Struggle for Mastery*, 167–68. For the text of the new law (emphasis in quote is mine), see North Carolina General Assembly, "An Act to Provide for the Holding of Elections in North Carolina," 246. The new law became effective in the state election of 1902.

24. "New Registration," *FT*, October 10, 1902, 2.

25. "Local Board of Managers" and "Advisory Board," Albion Academy catalogue, 1901–2, 2–3. Thomas had earlier served as president of Albion's board of directors. See "Tar Drops," *FT*, August 4, 1893, 3. Savage's leadership in the Republican Party and his walkout from the 1900 state convention are noted in "The Republican Convention," *FT*, July 22, 1898, 3; "The Pow-Wow, Long and Savage Take Charge and Run the Whole Machine," *FT*, September 16, 1898, 3; "The Negroes Won't Be Downed, Resent Attempts of White Republicans to Hold Them Back, Bolted Convention," *Morning Post*, May 2, 1900, 2; and "Republican Row," *FT*, May 4, 1900, 2.

26. The superintendent of public instruction for North Carolina reported the date of Franklinton Colored Normal School's abolishment as June 1905. See North Carolina Department of Public Instruction, *Biennial Report of the Superintendent of Public Instruction of North Carolina*, 1904–6, 40. Examples of Mary Dover Savage's fundraising efforts are described in "Mrs. Savage Speaks for Freedmen Work," *HMM*, July 1916, 213; and "Educational Work Among Negroes," speech of Mary Savage, reprinted in *HMM*, July 1920, 209.

27. Entry for [Tena] Elizabeth Drye in "Grammar School Course, Second Year," Scotia Seminary catalogue, 1896–97, 9. Tena is listed as a teacher at Albion Academy for the first time in "Missions and Missionaries for the Year Ending March 31, 1903, Cape Fear Presbytery, Schools," in Board of Missions for Freedmen, *Thirty-Eighth Annual Report*, 30. Luther A. Hayden [Lucean A. Headen] and T. Elizabeth Drye, marriage record, September 8, 1903, New Hanover Co., N.C., Ancestry.com, *North Carolina, Marriage Records*. Note: Although Luther A. Hayden appears on the actual marriage certificate, a printed copy of the full record, supplied by the Register of Deeds of New Hanover County, shows that the certificate's outer cover spells Headen's name correctly, as Lucean A. Headen.

28. Tena's birth date has not survived in the records. However, she was age one in the 1880 Census. See *Tenth United States Census: 1880*, Household of James D. Dry[e], Wilmington, New Hanover Co., N.C., ED 144, 14. For a biographical sketch of Tena's father and discussion of his business, social, and religious activities, see Reaves, *Strength through Struggle*, 295, 386–87. Drye, who started his tailoring concern in 1880, helped found the Business League and the United Charities Association in Wilmington, and served as president of the social Carolina Club. He was also an officer of the Giblem Lodge of Free Masons and the Republican Party. See "The 'Independent Republicans,'" *WMS*, August 21, 1888, 1; "Giblem Lodge, F. and A. M.," *WMS*, July 4, 1886, 1 (F. and A. M. is Free and Associated Masons); and untitled clipping, *Wilmington Dispatch*, May 15, 1903, Series II, Family Files, folder (Dry[e] Family), Reaves Collection, New Hanover Public Library, Wilmington, N.C., Mention of Drye's activities can also be found in "Local Dots," *Wilmington Star*, November 14, 1880, 1; untitled item, *WM*, September 24, 1889, 5; "Business League," *WM*, September 2, 1894, 8; "More Essential Than Politics, Business," *WMS*, September 2, 1894, 1; and "United Charities, A Benevolent Association of Colored People to Aid the Suffering Poor of Their Race," *WMS*, January 6, 1895, 1. Drye's representation of his presbytery in Los Angeles is noted in "Roll of the Assembly, IV. Synod of Catawba, Cape Fear Presbytery," *GAMPCUSA*, 1903, 4.

29. James Drye's mother, Sarah Drye Bryant, died in April 1887. See "Died: Bryant," *WMS*, April 17, 1887, 1. The date of Amelia Hill Drye's death is unknown, but it occurred sometime between June 1880, when she appeared in the 1880 census, and December 1889, when James Drye remarried to Jennie Scull. See *Tenth United States Census: 1880*, Household of James D.

Dry[e], Wilmington, New Hanover Co., N.C., ED 144, 14; and Jas. D. Dry[e] and M. J. Scull, marriage certificate, December 31, 1889, New Hanover Co., N.C., Ancestry.com, *North Carolina, Marriage Records*. Jenny Drye worked as a seamstress in Drye's tailoring business. For an account of William Drye's death, see "Colored Man Instantly Killed by Falling from a Train on the W., N. B., & N. Railroad," *Weekly Star*, October 27, 1893, 1. The W., N. B., & N. was the Wilmington, New Bern, & Norfolk Railroad.

30. For example, in 1897 Tena attended a dance in New Bern where she hobnobbed with Congressman George H. White and a host of doctors, judges, professors, and journalists. See "Social Event at the New Berne Fair—A Brilliant Affair at Lawthrop Hall Thursday Evening," *The Gazette*, September 4, 1897, 3. A reporter in 1917 called Headen "a man of very few words." See "Chicagoan Invents Submarine Device, Undersea Craft Made Invisible, L. A. Headen, Local Inventor, Will Startle World with New Invention," *Chicago Defender* (Big Weekend ed.), May 12, 1917, 1, 7; entries for Elizabeth E. [Tena Elizabeth] Drye and Connie [Constance] Catus in "Grammar School Course, Fourth Year, A," Scotia Seminary catalogue, 1898–99, 6; "City Paragraphs," *WB*, September 16, 1899, 8.

31. Tena's work with United Charities is noted in "Directors' Meeting Tomorrow," *WM*, April 8, 1900, 8; "The United Charities Association," *WM*, January 2, 1901, 4; "The United Charities Fair," *WM*, January 27, 1901, 4; and untitled item, *WM*, March 31, 1901, 5.

32. Although some businesses on James Drye's block were burned during the riot, his tailor shop was spared, perhaps because, unlike his son George, he posed no direct threat to white power. Although energetic in civic affairs he, like Henry Wood, expressed less interest in politics. For background on George Drye's activities, see "Republican Primaries, Meetings Held in the Various Wards to Nominate Candidates for Aldermen," *WMS*, March 17, 1897, 1; "Republican Primaries, Four Wards Out of Five Nominate Colored Aldermen, Satton Endorsed for Mayor by All the Meetings, He Is Confident of His Election," *WM*, March 17, 1897, 4; "County Commissioners, Registrars," *WMS*, July 7, 1897, 1; and "Regular Meeting of the Board of Aldermen," *WM*, April 6, 1897, 4.

33. Both Will and Nannie graduated in 1900. Will, a former graduate of Hampton Institute, completed his doctorate in pharmacy at Shaw, while Nannie completed a Normal degree. See "Negro Must Face the Inevitable, Movement in the South for Disfranchisement, Meserve's Sage Advice, Let Politics Alone and Foster Your Schools, Make Friends with the White People, Commencement Exercises at Shaw University, Seventeen Graduates, Annual Address by Mr. Brown, Speech by Gov. Jarvis," *N&O*, May 11, 1900, 3; and "Shaw University Graduates," *Virginian-Pilot*, March 17, 1900, 7. After graduating from Shaw, Nannie taught at Dayton from 1900 to 1904. See "Missions and Missionaries for the Year Ending March 31, 1903, Yadkin Presbytery, Schools," in Board of Missions for Freedmen, *Thirty-Eighth Annual Report*, 33; "Affiliated Schools of Biddle University, Dayton Academy, Faculty 1903–1904," in Biddle University catalogue, 1903–4, 60. Nannie married Will Jones on October 25, 1904. See "Wedding," *CB*, October 27, 1904, 3; "Fashionable Colored Wedding," *Western Sentinel*, October 27, 1904, 2; W. A. Jones and Nannie K. Headen, marriage certificate, October 25, 1904, Moore Co., N.C., Ancestry.com, *North Carolina, Marriage Records*. Jones opened his drug store in Winston in May 1903 and operated it until his death in 1927.

34. White's decision to leave North Carolina and his advice to others are noted in Mabry, "'White Supremacy,'" 7; and Justesen, "Black Tip, White Iceberg," 214. The *Carthage Blade* noted Guy's position at Wanamaker's in "Many Comers and Goers," *CB*, September 27, 1905,

3. See also entry for Guy Tyson in Philadelphia city directory, 1905, 2549; and *Thirteenth United States Census: 1910*, Household of Adam G. Tyson, Philadelphia (part of 13th district), Philadelphia Co., Pa., ED 830, sheet 8B. For Annie Wood's death, see "Mrs. Annie M. Wood Dies in the South, She Was Wife of Rev. Dr. Henry D. Wood—Other Deaths," *Trenton Evening Times*, August 4, 1904, 7. Marie Tyson was still teaching in Carthage during the 1905–6 school year. See "Closing Exercises," *CB*, May 24, 1905, 3; Seawell, *Edgehill Entry*, 118–19. Guy and Edith Tyson's membership at First African is documented in "Register of Members, Baptisms, and Deaths, VI. Alphabetical Index to Roll of Communicants, 1904," n.p. [line no. 105 on the roll], box 3, folder 2, RG 314, First African Presbyterian Church (Philadelphia, Pa.) Records, PHS. First African Presbyterian Church, founded in 1807, was the first black Presbyterian congregation in the country. When the Tysons joined, the prestigious church was located at 17th and Fitzwater Streets. Marie Tyson would also take an active part in Lombard Central Presbyterian Church, especially after it moved across the street from her home on Powelton Avenue in 1940. See "Rev. Imes Addresses Favorite Church Club," *Philadelphia Tribune* (hereafter *PT*) June 2, 1932, 1; and "Tea Climaxes Dedication at New Central Church," *PT*, May 16, 1940, 9. Guy Tyson's position at the post office is noted in [Adam] Guy Tyson, Registration Card, September 12, 1918, in Ancestry.com, *U.S. World War I Draft Registration Cards, 1917–1918*.

35. After working at the Hotel Walton for eleven years, George started (with partner George E. Johnson) the Philadelphia Tailoring and Wardrobe Company on Locust Street. See "To Take Proper Care of Clothing," *PT*, December 13, 1913, 5. By 1917, he and his wife had relocated to New York. See "Flashes & Sparks, Social and Otherwise During the Week," *PT*, January 27, 1917, 5. Samuel Stanley's employment by the Pullman Company is documented in entry for Sam J. Stanley, *Vol. E, Index, 1901–1903*, P.P.C. Co., 417, in 06/02/06, Employee and Labor Relations, Personnel Administration Department, Discharge and Release Records, 1880–1957, All Jobs Release Registers, in Pullman Company Records, NL. James's death is noted in James Festus Drye, death record, October 22, 1916, Ancestry.com, *North Carolina Deaths*.

Chapter Three

1. For discussion of early aviation activities on Long Island, see Robie, *For the Greatest Achievement*; and Dade and Strnad, *Picture History of Aviation on Long Island*. For a detailed description of the Aero Club of New York's facilities on Nassau Boulevard, see "The Life Worth Living at Garden City Estates, Nassau Boulevard Station," *Country Life in America: The Vacation Guide*, June 1, 1911, 3. Confusion has surrounded the name of the Aeronautical Society. The society was first established in 1908 as the Aeronautic Society of New York, but when it reincorporated in April 1910, it had to choose a different name, so it simply extended Aeronautic to Aeronautical. See "Club News, The Aeronautical Society," *Aeronautics*, May 1910, 180.

2. "Moisant Wins Statue Race, American Beats Grahame-White for the $10,000 Flight in Fast Time," *NYT*, October 31, 1910, 1; "Atwood Tours to New York," *Aero*, July 8, 1911, 306.

3. Electrician Joseph Crabb was hired by the Erie Railroad in 1899. See "Crabb, Edward Joseph," in Mather, *Who's Who of the Colored Race*, 79. In 1916, the Erie promoted Crabb to the position of foreman of electricians in its Jersey City shops. See "Appointments," *Erie*

Railroad Employes' Magazine (hereafter *EREM*), January 1916, 669. Crabb retired from the Erie after almost thirty-eight years of service in 1937. See "Erie Employes Retired," *EREM*, June 1937, 13. For examples of the *Age*'s coverage of black inventors, see "The Afro-American Inventor, in Face of Handicaps, His Achievements Show Creative Talent," *NYA*, August 17, 1905, 7; and "Inventors Not a Rarity, Negroes Have Secured Over 1,000 Patents Since Civil War," *NYA*, September 10, 1908, 1.

4. Muirheid, *Jersey City of To-day*, 6; Member of No. 502, "The Brotherhood," letter to the editor, *Railroad Trainman*, September 1909, 793. "Table VIII. Total Males and Females 10 Years of Age and Over Engaged in Selected Occupations, By Age Periods and Color or Race, Nativity, and Parentage for Cities of 100,000 Inhabitants or More–1910," in U.S. Bureau of the Census, *Thirteenth Census of the United States Taken in the Year 1910, Volume IV, Population, Occupation Statistics*, 558–59.

5. Headen's work for Pullman while in Jersey City is documented in *Vol. F, 1904–1906, Releases, The Pullman Co.*, 202, 06/02/06, Employee and Labor Relations, Personnel Administration Department, Discharge and Release Records, 1880–1957, All Jobs Release Registers; and personnel card, L. A. Headen, in *Pre-1917 Personnel Cards, Porters & Maids, Bannister through McCowen, M.* (microfilm), reel #1433, n.p. (alphabetical), Pullman Company Records, NL. Although Headen initially worked for Pullman's New England Division in its New York department, he and Tena lived in Jersey City. Headen appears in the 1905 city directory (compiled in 1904), residing on Whiton Avenue. The Headens are noted as residents of a boarding house at 88 Tuers Avenue in the New Jersey State Census of 1905, taken in June. See entry for Arthur Headen, Jersey City city directory, 1906–7, 267; and *1905 State Census of New Jersey* (microfilm) reel #23, Household of John L. [sic] and Tena Headen, Hudson Co., Jersey City, N.J., 9th Ward, 4th Dist., sheet 18B. Note: The census taker mistakenly listed Headen as John L. Headen. In the entry itself, however, all of Lucean and Tena's personal information, including birth dates and ages, places of birth, places of parents' birth, and occupations match. The last person enumerated before Headen was named John, and the enumerator seems to have repeated the name in error. Samuel Stanley's work for Pullman is documented in personnel card, Samuel J. Stanley, in *Pre-1917 Personnel Cards, Porters and Maids, McCowan, N.–Zink, H. C.* (microfilm), reel #1434, n.p. (alphabetical), Pullman Company Records, NL. His employment on the Erie is noted in "Dining Car Department," *EREM*, May 1910, 172. In 1910, the Headens, Stanleys, and friend and fellow porter Andrew Davison all lived at 93A Kearney Avenue. See *Thirteenth United States Census: 1910*, Household of Lucean Headen, Jersey City, Hudson Co., N.J., ED 169, sheet 5A. Stanley was a native of Wilmington, where he was adopted by an aunt, Rebecca Stanley, a resident of Wrightsville Beach, just outside the city. Before moving to New Jersey, he worked as a butler in Wilmington. See *Twelfth United States Census: 1900*, Household of Rebecca Stanley, Harnett Township, New Hanover Co., N.C., ED 63, sheet 18; and entry for Rebecca Stanley, in Wilmington city directory, 1900, 191. Samuel would later become secretary to the chairman of the Jersey Central Porters' and Waiters' Beneficial Association. See "Jersey City Briefs," *CD* (Big Weekend ed.), May 31, 1919, 18. Sarah's nickname is taken from "Employer's Supplemental Report of Service and Compensation," March 3, 1947, in box 1 (Individual Pensioner Files), file no. 3284, Mrs. Sarah N. Stanley, 06/03/06, Employee and Labor Relations, Pensions and Group Insurance Department, Retired with Pension Files, 1916–80, Pullman Company Records, NL.

6. Lafayette applied for incorporation in 1898 and received its certificate in 1901. See "Lafayette Presbyterian Church of Jersey City, New Jersey," in New Jersey Secretary of State, *Corporations of New Jersey*, 133. For information on the original founders, see Dickerson, "George E. Cannon: Black Churchman," 411–32. Among early railroad men, besides Cannon, active in the founding of the church were John Royall and Forrest Hayes. See entry for John Mabery Royall, Mather, *Who's Who of the Colored Race*, 235. Lafayette, then located between Grand Street and Manning Avenue, often adapted its calendar to accommodate trainmen. See "Out of Town Correspondence, Jersey City, N.J.," *NYA*, March 6, 1913, 3. For Sarah's choir activities, see, for example, "Out of Town Correspondence, Jersey City, N.J.," *NYA*, December 11, 1913, 3; and "Out of Town Correspondence, Jersey City, N.J.," *NYA*, March 19, 1914, 3.

7. Headen's dining car abilities are noted in "Erie Waiter an Aviator," *EREM*, January 1912, 669. Robinson quote is from Cornelius H. Robinson, "Opportunity," *CD*, June 10, 1911, 4. His inventive genius and mark quotes are from "Dining Car Department," *EREM*, June 1910, 227.

8. For any employee they wished to discharge *permanently*, the Pullman Co. recorded "Not to be rehired" next to their names in discharge registers. The claim that Headen had invented the ash cart cover and that it was adopted by New York City appears in "Negro Automobile Company to Manufacture Fine Car," *Dallas Express*, October 14, 1922, 1. The *New York Age* noted in 1912 that the city was replacing its old ash arts with a new one featuring a canvas cover, although it did not mention the inventor. See "Snow Contract Rescinded, Result of Dispute Over Petitions, City to Get New Ash Carts," *NYA*, December 24, 1912, 12.

9. The bulletin was available to anyone who wrote to request a copy. See "Aeronautical Society Lectures Printed," *Aeronautics*, September 1910, 83. For samples of bulletin topics, see "Club News," *Aeronautics*, September 1910, 109; "Club News," *Aeronautics*, December 1910, 225; "Club News," *Aeronautics*, February 1911, 79; and "Aeronautic Society's Monument and Medal," *Aeronautics*, April 1911, 145.

10. For discussion of the quest for a better equalizer, see "Looking Forward," *Aero*, April 1, 1911, 250.

11. The pay for waiters is noted in I. A. Canning (Supt. of Dining Cars), "Some Erie Dining Car Facts," *EREM*, May 1916, 16. The cost of the Wright and Curtiss planes is noted in Henry Woodhouse, "American Amateur Aviators," *Pearson's Magazine*, February 1911, 204.

12. S. H. Gladden, quoted in J[ohn] R. Winston, "In the Rail-Road Center," *CD*, July 29, 1911, 2.

13. Adam Kelly, son of John B. Kelly, graduated from Bennett Seminary and Meharry Medical College before opening his office in Covington. He later helped found the Kentucky State Society of Colored Physicians, Surgeons, Dentists, and Pharmacists. See Harris, "Kelly, Adam David," 501. Charles Kelly earned degrees from Albion, Lincoln University, and Meharry Medical College before establishing his Clarkesville practice. See "Kelly, Charles A.," in Lincoln University biographical catalogue, 1918, 46–47. Nathaniel Jackson, son of Albert and Mary Jackson, after leaving Dayton Academy, earned degrees from Greensboro A&M College and Shaw University's Leonard Medical School. He practiced in Laurinburg for many years. See sketch of Jackson in Caldwell, *History of the American Negro*, vol. 4, 482–83. James Garland McRae graduated from Biddle University in 1910 and from Howard Medical School in 1915 before joining the medical staff of the Baltimore City Department of Health. See

"School of Arts and Sciences, Senior Class," in Biddle University catalogue, 1909–10, 26; Howard University catalogue, 1914–15, 244; "Howard's Honor Graduates Receive Their Degrees," *Oakland Sunshine*, August 7, 1915, 1; entry for Jay [James] G. McRae, physician in Baltimore city directory, 1923, 1204; and City of Baltimore, *One Hundred and Twenty-Fifth Annual Report of the Department of Health, 1939*, 6. Robert Taylor was principal of the Dickinson School from 1901 to 1904 and founded the Academy Heights School in the 1910s. Robert's second wife, Edna Covington Quick, taught at Academy Heights and later served for forty-two years as principal of the nearby Eastwood School. See "A Negro School," *Pinehurst Outlook*, December 13, 1901, 1; "Eastwood's Little Colored School Sells $31.75 of Christmas Seals," *The Pilot*, December 24, 1937, 1; and "Edna B. Covington," in "AAERO Memorial Awards," African American Education & Research Organization, https://aaero.org/aaero-memorial-awards/. Charles W. Foushee first taught in Glendon outside Carthage before serving as principal of Sanford's Colored Graded School from 1902 to 1905. He then relocated to Statesville, where he headed the graded school (later named the Morningside School) for thirty years. See sketch of Foushee in Caldwell, *The History of the American Negro*, vol. 4, 223–25; untitled item, *CB*, July 31, 1902, 4; and T. E. Allison Jr., "News of Statesville's Colored People [Obituary]," *Statesville Record & Landmark*, August 2, 1935, 3.

14. Edwin French Tyson (1885–1962) was often touted as a model student at the M Street School in D.C. For discussion of his high school career, see "Closing Exercises, Colored School Pupils and Their Parents Entertained," *Evening Star*, December 24, 1903, 5; "High School Defended," *Evening Star*, February 1, 1905, 6; "Board of Education," *Evening Star*, October 4, 1905, 2. For his distribution of Chesnutt's novels at Harvard, see McElrath and Leitz, *To Be an Author*, 135; and Ashe, *From Within the Frame*, 13. Tyson's hosting of Washington at Harvard in 1907 is discussed in Sollors, Titcomb, and Underwood, *Blacks at Harvard*, 110. Tyson graduated from Harvard in 1907, winning the Boylston Prize for Elocution that year. Four years later, in 1911, he completed Howard University Medical School and interned at Freedmen's Hospital in Washington, D.C. For his record at Harvard, see Harvard University, "Reports of Departments," in *Report of the President*, 97; and "Local Graduates at Harvard," *Evening Star*, June 24, 1907, 10. For his record at Howard, see entry for Edwin French Tyson in Howard University catalogue, 1910–11, 61. Tyson joined the surgical staff of Good Samaritan Hospital in Charlotte, North Carolina, in November 1912. In 1920, he married Scotia Seminary graduate Ada Estelle Tate, daughter of prosperous Charlotte barber and real estate developer Thaddeus Tate. The couple had one child, May Beze Tyson, who in 1943 married Ellard Norwood Jackson of Charlottesville, Virginia. The Tysons also adopted a daughter named Ethel. Several years after Estelle's death, French remarried in 1943 to Lucille Henry. See *Fifteenth United States Census: 1930*, Household of Edwin F. Tyson, Charlotte, Mecklenburg Co., N.C., ED 60-6, sheet 2A; "Historical News," *Journal of Negro History*, July 1962, 215; Edwin F. Tyson and Ada Estelle Tate, marriage certificate, September 1, 1920, Mecklenburg Co., N.C., Ancestry.com, *North Carolina, Marriage Records*; "Wife of Charlotte Surgeon Passes," *Carolina Times*, May 28, 1938, 1; E. French Tyson and Lucille Henry, August 26, 1943, marriage register, 242, Mecklenburg Co., N.C., Ancestry.com, *North Carolina, Marriage Records*. Will A. Jones was one of Winston-Salem's most prominent black residents, helping establish, besides the Jones Drug Store, a local ice and coal company, insurance company, and bank. See "Colored Drug Store," *Winston-Salem Journal* (hereafter *WSJ*), May 29, 1903, 1; "Negroes Here Form Insurance Company," *Twin*

City Daily Sentinel, August 18, 1906, 1; "To the People of Winston-Salem," *WSJ*, June 26, 1913, 8; "Report of the Conditions of the Citizens Bank & Trust Company," *WSJ*, September 20, 1921, 6. For an obituary outlining his achievements, see H. A. Wiseman, "News of Colored People, Prominent and Respected Citizen Dies," *WSJ*, April 13, 1927, 17. For Jones's speech before the NNBL, see Dr. W. A. Jones, "The Negro Druggist," in S. Laing Williams, comp., *Report of the Sixth Annual Convention of the National Negro Business League Held in New York City, August 16th, 17th and 18th, 1905*, 1905, 68–69 (microfilm) reel # 1, frames 481–82, Records of the NNBL, Part 1: Annual Conference Proceedings and Organizational Records, 1900–1919, LC. The Jones brothers' hosting of Washington in Winston-Salem in 1910 is noted in "Negro Gives Good Advice, Dr. Booker T. Washington Makes Favorable Impression Here, South Negro's Place, Declares That the South Is the Best Place for His Race to Develop Itself," *WSJ*, November 1, 1910, 1; Horace T. Slatter, "Booker Washington Visits Winston-Salem and Makes Talk," *Western Sentinel*, November 1, 1910, 1; and Jackson Jr., *Booker T. Washington and the Struggle Against White Supremacy*, 113.

15. Baker, *The Colored Inventor*, 3. Forrest Hayes was an early officer in the Volunteer Subscription Fund and became vice president of the new Pullman benefit organization that grew out of it, serving alongside Gunnell and George R. Cannon, both on the board of directors. See "The Pullman Palace Car Porters and Railway Employees Beneficial Association," advertisement, *NYA*, July 23, 1908, 2; and "Jersey City Notes," *NYA*, July 29, 1909, 3. For discussion of the fund as the precursor to the Pullman organization, see "Pullman Employees in New Benefit Society," *NYA*, March 18, 1915, 1; and "Capacity for Organization," *NYA*, November 21, 1925, 4. In addition to serving side by side in the Volunteer Subscription Fund, Tena, Forrest, and Forrest's wife Ardenia taught Sunday School together at Lafayette and socialized as part of the Scotia Scholarship Society. See "Jersey City," *NYA*, December 28, 1911, 2; "Out of Town Correspondence, Jersey City, N.J.," *NYA*, January 23, 1913, 3; "Out of Town Correspondence, Jersey City, N.J.," *NYA*, April 17, 1913, 3.

16. For a discussion of the Wrights' extensive litigation to protect their patents, see Crouch, *The Bishop's Boys*, 402–23, 440–67.

17. "An Ingenious Gauge Cock," *EREM*, July 1910, 30. The decline in patent rates by independent inventors and the delayed receipt of patents are discussed in Lamoreaux and Sokoloff, "The Rise and Decline of the Independent Inventor, A Schumpeterian Story?" 61–66; and in Lamoreaux and Sokoloff, "Inventors, Firms, and the Market for Technology in the Late Nineteenth and Early Twentieth Centuries," 19–60.

18. Tena and Ardenia Hayes's service as officers is documented in "Railroad Men's Auxiliary Received," *NYA*, April 28, 1910, 7. After its founding in 1898, Lafayette Presbyterian held services in the cramped "old John Knox Church" at Grand Street and Manning Avenue. In April 1909, the congregation purchased the spacious Universalist Church at Summit Avenue and Ivy Place. See "New Church for Jersey City," *NYA*, May 6, 1909, 4. Tena's fundraising activities are documented in "Jersey City Notes," *NYA*, June 27, 1912, 2; and "Out of Town Correspondence, Jersey City, N.J.," *NYA*, January 23, 1913, 3. Her other organizational work for the church is documented in "Jersey City," *NYA*, September 28, 1911, 2; "Jersey City Notes," *NYA*, June 27, 1912, 2; "Out of Town Correspondence, Jersey City, N.J.," *NYA*, November 7, 1912, 2. Quote on Lafayette's status is from "New Life in Church Work, Progress of Lafayette Presbyterian Church at Jersey City, N.J., Manifest—Harmony Among the Members Under Rev. Dr. Trusty's Able Leadership," *Iowa State Bystander*, April 16, 1909, 1.

19. Dickerson, "George Epps Cannon," 514–16. Clorena Cannon graduated from Scotia in 1889 and was on the faculty from at least 1894–99, first as supervisor of the sewing room and later as head of the industrial department. Mary A. Cannon (later Scraggins) entered Scotia in 1888 and graduated three years later in 1891. See "Alumnae Roll," in Scotia Seminary catalogues, 1894–95, 25–26; 1895–96, 3; 1897–98, 5; and 1898–99, 5. The year 1908 is given as the date the society was first organized. See "Jersey City, N.J.," NYA, June 1, 1919, 5. The Scotia Literary Society became the Scotia Scholarship Society in 1910 in response to an appeal from an alumnae group in Concord, North Carolina, for funds to help their alma mater. The Concord group proposed the establishment of a number of societies across the country to achieve the fundraising goal. See "Our Freedmen Field and Its Work, from Address by Mrs. H. L. McRory," HMM, August 1910, 240. Early activities and leadership of the Jersey City club are documented in the NYA, especially in its regular "Out of Town Correspondence" column.

20. "Out of Town Correspondence, Jersey City," NYA, October 14, 1906, 8; "Out of Town Correspondence, Jersey City," NYA, November 8, 1906, 8. Henry Tyson and Mary Church Terrell were fellow members of the Bethel Literary and Historical Association (of which Terrell served as president in 1894), beginning in the early 1890s. See untitled flyer, January 1, 1892, in subject file 1884–1962, folder (Bethel Literary and Historical Association), microfilm reel #13, counter 691–93, Terrell Papers, LC. The friendship forged there would carry throughout their lives. In 1904, Tyson chaired the official welcoming committee for Terrell when she returned home from Germany after attending the International Women's Conference in Berlin. See "Cordially Greeted, Reception Tendered Mrs. Mary Church Terrell," The Evening Star, August 11, 1904, 16; "City Paragraphs," CA, August 13, 1904, 8; "Mrs. M. C. Terrell Honored," CA, August 20, 1904, 5. George White's appearance at Lafayette is noted in "Address at a Jersey Church by a Former Congressman," NYA, May 30, 1907, 1. White in 1906 was practicing law in Philadelphia, where he socialized with Guy and Marie at Lombard Central Presbyterian Church. Henry and Jane Tyson were also close friends with White's mother, witnessing her will. See Justesen, George H. White, 400–401, and "Last Will and Testament drafted for Mary Anna Spaulding White," in Justesen, In His Own Words, 286–87.

21. Attorney Traverse A. Spraggins was appointed in 1911 to serve as New Jersey's representative to the National Negro Educational Conference. See untitled article, CD, July 29, 1911, 3, "Jersey City, N.J.," NYA, August 3, 1911, 7. Cannon would become a national leader in the Republican Party. See discussion of his Republican activities during the 1920s in Avery, Up from Washington, 86; and Schneider, We Return Fighting, 185–87. In the 1920s, Spraggins and Cannon, with eight others, founded the Douglass Film Company. See "The Douglass Film Company," PC, September 19, 1925, 14. Lizzie Berry was married to John C. Berry, private car steward for Harold Gould, the millionaire brother of railroad magnate Jay Gould (see "Out of Town Correspondence, Jersey City, N.J.," NYA, February 13, 1913, 3). In addition to founding a chapter of the Eastern Star Order, she was active in the New Jersey Federation of Women's Clubs, rising quickly to become state president. See "Out of Town Correspondence, Jersey City, N.J.," NYA, June 26, 1913, 3; "Jersey City, N.J.," NYA, December 20, 1919, 5; and "New Jersey Colored Women's Federation," NYA, October 28, 1922, 2. Fred Moore was the guest speaker of the Lafayette Presbyterian Lyceum on April 2, 1911. See "Jersey City Notes," NYA, March 30, 1911, 3; and "Jersey Doctors Entertain," NYA, April 6,

1911, 7. Barrett appeared before the lyceum several times between April and July 1913. See "Out of Town Correspondence, Jersey City, N.J.," *NYA*, April 24, 1913, 3; "Out of Town Correspondence, Jersey City, N.J.," *NYA*, May 29, 1913, 3; "Out of Town Correspondence, Jersey City," *NYA*, July 13, 1913, 3; "Out of Town Correspondence, Jersey City, N.J.," *NYA*, April 9, 1914, 3; "News of Greater New York," *NYA*, May 7, 1914, 8. In 1911, Walter Quinn's son, Walter Quinn Jr., moved to Chicago, where he opened a real estate and insurance brokerage business with H. David Murray and William. H. Terrell. Terrell was real estate partners with Walter B. Anderson, who became an investor in Headen's Spring-in-a-Tube Co., founded in Chicago in 1916. See untitled article, *CD*, July 29, 1911, 3. Cannon's membership in the North Jersey Medical Association's auto club and his motor trips with Benjamin F. Thomas, William MacDonald "Mack" Felton, and others are noted in "Jersey City Notes," *NYA* June 22, 1911, 3; and "Motor to Asbury Park," *NYA*, July 18, 1912, 7.

22. Tena Nichols, quoted in Gilmore, *Gender and Jim Crow*, 31 (original source of quote, "Higher Education for Women," *The Gazette*, May 12, 1892). Robinson quote from Cornelius H. Robinson, "Opportunity," *CD*, June 10, 1911, 4.

23. Lee A. Pollard served as president of the Cosmopolitan Automobile School, organized in September or October 1909 and headquartered at the Hotel Maceo. Other principals besides Pollard and Benjamin Thomas were William Felton (owner of the Auto Transportation Co.), Elijah J. Scott (former president of the Coachman's Union and a partner in the Hudson-Fulton Garage), U.S. Post Office employees William Brown and W. W. Waller, University of Virginia student A. W. Willis, and a J. H. A. Davis. See "Organize Auto School," *NYA*, December 23, 1909, 7. For information on William "Mack" Felton, who had operated auto-related companies in New York since 1898, see "Conduct Automobile Schools in New York," *NYA*, February 13, 1913, 1. For information on J. Albert Robert's Automobile School (at 67 West 66th Street), see "U Auto Learn More to Earn More," advertisement, *NYA*, April 13, 1911, 3. Scott's work at the P&S Garage and at the Aeronautical Society is described in Henry Winter's unpublished autobiography. See "The Autobiography of Henry Winter of His Participation in Early Aviation," unpaginated chapter in Winter, "Early Aviation, U.S.A.," chapter pp. [7–17], MCNY. Winter also discusses Scott in letter, Henry Winter to Robert B. Wood, July 17, 1971, in biographical file, Henry J. Winter, NASM, UHRC. Marketing and other materials on the Aeronautic School of Engineers are housed in the Henry J. Winter Collection, Series 1, Scrapbook, 3, Special Collections Branch, USAFAL, USAFA. Aeronautical publications and New York newssheets gave Scott and Winter's Aeronautic School of Engineers wide coverage. See, for example, "Aero Engineers' School Opens," *Aero*, February 4, 1911, 97; "Aero Show at New York," *Aeronautics*, February 1911, 52; "Aviators Wanted," advertisement, *Brooklyn Eagle*, February 3, 1911, 14; and "Aeronautic School of Engineers," advertisement, *Evening Telegram*, January 7, 1911, 11. Winter had been an observer at the "P&S," and Scott hired him as an assistant. When the flying season ended, Winter convinced Scott to go into business with him. Their school, in which Scott offered motor and construction classes and Winter handled the administrative affairs, immediately enrolled sixty white students. Winter continued the Aeronautic School of Engineers with new partners after Scott's death, and eventually became the manager of the Aeronautical Society before retiring from aviation. See "The Autobiography of Henry Winter of His Participation in Early Aviation," unpaginated chapter in Winter, "Early Aviation, U.S.A.," chapter p. [34], MCNY. For Chappelle's early activities, see "Negro Aviator," *NYA*, January 12, 1911, 1. This

story was reprinted and abstracted in numerous publications. See, for example, "Race News," *Colorado Statesman*, February 4, 1911, 1; and "Social Uplift," *The Crisis*, May 1911, 12.

24. For further coverage of Thomas and Pollard, see, for example, "Motor to Asbury Park," *NYA*, July 18, 1912, 7. For details on Chappelle's plane, which the *The Air-Scout* described as "equipped with safety devices for long distance passenger-carrying flights," and praised as embodying "some very interesting features," see untitled news item, *The Air-Scout*, December 1910, 44. Chappelle, with Benjamin Thomas and five others, incorporated the Meteoric Aeroplane Co. in February 1911 to manufacture the plane. See Certificate of Incorporation, Meteoric Aeroplane Company, No. 3051, filed and recorded February 11, 1911, State of New York, Book 342, 215. The Meteoric's owners planned to "build and operate aeroplanes for profit" and to "teach aeronautics." The founding officers were attorney Louis A. Leavelle, president, Chappelle, vice president, and Benjamin F. Thomas, secretary. Other incorporators were Cosmopolitan Automobile School manager Lee Pollard, funeral home owner Rodney Dade, decorating store owner Samuel Moran, real estate agent John T. Birch, and actor and writer Harrison Stewart. For general information on Thomas's business activities in New York, see "The Automobile that Won a Prize in Carnival," *NYA*, May 13, 1909, 3; "Race News," *Colorado Statesman*, July 23, 1910, 2; "Conduct Automobile Schools in New York," *NYA*, February 13, 1913, 1–2; "Ben Thomas Invents an Auto Enclosure," *NYA*, September 16, 1915, 1; and "Cosmopolitan Automobile School," advertisement, *NYA*, October 13, 1910, 3. For information on Pollard, see "Lee A. Pollard," *NYA*, July 2, 1914, 1. For information on Rodney Dade, see "Rodney Dade & Bros., Undertakers and Embalmers," advertisement, *The Crisis*, November 1912, 41. For documentation of Samuel Moran's ownership of a decorating firm, see *Thirteenth United States Census: 1910*, Household of Samuel Moran, Manhattan, New York Co., N.Y., ED 1284, sheet 12A. For documentation of John T. Birch's occupation, see *Thirteenth United States Census: 1910*, Household of John Birch, Brooklyn, Kings Co., N.Y., ED 647, sheet 1B. A description of Harrison Stewart's career appears in Lester A. Walton, "Harrison Stewart," *NYA*, July 9, 1908, 6. For discussion of the company's early formation, see "To Form Aeroplane Company," *NYA*, January 26, 1911, 7; and "Aeroplane Company Formed," *NYA*, February 2, 1911, 1. The *Defender*'s eulogy to Scott appeared in "The First Aeroplane School," *CD*, February 25, 1911, 1. Quote concerning the *Defender*'s popularity in Jersey City is from John R. Winston, "Rail Road Center," *CD*, March 25, 1911, 2.

25. Latimer's artisanal origins and career as an inventor are documented in Fouché, *Black Inventors in the Age of Segregation*, 84–86. The occupation of Thomas's stepfather, an Italian immigrant, is noted in *Tenth United States Census: 1880*, Household of Philip Fortunata, Pocotaligo, Hampton Co., S.C., ED 121, 6. See also entry for Benjamin F. Thomas in Boris, *Who's Who in Colored America, 1930-1931-1932*, 416; and "Ben Thomas Invents an Auto Enclosure," *NYA*, September 16, 1915, 1. A short biography of Chappelle's life appears in entry for Charles Ward Chappelle, in Mather, *Who's Who of the Colored Race*, 63. For discussion of Chappelle's later business activities in Ghana, see Dailey, "The African Union Company," 528–29. Chappelle's father was a minister and his mother a grocer in Atlanta. See *Tenth United States Census: 1880*, Household of George W. Chappelle, Decatur District 531st G. M., DeKalb Co., Ga., ED 47, 27; and entries for Anna Chappelle in Atlanta city directories, 1886, 146; 1887, 147; and 1893, 489. Although the Alexandria, Virginia, census lists Scott's father as a "laborer," the city directory notes he worked as a tinner. See *Tenth United States Census: 1880*, Household of Warren Scott, Alexandria, Va., ED 3, 20; and entry for Warren Scott, in Alexandria

city directory, 1881–82, 134. Scott's uncle, John Randolph Marshall, apprenticed as a bricklayer. See sketch of John R. Marshall, in Yenser, *Who's Who in Colored America*, 1933, 295; A. N. Fields, "Intimate Glimpses of Early Chicago, Louis B. Anderson and John R. Marshall Come to Windy City and Join Colony of Early Settlers," *CD* (nat. ed.), December 3, 1932, 11; and "Col. John Marshall, Former Head of 8th Illinois Infantry, Dies," *CD* (nat. ed.), February 5, 1938, 1, 5. Before moving to New York, Scott had operated a cycle shop and auto garage in Newport, Rhode Island. He first earned notice in sports circles when he competed in motorcycle races sponsored by William K. Vanderbilt in Newport and later raced bicycles in New York's popular cycling event "The Six Days of New York." Scott opened his first shop in 1897 at 153 Prospect Hill Street in Newport. See Newport city directory, 1897, 243. The following year he moved his shop to 7 Touro Street. See Newport city directory, 1898, 245. By 1899 Scott, was running two shops, the one on Touro Street and another on Thames Street, in the heart of the city's business district. See Newport city directory 1899, 251. In 1901, he opened a popular bicycle shop and sporting goods store on Bellevue Avenue (the local equivalent of New York's Fifth Avenue), where he catered to the wealthy occupying summer mansions nearby. See advertisement, Newport city directory, 1901, 439. In 1892, he opened the Baker Automobile Storage, Repair and Supply Station, which specialized in renting and repairing the Baker Electric Car. See Newport city directory, 1902, 212, 267, 435, and advertisement, Newport city directory, 1903, 431. For information on Scott's motorcycle racing, see "Entries for Newport Motor Races," *NYT*, August 29, 1901, 7; and "Newport's Motor Races; Society Witnessed Thrilling Contests by Wealthy Amateurs," *NYT*, August 31, 1901, 3. For coverage of his bicycle racing see "Six-Day Cycle Race Far Behind Record," *NYT*, December 5, 1905, 10. Lee Pollard's career between 1900 and 1909 is detailed in "Organize Automobile School," *NYA*, December 23, 1909, 7. His father's occupation is noted in *Twelfth United States Census: 1900*, Household of William Pollard, Richmond, Henrico Co., Va., ED 109, sheet 15B.

Chapter Four

1. Rodgers's flight is described in LeBow, *Cal Rodgers and the Vin Fiz*, 107, 114; and in Fred Howard, Passenger Agent, untitled notes, p. 3, box 1, folder (Misc. Notes), Vin Fiz Special Papers, NASM, UHRC. For Ward's flight, see "Off for the Pacific, Ward Starts from Governor's Island," *Boston Evening Transcript*, September 13, 1911, 14.

2. Pullman employees' names are from "Log of Vin Fiz Flight," 1; and Telegrams, September 23, 1911, D. W. Morrison, Erie Railroad, to FDH [*sic*, Fred S. Howard], and reply, September 23, 1911, F. S. [Fred S.] Howard to D. W. Morrison, box 1, folder (Telegrams, 9/22/1911–9/27/1911), Vin Fiz Special Papers, NASM, UHRC. For coverage of the flights in the Erie's employee magazine, see "Many Thanks Mr. Bowen," *EREM*, October 1911, 460; "Rodgers' Flight Over Erie," *EREM*, October 1911, 472; "Erie Dispatchers Praised," *EREM*, October 1911, 472; "Delaware Dots," *EREM*, October 1911, 486; "From Airman C. P. Rodgers," *EREM*, November 1911, 520; "Dispatcher's Air Orders," *EREM*, December 1911, 595.

3. Aeronautical Society quote from Tandy, *An Epitome of the Work of the Aeronautic Society*, 7. Winter quote from Winter, untitled, unpaginated draft autobiography, p. [8], NASM UHRC. Information on cheap gas from Winter, "The Birth of Aviation in the United States December 17th 1903," unpaginated chapter in Winter, "Early Aviation, U.S.A.," chapter pp. [3–4], MCNY.

4. Todd was listed as housing her plane in the Aeronautical Society's main shed as early as July 1910. See "Lots of Flying at Mineola," *Aeronautics*, July 1910, 12. Todd's plane successfully flew in December 1910. See "First Aeroplane Built by Woman," *Aeronautics*, December 1910, 197. The date given for the successful flight of François Raiche's machine was September 16, 1909. See "Raiche Makes First Flight," *Aeronautics*, November 1909, 176. Acknowledgment of Bessica Raiche's solo flight appears in Ada Gibson, "News in General," *Aircraft*, November 1910, 328. Coincidentally, the solo flight occurred one year to the day of her husband's. Bessica Faith Medlar was born in April 1875 in Wisconsin. The daughter of James and Elizabeth Curtiss Medlar, when her parents separated, Bessica moved with her mother to Boston, where she entered Tufts University Medical School. After graduating in 1903, she found work in a dental office. Soon afterward, she met François Raiche (aka Frank C. Wright), a 1902 Yale law graduate and partner in Wright & Leighton of Lowell, when he visited her office as a patient. She and Raiche married soon afterward and the couple relocated to Staten Island, where Raiche opened a law practice and Bessica practiced medicine. In 1907, they purchased a summer home on Long Island to follow aviation activities there and joined the Aeronautical Society. For further biographical details on Raiche, see Gerald B. Burtnett, "America's First Flying Sportswoman," *Sportsman Pilot*, June 1931, 25; Dean Todd, "Bessica Raiche, First to Solo, 80 Years Later, Rockford Claims Nation's First Lady of Aviation," manuscript, biographical file, Bessica Faith Raiche (Dr.), NASM, UHRC. Raiche herself discusses her love of sports and driving in Holden, with Griffith, *Ladybirds*, 17. François Raiche's use of the name Frank Wright is reflected in *Twelfth United States Census: 1900*, Household of Frank C. Wright, Lowell, Middlesex Co., N.H., ED 824, sheet 7B. Entry for Frank C. Wright (Wright & Leighton), Lowell city directory, 1898, 894. Baldwin first arrived on Long Island in the summer of 1910. In June of that year he housed his plane at the Aero Club field. See "The Month Past at Mineola," *Aeronautics*, June 1910, 200. By June 1911, however, he had rented space at the Aeronautical Society. See "General News, Mineola and Belmont Park, Aeronautical Society Sheds," *Aircraft*, June 1911, 124. For short sketches of Baldwin, see Longyard, *Who's Who in Aviation*, 15; and "Tom Baldwin Sixty-five Years Young," in "The Personal Side of Talked-of Aviators," *The Air-Scout*, November 1910, 9.

5. Henry Winter claims that Scott taught both Stevenson, who owned an auto parts store next to the P&S Garage, and George Russell how to fly. See "Aeronautic School of Engineers" (brochure), in Henry J. Winter Collection, Series 1, Scrapbook, 3, Special Collections Branch, USAFAL, USAFA. Information on Stevenson's store can be found in "The Autobiography of Henry Winter of His Participation in Early Aviation," unpaginated chapter in Winter, "Early Aviation, U.S.A.," chapter p. [61], MCNY. A photograph of Scott adjusting Baldwin's Red Devil's steering mechanism appears in Dade and Strnad, *Picture History of Aviation on Long Island*, 14. The original photograph, taken by Otto Korten, temporarily was housed in the Nassau County Museum Reference Library Collection, Special Collections Department, Hofstra University, Hempstead, N.Y. However, when Korten's photographs were transferred to the Nassau County Library, the original of the photograph was subsequently lost. Walden quote is from Dr. Henry W. Walden, "The Walden Story: I Built and Flew America's First Monoplane," *Flying*, January 1958, 61. Charles Wesley Peters, a Pittsburgh glider pilot, had been scheduled to fly at the fair, but he was forced to withdraw when the tent holding the new biplane he was constructing caught fire. See "Successful Negro Fair; Successful Exhibition Held at Macon, Ga., by Progressive Colored Citizens," *Colorado Statesman*, December 16,

1911, 8; David Lurie, "Negro World War Vet, Plane Pioneer Sees Red Army 'Cornerstone of Victory,'" *Sunday Worker*, January 25, 1942, 4. Walden agreed to complete the flight, arriving in Macon in early November. Although ultimately replaced by another white flyer after he had a disagreement with the fair organizers, Walden's initial acceptance of the contract and his willingness to travel so far to keep the engagement spoke to his racial views or at least to his willingness to profit from black as well as white audiences. See "Another Aviator for the Negro Fair Today, Atlanta Man to Make Flights in Macon," *Macon Telegraph*, November 14, 1911, 10; "Aviator Leaves City; Machine Is Attached, Negro Fair Advanced $250 to Dr. Walden," *Macon Telegraph*, November 13, 1911, 3.

6. Henry Woodhouse discusses Bessica Raiche in Woodhouse, "American Amateur Aviators," *Pearson's Magazine*, February 1911, 203–9, contd. Adv. Sect. 32, 34. Mention of the $10,000 outlay for her plane is from Adv. Sect., 34. François Raiche sold a Bleriot monoplane he had constructed in the fall of 1911 to John Leitenberger and Anton Heindl of Johnstown, Pennsylvania. See "Aviator and Builder," *Aero*, November 11, 1911, 122. Raiche had begun teaching pupils the previous summer. See "Flight Progress About the Country," *Aeronautics*, June 1911, 217. He continued to advertise through the fall (see, for example, advertisement, Française Americaine Co., *Aero*, October 7, 1911, 18). For an advertising brochure published by the Raiches during this time, see, "Francaise Americaine Aeroplane Cie," in Institute of Aerospace Sciences Archives, Biographical File series, box 104, folder (Raiche, Bessica), LC. Details of Headen at Mineola appear in "Negro Aviator Gets Medal," *NYA*, January 18, 1912, 1. The medal Bessica Raiche received in October 1910 is described in detail in "Individualities," *The Argonaut*, January 7, 1911, 5. Bessica placed the medal on public display in the spring of 1911 at the Pittsburgh Automobile and Aeroplane Show. See "Exposition Show Most Unique in All History," *Pittsburgh Gazette Times*, March 19, 1911, Auto. Sect., 2.

7. Lucean's resignation was noted in "Erie Waiter an Aviator," *EREM*, January 1912, 669. Fred Moore's appearance before the Presbyterian Lyceum was noted in "Jersey Doctors Entertain," *NYA*, April 6, 1911, 7. The *Age*'s article was "Negro Aviator Gets Medal," *NYA*, January 18, 1912, 1. *Aero* magazine noted that in November 1911 Raiche had completed a new "Curtiss-type machine" fitted with a Smalley motor. See "Mineola Sees Much Winter Flying," *Aero*, December 9, 1911, 193. Richmond as Headen's first destination is from "Erie Waiter an Aviator," *EREM*, January 1912, 669. The blizzard conditions are noted in "Mercury at 12; Coldest Weather for 12 Years," *Virginian-Pilot and Norfolk Landmark* (hereafter *VPNL*), January 6, 1912, 1, 9; "6 Inches of Snow, Sleighing and Ice in Tidewater," *VPNL*, January 8, 1912, 1; "Bitterly Cold All Over Country," *N&O*, January 6, 1912, 3. The sale of a Curtiss-type plane in Norfolk was advertised in "Aero Mart," *Aero*, January 20, 1912, 326. The Raiches' new position in Chicago is noted in "Among the Aviators," *Aero*, February 17, 1912, 401. The Raiches remained in Chicago at least through October 1912. See "Fox Deluxe Aero Motors," advertisement, *Fly Magazine*, October 1912, 34.

8. "Entire South and Atlantic Coast in Grip of Severe Blizzard," *VPNL*, January 14, 1912, 1; "Foot of Snow in Carolinas; Trains Late; Winter's Grip Tightens," *VPNL*, January 16, 1912, 2. Headen's arrival in Charleston is noted in "A Colored Aviator," *Baltimore Afro-American* (hereafter *BAA*), January 20, 1911, 5. Snow in Charleston is documented in Edward H. Bowie, "Weather, Forecasts, and Warnings for the Month," *Monthly Weather Review*, January 1912, 147; and "Stop Work to Watch Snow, Charleston, S.C., Has Unusual Spectacle—South Under White Mantle," *NYT*, January 14, 1912, pt. 2, 2.

9. Clearing Field's location is from Hill, *The Little Known Story of a Land Called Clearing*, 220. Bessica's activities at Clearing are noted in "Clearing," *Aero*, April 6, 1912, 4. Headen's presence at Clearing and Tena's trip there are noted in "Jersey City Notes," *NYA*, June 13, 1912, 7.

10. "Out of Town Correspondence, Jersey City," *NYA*, November 28, 1912, 3; "Out of Town Correspondence, Jersey City, N.J.," *NYA*, January 23, 1913, 3.

11. Headen quote from "Sole Negro Aviator Due, Only Licensed Member of Race in World to Fly at Emancipation Event," *Globe-Democrat*, September 20, 1912, 7. Most flyers not licensed quote from "Is Simmons a Pilot[?]," *Aeronautics*, March 1912, 88.

12. For mention of the Triple City Aviation Meet (May 30–June 2, 1912), see Gray, "Cicero Flying Field," pt. 2, 14. For a description of the "Aviation Play" in Grant Park, see "Plan Aero Meets for the Summer, Illinois Club Begins Arrangements for Five Big Events; $100,000 Pledged," *Chicago Tribune* (hereafter *CT*), April 25, 1912, 10; "Plan Pageant for Aero Show, War Play Scheme May Be Abandoned as Part of 1912 Program," *CT*, July 8, 1912, 11; "Going to the Water Races? Here Are Some Carnival Sights to See," *CT*, August 10, 1912, 3.

13. The Cicero-Aurora Aviation Meet is discussed in Gray, "Cicero Flying Field," Part 2 of 3, 187. *Aero* magazine noted that in April 1912 the Raiches were operating three aircraft, all Curtiss models, at the Standard Aviation School. Two of the machines had 50-horsepower, 4-cylinder Maxi-Motors and one a 50-horsepower, 4-cylinder Smalley motor. See "Clearing," *Aero*, April 6, 1912, 4.

14. This pedagogy is noted in "Editorial." *Aerial Age*, June 1912, 14. Specific claims against the Raiches appear in George T. Bindbeutel, "7 Schools (?)—All in a Row," *Aerial Age*, October 1912, 8, and Bindbeutel, "More Notes, 'On the Trail', Report No. 3 of the AERIAL AGE Inquiry into 'N.G.' Aviation Schools Has to Deal with Ones in Milwaukee, Wis., Chicago, Girard, Kas., and Mt. Clemens, Mich., Are There Any More?" *Aerial Age*, November 1912, 6.

15. "Total Claimed by Aviation During the Past Five Years," *Asheville Citizen-Times*, December 29, 1912, 14; "Aviation Claims Big Toll in 1911," *Palladium and Sun Telegram*, December 14, 1911, 8.

16. The Raiches' activities in California are noted in Todd, "Bessica Raiche, First to Solo, 80 Years Later," n.p. The Standard Aviation School lawsuit is discussed in Bindbeutel, "'Now Comes the Defendant,'" *Aerial Age*, December 1912, 16.

17. Lucean's report that he had been refused membership in the Aero Club of Illinois is from "Interest Shown in Johnson Gala Day," *Inter-Ocean*, August 3, 1912, 4.

18. Although advertisements for the race did not mention a car type, the publication *Town Talk* noted that Johnson owned two Chalmers-Detroit automobiles that he raced in late 1909. See "Auto Notes," *Town Talk*, October 2, 1909, 34. For examples of the national coverage of the Gala Day, see "Sporting News Notes," *CT*, August 3, 1912, 10; Sylvester Russell, "Musical and Dramatic, Chicago Weekly Review," *The Freeman*, August 3, 1912, 5; "Jack Johnson to Race Auto Against Airship," *Reno Evening Gazette*, August 2, 1912, sect. 2, 6; "Johnson to Drive Racing Car," *NYT*, August 3, 1912, 8; "Johnson to Race," *Atlanta Journal Constitution*, August 4, 1912, 26; "Jack Johnson May Take Up Aviation," *El Paso Herald*, August 7, 1912, 10. Local coverage of the Gala Day included "Interest Shown in Johnson Gala Day," *Inter-Ocean*, August 3, 1912, 4; "Hawthorne Race Track, Sunday, Aug. 4, Jack Johnson Gala Day, L. Arthur Headen, Only Negro Aviator in the World," advertisement, *Inter-Ocean*, August 3, 1912, 4.

19. Headen's plans to fly in Kansas City and Louisville are mentioned in "Sole Negro Aviator Due," *Globe-Democrat*, September 20, 1912, 7. Headen's appearance in Memphis is noted in "Out of Town Correspondence, Jersey City," *NYA*, November 28, 1912, 3.

20. Description of the Gala Day is from "Interest Shown in Johnson Gala Day," *Inter-Ocean*, August 3, 1912, 4. Headen's failure to appear is noted in "Is This the Mr. Hayden?" *CD* (Big Weekend ed.), October 3, 1914, 8. The *Freeman*'s joke appears in untitled editorial, *The Freeman*, August 10, 1912, 4.

21. Bradford was advertised as appearing at the Gala in Sylvester Russell, "Musical and Dramatic," *The Freeman*, August 3, 1912, 5. Bradford's complaint appears in Russell, "Musical and Dramatic," *The Freeman*, August 17, 1912, 5. Mills Aviator claim from Russell, "Musical and Dramatic, Chicago Weekly Review," *The Freeman*, March 30, 1912, 5; and Russell, "Musical and Dramatic, Chicago Weekly Review," *The Freeman*, April 13, 1912, 5.

22. Crushing us quote from Mr. Arnold, "Lexington, Mo., Notes," *CD*, February 25, 1911, 3.

23. "The First Aeroplane School," *CD*, February 25, 1911, 1.

24. Scott quoted in Winter, "The Autobiography of Henry Winter of His Participation in Early Aviation," unpaginated chapter in Winter, "Early Aviation, U.S.A.," chapter p. [12], MCNY. James Harrington was fined $10 for assaulting Scott. See "Police Notes," *Newport Daily News*, August 17, 1896, 5. In 1899, Scott won a suit filed against him by cycle shop owner Julius Engel. See Docket No. 825, *Engel v. Scott*, Common Pleas Court, District Court of the 1st Judicial, Newport County, Rhode Island (filed April 1898, verdict January 19, 1899), Rhode Island Supreme Court Judicial Records Center, Pawtucket, R.I. Scott's participation in motorcycle races sponsored by William Vanderbilt in Newport is noted in "Entries for Newport Motor Races," *NYT*, August 29, 1901, 7; and "Newport's Motor Races; Society Witnessed Thrilling Contests by Wealthy Amateurs," *NYT*, August 31, 1901, 3. Scott also competed against whites in the famed Six-Day Bicycle Race in New York, receiving praise from the white sports reporter covering it. See "Six-Day Cycle Race Far Behind Record," *NYT*, December 5, 1905, 10. The story of Scott's car being hit by a woman cyclist is told in "A Bicycle-Automobile-Collision," *Newport Daily News*, October 1, 1903, 5.

25. Color line quote from "Sole Negro Aviator Due," *Globe-Democrat*, September 20, 1912, 7. For information on Taylor's career, see Ritchie, *Major Taylor*; and Taylor, *The Fastest Bicycle Rider in the World*. In response to Headen, other newspapers too began to reflect a more aggressive demeanor, including the conservative *Colorado Statesman* of Denver. The *Statesman* regularly pirated articles from the *New York Age* and other uplift-minded organs. In 1913, having already twice reprinted the *Age*'s account that Headen had learned to fly at the Aeronautical Society, the paper now picked up on the more inflammatory version. It published a synopsis of the *Globe-Democrat*'s piece, repeating Headen's claims that he had been banned from American schools and had earned a license in France. See "Afro-American Cullings," *Colorado Statesman*, March 1, 1913, 7.

26. "Nonflying Negro Aviator Spoils Emancipation Day," *St. Louis Post-Dispatch*, September 22, 1912, 1.

27. "Crowd Goads Airman to Flight and Death, J. J. Frisbie Goes Up in Crippled Machine Because Kansas Spectators Call Him a Faker," *NYT*, September 2, 1911, 1; Scamehorn, *Balloons to Jets*, 65–66.

28. Tom Farrel, "Let Me Down Easy, or the Machinery Man" (Chicago: Will Rossiter, 1906), in Sam DeVincent Collection, Series 1.1, box 6, folder (CC), Archives Center, NMAH.

The stereotype of African Americans as aeronautical interlopers lacking the courage, intelligence, and natural ingenuity required to master machines such as the balloon, and later the airship and the airplane, had its seeds in the narratives of early white aeronauts such as Charles Durant, George Elliott, Hugh Parker, Peter Carnes, Jane Warren, and John Wise, all of whom described blacks as uncomprehending, horror-struck, or comically "scampering" away in terrified amazement at the sight of a balloon. Almost as soon as such descriptions appeared in balloonists' accounts, they found their way into the stage lyrics of songsters such as Thomas Rice. Known as the "father of blackface minstrelsy," Rice penned a popular skit in 1832 entitled "Jim Crow's Peep at the Balloon," in which Jim Crow declared, upon seeing a balloon ascend, "De Balloon I saw go up, and mounting to de sky, But rader you dan I." For sample narratives by Elliott, Durant, and others, see clippings, broadsides, and advertisements in various scrapbooks in Scrapbook series, boxes 177, 181–82, and Oversize series, OV44, Institute of Aerospace Sciences Archives, LC. See Wise, *Through the Air*, 404. For Rice lyrics, see Thomas D. Rice, "Jim Crow's Peep at the Balloon," in "Jim Crow as Sung by Mr. T. D. Rice at the Theatre Royal, Adlephi," 34th ed., London: D'Almaine & Co., [1836], Minstrel Sheet Music Collection, Harvard Theatre Collection, Harvard University, Cambridge, Mass. The images these aeronauts created persisted in American culture, becoming standard fare in the entertainments of the late nineteenth and early twentieth centuries, and appearing in every imaginable form of popular culture, from blackface minstrel songs to novels and short stories, to lithographs, vaudeville skits, and radio shows. By the 1910s, they had developed into a full-blown myth that blacks were not simply afraid to fly but incapable of it. In World War II, debunking this myth would become a central goal of many of America's first black military pilots. As Tuskegee Airman Charles De Bow claimed in 1942, he hoped that by succeeding as a pilot he could ensure once and for all "that nobody can ever again say, 'Oh, Negroes are all right as janitors and handymen, but they can't learn to fly.'" See Lieut. Charles De Bow, "I Got Wings," *American Magazine*, August 1942, 28–29, 104, quote on 28.

29. "What the Papers Say, an Eclipse for St. Louis," *Aerial Age*, November 1912, 11; "Up in the Clouds, a Dark Cloud a-Rising," *Aerial Age*, December 1912, 11.

30. "Negro to Make Flights, Exhibition Arranged for South Kinloch Park Residents," *St. Louis Post-Dispatch*, October 30, 1912, 6; "Free Flying Exhibition at South Kinloch Park, Sunday, November 3d, 1912, 2 O'clock," *St. Louis Post-Dispatch*, November 1, 1912, 10; "Free Flying Exhibition at South Kinloch Park, Sunday, November 3d, 1912, 2 O'clock," *St. Louis Post-Dispatch*, November 2, 1912, 12; "Out of Town Correspondence, Jersey City, N.J.,"*NYA*, November 28, 1912, 2. Figures on subsequent development of the neighborhood are from Kinloch History Committee, *Yesterday, Today, and Tomorrow*, 10, State Historical Society of Missouri, St. Louis.

31. The St. Louis makeup flight and Headen's engagement in Memphis are noted in "Out of Town Correspondence, Jersey City," *NYA*, November 28, 1912, 3. The percentage of those making a living from flying is from "More Birdmen Than Machines, Position of Aviator Already Crowded and Others Anxious to Fly, Few Earn Expenses," *Charlotte Observer*, September 1, 1912, 18.

32. "Negro Aviator Gets Medal," *NYA*, January 18, 1912, 1; untitled editorial, *NYA*, January 25, 1912, 4. Work's mention of Headen appears in "Inventions by Negroes in 1912," in Work, *Negro Year Book* (1912), 208.

33. "Negro Aviator Is from North Carolina," *Salisbury Evening Post*, August 5, 1912, 4 (reprinted from *Winston-Salem Journal* of August 4); J[ohn] M. Gaston, D. D., "The Colored Man as a Soldier," *Assembly Herald*, April 1918, 208.

Chapter Five

1. "Hughitt Says Must Know Men to Succeed," *Savannah Tribune*, September 28, 1912, 3.

2. The beginning date of Headen's work for Hawkins is noted in letter, September 19, 1917, Wilmot C. Hawkins, The Strauss Yielding Barrier Company, Chicago, Ill., to Bureau of Citizenship, Department of State, Washington, D.C., attachment, passport application of Lucean Arthur Headen, 1917, Ancestry.com, *U.S. Passport Applications*. Hawkins, the son of Wilmot and Addie C. Hawkins, was baptized in the First Presbyterian Church of Hamptonburgh in Campbell Hall, N.Y., on September 4, 1885. See entry for Wilmot Comfort Hawkins, in Ancestry.com, *U.S. Presbyterian Church Records, 1701–1970*, 63.

3. Headen first placed his ad for a chauffeur's position in mid-1914. See "Situations Wanted—Chauffeur," *Chicago Daily News*, June 27, 1914, 15. For the McCormicks' involvement in the Presbyterian Church North and philanthropy, see Burgess, *Nettie Fowler McCormick*, 47; and Murray, *Presbyterians and the Negro*, 109. Cyrus McCormick Sr.'s role in the establishment of McCormick Seminary is discussed in Arpee, *Lake Forest, Illinois*, 69. Cyrus Hall McCormick Jr. served on the Board of Aid for Colleges and Academies from its inception in 1884 until 1892. See "IX. Board of Aid for Colleges and Academies," *GAMPCUSA*, 1884, 217; and "Presbyterian Board of Aid for Colleges and Academies, Tenth Annual Report," 14, in PCUSA, *Reports of the Missionary and Benevolent Boards and Committees to the General Assembly of the Presbyterian Church in the U.S.A.*, 1893. Both the Sabbath school of the McCormicks' home church, Fourth Presbyterian in Chicago, and Cyrus Jr. made direct contributions to Albion Academy. See "XI. Board of Aid for Colleges and Academies," *GAMPCUSA*, 1884, 217; "Appropriations and Payments of 1884–5," in "XI. Board of Aid for Colleges and Academies," *GAMPCUSA*, 1885, 805–6; and "Receipts for Colleges and Academies in June, 1885," *PMR*, August 1885, 332. Cyrus McCormick's and Henry Wood's service together on Albion's board of trustees is documented in "Board of Trustees," Albion Academy catalogue, 1884–85, 3.

4. Both Robert and Cyrus Jr. were regulars at the University Club and often made family visits. See "University Club of Chicago, Members," *Chicago Blue Book*, 1913, 521; and correspondence in series 1C, Cyrus Hall McCormick, Jr., Correspondence, 1870–1936, Wisconsin Historical Society, Madison, Wisc. In 1912, McCormick took a luxury apartment at 1446 N. Dearborn Street. Lucean, who had upon his first arrival listed his residence at 3825 S. Dearborn Street, at about the same time moved to 214 Hill Street, a few blocks from McCormick. Headen lived on West Hill alongside mostly Swedish, Italian, Greek, Irish, and German immigrants who worked as chauffeurs, valets, maids, cooks, and butlers for the McCormick clan and other Gold Coast denizens. See entry for R. R. McCormick in the *Chicago Blue Book*, 1913, 235, 686; Entries for Lucean Headen in Chicago city directories, 1913, 592; 1914, 689.

5. In late January 1913, Tena accepted reelection as president of her Jersey City Sunday School Club for the upcoming year. See "Out of Town Correspondence, Jersey City, N.J.," *NYA*, January 23, 1913, 3. By January 1914, however, she had moved to Chicago. On January 29, 1914, the *Age* noted that "Mrs. Heading [sic] of Chicago is visiting her sister, Mrs. Stanley, 294 Forest street." See "Out of Town Correspondence, Jersey City, N.J.," *NYA*,

216 Notes to Chapter Five

January 29, 1914, 3. The Headens do not appear in the 1915 city directory, but a *Defender* article in November 1915 gives their address as 1507 S. Dearborn, and it notes Headen's employment with McCormick. See "Wife of Aviator Headen Visits South," *CD* (Big Weekend ed.), November 13, 1915, 3. McCormick moved in mid-1913 to the Pullman Building several blocks east of the *Tribune* offices. See *Chicago Blue Book*, 1914, 708; Smith, *The Colonel*, 144.

6. Edith McCormick's relationship with her chauffeur is noted in Johnson, with Sautter, *The Wicked City*, 122. Play anecdote from Walter Trohan, "My Life with the Colonel," *Journal of the Illinois State Historical Association*, winter 1959, 487. Note: McCormick's personal views on race at the time Headen worked for him are unclear, but later correspondence indicates he was prone to a genetic reductionism that may actually have worked in Headen's favor. Believing, as many whites, that those of mixed race showed greater intelligence than those who were darker skinned, McCormick included a twist in his logic, arguing in the mid-1930s that, as in animal breeding, "the first cross produces issue superior to either parent." The notion that miscegenation could create a man superior to a white person would have been anathema to his Gold Coast family. McCormick, more iconoclast than liberal, however, did not stray too far from their views. He believed that if racial mixing continued over a long period, "subsequent generations become mongrel." However flawed McCormick's reasoning, it may have allowed him to make sense of a mechanically gifted Headen—whose brown skin evidenced racial mixing, but who apparently was not so many generations removed to yet be considered "mongrel"—without actually having to embrace full racial equality. For McCormick quote, see letter, Robert R. McCormick, Chicago, to Dr. Irving S. Cutter, Chicago, November 18, 1935, Series I-60: Robert R. McCormick–Business Correspondence, box 59, folder (Negro, 1919–1939), in McCormick Papers, CRRMcCRC, Wheaton, Ill.

7. Headen described in "Chicagoan Invents Submarine Device," *CD* (Big Weekend ed.), May 12, 1917, 1, 7. McCormick described by Trohan, "'My Life with the Colonel' Gives Vivid Picture of the Editor," *Daily Illini*, March 17, 1960, 7. God a Presbyterian quote from Smith, *The Colonel*, xviii. McCormick formally joined the Presbyterian Church in 1946 (Smith, 467).

8. McCormick's passion for flying is discussed in Morgan and Veysey, *Poor Little Rich Boy*, 107. A description of McCormick's trip to Fort Myer appears in Longworth, *Crowded Hours*, 67–68. For McCormick's time in Texas, see Smith, *The Colonel*, 245. McCormick's Texas hangar is noted in "America Now Has Forty Flying Fields," *Aero*, April 13, 1912, 66. Mention of a black pilot flying at Cicero Field sometime before the field's closure in 1915 appears in Gray, "Cicero Flying Field," Part 1 of 3, 41. Gray gives no specific date for the flights, but I estimate 1914. Headen claimed in 1912 to have received "no consideration" from Chicago's white flying community, and no newspaper mentions him as flying in 1913 or early 1914. However, beginning in September 1914, soon after Headen went to work for McCormick, the writer of the *Defender*'s "Lake Forest" column began referring to Headen as an aviator. For Headen's comment, see "Sole Negro Aviator Due," *Globe-Democrat*, September 20, 1912, 7. For the first mention of Headen as an aviator in the *Defender*, see "Lake Forest, Ill.," *CD* (Big Weekend ed.), September 26, 1914, 3. McCormick earned seven patents between 1917 and 1930, most for printing presses. See Smith, *The Colonel*, 195.

9. Smith, 153.

10. "Robert M'Cormick, Tribune Head, Named in Big Damage Suit," *Day Book*, September 25, 1914, 1–2; "Use of Dictagraph Is Charged in Adams-M'Cormick Case," *Day Book*, November 4, 1914, 1–2.

11. Sloan's business in Lake Forest and Headen's visits with Sloan and others in the suburb are noted in "Lake Forest, Ill.," *CD* (Big Weekend ed.), July 26, 1913, 7; George Jiles, "Lake Forest, Ill.," *The Freeman*, May 16, 1914, 1; "Lake Forest, Ill.," *CD* (Big Weekend ed.), September 26, 1914, 3; and "Lake Forest, Ill.," *CD* (Big Weekend ed.), October 3, 1914, 2. Sloan by 1918 had built a two-story auto garage in Lake Forest. See "Contracts Awarded, Lake Forest, Ill., Garage and Flat Building," *American Contractor*, April 13, 1918, 47.

12. Laura Frank's leaving for Scotia is noted in "Lake Forest, Ill.," *CD* (Big Weekend ed.), September 26, 1914, 3. Proud of him quote from "Lake Forest, Ill.," *CD* (Big Weekend ed.), October 3, 1914, 2.

13. A family friend since the McCormicks' own days in St. Petersburg, where Robert's father had been the American ambassador, the Russian ambassador could hardly refuse. See Smith, *The Colonel*, 153.

14. McCormick's plan is discussed in Smith, *The Colonel*, 154–55. [Lucean] Arthur Headen, certificate no. 51370, February 16, 1915, Ancestry.com, *U.S. Passport Applications*. In the Lake Forest column of the *Chicago Defender*, Henrietta Holland claimed, "Mr. H[e]aden will soon be leaving for Russia, to take some actual war pictures." See Henrietta Holland, "Dr. Hudson Sermonizes, Lake Forest Sunday School Hears Interesting Debate," *CD* (Big Weekend ed.), January 23, 1915, 2. McCormick had no need of a chauffeur on his trip. He had diplomatic and military drivers supplied throughout his time abroad. He describes several of his drivers in McCormick, *With the Russian Army*, 11–13, 72–73. McCormick applied for his passport on February 4, and sailed aboard the *Adriatic* four days later, filing his first cable from Liverpool a week after his arrival. See Robert R. McCormick, passport application, certificate no. 49647, February 4, 1915, Ancestry.com, *U.S. Passport Applications*; Robert R. McCormick, "News from the Tribune's War Correspondents, Met No Submarines," *CT*, February 19, 1915, 1.

15. Amie Irwin Adams, passport application, certificate no. 51516, February 19, 1915, Ancestry.com, *U.S. Passport Applications*; entries for Amie Irwin Adams and Ida Small, in "Names and Descriptions of Alien Passengers," Ship's Manifest, *R.M.S. Lusitania*, arrived Liverpool, England, March 6, 1915, Ancestry.com, *UK, Incoming Passenger Lists, 1878–1960*; entries for R. R. McCormick, Mrs. A. McCormick, D. Thompson, and August Samuelson, in "Names and Descriptions of Alien Passengers Embarked at the Port of London," Ship's Manifest, *R.M.S. Kaisar-i-Hind*, embarked Liverpool, England, March 13, 1915, Ancestry.com, *UK, Outward Passenger Lists, 1890–1960*.

16. Bert [Robert R. McCormick], London, letter, May 5 [1915], to Joe [Joseph Patterson], Chicago, Ill., in Series 2, box 51, folder 1, Joseph Medill Patterson Papers, Lake Forest College, Lake Forest, Ill. Frank Dean is listed as the owner of a repair shop on Washington Avenue in the 1910 census. See *Thirteenth United States Census: 1910*, Household of Frank Dean, Chicago, Cook Co., Ill., 7th Ward, ED 420, sheet 2. He still lived at the Washington Avenue address in 1914 and was listed as a garage owner in the Chicago city directory, 1914, 1980.

17. Headen was described as a "machinist" in "Wife of Aviator Headen Visits South," *CD* (Big Weekend ed.), November 13, 1915, 3. The disappearing tower is described in *Chicago Tribune, W.G.N. Handbook*, 174.

18. Headen Motor Company (brochure, 1922), in Name File, 1896–1968, box 5, folder (Headen, L. A., 1918–22), Green-Driver Collection, LC (hereafter Headen Motor Co. brochure, 1922). According to Edward Adams, in 1914 McCormick kept two cars at Adams's

home in Lake Forest. See "Both Bert M'Cormick and Adams Appear Before Judge Landis," *Day Book*, November 17, 1914, 1–3. He may have also maintained an auto at his apartment in the city. It was not unusual for chauffeurs to take responsibility for a variety of motorized vehicles. Harold McCormick's driver, R. J. Hull, frequently worked on the Aero Club president's planes. Hull tragically lost a hand to a spinning propeller while helping test a new hydroplane Harold had purchased in 1913. See "M'Cormick's New Air Boat Cuts Off Passenger's Hand, Chauffeur Victim of Accident as He Tries to Hurl Cap into Hangar Just Previous to Trial Flight," *CT*, September 30, 1913, 1.

19. In 1910, Jones served as chairman of the National Medical Association's Pharmaceutical Section, in which Porter was active. See untitled article, *Journal of the National Medical Association*, 1910, 347. Their personal collaborations are noted in "Of Interest to Pharmacists, Pharmaceutical Section, Afternoon Session, August 25, 1915," *Journal of the National Medical Association*, April–June 1916, 117. In 1915, when Headen applied for a passport, Porter wrote a letter attesting to having known Headen since his arrival in Chicago. See letter, Dr. George M. Porter, Chicago, Ill., to Bureau of Citizenship, Department of State, Washington, D.C., attachment, [Lucean] Arthur Headen, certificate no. 51370, February 16, 1915, Ancestry.com, *U.S. Passport Applications*. Quote is from Simms, *Simms' Blue Book*, 1923, 35. This publication contains a full biographical sketch and photograph of Porter.

20. According to Grace Presbyterian's session minutes, on October 18, 1914, "The moderator reported that Mrs. T. E. Headen had handed him the church letter of herself and her husband, Mr. L. A. Headen, from the Lafayette Presbyterian Church, of Jersey City, N.J., and asked that their names be placed on our roll. On motion, the letter having been found in order, their names were enrolled, and the clerk was requested to notify them to be present to be acknowledged at the next communion." See "October 18, 1914 [Session]," Grace Presbyterian Session Minutes, vol. 1, 1895–1923, 221, Grace Presbyterian Church Records, CHS. Because of confusingly similar names, Grace Presbyterian has often been mistaken for other local churches. The black-founded Grace Presbyterian Church was established in July 1888 and held its first meetings in a storefront at 3233 South State Street. By 1907 it had moved to 4707-09 South Dearborn. In October 1918, the congregation purchased the church building of the Sixth Presbyterian Church (white) and moved into this building at 3600 South Vincennes Avenue. In 1969, Grace Presbyterian merged with Sixth United Presbyterian Church (black) of 62nd and South Woodlawn Street to form the present-day Sixth Grace Presbyterian, located on E. 35th Street near S. Cottage Grove Avenue. See Sixth Grace Presbyterian Church, *Sixth Grace Presbyterian Church, U.S.A.*; Stevenson, *Chicago: Pre-eminently a Presbyterian City*, 113; "Grace Presbyterian Church," in Black, *Black's Blue Book*, 1918, 38; "Real Estate Transfers, South Town" and "Various Real Estate Matters, Miscellaneous," *The Economist*, November 23, 1918, 845–46. Robert Abbott joined Grace Presbyterian in March 1898. See "March 23, 1898 [Session]," Grace Presbyterian Session Minutes, vol. 1, 1895–1923, 45, Grace Presbyterian Church Records, CHS. George Cleveland Hall's membership in and service as a trustee for Grace Presbyterian is documented in "Dr. George Cleveland Hall, '86," obituary, *Lincoln University Herald*, September 1930, 3. The membership of John Randolph Marshall and Ida Wells-Barnett is documented in "Celebrate the Journey" (typescript), Grace Presbyterian Church Records, CHS. Dr. Hall was identified as Tena's physician in "Mrs. Headen Returns," *CD* (Big Weekend ed.), January 17, 1920, 12.

21. Black newspapers of the period had few resources to research stories and often relied on individuals to provide content. Ulysses Scott, for example, had received attention in the *Defender* because his uncle John Marshall could supply Robert Abbott a photo and information on his nephew. Scott went unremarked upon, however, in his home paper, the *New York Age*, with which he had no connections. At the same time, the *Age* touted the career of Charles Chappelle because Chappelle's associate, Benjamin Thomas, was a major advertiser in the paper. Quote is from "Wife of Aviator Headen Visits South," *CD* (Big Weekend ed.), November 13, 1915, 3. Note: Although Headen was mentioned as an aviator in the *Defender*'s "Lake Forest" column, he received no attention as such from the *Defender*'s reporters until after he and Tena joined Grace Presbyterian.

22. McCormick served in Mexico from July to August 1916. See Smith, *The Colonel*, 175–78. Headen's application was assigned number 86546. The firm's incorporation and its officers are documented in Illinois Office of Secretary of State, "Corporations for Profit," in *Biennial Report of the Secretary of State*, 54, and in incorporation records for the company. See Articles of Incorporation, Headen Spring-in-a-Tube Manufacturing Company, Certificate No. 3207, filed May 16, 1916; Certificate of Increase of Stock, Headen Spring-in-a-Tube Mfg. Co., filed May 27, 1916; and Affidavit of Louis F. Emmerson, Secretary of State, September 15, 1920, Corporations, Headen Spring-in-a-Tube Company, box 1376, no. 87766, Records of the Secretary of State, State of Illinois, Cook Co., Ill.

23. Walter Desire Allimono, born in the American-occupied portion of Cuba, held liberal arts, commercial science, and accounting degrees from Straight University in New Orleans, Bryant & Stratton Business College in Chicago, and Northwestern University. Early an instructor at Tuskegee, he also for several years served as the university's chief accountant. Allimono was a devoted supporter of Booker T. Washington's philosophy. By 1915 he had begun to test the waters of South Side business life, working as a salesman for the Overton Hygienic Manufacturing Company, and as head cashier for the local R. W. Hunter & Co. bank chain. He also became a partner in a Chicago contracting business and co-owned a confectionery at 3605 S. State Street. For Allimono's business philosophy, see W. D. Allimono, "The Science of the Booker T. Washington Theory," *Champion Magazine*, November 1916, 140–43. For a biographical sketch of Allimono, see Robb, *The Negro in Chicago, 1779–1929*, vol. 1, 104. For his early business activities, see entry for Allimono in Chicago city directory, 1913, 104; entry for Allimono and Smith, Confectioners, in Chicago city directory, 1916, 99; and "In Training at R. W. Hunter & Co., Bankers, 4757 State St., Chicago," *CD* (Big Weekend ed.), November 1, 1919, 11. For his position as Tuskegee's accountant, see Walter Desire Allimono, draft registration card, Ancestry.com, *U.S., World War I Draft Registration Cards*. See also Simms, *Simms' Blue Book*, 1923, 53. *The Negro in Chicago* and *Simms' Blue Book* both contain good photographs. See "Anderson and Terrell Are Fast Forging to the Front as the Leading Real Estate Brokers and Agents on the South Side," *The Broad Ax*, September 7, 1918, 12. According to the *Defender*, "Walter C. Quinn, Jr., formerly of Jersey City, N.J.," had in 1911 opened, with Terrell and another partner, H. David Murray, "one of the largest real estate and insurance brokerage businesses on the south side." See untitled article, *CD* (Big Weekend ed.), July 29, 1911, 3. Anderson was also secretary of the Sphinx Safe Deposit Co., of which Joseph Jordan was president, William H. Terrell treasurer, and W. T. Browne director. For a photo of Anderson & Terrell's real estate office and the Sphinx Safe Deposit Co., see Simms, *Simms' Blue Book*, 1923, 48. See biographical sketch of James S. Nelson in

Goode, *The Eighth Illinois*, 78. Nelson, a native of British Canada, was a naturalized citizen. See also Black, *Colored People's Guide Book for Chicago* (1915–16), 39. John F. "Jack" White was a partner with Montrose Rankin in the Rankin & White Drugstore between at least 1906 and 1917. See "Chips," *Broad Ax*, April 14, 1906, 2; Chicago city directories, 1913, p. 1434; 1914, p. 1723; 1915, p. 1345; 1916, p. 1989; and 1917, p. 1909. Initial shares of Headen Spring-in-a-Tube Co. were purchased by Headen, who held seven, and Allimono, Anderson, and Nelson, who each owned one.

24. The business was listed in 1916 as offering auto supplies. See Chicago city directory, 1916, 788. The claim of Army orders appears in "Chicagoan Invents Submarine Device," *CD* (Big Weekend ed.), May 12, 1917, 7. Allimono quote is from Annual Report of the Headen Spring in a Tube Mfg. Co., filed March 12, 1917, box 1376, no. 87766, Records of the Secretary of State, State of Illinois, Cook Co.

25. The Headen Spring-in-a-Tube Co.'s charter was officially canceled in April 1918 and the firm was dissolved by the state in October 1926. See Certificate of Cancellation of Charter, the Headen Spring In a Tube Manufacturing Co., filed April 30, 1918, and Papers of Dissolution, filed November 26, 1926, box 1376, No. 87766, Records of the Secretary of State, State of Illinois, Cook Co.

26. "Device Wraps U-Boat Chasers in Magic Cloak, Invention to Be Tried Out by Navy Chief Here Tuesday," *CT*, May 6, 1917, 3. By February 1917, when Germany declared "all-out submarine warfare," Britain's Board of Invention and Research and the U.S. Naval Consulting Board (both established to test new inventions related to the war) had identified antisubmarine measures as their top priority. See MacLeod and Andrews, "Scientific Advice in the War at Sea, 1915–1917," 18–19; and Weir, "Surviving the Peace," 86. Headen also believed submarines could be cloaked when surfacing using his method.

27. "Chicagoan Invents Submarine Device," *CD* (Big Weekend ed.), May 12, 1917, 1, 7. Liebrandt became the president of Lincoln State Bank in 1912. See "Lincoln State Savings Bank Is Opened," *CD* (Big Weekend ed.), May 11, 1912, 1. His role in the Liberty Insurance Company is discussed in entry for Frank L. Gillespie, Insurance Executive, Liberty Life Insurance Company, in Ingham, comp., *Biographical Dictionary of American Business Leaders*, vol. 1, 458. The *Pittsburgh Courier* would later describe Liebrandt as a man who had "weathered the storm for a number of business men of the race" and he was known for having "come to the rescue of hundreds in the renewal of mortgages on homes." See "Louis B. Anderson Director of Lincoln State Bank," *PC*, January 21, 1928, 8. Among Joseph (Joe) Jordan's holdings was the Jordan Building on the corner of S. State and 36th Streets. The baptism of Jordan's daughter, Irene Josephine Jordan, is noted in "May 3, 1925 Session," Grace Presbyterian Session Minutes, vol. 2, 1923–August 1936, 75, Grace Presbyterian Church Records, CHS.

28. The description of Headen's model boat and its test appears in "Device Wraps U-Boat Chasers in Magic Cloak," *CT*, May 6, 1917, 3. Josephus Daniels established the Naval Consulting Board in October 1915. See Paxson, "The American War Government, 1917–1918," 57. Headen wrote Daniels on March 5, 1917. See letter, Lucean A. Headen, Chicago, Ill., to Josephus A. Daniels, Secretary of the Navy, Washington, D.C., entry #UD-155, box 327, folder (Headen, L. A., Invisible Submarine Boat Chaser), Case Files, 1915–34, Records of the Office of Inventions, RG 80, General Records of the Department of the Navy, NARA, Washington (hereafter Headen Navy Office of Inventions case file).

29. For Daniels's role in the politics that led up to the armed coup in Wilmington and his subsequent "Redemptionist" activities, see Craig, *Josephus Daniels: His Life and Times*, 183–91. Letter, Lucean A. Headen, Chicago, Ill., to Josephus A. Daniels, Secretary of the Navy, Washington, D.C., March 5, 1917, Headen Navy Office of Inventions case file.

30. Letter, Lucean A. Headen, Chicago, Ill., to Josephus A. Daniels, Secretary of the Navy, Washington, D.C., March 20, 1917, Headen Navy Office of Inventions case file.

31. Carey was long a political figure on the South Side. See Reed, *Knock at the Door of Opportunity*, 124, 188. Madden's popularity among black constituents is noted in Michaeli, *The Defender*, 171. Letter, Lucean A. Headen, Chicago, Ill., to Hon. Martin B. Madden, Washington, D.C., March 31, 1917; and letter, Hon. Martin B. Madden, House of Representatives, Washington, D.C., to Josephus Daniels, Secretary of the Navy, Washington, D.C., April 7, 1917, Headen Navy Office of Inventions case file. Medill McCormick's name is written on the back of Headen's blueprint, included in his case file, for contact purposes. McCormick served in the House of Representatives from March 4, 1917, to March 3, 1919, and in the U.S. Senate from March 4, 1919, until his death on February 25, 1925. See entry for Joseph Medill McCormick, U.S. Congress, *Biographical Dictionary of the United States Congress, 1774–2005*, 1534. His correspondence with Daniels concerning submarine chasers include letter, Josephus Daniels, Washington, D.C., to Medill McCormick, Washington, D.C., May 5, 1917; letter, Medill McCormick, Washington, D.C., to Josephus Daniels, Washington, D.C.; and letter, Josephus Daniels, Washington, D.C., to Medill McCormick, Washington, D.C., May 11, 1917, in Medill McCormick Correspondence Series, box 5, folder (Jan.–Oct. 1917), Hanna-McCormick Family Papers, LC. McCormick, like Madden, owed his election in large part to black support, and many of those who campaigned for him on the South Side were Headen's fellow congregants at Grace Presbyterian. They included Major R. R. Jackson, Hon. B. F. Moseley, and Charles B. Travis. A member of the U.S. House of Representatives, McCormick had earlier been instrumental in funding Chicago's Semi-Centennial Exposition in 1915 and had supported antilynching legislation. See "Medill McCormick Is Endorsed by Leaders," *CD* (Big Weekend ed.), September 9, 1916, 4.

32. Harold McCormick and Julius Rosenwald were in close touch as fellow members of the Board of Trustees of the University of Chicago. See "The Board of Trustees of the University, 1915–1916," Appendix, in Goodspeed, *A History of the University of Chicago*, 500. The *Defender* confused Howard Coffin with the aviator Frank Coffyn, and the National Defense Council for the National Defense Guard. See "Chicagoan Invents Submarine Device," *CD* (Big Weekend ed.), May 12, 1917, 1, 7. Rosenwald and Coffin's roles on the advisory committee of the National Defense Council are discussed in Paxson, "The American War Government, 1917–1918," 57–58. The two men served together on the council's newly formed general munitions board between April and May 1917, just as Headen made his appeal. See Council of National Defense, Washington, April 9, 1917, "Immediate Release—p. 2"; and Meeting Minutes (April 24, 1917, 60; April 25, 1917, 68; April 26, 1917, 68; May 5, 1917, 95; May 12, 1917, 101; and May 19, 1917, 114), entry 5-B1 (Minutes, April–August 1917), box 290, *Volume 1, Minutes, General Munitions Board* (April 9, 1917–August 9, 1917), RG 62, Records of the Council of National Defense, General Munitions Board & Munitions Standards Records, NARA, College Park. Coffin's additional service on the Naval Consulting Board is discussed in Noble, *America by Design*, 81. Liebrandt's efforts are documented in letter, John F. McCarron, Secretary to James Hamilton Lewis, U.S. Senate, Washington, D.C., to Frank Smith, Secretary

to the Secretary of the Navy, May 1, 1917, Headen Navy Office of Inventions case file. William Strother Smith is identified as the navy's liaison to the board in Scott, *The Naval Consulting Board of the United States*, 124.

33. "Device Wraps U-Boat Chasers in Magic Cloak," *CT*, May 6, 1917, 3. According to Maxim, the Naval Consulting Board met on April 28. See letter, Hudson Maxim to Josephus Daniels, April 21, 1917, folder (Civilian Naval Consulting Board, 1917 Jan–Apr), Navy Files (microfilm), reel #28, Josephus Daniels Papers, LC.

34. The agreed meeting was first noted in "Device Wraps U-Boat Chasers in Magic Cloak," *CT*, May 6, 1917, 3. Moffett's response is documented in letter, William A. Moffett, Commandant, U.S. Naval Training Station, Great Lakes, Ill., to Josephus Daniels, Secretary of the Navy, Washington, D.C., May 21, 1917, Headen Navy Office of Inventions case file. Headen's invitation back to Washington is noted in "Headen Leaves for Washington," *CD* (Big Weekend ed.), May 26, 1917, 1. On June 8, Headen requested that all correspondence concerning his invention be sent to him at his Uncle Henry's address, 2124 K Street, Northwest. See letter, Lucean A. Headen, Washington, D.C., to Capt. Frank Smith, Secretary to the Secretary of the Navy, Washington, D.C., Headen Navy Office of Inventions case file.

35. Letter, Josephus Daniels, Secretary of the Navy, Washington, D.C., to L. A. Headen, Washington, D.C., June 18, 1917, Headen Navy Office of Inventions case file. The discussion of carrying capacity appears in Scott, *Naval Consulting Board of the United States*, 108. Number of inventors rejected is from McBride, "The 'Greatest Patron of Science'?," 12.

36. Only 110 of the 110,000 inventions sent to the Naval Consulting Board and directly to the Navy Department were considered worthy of serious consideration. See Scott, *The Naval Consulting Board of the United States*, 125. Headen's request for the return of his plans appears in Lucean Headen, Chicago, Ill., to Josephus Daniels, Secretary of the Navy, Washington, D.C., July 7, 1917, Headen Navy Office of Inventions case file.

37. Number of ships lost is from "Handelskreig," in Pope and Wheal, *Dictionary of the First World War*, 221. For a report of the delegation's visit, see "Report by Professor Sir Ernest Rutherford FRS and Commander Cyprian Bridge, RN, on Visit to the USA in Company with French Scientific Mission, May 19th to July 9th, 1917," Board of Invention and Research, BIR 28208/17, Public Record Office, ADM 293/10, National Archives, Kew. Statement that they had met with inventors from the public appears in Sir Ernest Rutherford and Commander Cyprian D. C. Bridge, "Report by Professor Sir Ernest Rutherford, F.R.S., and Commander Cyprian Bridge, on Visit to the United States of America in Company with the French Scientific Mission, May 19th to July 9th, 1917," Report No. BIR 28208/17, July 18, 1917, 7, in ADM 293/10, *B.I.R. Sec. II. Reports, 1917* [hand-numbered p. 38], National Archives, Kew.

38. Wilmot Hawkins began working for the Strauss Yielding Barrier Co. in August 1916. See letter, Charles R. Cook and J. B. Strauss, Strauss Yielding Barrier Co., Chicago, Ill., to Bureau of Citizenship, Department of State, Washington, D.C., attachment to Wilmot Comfort Hawkins, certificate no. 66644, September 18, 1917, Ancestry.com, *U.S. Passport Applications*. In his negotiations with Cook and Strauss, Lucean may also have called on Robert McCormick to vouch for him. McCormick, prior to joining the *Tribune*, had served as head of the Chicago Sanitary District. In this role, he held control over all bridge-building contracts for the city. Thus, Strauss and McCormick had found themselves across the table from each other on numerous occasions as the board approved and reviewed bridge-building contracts.

39. The trip's purpose and Headen's salary are from letter, September 20, 1917, Chas. R. Cook and J. B. Strauss, The Strauss Yielding Barrier Co., Chicago, Ill., to Bureau of Citizenship, Department of State, Washington, D.C.; letter, September 19, 1917, J. B. Strauss to Bureau of Citizenship (attachment to William Comfort Hawkins's passport application); and letter, September 19, 1917, Wilmot C. Hawkins, The Strauss Yielding Barrier Co. to Bureau of Citizenship (attachment to Lucean Arthur Headen passport application). Passage for the Hawkinses and Headen is documented in entries for L. A. Headon [sic], W. C. Hawkins, and Anna M. Hawkins in "Names and Descriptions of Alien Passengers," Ship's Manifest, *S.S. Lapland*, Arrived Liverpool, England, October 9, 1917, from New York, Ancestry.com, *UK, Incoming Passenger Lists, 1878–1960*.

40. Headen notes he had an Admiralty office from which he could view Trafalgar Square in Headen Motor Company brochure, 1922. The Admiralty's name for Headen's device was noted in E. W. Nelson, "Section II. Report for Week Ending November 23rd, 1918," 1, in ADM 293/20, "Reports of Director of Experiments and Research, Sectional Weekly Reports, 1918," National Archives, Kew. Just prior to Headen and Hawkins's arrival to give a demonstration to the BIR, the Holland Skinner Report was issued, recommending that the BIR be abolished or diminished in its role. The Admiralty chose to phase out the BIR's activities rather than eliminating them outright, and it began with a reorganization that placed the BIR under a newly created director of experiments and research. Not until almost two months later, however, was a director (Charles H. Merz) appointed, and in the months that followed, the BIR and Merz and his staff were preoccupied with working out logistics among themselves.

41. Headen's and the Hawkinses' return date is documented in entries for Lucian [sic] Arthur Headen, Wilmot Comfort Hawkins, and Anna Mary Hawkins in "List of United States Citizens," Ship's Manifest, *S.S. St. Paul*, Arrived New York, New York, November 26, 1917, from Liverpool, England, Ancestry.com, *New York, Passenger and Crew Lists*. Headen's employment at the British Ministry of Shipping is documented in Lucean Arthur Headen, draft registration card, Ancestry.com, *U.S. World War I Draft Registration Cards*. Headen noted his specific duties at the ministry in Headen Motor Company brochure, 1922.

42. Nelson noted in his weekly report to the Admiralty that, "The following proposals are being considered in conjunction with the Admiralty Departments concerned: L. H. [sic] Headen and Wilmot C. Hawkins, Headen system of mirror Camouflage (Extracts of Sir R[ichard] Paget's report B.I.R. 14966d), Referred to D.E.R." See "Section II. Report for Week Ending November 23rd, 1918," 1, ADM 293/20, in "Reports of Director of Experiments and Research, Sectional Weekly Reports, 1918," National Archives, Kew. According to official Admiralty Memorandum No. 18, proposals from outside inventors were first assessed by the BIR, and those that appeared "deserving of further investigation" were referred to the DER for action. See "Office Memorandum No. 18, as Amended by No. 31, Organisation of Scientific Research and Experiments, Appointment of a Director of Experiments and Research," in Office of the Director of Experiment and Research, Admiralty, 31st December 1918, "Report on the Position of Experiment and Research for the Navy," 5, Attachment to the Holland-Skinner Report, ADM 116/1430 (volume labeled Case 5S45), National Archives, Kew.

43. Wood, "From Board of Invention and Research to the Royal Naval Scientific Service," 40–41.

44. "L. A. Headen in London," *CD* (Big Weekend ed.), November 3, 1917, 6. The poem "A Man's a Man for A' That," penned by Robert Burns in 1795, was often referenced by individuals and groups, including British labour, to assert the ideal of equality.

45. Andrew Louis Davison was listed as the proprietor of a restaurant, living at 570 Lennox Avenue (the address Headen listed on his WWI draft registration card) in 1920. See *Fourteenth United States Census: 1920*, Household of Lewis Davidson [Andrew Louis Davison], Manhattan Borough, New York, N.Y., ED 1410, sheet 6A. Davison, born October 11, 1871, was a native of Oberlin, Ohio, and was listed as a caterer on his death certificate. He died on February 23, 1923. See Andrew Louis Davison, death record, February 23, 1923, FamilySearch.com, *New York, New York City Municipal Deaths*. Headen's talks at the church are noted in "St. James Presbyterian," *NYA*, December 29, 1917, 8. He would continue to stop in at the church on occasion, exciting the congregation with his presence at a service in July 1918. See "St. James Church," *NYA*, July 6, 1918, 8.

46. "Editor R. S. Abbott Dined at the Famous Libya," *CD* (Big Weekend ed.), June 22, 1918, 3. Tena accompanied Lucean from Chicago to New York when he relocated to take up his new position. See "Only Race Aviator Visits New York," *CD* (Big Weekend ed.), May 18, 1918, 2. Their stop in West Chester is noted in "West Chester," *PT*, August 31, 1918, 6. Sarah and Samuel moved to Philadelphia sometime between 1914 and 1916. See entry for Samuel J. Stanley in Philadelphia city directory, 1916, 1582. By the following year, however, George Drye and his wife had left Philadelphia for New York. See "Flashes & Sparks, Social and Otherwise During the Week," *PT*, January 27, 1917, 5. Samuel and Sarah soon themselves returned to Jersey City. See *Fourteenth United States Census: 1920*, Household of Samuel Stanley, Jersey City, Hudson Co., N.J., ED 186, sheet 1A. By 1920, however, George again returned to Philadelphia. See *Fourteenth United States Census: 1920*, Household of George Drye, Philadelphia, Philadelphia Co., Pa., ED 990, sheet 7B.

47. The *Defender* inaccurately claimed in October 1917, when Headen first sailed for England, that the purpose of his trip was to "'do his bit' in the English aviation corps." See "Aviator Sails for England," *CD* (Big Weekend ed.), October 6, 1917, 6. Upon his move to New York, the *New York Age* asserted that Headen was an officer in the Royal Air Force. See "Britain Uses His Invention," *NYA*, April 27, 1918, 1. The *Defender* again asserted that Headen had received "a commission in the British flying service" a month later. See "Only Race Aviator Visits New York," *CD* (Big Weekend ed.), May 18, 1918, 2. Other publications, such as Monroe Work's *Negro Year Book*, repeated these claims. See Work, *The Negro Year Book* (1918–19), 5. No proof exists, however, that they are true, or that Headen trained personnel on Long Island. The U.S. Army Signal Corps trained American flyers at Hazelhurst Field in Mineola and the U.S. Navy trained pilots at Bay Shore Naval Air Station, but British personnel took no part in instruction at either location. Other military outposts on the island, including Rockaway Naval Air Station and Montauk Naval Air Station, and the army's Fort Tilden, provided dirigible and other air surveillance of the coastline during the war, but they had no flight schools. See Van Ells, *America and World War I*, 3–4; and Whitehouse, *Fire Island*, 103–12.

Chapter Six

1. The location of Headen's shop was noted as 71 E. 36th St. in "The Headens Entertain," *CD* (Big Weekend ed.), November 29, 1919, 17. The advertising brochure Headen created

for his company recorded 1918 as the year that the company was founded. This date, however, actually referred to the establishment of Headen's auto garage rather than Headen Motor, which was not incorporated until 1921. See Headen Motor Company brochure, 1922.

2. In July 1917, just before Lucean left for England, the couple had moved to 636 E. 38th Street, where Tena began taking in boarders. By 1920, she was managing a household that included a pharmacist and his younger brother and a mail carrier and his wife. See *Fourteenth United States Census: 1920*, Household of Lucian [*sic*] Headen, Cook Co., Chicago, Ill., ED 96, Sheet 1A. Abbott and Walter Jones knew each other from music activities at Hampton, where Abbott was a member of the famed Hampton Quartet and Jones performed with less prominent groups. Both men remained interested in music after graduating. Jones regularly gave concerts in Richmond, and during Headen's visit directed a local "Victory" sing to celebrate the end of the war. He later led his own quartet and became Minister of Music for Ebenezer Baptist Church in the city. See "Victory Sing in Reformer Hall Sunday," *Richmond Times-Dispatch*, November 22, 1918, 12; "The Y.M.C.A. Notes," *Richmond Planet* (hereafter *RP*), December 23, 1923, 7; obituary, "Mary Pollard" (Jones's daughter), *Richmond Times-Dispatch*, January 22, 2016, https://www.google.com/amp/s/www.richmond.com/obituaries/pollard-mary/articles_f9d815-b8cb-5889-a598-4d3c03f671cc.amp.html. Both men also retained strong ties to Hampton. In 1918, Jones served as president of the Richmond chapter of the Armstrong League, an alumni group Abbott also gave strong support. In 1906, Jones had helped incorporate and assumed the office of vice president for Richmond's Young Men's Investment Association. For information on Jones's carriage-building business and his status in the Armstrong League, see "Graduates and Ex-Students," *Southern Workman*, August 1914, 471; "Graduates and Ex-Students," *Southern Workman*, May 1918, 255. For the founding of the investment association, see "Virginia Assembly Ending," *RP*, March 8, 1906, 1. Headen's weeklong stay with Jones is noted in untitled item, *RP*, November 23, 1918, 2.

3. For Headen's arrest, see "Fake Auto Tank Speeds Driver to Jail," *Detroit Free Press*, December 24, 1918, 14. For arrest statistics and a discussion of bootlegging between Toledo and Detroit, see Frank B. Elser, "Keeping Detroit on the Water Wagon," *The Outlook*, April 2, 1919, 560–62, 567. Although the author of the *Outlook* article greatly disapproved of Headen's actions as a bootlegger, he nonetheless could not resist praising his method, calling it a "nifty, if shifty, piece of work," and marveling at its ingenuity.

4. Chicago's automotive district featured auto showrooms, accessory and parts stores, filling stations, and garages. For a description, see Chicago Commission on Race Relations, *The Negro in Chicago*, 214. Between 1910 and 1920, the black population of Chicago increased from 44,103 to 109,458. See "Table 32–Negro Population and Increase in Negro Population of Cities Having, in 1920, More than 25,000 Negro Inhabitants: 1920, 1910, and 1900," in Rossiter, *Increase of Population in the United States, 1910–1920*, 128. The name "Bronzeville" was created in 1930 by *Chicago Bee* theater editor James J. Gentry. See Travis, "Bronzeville," in *The Electronic Encyclopedia of Chicago*, http://www.encyclopedia.chicagohistory.org/pages/171.html.

5. "Dr. A. W. Williams Purchases Big Car," *CD* (Big Weekend ed.), April 17, 1915, 4.

6. "Five People Slain as Lawless Mob Storms City Jail, Many Others Are Injured in Riot at Winston-Salem, Police and Home Guards Fail to Hold Back Gang," *RP*, November 18, 1918, 1; "Reign of Terror in Winston-Salem," *RP*, November 23, 1918, 9; "Five Are

Killed and 25 Were Injured Here Last Night in Tragedy Following an Attempt to Lynch Negro at City Jail," *WSJ*, November 18, 1918, 1; "Southern Race Riot Costs Five Lives; Army Tank Corps Called to Quell Lynching Mob in Winston-Salem, N.C., Battle with Home Guards, Jail-Storming Crowd Overcomes Them, as Well as Police and Fire Companies," *NYT*, November 17, 1918, 8. Location of shooting near Jones Drug Store from James A. Morris, letter to the editor, "Colored Man Expresses Sincere Appreciation," *WSJ*, November 21, 1918, 10.

7. Bombings in the city between 1917 and 1921 are discussed in Chicago Commission on Race Relations, *The Negro in Chicago*, 122–35.

8. Voogd, "Washington (D.C.) Riot of 1919," 681–82.

9. Twenty-three blacks and fifteen whites died in the Chicago riot. See Stolz, "Chicago (Ill.) Riot of 1919," 100–106; and Krist, *City of Scoundrels*, 205.

10. The deaths of Henry Baker, a black man shot while standing next to his window, and David Marcus, a white man stabbed on the street by a black attacker, occurred at 511 E. 37th and 534 E. 37th, respectively. Insurance agent G. L. Wilkins of the Metropolitan Life Insurance Agency was killed at 38th Street and Rhodes Avenue. Oscar Dozier was clubbed and stabbed to death at W. 39th Street and Wallace Avenue. Dozier's death is not to be confused with that of William A. Dozier, also killed in the riot. William Dozier's death occurred at Exchange Ave. near Cook St. in the Stockyards district. See Chicago Commission on Race Relations, *The Negro in Chicago*. Appendix, 656 (Oscar Dozier), 657 (Baker), 658 (Marcus), 665 (Wilkins), and 667 (William Dozier). The murder of "Mr. Oscar A. Dozier" was noted in the session for "September 4, 1919," Grace Presbyterian Session Minutes, vol. 1, 1895–1923, 307, Grace Presbyterian Church Records, CHS.

11. Quote from "R. W. Hunter & Company, Bankers, Chicago, Ask the Colored American Citizens This Great Question," advertisement, *Broad Ax*, October 25, 1919, 4. Although real estate broker Jesse Binga had lent money and financed mortgages for blacks on the South Side since 1908, he made his activities official in 1921, opening the newly chartered Binga State Bank in early January 1921 on South State Street. The following year Anthony Overton opened the Douglass National Bank. See "More Than Two Hundred Thousand Dollars Was Deposited in the Bank on Opening Day," *Broad Ax*, January 15, 1921, 3; Smith, "Anthony Overton," 626. Binga's home and office had been bombed no less than six times between 1919 and 1921. See Chicago Commission on Race Relations, *The Negro in Chicago*, 124–33; and "Bombing Binga," *CD* (nat. ed), September 3, 1921, 16.

12. Poindexter was identified as the head mechanic for Headen in 1919 in "Miss Alexander on a Visit," *CD* (Big Weekend ed.), August 30, 1919, 12. See also *Fourteenth United States Census: 1920*, Household of Henry Poindexter, Chicago, Cook Co., Ill., ED 89, sheet 8A. Fred Walls was identified as head mechanic in October 1920. See "Society," *CD* (Big Weekend ed.), October 2, 1920, 10. Walls continued as manager at the new location, and William Smith became assistant manager. See "Auto Repair Shop Moves," *CD* (nat. ed.), April 2, 1921, 15. Edward G. Shaw was an active member of the Associated Business Club (ABC), a group led by Robert Abbott (president) and Jesse Binga, and affiliated with Booker T. Washington's NNBL. The group also included Headen's close friend George Porter, as well as Phil A. Jones, managing editor of the *Defender*. See "New Ideas Are Outlined to Business Men at Luncheon," *CD* (nat. ed.), December 15, 1923, 11; Ethel Minor Gavin, "Business League Officers Welcomed at Huge Banquet," *CD* (nat. ed.), August 23, 1924, 2.

13. "Wizard Automobile Co. Assets Sold for $105,500," *Automotive Industries*, April 27, 1922, 943; "Hanson Doubles Production," *Automotive Industries*, May 18, 1922, 1089; "Columbia Makes 40 Cars Daily," *Automotive Industries*, May 11, 1922, 1042.

14. For information on Patterson's carriage and auto business, see May, *First Black Autos*; and Nelson, *The C. R. Patterson and Sons Company*.

15. For the *Defender*'s coverage of Patterson's business, see "The New Car Built by Patterson & Sons," *CD* (Big Weekend ed.), October 2, 1915, 1; and "Race Firm in Auto Industry, Patterson & Sons Keeping Abreast of Times, Leading Wagon and Carriage Makers of Ohio," *CD* (Big Weekend ed.), January 8, 1916, 1. The cost of the ReVere in 1918 is noted in "The 'Racy' Revere," *Cycle and Automobile Trade Journal*, July 1, 1918, 60. For additional information on the ReVere, see Cass County Historical Society, "ReVere Motor Car Company," http://casscountyin.tripod.com/CCHS/ReVere.html; and Daniel Strohl, "ReVere's Ride: This Classic Had It All, Including a Man Who Doomed It," *Hemmings Classic Car*, vol. 17, February 2006, https://www.hemmings.com/magazine/hcc/2006/02/ReVere-s-Ride/1282137.html. In 1918, Fred and August Duesenberg, designers of the Duesenberg engine, had sold the rights to its production to the Rochester Motor Company, Rochester, N.Y. This company produced the engine installed in the 1921 ReVere. See Phillips, *Cars, 1895–1965*, 228. The trip to the Indy 500 by Headen and his friends is described in "City News in Brief, Motor to Speedway Races," *CD* (nat. ed.), June 4, 1921, 4.

16. Stretch was the son of German immigrants and was listed as a "commission salesman" living on Ainslie Street in the 1910 Census. See *Thirteenth United States Census: 1910*, Household of Charles Stretch, Chicago, Cook Co., Ill., ED 280, sheet 16A. In 1920, he was listed as a "wholesale salesman." See *Fourteenth United States Census: 1920*, Household of Charles Stretch, Chicago, Cook Co., Ill., ED 774, sheet 3B. Dwyer's affiliation with the Eighteenth Ward organization is noted in "Mrs. Grogan Saw Murder in Club Run by Husband," *CT*, January 29, 1919, 1. Dwyer is noted as a clerk for the Election Commission in the 1920 Census. See *Fourteenth United States Census: 1920*, Household of Patrick Dwyer, Chicago, Cook Co., Ill., ED 1048, sheet 4B. Dwyer's involvement in the burglaries in 1918 and his arrest for the murder of Charles Stillwell are noted in "Art Institute Gems Clew to Club Murder, Slaying at Grogan's Is Traced by Mystery Phone Calls," *CT*, January 20, 1919, 1, 6. Dwyer's indictment for cracking the safe of the Waiters Association Club at 105 West Madison Street in 1923 is discussed in Testimony (Resumed) of Virgil W. Peterson, Operating Director, Chicago Crime Commission, in U.S. Superintendent of Documents, *Investigation of Improper Activities in the Labor or Management Field*, 12532.

17. Articles of Incorporation of Headen Motor Company, Certificate No. 109691, filed December 1, 1921, box 1628, no. 109691, Records of the Secretary of State, State of Illinois, Cook Co. The South Wood Street address Dwyer gave on the incorporation papers matches that of the Patrick Dwyer charged with burglary and murder in 1918–19.

18. "When You Come to Chicago, Exhibitors in the Greer Bldg., Adjoining Coliseum," *Motor Age*, January 1922, 9–10; Patrick J. Dwyer, Annual Report of Headen Motor Company, filed March 21, 1923, box 1628, file 691, Records of the Secretary of State, State of Illinois, Cook Co., Ill. White and Wilson are identified as the officers for 1922 in "C. M. White Entertained," *CD* (nat. ed.), July 8, 1922, 3. Wilson was a member of the executive committee of the Colored Commercial Club in Omaha. See "Colored Commercial Club Has Heavy Concert Sale, Half of Auditorium Already Sold Out for Program to Be Given May 31," *Omaha World*

Herald, May 21, 1922, 12; "Spirituals to Be Sung," *Omaha World Herald*, May 21, 1922, 37. In 1918, Wilson was elected secretary of the Douglas County Republican League. See "Douglas County Republican League," *Omaha World Herald*, July 24, 1918, 6.

19. A top speed for the Model T Ford of 40–45 mph is noted in Tata, *How Detroit Became the "Automotive Capitol [sic] of the World,"* 42. The ReVere's top speed is noted in "The New Re Vere Motor Car, Manufactured by The Re Vere Motor Car Corporation of Logansport, Indiana," *The Dragon*, November 1919, 9–12.

20. See Headen Motor Company brochure, 1922. The design of the Temme Heater is described in "A New Automobile Exhaust Heater for Protection Against Cold," *American Garage and Auto Dealer*, November 1919, 58; "Temme Exhaust Heater, "*Motor Age*, December 1920, 40; and "New Products," *Motor Record*, December 1920, 43. The new device would prove extremely popular with car buyers, and it soon was considered a necessity in cold climates such as Chicago's.

21. Roberts' showroom is discussed in Coulter, *Take Up the Black Man's Burden*, 119, and in Restuccia, with Gibson and Sanders, *An Extraordinary Man*, 29, 47, 59–61. Cary Lewis's role in the National Negro Business League is noted in Lester, *Rube Foster in His Time*, 114–15. See also Bruce, *The Kansas City Monarchs*, 18; and Jules Tygiel, "Unresolved Strivings," 82. For an example of the *Defender's* coverage of the new league, see "Baseball Men Write League Constitution: Western Circuit Organized, to Become Effective April 1, 1921," *CD* (Big Weekend ed.), February 21, 1920, 9. Howard had previously been an owner in the league. In December 1920, he, along with Harry St. Clair, purchased the team known as the Dayton Marcos. The Marcos, one of the league's original teams, finished in the cellar in the first season and subsequently withdrew. Moving to Columbus, Ohio, and reorganized by the new owners, the team played in the league under the name of the Columbus Buckeyes before being disbanded in 1921. Howard's purchase of the team and its move to Columbus are noted in untitled article, *Kansas City Sun*, December 25, 1920, Sports-Theatricals-Athletics Page, 4; and "From Harry St. Clair and Dock Smith, the New Owners of the Columbus, Ohio Team Formerly the Dayton Marcos" (letter), *Kansas City Sun*, December 25, 1920, 4. The failure of the Buckeyes is noted in Lanctot, *Fair Dealing and Clean Playing*, 91.

22. "Headen Breaks Record Running to Kansas City, in the 'Headen,' Car of Own Make and Design, Shatters Previous Auto Marks," *CD* (city ed.), July 8, 1922, 3. Whether 20.1 hours was a road record, as claimed by the *Defender*, is difficult to validate. The bulk of pre-1931 files maintained by the Contest Board of the American Automobile Association, which sanctioned all records, have been lost.

23. The trip to Long's farm and accommodations afforded Phil Jones and Jack White are noted in "Entertained," *CD* (nat. ed.), July 8, 1922, 3. Accommodations afforded Headen, Wilson, and Thomas and Roberts's agreement to put the Pace Setter in his showroom are noted in "New 'Green Dragon' in Record Run," *CD* (nat. ed.), August 5, 1922, 11. Headen's address at the Woodmen banquet is noted in "C. M. White Entertained," *CD* (nat. ed.), July 8, 1922, 3. Baker's role in the Woodmen is described in "Kansas City Camp No. 5 of American Woodmen Organized at Y.M.C.A," *Kansas City Sun*, December 2, 1916, 1. His agreement to become western representative is discussed in "Headen Breaks Record Running to Kansas City, in the 'Headen,' Car of Own Make and Design, Shatters Previous Auto Marks," *CD* (city ed.), July 8, 1922, 3; and "New 'Green Dragon' in Record Run," *CD* (nat. ed.), August 5, 1922, 11.

24. Richardson's ride with Headen is noted in "City News in Brief," *CD* (nat. ed.), August 12, 1922, 4. Sarah Rector's parents, Joseph and Rosa Rector, were citizens of the Creek Nation by virtue of their own parents having been owned by Creek slaveholders. Sarah, too, was a citizen. Thus when Indian-held lands were broken up under the Dawes Allotment Act, between 1887 and 1907, all members of Sarah's family, including herself, received parcels of land. Oil was discovered on Sarah's allotment in 1912 and eventually yielded enormous wealth. By 1921 Sarah's mother Rosa owned three cars, and when Sarah turned twenty in March 1922, gaining control of her own money, she quickly followed in her mother's footsteps. See "Richest Negress in U.S. Pays $25 Fine for Son," *Moberly Evening Democrat*, September 29, 1921, 1; Bolden, *Searching for Sarah Rector*, 39, 47.

25. "Sarah Rector Orders Car from Headen Motor Works," *CD* (nat. ed.), September 30, 1922, 3.

26. Headen Motor Company brochure, 1922. Johnson's presence in Birmingham is noted in Katherine Kent Lambert, "Alabama, Birmingham, Ala.," *CD* (nat. ed.), September 16, 1922, 19. The initial cost of shares is noted in "Headen Motor Company," *CD* (nat. ed.), August 26, 1922, 2. The cost paid in November is taken from receipt, November 8, 1922, The Headen Motor Company, Inc., to John Benj. Green, Name File, 1896–1968, box 5, folder (Headen, L. A., 1918–1922), Green-Driver Collection, LC.

27. Joseph Jones described the car Headen drove on this trip as Headen's "sport model." See "Says Jonesy: The Liberty," *CD* (nat. ed.), December 2, 1922, 6. Barrett spoke at the Lafayette Presbyterian Lyceum several times between April and July 1913, while Tena was still living in Jersey City. See "Out of Town Correspondence, Jersey City, N.J.," *NYA*, April 24, 1913, 3; "Out of Town Correspondence, Jersey City, N.J.," *NYA*, May 29, 1913, 3; "Out of Town Correspondence, Jersey City, N.J.," *NYA*, July 13, 1913, 3; "Out of Town Correspondence, Jersey City, N.J.," *NYA*, April 9, 1914, 3; "News of Greater New York," *NYA*, May 7, 1914, 8; "Important Conference," *NYA*, September 25, 1913, 2. For biographical information on Barrett, and mention of his religious activities, see entry for Harold W. Barrett, in Mather, *Who's Who of the Colored Race*, 20; and "Important Conference," *NYA*, September 25, 1913, 2. Barrett's appearance at Grace Presbyterian is noted in "H. W. Barrett to Speak at Grace Lyceum Sunday," *CD* (nat. ed.), October 15, 1921, 4.

28. *The Freeman*, quoted in "Comments by The Age Editors on Sayings of Other Editors," *NYA*, October 21, 1922, 7; *St. Louis Globe-Democrat*, quoted in "New 'Green Dragon' in Record Run," *CD* (nat. ed.), August 5, 1922, 11.

29. "Sarah Rector Orders Car from Headen Motor Works," *CD* (nat. ed.), September 30, 1922, 3; *Fourteenth United States Census: 1920*, Household of John P. Crawford, Nashville, Davidson Co., Tenn., ED 16, sheet 19B; "Tennessee, Nashville, Davidson Co.," in Patterson, *Patterson's American Educational Directory*, 468. Crawford had served as Tennessee's Grand Chancellor for at least a decade. See "Dr. J. P. Crawford Re-Elected," *Nashville Globe*, July 19, 1912, 1, 5; "Tennessee Pythians to Erect Widows' Home," *NYA*, July 22, 1915, 7; "Trail of the National Negro Business League in the South," *NYA*, August 12, 1922, 2; "Hutto, G. C., K. of P., Ga., Died Attending Grand Lodge," *NYA*, July 29, 1922, 2. Crawford was a contemporary of John W. Jones, whose position as North Carolina Grand Chancellor is discussed in "Funds Mis-Handled, Investigation into Condition of Fraternal Insurance," *Raleigh Times*, July 27, 1911, 7; "Public Meeting of Colored Pythians," *Raleigh Times*, July 23, 1912, 5; "Dr. J. W. Jones of Twin-City Re-Elected Grand Chancellor," *WSJ*, July 19, 1913, 8;

"Dr. J. W. Jones Is Re-Elected," *WSJ*, July 12, 1914, 8; "Negro Knights Here," *The Advance*, July 23, 1915, 1; "Colored Pythians in Indignation Meeting," *Twin-City Sentinel*, August 9, 1916, 15; "Colored K. of P. Lodge Adjourns, Dr. J. W. Jones Re-elected Grand Chancellor," *WSJ*, July 20, 1917, 6; Charles Stewart, "Negro Pythians on Second Day," *Charlotte News*, July 16, 1919, 15; "Jones Re-Elected Head of Negro Pythians," *WSJ*, July 25, 1920, 21; "Negro Pythians Close Sessions, Dr. J. W. Jones Chosen Grand Chancellor, Big Parade and Barbecue," *Twin-City Sentinel*, July 21, 1922, 12; and H. A. Wiseman, "News of Colored People, Pythians Requested to Assemble," *WSJ*, April 14, 1927, 15. As early as 1909, Barrett held the position of "grand inner guard" for the New Jersey Pythians. See "Our Secret Societies, News and Gossip Concerning the Fraternities," *Trenton Evening Times*, October 24, 1909, 27.

30. Jones, "Says Jonesy," *CD* (nat. ed.), December 2, 1922, 6; "Negro Automobile Company to Manufacture Fine Car," *Dallas Express*, October 14, 1922, 1. Jordan, too, provided Headen fraternal connections. He had in 1919 served as vice supreme commander of a group of men and women known as the Golden Chain of the World and he was a member of the Pilgrim Grand Lodge, also a mixed group whose organizational affiliations are unclear. See "Marshall," *Dallas Express*, July 12, 1919, 8.

31. The *Defender* mistakenly reported the stock amount as $225,000. The actual certificate of increase shows it was $250,000. See "Headen Motor Company Elects New Officers," *CD* (nat. ed.), January 12, 1923, 2; Certificate of Inc. in Stock $40,000 to $250,000 of Headen Motor Company, filed February 7, 1923, Certificate No. 15764, box 1628, no. 109691, Records of the Secretary of State, State of Illinois, Cook Co. Searetta Jane Garner was born in 1892 in Logansport, Indiana. In 1917, she married barber Felix Sawyer. See *Fourteenth United States Census: 1920*, Household of Ciretta [Searetta] Sawyer, Chicago, Cook Co., Ill., ED 1901, sheet 3A; *Fifteenth United States Census: 1930*, Household of Searetta Sawyer, Chicago, Ward 5, Cook Co., Ill., ED 16-193, sheet 35B. Sawyer's relationship to Salem Tutt Whitney is noted in L. Baynard Whitney, "Simple Rites Mark Funeral Services for Late S. T. Whitney," *NYA*, February 24, 1934, 2.

32. Advertisement, T. H. Pinckney, *Southern Indicator*, November 14, 1914, 5; "Locals and Personals," *Southern Indicator*, February 3, 1923, 3. Identification of Murray as an agent for Headen Motor appears in untitled item, *NYA*, March 24, 1923, 4, reprinted from *Southern Indicator*. Henry Tyson was on the advisory board of the Bethel Literary and Historical Association, which selected speakers for the organization, when Murray spoke before it in 1892. See untitled flyer, January 1892, in subject file 1884–1962, folder (Bethel Literary and Historical Association), microfilm reel #13, counter 691–93, Terrell Papers, LC. Three years later, in 1896, Murray gave the keynote address for a YMCA fundraiser Tyson helped organize in Washington. See "Carnival of Athletes," *Washington Evening Star*, February 25, 1896, 10. The two men more than a decade later served together on the Terrell reception committee in June 1914. See "Judge Terrell Given Reception by Citizens," *NYA*, June 4, 1914, 1. Murray's life, political career, and his patents, all for agricultural implements, are documented in Marszalek, *A Black Congressman in the Age of Jim Crow*; and Rosenberg, "George Washington Murray," 388–90. Headen and Murray's presence in Camden is noted in "No. Carolina, Camden, N.C.," *CD* (nat. ed.), April 7, 1923, 19.

33. Street is named as vice president of the Central Industrial Insurance Co. in the Tampa city directory, 1924, 761. His marriage to Idella Armwood is documented in James L. Street

and Idella S. Armwood, marriage record, September 26, 1900, Hillsborough Co., Fla., FamilySearch.com, *Florida, Marriages*. His role (along with that of Idella, Idella's father Levin, and her sister Blanche Armwood Beatty) in organizing the Tampa chapter of the National Urban League in 1922 is discussed in "The Community Chest, The Urban League," *Tampa Tribune*, March 22 1924, 19. Blanche was elected the organization's first executive secretary. The Central Industrial Insurance Co. was formed in 1922. See State of Florida, Office of the Secretary of State, "Domestic Corporations," 60. For a history of the company, see the *Florida Sentinel*, October 11, 1947. Street and Beatty joined Headen Motor Company in January 1924. See "Headen Motor Co. Elects Officers," *CD* (city ed.), January 19, 1924, 9.

34. Dr. Jerry lodged with the principal of Tampa's Harlem School, Christine Meachem, with whom Beatty had long worked. See *Fourteenth United States Census: 1920*, Household of Robert Meachem, Tampa, Hillsborough Co., Fla., ED 47, sheet 19A. In 1922, Beatty and Genevieve Cannon served together on the executive committee of the Anti-Lynching Crusaders, and Beatty and George Cannon worked together in the national Republican Party. See "The Ninth Crusade," *The Crisis*, March 2, 1923, 214–17. They also worked side by side as delegates to the 1924 Republican National Convention. See Melvin Chisum, "The Republican Party and Colored America," *California Eagle*, June 27, 1924, 8. Lizzie Berry and Beatty were acquainted through women's club work. In early 1919, when Berry visited New Orleans, Beatty was employed in the city as a home extension agent and club organizer. She was among the New Orleans clubwomen who proffered Berry "much social attention" and "an ovation" on her trip. See "Out of Town Correspondence, Jersey City, N.J.," *NYA*, May 3, 1919, 2. Both Berry and Beatty were also active in the National Federation of Women's Clubs and antilynching work. See "Women Deplore Lynching; Northeastern Federation Believes Government Can Stop Mob Violence," *Broad Ax*, August 24, 1912, 4; and "National Colored Women's Clubs in Biennial Meeting," *NYA*, August 19, 1922, 2. Tena remained friends with the Cannons and Lizzie Berry, visiting frequently over the years, and by October 1922 Berry and her husband John had joined the Headens in Chicago. See, for example, "The Headens Entertain," *CD* (Big Weekend ed.), November 29, 1919, 17; and (for Berry's move to Chicago) "New Jersey Colored Women's Federation," *NYA*, October 28, 1922, 2. The identity of Larramore remains a mystery. Although noted to be a Tampan, he could not be located in any extant records.

35. Headen Motor Co. brochure, 1922.

36. "Routes for the Autos, Nashville Citizens Plan to Perfect Street Car Boycott," *NYA*, September 28, 1905, 2; "The Automobiles Dedicated, Joyous Festivals Crown Fight Against Nashville 'Jim Crow,'" *NYA*, October 12, 1905, 1. For a discussion of the use of jitneys by blacks to avoid segregation and as the basis for business opportunities, see Franz, "The Open Road," 140. For discussions of local jitney efforts, see, for example, Chambliss, "A Question of Progress and Welfare," online; Cassanello, "Avoiding 'Jim Crow,'" 435–57; Dressman, "Yes, We Have No Jitneys!" 116–24. For a good discussion of the use of jitneys in St. Louis, see Pointer, "Reinventing the Jitney in St. Louis." Writers frequently felt torn between the appeal of the automobile and its inordinate costs. See, for example, William H. Ferris, "The Automobile Craze," *Negro World*, June 10, 1922, 6. But a great many ultimately embraced it. Quotes from "Automobiles and the Segregation Problem," *Negro World*, September 20, 1924, 4; and George Schuyler, "Traveling Jim Crow," *American Mercury*, August 1930, 423–32.

232 Notes to Chapter Six

37. The search for "friendly" towns when on the road is noted in "Pleasant Automobile Trip to Wilmette Last Sunday Afternoon, Eight Autos Joined the Cavalcade," *Broad Ax*, August 11, 1923, 3. When the National Negro League was formed in 1920, several of those attending stayed at the YMCA in Kansas City. See Lester, *Rube Foster in His Time*, 114. Headen himself stayed at black YMCAs, and sportswriter Frank Young noted that he called the black YMCA in Indianapolis from Danville, Indiana, to get a report on the weather when on his way to the inaugural Gold & Glory Sweepstakes in 1924. For Headen's stay at the 12th Street YMCA when he visited Washington, D.C., in 1917, see "Society," *CD* (Big Weekend ed.), May 5, 1917, 5. For Young's reliance on the Indianapolis YMCA, see Frank Young, "Sidelights of the Big 100-Mile Derby," *CD* (city ed.), August 9, 1924, pt. 1, 10. The National Urban League of Tampa's request to the Traveler's Aid Society, and the leadership positions of the branch held at that time by Levin Armwood and Idella Street, are noted in "Tampa Urban League Holds Its Annual Meeting and Election," *Tampa Tribune*, March 13, 1924, 9.

38. "Form Automobile Assn.," *CD* (city ed.), September 27, 1924, pt. 1, 4.

39. Untitled item, *Colorado Statesman*, November 20, 1909, 4; Lee A. Pollard, "Automobiling as a Profession," *NYA*, May 26, 1910, 7; "Learn to Repair Automobiles and Aeroplanes," advertisement, *CD* (nat. ed.), November 26, 1921, 12. Felton would advertise regularly in the *Defender*, *The Crisis*, and other national publications in the 1920s.

40. "Negro-Built and Foreign Autos to Be Featured in Election Day Auto Races," *NYA*, October 25, 1924, 6; "First Auto Race Meet in the East," *Negro World*, October 25, 1924, 2; "Speakers Arouse Big Luncheon Club," *PC*, October 25, 1924, 3.

41. "Negro-Built and Foreign Autos to Be Featured," *NYA*, October 25, 1924, 6.

42. Bradford's residence at 3111 S. State, the same address as the Goins Tonsorial Parlor, is noted by Sylvester Russell. Bradford committed suicide there in January 1915, only months after Coleman began working at Goins's. See Russell, "Chicago Weekly Review," *The Freeman*, November 14, 1914, 5; and December 12, 1914, 5. For descriptions of the newly renovated barbershop, see Cary B. Lewis, "Goins Tonsorial Parlor," *The Freeman*, July 4, 1914, 1, and "Clifford Clark an Expert," *The Freeman*, June 18, 1914, 1. Coleman was already working at Goins's by September 1914. See "[The] Cream of Chicago Manicurists, Young Ladies Who Have Put [the] City's Tonsorial Parlors on a Plane with the [Best in the World]," pt. 1 of 2, *CD* (City ed.), March 3, 1917 [2]. For Bradford's obituary, see "Fred S. [sic] Bradford, Aviator Commits Suicide," *CD* (Big Weekend ed.), January 16, 1915, 4.

43. For biographical accounts of Coleman's life and career, see Rich, *Queen Bess*, and Snider, "Flying to Freedom," 134–237. For a description of the airplane's use in the Tulsa Race Riot, see Snider, "'Great Shadow in the Sky,'" 105–46. Quotes from Coleman are from "Aviatrix Must Sign Away Life to Learn Trade," *CD* (nat. ed.), October 8, 1921, 2; Ralph Eliot, "Bessie Coleman Says Good Will Come from Hurt, Wants World to Know She Is Going to Fly Again; Says Escape Proves It's Tame," *CD* (nat. ed.), March 10, 1923, 3; Robert Paul Sachs, letter to the editor, *California Eagle*, March 4, 1923, 1; and "Flying Circus Unusual Event to Be Repeated," *Houston Informer*, June 27, 1925, 1.

44. William Jenifer Powell was the son of hairdresser Lula Jenifer Powell and the stepson of barber Louis N. Powell. See *Thirteenth United States Census: 1910*, Household of Louis Powell, Chicago, Cook Co., Ill., ED 242, sheet 7B; *Fourteenth United States Census: 1920*, Household of Louis Powell, Chicago, Cook Co., Ill., ED 172, sheet 5A. Louis Powell and Lulu Jenifer

married in 1907 and soon moved to 3513 S. Dearborn Street. By 1915 they had relocated to East 36th Street, where they opened a barber shop and salon in their home. See entry for Louis N. Powell and Lulu Jenifer, marriage record, September 25, 1907, Ancestry.com, *Cook County, Illinois, Marriage Index*; *Thirteenth United States Census: 1910*, Household of Louis Powell, Chicago, Cook Co., Ill., ED 242, sheet 7B; entry for Louis Powell, Chicago city directory, 1915, 1320; and entry for Mme. I. [L.] N. Powell, "Hairdressing Parlors," in *Black's Blue Book: Directory of Chicago's Active Colored People*, 1917, 18. For William Powell's service as a lieutenant in the 365th Infantry, see Scott, *Scott's Official History*, 478; and "Soldier Gives Facts on Slur to 365th Flag," *CD* (city ed.), July 14, 1923, 2.

45. Powell graduated from the University of Illinois in 1922. See "Chicago Boys Receive Degrees at Illinois," *CD* (city ed.), June 17, 1922, 4. His filling stations are described in "Automatic Air-Meters at Powell's Garage," *CD* (city ed.), May 24, 1924, 10; "Powell Opens Service Station Number 3," *CD* (city ed.), June 27, 1925, 10; and "William Powell Opens New Greasing Station," *CD* (city ed.), June 26, 1926, 3. Plans for his garage are noted in "A Sign of Progress," *CD* (city ed.), August 23, 1924, pt. 2, 5. Powell incorporated his garage in 1925, See certificate no. 21641, Articles of Incorporation of Powell's Auto Service (Inc.), June 13, 1925, Chicago, Ill., box 1814, no. 128091, Office of the Secretary of State, State of Illinois, Cook Co. Photographs of Powell, his garage, and one of his filling stations appear in Taitt, *Souvenir of Negro Progress*.

46. For the best discussion of Powell's West Coast aviation activities, see Von Hardesty's introduction to the reissue of Powell's autobiography (Powell, *Black Aviator*). See also Snider, "William Jenifer Powell," 458–60. For the first articulation of Powell's full vision, see his 1934 autobiography, *Black Wings*, and his 1935 film "Unemployment, the Negro, and Aviation."

Chapter Seven

1. Alvin D. Smith, "Racing Association Elects Officers; Bars Chicagoan," *CD* (nat. ed.), April 18, 1925, 10.

2. The crowd at the 1924 Indy 500 was estimated at between 135,000 and 145,000 spectators. See "Record Crowd Sees Race at Speedway," *Indianapolis Star*, May 31, 1924, 1.

3. The Savannah association is noted in "Colored Auto Race Drivers in Own Cars in Competition, Negro Men's Automobile Racing Association of Savannah, Ga., Holds Semi-Annual Auto Races on Thanksgiving Day," *NYA*, December 10, 1921, 5. The early Detroit association is mentioned in Smith, "Racing Association Elects Officers," *CD* (nat. ed.), April 18, 1925, 10.

4. Alvin D. Smith, "Malcolm Hannon Winner in Big Auto Derby," *CD* (city ed.), August 9, 1924, pt. 1, 10.

5. Descriptions of Headen's leading the parade appear in "Ten Thousand See First National 100-Mile Event Go to Indianapolis Driver," *CD* (city ed.), August 9, 1924, 10; "Sidelights of the Big 100-Mile Derby," *CD* (city ed.), August 9, 1924, pt. 1, 10; and "First Auto Derby Successfully Run at Indianapolis," *California Eagle*, August 15, 1924, Sport Page [9]. Harry Earl was a steam-engine specialist for the CI&W and also managed the Walnut Gardens Speedway outside the city, and Oscar Schilling was a mechanical engineer for the CI&W. For information on Rucker, Dunnington, Earl, and Schilling, see Gould, *For Gold and Glory*, 36–41. Earl and Schilling's employment by the CI&W Railroad is noted in Wiggins, "'Black Athletes in White Men's Games,'" 189.

6. "Change 100-Mile Derby to 100-Miles of Auto Racing," *CD* (city ed.), August 30, 1924, 10.

7. "Entries Pour in for Auto Race at Hawthorne, Sept. 14," *CD* (city ed.), September 6, 1924, 12; Armstrong, *Louis Armstrong, in His Own Words*, 56.

8. "Two Killed in Chicago Auto Race, Driver and Spectator Who Ran Across the Track Dead from Collision," *CD* (city ed.), September 20, 1924, 1, 11.

9. Armstrong, *Louis Armstrong*, 57. For a discussion of Wiley's racing activities and death, see Gould, *For Gold and Glory*, 62–65.

10. In 1917, Bottoms was a retail liquor dealer. See William Bottoms's draft registration card, Ancestry.com, *U.S., World War I Draft Registration Cards*. He may later have been a business partner with Jefferies in the illegal distilling of alcohol once Prohibition took effect in 1920. Jefferies's backdoor activities are noted in Baldwin, *Chicago's New Negroes*, 48–49. The Chicago Colored Auto Racing Association, headquartered at the Dreamland Café (3518 S. State Street), was at times called the Chicago Colored Speedway Association. For a description of derby events, see "Change 100-Mile Derby to 100-Miles of Auto Racing," *CD* (city ed.), August 30, 1924, 10; and "Entries Pour in for Auto Race at Hawthorne, Sept. 14," *CD* (city ed.), September 6, 1924, 12. Jefferies was identified as general manager in "Two Killed in Chicago Auto Race," *CD* (city ed.), September 20, 1924, 1, 11. Bottoms and Jefferies sublet Hawthorne Racetrack from John Owen, head of the National Motor Speedway Association, who the previous spring contracted for sole use of the track for 1924. See "New Body Plans Auto Races at Hawthorne," *Chicago Sunday Tribune*, April 20, 1924, pt. 2, 4. Dunnington's criticism is discussed in Gould, *For Gold and Glory*, 63. The *Defender*'s mocking response appears in "Auto Drivers Ready for Wave of Starter's Flag Sunday," *CD* (nat. ed.), September 13, 1924, 9.

11. James L. Street, death certificate, March 30, 1924, Tampa, Hillsborough Co., Fla., FamilySearch.com, *Florida, Deaths*. (Note: FamilySearch.com contains a transcription error that lists Street's name as W. S. Street. However, viewing the original record confirms the name as Jas. L. Street.) Barrett's death is noted in Ancestry.com, *Illinois, Deaths and Stillbirths Index*. Roland Tyson's death is noted in Eve Lynn, "Young Philadelphia Boy Drowns at Asbury Park," *PC*, June 28, 1924, 12. Marie's stay in Greensboro is noted in Lynn, "Eve Lynn Chats 'Bout Society and Folks," *PC*, July 12, 1924, 12; and "Greensboro," *NYA*, July 26, 1924, 8. Guyrene Tyson met Dr. George Simkins of Greensboro in 1922, when she was teaching in the city schools. They married June 30, 1923 (see "Greensboro, N.C.," *NYA*, July 14, 1923, 5).

12. "Speakers Arouse Big Luncheon Club," *PC*, October 25, 1924, 3.

13. For coverage of the race in the *Defender* and in New York papers, see "Speed Kings Will Invade Gotham Nov. 4," *CD* (city ed.), October 18, 1924, pt. 2, 10; "New York Prepares for the Auto Races," *CD* (city ed.), October 25, 1924, pt. 2, 10; William E. Clark, "Sport Comment, New York to See All Colored Auto Race on Election Day at Ho-Ho-Kus Race Track, N.J.," *NYA*, October 18, 1924, 6; "Negro-Built and Foreign Autos to Be Featured in Election Day Auto Races," *NYA*, October 25, 1924, 6; and "First Auto Race Meet in the East," *Negro World*, October 25, 1924, 2. "Wonders" quote from "Plan Eastern Auto Races on Election Day in Jersey," *PC*, October 18, 1924, 12. Encouragement to come see Headen appeared in untitled advertisement, *CD* (nat. ed.), November 1, 1924, A4.

14. "Speakers Arouse Big Luncheon Club," *PC*, October 25, 1924, 3; Alvin D. Smith, "Indiana State News, Indianapolis News," *CD* (nat. ed.), October 27, 1924, 11.

15. "Officials in Big Eastern Auto Races at Hohokus, N.J., Nov 4," *PC*, November 8, 1924, 6; "W. S. Morgan of New York Was Winner of the World Auto Race Championship," *NYA*, November 3, 1924, 3; Floyd G. Calvin, "Thousands Witness Election Day Auto Races," *PC*, November 8, 1924, 6.

16. "W. S. Morgan of New York Was Winner," *NYA*, November 3, 1924, 6.

17. "Auto Races Draw Good Crowds to HoHoKus Track," *NYA*, December 6, 1924, 6.

18. In 1920, Drye was resident at the Benning Race Track Barns. See *Fourteenth United States Census: 1920*, entry for Ollie Drye, Benning Race Track Barns, Washington, D.C., ED 255, sheet 2A. His presence on Headen's team is noted in "Joe Bruen Wins Auto Championship," *NYA*, January 31, 1925, 6. Blackman, when racing at the Louisiana State Fair in 1914, was described as from "one of the best families of Shreveport." See Salem Tutt Whitney, "Seen and Heard While Passing," *The Freeman*, November 21, 1914, 6. His participation in the Hawthorne race is recorded in "2 Killed in Chicago Auto Race: Driver and Spectator Who Ran Across Track Dead from Collision," *CD* (nat. ed.), September 20, 1924, 1, 11. His win in Minnesota is noted in Aho, "The History of Motor Sports in Northern Minnesota," 2012, http://www.racehibbing.com/Timeline4.html. Entered in the Ho-Ho-Kus race, Blackman withdrew after crashing his Duesenberg in a preliminary run. See "W. S. Morgan of New York Was Winner," *NYA*, November 3, 1924, 3. He would later race in Louisville in 1925. See Smith, "Bill Blackman Enters Blue Grass Derby," *CD* (nat. ed.), April 25, 1925, 11. Headen's southern itinerary is noted in "Plan Eastern Auto Races on Election Day in Jersey," *PC*, October 18, 1924, 12; and "Savannah All Agog for New Years Races," *BAA*, January 3, 1925, 5. The circuit already established is noted in "Colored Auto Races in Own Cars in Competition, Negro Men's Automobile Racing Association of Savannah, Ga., Holds Semi-Annual Auto Races on Thanksgiving Day—Two Autos, One Motorcycle Smashed," *NYA*, December 10, 1921, 5.

19. The date the NCAA was established is noted in "Louisville All Set for Auto Grind," *CD* (nat. ed.), May 16, 1925, 9. Headen's role as a "joint promoter" is noted in Smith, "Racing Association Elects Officers," *CD* (nat. ed.), April 18, 1925, 10.

20. "Savannah to Have Races on New Year," *BAA*, December 27, 1924, 4; "Joe Bruen Wins Auto Championship," *NYA*, January 31, 1925, 6.

21. Garland Ashcraft, "Darktown Stages Own Racing Classic; Finds Thrills Galore, African Speed Demons Do Their Stuff on Central City Park Track," *Macon Telegraph* (hereafter *MT*), February 8, 1925, 6; "Negroes Race, More Auto Contests Will Be Staged at Macon Park," *MT*, February 15, 1925, 7; "Negro Championship Automobile Races," advertisement, *MT*, February 15, 1925, 26. For a description of the Central City Park track, see Brown, *History of America's Speedways*, 175.

22. "Large Damage to School, Negro Normal Institute in Albany Flooded by Rains," *MT*, January 31, 1925, 6; "Negro Auto Races at Fair Grounds Mar. 20, Noted Negro Automobile Manufacturer Will Drive One of His Own Cars," *Albany Herald* (hereafter *AH*), March 11, 1925, 3. Headen likely knew Holley prior to going to Albany. Holley was a close friend of the Headens' personal physician in Chicago, George Cleveland Hall. Hall is noted as having treated Tena after she sprained her ankle in 1920. See "Mrs. Headen Returns," *CD* (Big Weekend ed.), January 17, 1920, 12. A fellow Lincoln University graduate of Hall's, Holley described Hall as "a warm personal friend" in his autobiography. See Holley, *You Can't Build a Chimney from the Top*, 50. Hall also gave the dedication speech for the first brick building

erected at Holley's school in 1911 and made regular trips thereafter. See, for example, "Dr. Hall's Southern Trip," *CD* (Big Weekend ed.), February 21, 1914, 2.

23. "Negro Auto Races at Fair Grounds Mar. 20," *AH*, March 11, 1925, 3; "Colored Auto Races Here Next Friday, Much Interest Shown by Negro Population in Great Event," *AH*, March 16, 1925, 3. Description of the track is from "Automobile Races to Be Held Friday, Program Which Rain Prevented to Be Offered," *AH*, January 5, 1925, 2. The Albany Fairgrounds track was located west of the city. See Brown, *History of America's Speedways*, 173.

24. Smith, "Racing Association Elects Officers," *CD* (nat. ed.), April 18, 1925, 10; Smith, "Bill Blackman Enters Blue Grass Derby," *CD* (nat. ed.), April 25, 1925, 11.

25. See, for example, Ashcraft, "Darktown Stages Own Racing Classic," *MT*, February 8, 1925, 6; and "Negro Auto Races at Fairgrounds," *AH*, March 11, 1925, 3.

26. "Indianapolis Driver Wins 75-Mile Devonshire Race," *Border Cities Star*, June 1, 1925, 12; "West Begins Series of Automobile Races," *BAA*, May 23, 1925, 8; "Louisville All Set for Auto Grind," *CD* (nat. ed.), May 16, 1925, 9.

27. Plummer was the son of Henry Vinton Plummer Sr., an army chaplain court-martialed in 1894 for his civil rights activism. The elder Plummer's experiences are discussed in a biographical sketch in Hawkins, *Black American Military Leaders*, 370. For information on the younger Plummer and his relationship with Garvey, see Vincent, *Black Power and the Garvey Movement*, 155–56, 212; Robert Hill, editor, *Marcus Garvey Papers*, vol. 2, 1982, 202; and Harold, *The Rise and Fall of the Garvey Movement in the Urban South*, 84, 93. For discussion of the UNIA's view of transportation technologies, see Snider, "'Great Shadow in the Sky,'" 105–46.

28. Plummer's tour of Savannah is noted in "Representative Negro World in City," *Savannah Tribune*, September 28, 1922, 4. The location of fourteen UNIA divisions in close proximity to Albany is noted in Rolinson, *Grassroots Garveyism*, 96.

29. Plummer's legal woes are documented in "Judge Crawford Scores Henry Plummer Hard," *Omaha Daily Bee*, February 16, 1910, 12; "Lawyer Fined; Is Sent to Jail, Henry E. [sic] Plummer Found Guilty of Obtaining Money Fraudulently in Police Court," *Omaha Daily Bee*, May 14, 1910, 4; "Pleads Guilty on Three Charges," *Evening Star*, August 13, 1915, 3; "District Court News," *Washington Post*, February 22, 1916, 5. Plummer is identified as General Counsel for Headen Motor Car Co. in entry for H. Vinton Plummer, Albany city directory, 1925, 153. For an account of the legal conflicts between Abbott and Garvey, see Michaeli, *The Defender*, 124–27, 130, 139–41, 171–72.

30. In 1925, Jefferies sponsored a race at Chicago's Thornton Speedway. See "Bill Wallace Winner of Big Auto Classic," *PC*, June 6, 1925, 13. For a list of the Four As' officers, see "Form Automobile Assn.," *CD* (city ed.), September 27, 1924, pt. 1, 4. By October 1924, J. H. Williams had also come on board as assistant secretary for the Four As. His identity, however, has not been confirmed. See "Officials in Big Eastern Auto Races at Hohokus, N.J., Nov 4," *PC*, November 8, 1924, 6. For a description of the gambling activities of Virgil Williams, Jefferies, Bottoms, and MacFarland, see Lombardo, "The Black Mafia," 47–48; Baldwin, *Chicago's New Negroes*, 48–49; Gould, *For Gold and Glory*, 48; Pacyga, *Chicago, A Biography*, 228; Lombardo, *Organized Crime in Chicago*, 72–73; "City Council Fight Bitter in Chicago, Present Incumbent Accused of Receiving $25,000 From Police-Protected Cabaret," *BAA*, December 29, 1922, 1; "Friendship Night," *CD* (Big Weekend ed.), July 12, 1919, 9; "Game, Unnoticed in 1915, Now One of the Richest Rackets in America," *NYA*, August 23, 1952, 29;

"Capt. Healy and De Priest to Be Arrested Today," *CT*, January 19, 1917, 13; "Alderman Oscar De Priest Stated at a Meeting at Bethel Church the First of This Week, That He Does Not Control Those Who Are Addicted to Vice Residing in the Second Ward," *Broad Ax*, January 20, 1917, 1; "Hoyne Cancels Graft Cases Against Healy, De Priest," *Broad Ax*, June 14, 1919, 8; "Graft and Riot Suspect Taken in Raids, Hoyne Rakes Black Belt," *CT*, August 24, 1919, 1–2; and "Frame New Laws to Help Chicago Banish Criminals," *Brooklyn Daily Eagle*, November 27, 1920, 1.

31. "New Ideas Are Outlined to Business Men at Luncheon," *CD* (nat. ed.), December 15, 1923, 11.

32. Description of the early drivers is from Averitte Corley, quoted in Gould, *For Gold and Glory*, 80. Bottle quote is from Armstrong, *Louis Armstrong*, 56. Roberta Wiggins's feelings toward Jefferies are described in Gould, *For Gold and Glory*, 50, 100, 110–12.

33. For Allimono's religious activities, see "People's Forum to Open Sunday Service at Avenue," *CD* (nat. ed.), September 2, 1922, 4. Allimono later worked for the National Baptist Publishing Board. See "Negro Bulk Plan Employees Demonstrate Their Selling Ability for Firm and Uncover Negro Purchasing Power," *NYA*, February 22, 1936, 8.

34. For mention of Lesta Bottoms and Henryene Stevens at the Indianapolis Gold and Glory race, see "Indianapolis, Ind.," *PC*, August 9, 1924, 14.

35. "Mrs. Headen Returns," *CD* (Big Weekend ed.), January 17, 1920, 12.

36. Constance Catus married Dr. Allen G. Gantt, a physician at the Home for Aged and Infirm Colored Women in Pittsburgh, in 1904. See entry for Allen G. Gantt, Lincoln University biographical catalogue, 1918, 46. Quote from "Mrs. L. A. Headen Left at Pittsburg by Train," *CD* (Big Weekend ed.), December 11, 1915, 5.

37. "The Headens Entertain," *CD* (Big Weekend ed.), November 29, 1919, 17.

38. Mrs. Cary B. Lewis was noted as president of the Grace Presbyterian Lyceum in "Grace Presbyterian Church," advertisement, *Black's Blue Book*, 1918, 38.

39. Lion quote is from Juli Jones, "How Things Have Changed," *CD* (nat. ed.), October 4, 1924, 10. Local color quote is from "Speed Kings Will Invade Gotham Nov. 4," *CD* (city ed.), October 18, 1924, pt. 2, 10.

Chapter Eight

1. For descriptions of the new growth in Albany, see "Spend Million for Buildings, Previous Record Exceeded by $350,000 in 1924 in Albany," *MT*, January 3, 1925, 7; "Romance of Development Seen in Cities' Building," *Augusta Chronicle*, February 8, 1925, 7; "Albany to Have New Hotel, Half-Million Dollar Building Project Will Begin Monday," *MT*, January 10, 1925, 2; "City Extended, Albany to Take on New Territory Because of Bill," *MT*, August 23, 1925, 3; "Albany School Gets Students," *MT*, February 8, 1925, 14; "Municipal Golf Course Planned," *MT*, January 3, 1925, 3; "Three Conventions Secured by Albany," *MT*, January 27, 1926, 7.

2. Albany's seven railroads, its population in 1925, and its being the home of several car manufacturers are noted in "Albany," Albany city directory, 1925, 6. For the addition of new trains, see "New Trains to Run," *MT*, September 27, 1925, 30. For additional information on auto manufacturers in Albany, see John H. Mock, "Albany, the Metropolis of Southwest Georgia," *MT*, May 8, 1923, 48. For Dougherty's minimal tax rate, see "Dougherty Tax Rate Very

Low, Progressive Albany Attracts Attention of Entire State," *MT*, September 1925, 8. McIntosh's and others' plans for Albany are described in "Editor McIntosh of Albany Herald Describes Value of Diversification," *Marietta Journal*, December 11, 1924, 12; and "Georgia Gleanings, Think About Georgia," *Augusta Chronicle*, March 6, 1925, 4. For the good roads movement in Albany, see "Highway Paved, Every Foot of Dixie in Dougherty County Is Improved," *MT*, July 30, 1924, 5; "Paving Contract Not Yet Awarded," *MT*, August 22, 1925, 3; "To Pave 59 City Blocks, Albany Plans Extensive Paving Operation in Fall," *MT*, August 2, 1925, 9; "Albany Plans More Paving," *MT*, January 16, 1926, 3; "Florida's Boom Offers Georgia Big Opportunity," *MT*, June 21, 1925, 9; "Motor Tour Is Planned, Albany Seeking to Arouse Interest in Florida Short Route," *MT*, February 1, 1926, 9. At least one other new car company, the Zettle-Jones Co., opened just before Headen's. See *Iron Age*, April 1, 1926, 1039.

3. U.S. Bureau of the Census, *Negroes in the United States, 1920–1932*, 2nd ed., 56–57, 189–90, 195, 692, 705. Holley's position in the Pythians is noted in "Georgia Pythians Hold Grand Lodge at Macon," *NYA*, July 18, 1925, 3, and Holley, *You Can't Build a Chimney from the Top*, 139. Types of black-owned businesses in Albany is from a survey of the 1920 U.S. Census for Albany, Georgia.

4. Born in Augusta, Georgia, Henry Aloysias Petit relocated with his family to Savannah as a young man. There, like his father Henry James Petit, he became an engineer on the SAL. (The elder Petit was killed in a train derailment outside Columbia, S.C., in 1917.) Petit moved to Albany in 1921 to work for the Atlantic Coast Line Railroad. See *Twelfth United States Census: 1900*, Household of Henry J. Petit, Savannah, Chatham Co., Ga., ED 55, Sheet 14A; entry for Henry A. Petit, Savannah city directory, 1916, 439; "Train Hits an Open Switch; Engineer Is Killed, Others Hurt," *Tampa Morning Tribune*, January 8, 1917, 1; Henry Aloysias Petit, draft registration card, Ancestry.com, *U.S. World War I Draft Registration Cards*; entry for Henry A. Petit, Savannah city directory, 1920, 425; *Fourteenth United States Census: 1920*, Household of Henry A. Petit, Savannah, Chatham Co., Ga., ED 65, Sheet 3B; entries for Henry A. Petit, Albany city directories, 1922 (194) and 1925 (151). Petit sold Paige cars as an independent agent and also worked as a salesman for the Kelley Chevrolet Company. See entries for Henry A. Petit, Albany city directories, 1928–29 (233) and 1930–31 (233), and *Fifteenth United States Census*, 1930, Household of Henry Petite [Petit], Albany, Dougherty Co., Ga., ED 48-8, sheet 17A.

5. Little is known of the origins of William and Emma V. Wynn. Both native Georgians, they married in 1901. In 1910, they were living in Thomasville, Georgia, but by 1919 had moved to Albany, where Emma opened her salon and William a café. See *Thirteenth United States Census: 1910*, Household of Willie Wynn, Thomasville, Dougherty Co., Ga., ED 150, sheet 5A; *Fourteenth United States Census: 1920*, Household of William Wynn, Albany, Dougherty Co., Ga., Militia District 945, ED 58, sheet 13B; *Fifteenth United States Census: 1930*, Household of William Wynn, Albany, Dougherty Co., Ga., Militia District 945, ED 48-10, sheet 7A; entries for William and Emma Wynn in Albany city directories, 1922 (256) and 1925 (203). The name of Emma Wynn's beauty parlor is documented in "Bottled Beauty for Everybody," *CD* (Big Weekend ed.), November 13, 1920, 11. She was identified as a state organizer for the Federation in "Georgia State, Gainesville, Ga.," *CD* (nat. ed.), August 23, 1930, 17. Her early charity activities are noted in "Georgia, Albany, Ga.," *CD* (nat. ed.), December 29, 1923, 14. William Wynn was identified as a founding member of the Albany chapter of the NAACP

in 1919, "Application for Charter of Albany, Ga., Branch of the National Association for the Advancement of Colored People," January 2, 1919, Part I: Branch Files, 1910–1947, Georgia, box I:G43, folder 1 (Albany, Ga., 1919–1933), NAACP Papers, LC. Note: William Wynn is not to be confused with William Anthony Wynne of Albany. William Anthony Wynne was born in the city in 1885 and earned a B.A. from Fisk University in 1905. Afterward he taught mathematics at the Theological and Industrial College in Holly Springs, Mississippi. In 1910, he was back in Albany, living with his mother and teaching in the city's public schools, but by 1918 had left again, this time to teach in Knoxville, Tennessee. He would remain in Knoxville until at least 1920. See *Twelfth United States Census: 1900*, Household of Jane Wynn[e], Albany, Dougherty Co., Ga., ED 45, sheet 17A; entry for William Anthony Wynn[e] in "Alumni, Class of 1905," in Fisk University catalogue, 1906–7, 86; *Thirteenth United States Census: 1910*, Household of Jane Wynn[e], Albany, Dougherty Co., Ga., Militia District 1097, ED 72, sheet 9A; William Anthony Wynne, draft registration card, Ancestry.com, U.S., *World War I Draft Registration Cards*; and *Fourteenth United States Census: 1920*, Household of William A. Wynne, Knoxville, Knox Co., Tenn., ED 82, sheet 5A. Wynne eventually moved to Jamaica, L. I. See William Anthony Wynne, draft registration card, Ancestry.com, *U.S. World War II Draft Registration Cards*. He died in Greensboro, N.C., in 1956, Ancestry.com, *North Carolina Death Certificates*.

6. Petition for Charter, Headen Motor Car Company, Dougherty Co. Superior Court, Albany, Ga., Filed June 30, 1925; and Secretary of State, *Business Services & Regulation, Corporations Registrations Ledgers, 1906–1941*, RGSGS 002-04-129, vol. 3-8689, 1924–29, in Original Document Collection, Georgia Archives, Morrow, Ga. Harris was the son of Orange and Harriet Tucker Harris, originally of Liberty County, Georgia. After marrying in 1879, his parents briefly relocated to Lincoln County before moving to Albany, where Edward was born on April 15, 1881. In 1925, Edward was employed by William A. Stokes of the Bunch Graham Company. He seems to have been the member of the group with the most resources, holding a number of local properties. See Orange Harris and Harriet Tucker, marriage certificate, December 1879, Liberty Co., Ga., Ancestry.com, *Georgia Marriage Records*; *Tenth United States Census: 1880*, Household of Orange Harris, Lincoln Co., Ga., 186 Dist. G.M., ED 69, 20; entry for Edward E. Harris of Albany, Georgia, Ancestry.com, *U.S. Social Security Applications and Claims Index* (the index lists Harris's birthdate as April 15, 1881, and identifies Orange and Harriet Harris as his parents); entry for Edward Harris in Albany city directory, 1925, 96; entry for E. E. Harris (wife Bessie), in "Return of Colored Tax Payers, Real Estate," *Dougherty County Tax Digests*, 1927, 1928, and 1929, Georgia Archives.

7. Headen's plans for an all-black company are noted in "Negroes Start Auto Plant Near Albany," *MT*, February 28, 1926, 21.

8. For Madame C. J. Walker's use of the automobile, see Bundles, *On Her Own Ground*, 52; and Baldwin, *Chicago's New Negroes*, 70–71. For Malone's purchase of the Rolls Royce, see Wilkerson, *Story of Pride, Power, and Uplift*, 74.

9. For Wynn's sale of Pearl Drops, see "Bottled Beauty for Everybody," *CD* (Big Weekend ed.), November 13, 1920, 11.

10. *Atlanta Independent*, quoted in "Comments by the Age Editors on Sayings of Other Editors," *NYA*, September 20, 1924, 4; *Norfolk Journal and Guide*, quoted in "Comments by the Age Editors on Sayings of Other Editors," *NYA*, November 7, 1924, 4; *Richmond Planet*,

quoted in "Comments by the Age Editors on Sayings of Other Editors," *NYA*, January 24, 1925, 4; *Savannah Tribune*, quoted in "Comments by the Age Editors on Sayings of Other Editors," *NYA*, July 19, 1924, 4.

11. "Noted Increase of Colored Owned Cars," *Brunswick News*, March 6, 1925, 3.

12. "Plainfield, N.J.," *NYA*, 28 March 1925, 9; Howard L. Jenkins, "Around and About Baltimore," *NYA*, August 1, 1925, 9; "Greensboro, N.C.," *NYA*, August 30, 1924, 3; "Greensboro, N.C.," *NYA*, August 30, 1924, 3.

13. Levin Armwood Sr.'s ownership of an automobile is noted in an article on an accident he had in Tampa in 1918. See "Victim of Collision Possibly Not [to] Recover," *Tampa Tribune*, August 13, 1918, 9. Armwood did recover, living another three years, but the accident prompted him to sell the orange grove and grocery store he was then operating. See "For Sale," *Tampa Tribune*, August 23, 1918, 10. For Armwood's death, see "Negro Centenarian Dies in Hospital; Head Large Family," *Tampa Tribune*, March 31, 1921, 13. For a discussion of Levin Armwood Sr., see Brown Jr., *African Americans on the Tampa Bay Frontier*, 42, 58–62.

14. For French Tyson's motor trip in 1924, see Eve Lynn, "Eve Lynn Chats 'Bout Society and Folks," *PC*, June 28, 1924, 12. Nannie, along with friend and former Scotia student Maude Young Ray, wife of Dr. Alexander Hamilton Ray, often traveled together. In January 1925, they "motored to the city of Charlotte to spend a few days with relatives and friends." The following week found them, along with Mrs. Irma D. Yancey of Charlotte, on the road to Raleigh to see Mrs. C. E. Craig. The following month Nannie and Maude drove to Greensboro to attend the christening of Guyrene's son, George Simkins Jr. See "Mrs. Jones and Mrs. Ray Return to the City," in H. A. Wiseman, "News of Colored People in the City and County," *WSJ*, January 3, 1925, 9; "Greensboro, N.C.," *NYA*, January 10, 1925, 9; and "Greensboro, N.C.," *NYA*, February 28, 1925, 9. In 1931, the *BAA* noted that "Jerry Headen and Hugh Mason motored to Winston-Salem, Sunday." See "North Carolina, Aberdeen," *BAA*, February 21, 1931, 18. Jerry, Nannie, and Louise frequently drove between Winston-Salem and Aberdeen and to nearby towns. See, for example, "Mrs. W. A. Jones Returns to City," in H. A. Wiseman, "News of Colored People in the City and County," *WSJ*, July 1, 1925, 11; "Personals," in H. A. Wiseman, "News of Colored People in the City and County," *WSJ*, February 17, 1926, 7; and "Raeford, N.C.," *New Journal and Guide*, July 14, 1934, 16. The trip between Winston-Salem and Aberdeen was 200-plus miles by train, with a change between the Southern Railroad and the Seaboard Air Line, but was less than 100 miles by car on state highway 311, which ran directly between the two cities. Routes mapped using *Map Showing Railroads & Package Car Service from Winston-Salem, N.C., to Points in the States of Virginia, North Carolina, South Carolina, & Georgia*, Winston-Salem, Industrial Commission of Winston-Salem, N.C., 1930, in "New Old Maps," https://northcarolinaroom.wordpress.com/2013/09/05/new-old-maps/; and map, *Winston-Salem, N.C., to Points in the States of Virginia, North Carolina, South Carolina, & Georgia*, Winston-Salem, Industrial Commission of Winston-Salem, N.C., 1930. Both map originals are housed in the North Carolina Collection, Forsyth Co. Library, Winston-Salem, N.C. For a description of the accident damaging Will and Nannie's home, see "Auto Cuts Down Telephone Pole, Also Brings Heavy Transformer into Dwelling House," *WSJ*, May 3, 1926, 8.

15. Louise's graduation from Winston-Salem Teachers College is noted in "Negro Director Talks on Work, Says State Has Five Institutions of Higher Learning for Colored, 51 Graduate," *WSJ*, June 4, 1926, 8. Her graduation from Pratt Institute is noted in "Mrs. Harold B. Chandler," *NYA*, March 16, 1929, 1. Her initial employment in the Colored Graded School

(later named the Morningside School) in Statesville is noted in "Teachers Named for City Schools," *Statesville Daily Record*, July 28, 1933, 1. The highway trip from Aberdeen to Statesville could be made via Routes 70/311, 90, and 26 in half the time of the train trip. The auto also gave Jerry, Nettie, and Nannie the flexibility to meet in Statesville to visit Louise together, because it freed them from having to coordinate differing train schedules and transportation from the station to Louise's home. Such a family gathering in Statesville is documented in T. E. Allison Jr., "News of Statesville Colored People," *Statesville Record & Landmark*, November 2, 1934, 2. The renaming of the Colored Graded School to Morningside School is noted in T. E. Allison Jr., "News of Statesville's Colored People," *Statesville Record & Landmark*, August 2, 1935, 3.

16. For student requests at Bordentown, see "Bordentown Students Are Attracted by Courses in Auto-Mechanics Trades," *NYA*, December 12, 1925, 9.

17. Headen's leading of the committee for the fair and Harris's assistance are noted in "Commission in Brief Session Tuesday Night," *AH*, August 26, 1925, 3; "Negroes Will Hold Fair," *MT*, August 28, 1925, 7; and "Build Race Auto Plant in Georgia," *PC* (city ed.), March 6, 1926, 2 (reprinted from *Albany Herald*). The first annual Albany South State Fair was held only six years earlier in 1919, and each year featured horse and auto racing. A separate day was set aside for blacks during the fair. In 1925, however, due to a lack of financing, no white fair was held. The lack of the white event gave Headen's efforts additional visibility. For notation of the fair's establishment, see Bacon, *Albany on the Flint*, 107. For mention of the fair's success, see "Headen Begins Work on Plant on Dawson Road, Colored Inventor Constructing Assembly Plant for Headen Car on Tom O'Connor's Property," *AH*, February 26, 1926, 1.

18. "Albany Loses 500 Negroes to the North," *MT*, December 8, 1916, 3. In 1915, Albany had over 1,700 black men of voting age. In 1920, it had 1,701 aged 21 or over. See Formwalt, "Albany," online; and "Table 10, Composition and Characteristics of the Population, for Cities of 10,000 or More: 1920," in U.S. Bureau of the Census, *Fourteenth Census of the United States Taken in the Year 1920*, 22. The *Herald*'s optimistic outlook appears in "Prosperity Picture," *AH*, reprinted in the *Atlanta Constitution*, April 4, 1920, 4.

19. The mass exodus between 1922 and 1925, and Congressman Bell's application for aid, are discussed in Grant, *The Way It Was in the South*, 295–96.

20. For the importing of unemployed white farmers to Albany, see "Farmers Find Employment," *MT*, November 4, 1925, 13.

21. Joseph H. Watson, editor, *Supreme Circle News*, quoted in "Again the Ready Letter Writer," *NYA*, January 6, 1923, 4. For mention of Albany's strict segregation, see David D. Jones, reprinted from *Opportunity Magazine*, in "James Crow and I," *BAA*, February 2, 1929, 5. For the burning of black churches and schools, see "Night Riders Burn Negro Churches," *Greensboro Patriot*, October 7, 1908, 13. For the Colquitt County mob's actions, see "Night-Riders Whip Ministers in South, Officials Fail to Make Arrest of Lawbreakers for Political Reasons," *CD* (Big Weekend ed.), December 25, 1920, 1.

22. McIntosh quoted in Williams, "The Negro Exodus from the South," 102. The meeting of black leaders is noted in "Labor's Exodus to Be Taken Up, Leaders Among Negroes in Albany to Continue Thursday, Many Leaving for North, Will Seek to Find Remedy, Prominent White People Invited," *MT*, May 24, 1923, 9. The move to deny the Klan is noted in "Albany Frowns on Klan," *Southern Cross*, August 15, 1924, 12. Calls for secession in Albany are described in Formwalt, "Albany," online. For a description of the Lincoln Day program,

see "Tribute Paid to Lincoln's Memory," *AH*, February 12, 1925, 1; "Albany Lincoln Day," *MT*, February 13, 1925, 10. The election of Dierberger is noted in "Albany C. of C. Gets Secretary, Paul W. Dierberger of South Haven, Mich., Selected for Post," *MT*, September 25, 1925, 5.

23. "Plan Drive to Advertise Albany, Real Estate Board to Take Leadership in Campaign," *MT*, August 23, 1925, 3; "The South the New Frontier," *Orlando Sentinel*, November 29, 1925, 4. The Skywater Resort was later renamed Radium Springs Resort after radium was discovered in the water. See "Name of Springs May Be Changed, Barron Collier Is One of Promoters of Albany Resort, Radium Found in Water," *MT*, December 2, 1926, 2.

24. The check amount is noted in "Build Race Auto Plant in Georgia," *PC* (city ed.), March 6, 1926, 2. Community spirit quote from "The Spirit of Albany," *MT*, January 27, 1926, 4. Secretary Mowry's quote from Don E. Mowry, "Civic Achievements, No. 26—Good Hotels an Asset," *Freeport Journal-Standard*, May 28, 1927, 1.

25. Descriptions of Headen's activities concerning his new factory appear in "Headen Begins Work on Plant on Dawson Road," *AH*, February 26, 1926, 1; H. A. Wiseman, "News of Colored People in the City and County, First Auto Factory," *WSJ*, March 8, 1926, 10; "Build Race Auto Plant in Georgia," *PC* (city ed.), March 6, 1926, 2; and "The First Negro Auto Assembly Plant Building," *Norfolk Journal & Guide*, March 6, 1926, 1. The former owners of the cannery building were a white couple named Tom and Marie Louise O'Connor, who incorporated the American Pimento Products Company in April 1922. See "Canning and Packing Plants," *Manufacturers Record*, April 27, 1922, 69. The dimensions of the plant and Armwood's hiring are noted in "The South Atlantic States," *Iron Age*, January–March 1926, 826; and "Headen Motor Car Company," *Iron Age*, April–June 1926, 971. The price of the land is noted in "Miami Realtor Moves to Albany," *MT*, October 25, 1925, 13. Walter Armwood's experiences in Trenton, and his feelings on being shut out of skilled work there, appear in "Union Forming to Help Negro Race," *Trenton Evening Times*, February 16, 1917, 2; and W. A. Armwood, letter to the editor, "Negro Asks North If It Is Sincere, Says He Was Refused Work in Trenton Because of His Race," *Trenton Evening Times*, May 4, 1917, 27. Headen's original Chicago-based company was dissolved by the state of Illinois in November 1926. See decree of dissolution, Headen Motor Company, filed November 26, 1926, box 1628, Records of the Secretary of State, State of Illinois, Cook County.

26. Headen's appearance in Columbus is noted in "Columbus, Ga.," *BAA*, April 3, 1926, 22. His claims of pressing orders appear in "Work Begun on Auto Factory," *BAA*, March 6, 1926, 18; "The First Negro Auto Assembly Plant Building," *Norfolk Journal & Guide*, March 6, 1926, 1; and "L. A. Headen Building First Auto Factory Owned by Negroes," *NYA*, March 6, 1926, 1.

27. L. A. Headen, quoted in "Headen Begins Work on Plant on Dawson Road," *AH*, February 26, 1926, 1; "The First Negro Auto Assembly Plant Building," *New Journal & Guide*, March 6, 1926, 1; Washington, "The Atlanta Address," 79.

28. The activities carried out by the garage are noted in the petition for charter, Headen Motor Car Company, Dougherty County Superior Court, Albany, Ga., filed June 30, 1925. For Holley anecdote regarding local garage owner, see Holley, *You Can't Build a Chimney from the Top*, 73. Tax records for Dougherty Co. list the property owned by value of Headen's company as $1,350, worth today about $42,000, not accounting for differences in regional property values (the relative value of $42,000 in Albany vs. Chicago would have been higher). See "Return of Colored Tax Payers, Real Estate," *Dougherty County Tax Digests*, 1927, 1928, and 1929, GA, Morrow.

29. Claim of Headen's genius is from "Negroes Start Auto Plant Near Albany," *MT*, February 28, 1926, 21. Characterization of him as an engineer of note is from "Invention by Albany Men Makes Use of Crude Oil in Motors Possible, Patent Is Issued for Vaporizer That Is Expected to Revolutionize Automotive Industry—Slight Change in Ordinary Gasoline Motor Transforms It into One Using Either Gasoline or Crude Oil," *AH*, August 21, 1929, 1–2.

30. Petit's seeking of Headen's help, and the two men's collaboration, are noted in "Invention by Albany Men Makes Use of Crude Oil in Motors Possible," *AH*, August 21, 1929, 1–2.

31. "A Good Right Arm!" *MT*, March 26, 1925, 4; "Thought of the Day, Gasoline Injunction Denied," *Columbus Daily Inquirer*, March 30, 1925, 4. Calculations derived using "UK Petrol Prices (1902–2008) and Diesel Prices (1989–2008)," Energy Institute (energyinst.org); and "Computing 'Real Value' Over Time with a Conversion Between UK Pounds and U.S. Dollars, 1774 to Present" (measuringworth.com).

32. Headen's bi-fuel motor contained a small auxiliary gasoline tank attached to the carburetor. When the engine grew hot, a throttle was used to close off the gasoline source and introduce the crude oil, and the spark plugs were disengaged.

33. Application date is from Headen and Petit, "Ignition Device," U.S. Patent 1,780,076. Description of the unveiling is from "Vaporizer Test Is Successful, Two Albany Men Show Use of Crude Oil as Fuel for Motors," *MT*, August 22, 1929, 5. Revolutionize the industry quote is from "Invention by Albany Men Makes Use of Crude Oil in Motors Possible," *AH*, August 21, 1929, 1–2. This claim was repeated in "Albany Men Patent Apparatus[,] Replace Gas with Crude Oil," *Thomasville Times Enterprise*, August 22, 1929, 5.

34. Remarkable genius quote from "Negroes Start Auto Plant Near Albany," *MT*, February 28, 1926, 21. Attribution of inventions to Petit is from "Albany Men Patent Apparatus[,] Replace Gas with Crude Oil," *Thomasville Times Enterprise*, August 22, 1929, 5; and "Vaporizer Test Is Successful, Two Albany Men Show Use of Crude Oil as Fuel for Motors," *MT*, August 22, 1929, 5. Petit's confirmation that the vaporizer was Headen's invention is from Henry A. Petit, affidavit, November 26, 1930, attachment to letter, December 8, 1930, Attorney Victor J. Evans to Commissioner of Patents, Washington, D.C., in Lucean Arthur Headen, U.S. Patent No. 2,017,497, Case File, RG 241, U.S. Patent and Trademark Office, Patent Case Files, NARA, Kansas City (hereafter Headen U.S. 2,017,497 patent case file). For the British and U.S. patents Headen received on his vaporizer, see Headen, "Improvements in or Relating to Vaporizers for Internal Combustion Engines," GB Patent 381,588; and Headen, "Vaporizer," U.S. Patent 2,017,497.

35. For biographical information on Koelliker, see "George Philip Koelliker," in McCray, *Representative Clevelanders*, 237; "George P. Koelliker," in Avery, *A History of Cleveland and Its Environs*, vol. 2, 356–57; and George Philip Koelliker, certificate no. 147540, Ancestry.com, *U.S. Passport Applications*. For general information on Canfield Oil, an independent refinery, see "Canfield Oil Co.," in Van Tassel and Grabowski, *Encyclopedia of Cleveland History*, 152. For Koelliker's position as a director of Canfield, see "The Canfield Oil Company," in Borton and Borton, *Borton's Pocket Manual of Cleveland Securities*, 26. Other 1920s patents assigned to Koelliker were Downer, "Storage Battery," CA Patent 259,854; Bensing, "Electrolytic Rectifier," U.S. Patent 1,628,785; and Lewis, "Electrolytic Rectifier," U.S. Patent 1,775,417. Koelliker continued to buy the rights to and manufacture inventions through the 1950s. Koelliker's relationship to Bagnall in Thomasville is noted in "Personal Mention," *Tallahassee Daily Democrat*, January 28, 1929, 5, and February 7, 1929, 5.

36. Headen's trips in a Model T are noted in "Use Crude Oil to Propel Automobiles, Georgia Invention Expected to Revolutionize the Motor Industry," *Raleigh Independent*, September 1, 1929, 26. Possible patent infringement was noted in "Albany Men Patent Apparatus[,] Replace Gas with Crude Oil," *Thomasville Times Enterprise*, August 22, 1929, 5; and "Georgians Seek to Save Motor, Crude Oil Machine Is Infringement," *Augusta Chronicle*, January 9, 1930, 3. Although the *Albany Herald* claimed that Headen and Petit had founded National Oil Manifolds and intended to manufacture their inventions in Albany, the official address listed for the company in patent paperwork was Koelliker's Rose Building office in Cleveland, and manufacturing, once started, took place there. A contemporary newspaper notice documents the incorporation of National Oil Manifolds, but it unfortunately does not list the principals, and the Delaware Secretary of State holds no record for the company. Since the *Herald* often made misstatements concerning Headen and Petit's work, and Headen later assigned his U.S. patent to Koelliker, I am inclined to believe Koelliker rather than Headen and Petit started the company. For the Rose Building address for the company, see "Final Fee Paid to the Commissioner of Patents" (receipt), September 18, 1935, Headen U.S. 2,017,497 patent case file. For public notice of the company's incorporation, see "Charters Filed at State House, 21 Companies Granted Articles of Incorporation; Two Increase Capital," *Morning News*, May 1, 1930, 15.

37. The application date listed on the patent for Headen's vaporizer was May 16, 1930. See Headen, "Vaporizer," U.S. Patent 2,017,497. Headen's trip to Tallahassee is noted in "Albany Inventors Produce Manifold to Cut Fuel Costs," *MT*, July 3, 1930, 3. Calculation of current cost is based on comparison of the Consumer Price Index (see measuringworth.com). Display of the vaporizer noted in "Invention of Albany Men Will Lower Cost of Motor Traveling, Several Models of New Oil Manifolds Are Now on Exhibit—Demonstrations Have Proven That New Invention Is a Success," *AH*, June 30, 1930, 1.

38. Headen was noted on his way to Philadelphia when he made a brief stop in Gainesville, Georgia (where Emma Wynn was at the time working to organize for the City Federation of Women's Clubs). See "Georgia State, Gainesville, Ga.," *CD* (nat. ed.), August 23, 1930, 17. Hamilton departed for England from Montreal in mid-September, arriving in Liverpool on September 21, 1930. See entry for George Hamilton, *Names and Descriptions of Alien Passengers, The Albertic*, departed Montreal, Quebec, Canada, arrived Liverpool, England, September 21, 1930, Ancestry.com, *UK, Incoming Passenger Lists*. George Dickinson Hamilton was born April 22, 1880 [or 1878], in Southwick, Sunderland, Tyne and Wear, England. He was the son of Thomas and Elizabeth Hamilton. A sailor in his youth, he emigrated to Canada, then moved to Cleveland. Hamilton served in the U.S. Army's Quartermaster Corps during World War I before going into the parking business. See George Dickinson Hamilton, U.S. citizenship petition, granted April 25, 1930 (certificate no. 3337132), Fold3.com, *Naturalization Petition and Record Books*; entry for George D. Hamilton, in State of Ohio, *The Official Roster of Ohio Soldiers, Sailors and Marines in the World War, 1917–18*, vol. 7, 6835. Hamilton died in Phoenix, Arizona, in January 1945. See Cleveland Necrology File, microfilm reel #034, Cleveland Public Library, Cleveland, Ohio. He is buried in Cleveland. See entry for George D. Hamilton, died January 18, 1945, in Alger Cemetery, Cleveland, Ohio, FindaGrave.com, https://www.findagrave.com/memorial/81820845/george-d-hamilton. Hamilton's parking garage holdings are documented in entries for Geo. D. Hamilton (Auto Parking, 1040 Superior Ave., N.E., 914 Walnut Ave., and 1227 Rockwell Ave.), in Cleveland city direc-

tory, 1929, 831; and George D. Hamilton (president and manager, Hamilton Parking, Inc., 914 Walnut) in Cleveland city directories, 1930, 826, and 1931, 766.

39. Hintz, "Portable Power," 24–57.

40. Bacon's ownership of the Tift Silica Brick Company is noted on his draft registration card. By 1928 he had also completed medical school and opened a practice in Albany. See records for Albert S. Bacon, Ancestry.com, *U.S. World War I Draft Registration Cards*; Albert S. Bacon, Albany city directory, 1928–1929, 108; and *Fifteenth United States Census: 1930*, Household of Albert S. Bacon, Albany, Dougherty Co., Ga., ED 48-8, sheet 9B. Headen's residence in Cleveland is noted in entry for Arth[ur] Headen, inventor, in Cleveland city directory, 1931, 787.

41. "Dr. J. W. Holley Threatened by a White Mob," *PT*, March 13, 1930, 2.

42. "Headen, Inventor, Sails for London," *CD* (nat. ed.), June 6, 1931, 11; certificates of evidence, December 1 and 4, 1929, and decree of divorce, filed December 17, 1929, Case B-188,221, *Tena E. Headen vs. L. Arthur Headen*, Circuit Court of Cook Co., Chicago, Ill.

43. Bertha Mosley Lewis, "Society," *CD* (nat. ed.), July 9, 1927, 5.

44. Prominent quote appears in "Announces Marriage of Sister, Lena [*sic*] E. Headen," *CD* (nat. ed.), January 4, 1930, 5.

45. For background on Norfleet Meares, see "Supervisor Meares Returns," *CD* (Big Weekend ed.), April 20, 1918, 6; "Supervisor Mears Sprains Ankle," *CD* (Big Weekend ed.), August 31, 1918, 10; "Pullman Company Rewards Employees," *CD* (Big Weekend ed.), March 20, 1920, 12; and "Norfleet Meares Promoted," *CD* (Big Weekend ed.), October 2, 1920, 9. For Tena and Norfleet's marriage, see Norfleet Meares and Tena E. Headen, marriage license, December 10, 1929, Lake Co., Ind., FamilySearch.com, *Indiana, Marriages*; "Announces Marriage of Sister," 5; and "Wedded, Mrs. Norfleet Meares," *CD* (nat. ed.), January 4, 1930, 10. For Norfleet Meares's joining of Grace Presbyterian, see "January 21, 1933, Session," Grace Presbyterian Session Minutes, vol. 2, 1923–August 1936, 281, Grace Presbyterian Church Records, CHS. William J. Meares was the son of Joshua and Mary Anna Meares. He and his sister Lucy grew up on Red Cross, between 7th and 8th Streets, just around the corner from the Drye family on 7th Street, between Chestnut and Mulberry. Tena and Lucy attended Scotia Seminary together between 1897 and 1899. See Scotia catalogues, 1897–1898 and 1898–1899. For documentation of William and Lucy's parents, see William Joshua Meares, death certificate, August 29, 1945, Greensboro, N.C., Ancestry.com, *North Carolina Death Certificates*; and Lucy Jane Meares and Richard L. Hutchins Jr, Laurinburg, Scotland Co., N.C., December 30, 1905, Ancestry.com, *North Carolina, Marriage Records*. For the proximity of the Meares and Drye families, see entries for James Drye and Mary Meares in Wilmington city directory, 1897, 143, 197.

46. Headen's reporting of himself as widowed appears in *Fifteenth United States Census: 1930*, L. A. Headen, enumerated in the Household of William Wynn, Albany, Militia District 1097, Dougherty Co., Ga., ED 48-10, sheet 7A. Headen was identified that year as a mechanical engineer in a machinery repair shop, indicating he was repairing machinery as well as vehicles. Headen's attendance at the auto show and his stay at the McAlpin Hotel are noted in "Headen, Inventor, Sails for London," *CD* (nat. ed.), June 6, 1931, 11. For the Abbotts' attendance at the Meares's wedding reception, see "Newlyweds Have Pretty Reception for Friends," *CD* (nat. ed.), March 1, 1930, 4. As an example of the *Defender*'s renewed admiration for Headen, see, for example, "Our Status as Inventors," *CD* (nat. ed.), July 11, 1931, 1.

Chapter Nine

1. Hamilton returned to the United States in late January 1931. See entry for George D. Hamilton, Garage Keeper, Age 52, in "Names and Descriptions of Alien Passengers Embarked at the Port of Liverpool," Ship's Manifest, *S.S. Laurentic*, Departed Liverpool January 17, 1931, for New York; and entry for George Hamilton, "List of United States Citizens, *S.S. Laurentic*, Sailing from Liverpool, 17 January 19[31], Arriving at Port of New York 1/27/31," Ship's Manifest, *S.S. Laurentic*, January 27, 1931, Ancestry.com, *UK, Outward Passenger Lists*. Four corners quote from McBeth, *British Oil Policy*, 4. For import figures, see "Table VII, The Changing Pattern of U.K. Oil Supplies, 1900–1939," in McBeth, 93. For discussion of Reza Shah Pahlavi's (Reza Kahn's) rise to power in Iran, and his subsequent negotiations over the country's oil profits, see Elm, *Oil, Power, and Principle*, 21–36; and Daniel Yergin, *The Prize*, 252–54. Headen also faced some resistance in the United States from those who feared what cheaper fuels could do to the U.S. economy. The very day he mounted his display at the National Auto Show, the *Miami Herald* warned that "the introduction of a crude oil engine would create an unwholesome economic upheaval." See "A Change Needed," *Miami Herald*, January 23, 1930, 6. Thanks to Peter Liebhold of the National Museum of American History for providing me guidance on Britain's oil sources.

2. For a discussion of Ford's production of the Fordson in Ireland and England, see D. S. Jacobson, "The Political Economy of Industrial Location: The Ford Motor Company at Cork, 1912–26," *Irish Economic and Social History* 4 (1977): 36–55. For the uptick in popularity of paraffin tractors, see "The Manufacture of Tractors in England," *Roadless News* (hereafter *RN*), February 1931, 29.

3. In 1912, the RAC conducted trials of experimental petrol-paraffin engines, and thereafter it encouraged designers of the engines to participate in the RAC's annual auto show. See "Paraffin Carbureter Tests, Stewart-Morris Instrument Gives Excellent Results with That Fuel on 2,000-Mile R.A.C. Trial," *The Automobile*, October 17, 1912, 800–801. In 1921, to spur research on fuels, the club helped fund an expansive effort at Manchester University, and in 1928 it sponsored an open trial of motors that could operate on propellants other than petrol, offering prize monies for the top contenders. For information on the Manchester University program, see "Motor Travel, the Royal Automobile Club," *Club Journal*, January 1921, 9–12. A description of the club's alternative fuel trials appears in "New Fuel for Motor Vehicles," *Gas Power*, May 1913, 60; and J. H. Nelson, "Foreign Trend in New Motor Fuels," *Oil and Gas Journal* 27, no. 27 (1928): 164. The Commercial Motor Users' Association was first formed in 1903 as the Motor Van, Wagon and Omnibus Users' Association. It eventually became an independent affiliate of the RAC, merging in 1944 with the National Road Transport Federation. For discussion of this association and of commercial vehicles at RAC trials, see "The Commercial Vehicle Aspect," in Noble, *The Jubilee Book of the Royal Automobile Club*, 175. In the mid-1920s, the Royal Agricultural Society began including a section for petrol-paraffin machines in its annual trials of British-built tractors, and it did so again in 1930 when it organized a world trial to assess general progress in farm machinery. See Williams, *Farm Tractors*, 89–90. The June date of Headen's demonstration is noted in "Headen, Inventor, Sails for London," *CD* (nat. ed.), June 6, 1931, 11; "Gets Chance," *CD* (nat. ed.), June 6, 1931, 11.

4. Lucean A. Headen, Power of Attorney, February 20, 1932, in Lucean Arthur Headen, U.S. Patent No. 2,017,497, Case File, NARA, Kansas City.

5. Entries for Lucein [Lucean] Headen, engineer, and George Hamilton, operator, "Names and Descriptions of Alien Passengers, *S. S. Majestic*," Arrived in Southampton, June 4, 1931, Ship's Manifest, *S.S. Majestic*, June 4, 1931, Ancestry.com, *UK, Incoming Passenger Lists*. Both men listed the address 8 Bloomfield Street, Southwick, Sunderland, as their "Proposed Address in the United Kingdom." The RAC first began using the Brooklands Track for trials in 1909 and continued to conduct trials there into the early 1930s. See "Standard Test of Performance, Royal Automobile Club of Great Britain Adopts a System of Certification—Its Purpose and Method," *Motor World*, March 4, 1909, 1060; Thackray, *The AEC Story*; and Noble, *The Jubilee Book of the Royal Auto Club*, 81–82. Headen's obituary states that he had arrived in England with only a business trip in mind, deciding only afterward to stay. See "An American Who Settled in Frimley Green Dies," *Camberley News* (hereafter *CN*), September 27, 1957, 6. Headen's residence at the Strand Hotel is noted on his National Registration Identity Card (in the possession of his son). "White, Langer, Parry & Rollinson" are listed as the patent agents in Headen, "Improvements in or Relating to Vaporizers for Internal Combustion Engines," GB Patent 381,588. The 60 Strand office location appears in a September magazine article and on Headen's February 23, 1932, application for a British patent. See Headen, "Improvements in or Relating to the Formation of the Charges Supplied to Internal Combustion Engines," GB Patent 396,834.

6. "An Oil-Vaporising Manifold, Device for Converting Petrol Engines to Run on Cheap Non-volatile Fuel," *Motor Transport*, September 21, 1931, 333.

7. Keil was from a long line of German master cabinetmakers. See biographical sketch, "James Richard McLean Keil," in J. R. McLean Keil business file, SHM. Information on Keil's RAF background can be found in his service file. See file for James Richard McLean Keil, in FindMyPast.com, *British Royal Air Force, Officers' Service Records*. Keil was listed as a builder in telephone directories beginning in 1923, and he advertised himself as a "Contractor to War Department" beginning in 1929. See advertisement, "J. R. McLean Keil, Builder and Decorator, Heating & Sanitary Engineer," advertisement, in *Norwich /Cambridge /(etc.)* telephone directory, 1929, p. 37, Ancestry.com, *British Phone Books*. For information on his early building activities, see Item Ref 6736/1-30, Collection Ref 6736, Deeds for Duke Villa, York Villa, and "The Bower" (also known as "Newlands"), Frimley Road (Camberley: Deeds, 1871–1967), SHC. St. Mary's Works was located between Bridge and Krooner Roads. For information on Rowlands Metal Windows, see William Lewis Rowlands, "Notice of Objection to Draft Special List by Person Aggrieved," July 10, 1929, in response to Rating and Valuation (Apportionment), in Rowlands business file SHM. By the late 1920s, Keil was publicly advocating for tax reform to promote businesses in Camberley. See "Local Government Reform," *Sussex Agricultural Express*, March 15, 1929, 5.

8. Although Headen's new location had the post address 15 Victoria Avenue, it did not directly face the street. It was situated between Victoria Avenue and Frimley Road in a lot that backed onto the rear of 15 Victoria. Located next to Headen's buildings were two carpenters' workshops and a stable, all owned by Thompson. Thompson sold his stable and horses in 1935 but retained the other buildings until 1947. According to tax books, the facilities Headen rented had four times the value of surrounding workshops. Headen's identity card gives January 16, 1932, as the date he moved into the Duke of York Hotel. Headen Hamilton Engineering's first appearance at the 15 Victoria Avenue site is noted in the 1932 local directory. See entry for Headen Hamilton Engineering Co. Ltd., Victoria Avenue, *Norwich/*

248   *Notes to Chapter Nine*

Cambridge/(etc.) telephone directory, 1932, 39, Ancestry.com, *British Phone Books*. The value of the workshop and premises owned by Thompson is noted in entry for Headen Keil Engineering Co., 15 Victoria Ave., in District Council of Frimley & Camberley, *The Rate Book for the General Rates for the Period Ending 30th September, 1945*, 219–20, SHM. For information on Thompson's stables, see clipping, "Sales by Auction, Thompson's Hunting Stables, Camberley, Surrey," in *Chancellor's Book, 1935–1939*, SHM.

9. Entry for George Hamilton in "Names and Descriptions of Alien Passengers Embarked at the Port of Southampton, Departed Southampton 10 February 1932 for New York," Ship's Manifest, *S.S. Majestic*, Ancestry.com, *UK, Outward Passenger Lists, 1890–96*. Hamilton arrived back in New York six days later. See entry for George D. Hamilton, "List of United States Citizens, *S.S. Majestic*, Sailing from Southampton, February 10th, 1932, Arriving at Port of New York, February 16th, 1932," Ship's Manifest, *S.S. Majestic*, Ancestry.com, *New York, Passenger and Crew Lists*.

10. Headen, "Improvements in or Relating to Internal Combustion Engines," GB Patent 396,834. For discussion of the pre-ignition problem, see "Problems of Kerosene Combustion," *Gas Engine*, March 1919, 74.

11. Although Headen Hamilton opened its factory on Victoria Avenue in 1932, Headen maintained the Finsbury Circus (River Plate House) office at least through 1934. See entries for Headen Hamilton Engineering Co. Ltd., 15 Victoria Avenue, in the *Norwich/Cambridge/(etc.)* telephone directory, 1932, 39; and 10 Finsbury Circus, E.C.2, *London Surnames A–K*, February 1933, 724; and *London Surnames A–K*, August 1933, 732, Ancestry.com, *British Phone Books*; and entry for Headen Hamilton Engineering Co., Ltd., 10 Finsbury Circus, in Great Britain, *London Post Office Directory*, 1934, 436. The name Headen Hamilton Engineering Co. was used in the *Norwich/Cambridge/(etc.)* directory through 1934, before being replaced by Headen Keil Engineering Ltd. See *Norwich/Cambridge/(etc.)* telephone directory, 1934, 37.

12. Headen's display of his kit in 1933 is noted in "Commercial Motor Transport Exhibition, Olympia, November 2–11," *World's Carriers and Carrying Trades' Review*, November 7, 1933, 69. Sample advertisements for the kit include: "Ford Models of the Headen Oil Manifold," *Belfast Telegraph*, August 4, 1932, 9; "Petrol Lorry Owners," *Derby Daily Telegraph*, October 8, 1932, 3; "Save 50% of Petrol," *Derby Evening Telegraph*, October 8, 1932, 3; "Motor Cars, Economy," *Nottingham Evening Post*, October 29, 1932, 3; "Ford Commercial Users," *Dundee Courier*, February 2, 1933, 1; "Ford Commercial Users," *Dundee Evening Telegraph*, February 15, 1933, 2; and "Engines, Machinery, Tools," *Yorkshire Evening Post*, March 23, 1934, 3. Quote concerning the manifold's wide adoption appears in "An Improved Automatic Vaporizer, Simplicity of Control a Feature of the Latest Headen-Hamilton Apparatus," *Commercial Motor* (hereafter *CM*), February 23, 1934, 53. Motor Accessments' role as a distributor is noted in "Headen Oil Manifold," *World's Carriers and Carrying Trades' Review*, January 15, 1935, 190.

13. Mary Ann Bennett, in her excellent history of Camberley, notes that Keil became partners with several of those carrying on manufacturing operations at St. Mary's Works. See Bennett, *Camberley, A History*, 8. February 1934 is the last known date that Headen Hamilton still operated at 10 Finsbury Circle. That was the address listed in "An Improved Automatic Vaporizer," *CM*, February 23, 1934, 53. Although Headen Hamilton Engineering ceased to operate after 1934, it was not officially dissolved as a corporation until 1937. See dissolution

of Headen Hamilton Engineering Co., Ltd. in "Dissolutions," *London Gazette*, April 12, 1937, 2386.

14. Close is listed as a director on the Headen Keil Engineering stationery. See L. A. Headen, letter, November 12, 1942, to National Institute of Agricultural Engineering, Silsoe Research Institute Records, SR SRI AD8/3/2/8, Correspondence with Manufacturing Company-H-1942-1957, MERL. Close's membership in the Masons is noted in *Freemason and Masonic Illustrated* 46 (1908): 56. Keil's membership is documented in "Recollections of V.W. Bro. M.E.P.," Camberley Lodge No. 5591, http://www.camberleylodge5591.org.uk/index.php/heritage. The year 1937 was estimated as the date Victoria Avenue was surfaced. See A Ratepayer, Camberley, letter to the editor, *CN*, April 21, 1939, 5.

15. For a good discussion of crankcase oil dilution, see Robert E. W. Wilson and Robert E. Wilkin, "A Suggested Remedy for Crankcase Oil Dilution," *SAE Transactions* 21, pt. 1 (1926): 81–115.

16. Innumerable efforts quote from "Internal Combustion Engines and the Problem of Crankcase Dilution," *RN*, March-April 1935, 9–11. Remarkable cure quote from "A Hermes on Heavy Oil," *The Aeroplane*, November 6, 1935, 565. The gasket is also described in "A Protection Against Dilution," *CM*, September 13, 1935, 34; and "Special Cylinder Gasket for Heavy Fuels," *Sydney Morning Herald*, November 12, 1935, 7. The gasket was tested in 1938 (Ministry of Agriculture and Fisheries, "Headen Keil Anti-Dilution Cylinder-Head Gasket," 1).

17. Quote from "More About Crankcase Oil Dilution," *RN*, May–June 1935, 15–16. Headen patented his gasket in Britain in October 1936 and in the United States in 1937. See Keil, "Improvements in or Relating to Charge Mixing and Heating Devices and/or Vaporisers for Use in the Cylinders of Internal Combustion Engines," GB Patent 437,020; and Headen, "Charge Mixing and Heating Device and/or Vaporizer for Use in Cylinders of Internal Combustion Engines," U.S. Patent 2,092,454. Note: The British patent for Headen's gasket bears Keil's name, but the U.S. patent bears Headen's. This discrepancy reflects a difference in British and U.S. patent law of the period. The British system, because a main purpose of the application was to announce the intent to manufacture, allowed an assignee to apply for a patent in his or her name. This occurred frequently, especially when the inventor was not a British citizen. U.S. law, however, required that all patents bear the inventor's name, regardless of the inventor's origins. Canadian law was similar, and Headen's name appears on the Canadian patent for the gasket. See Headen, "Engine Charge Device," CA Patent 362,088. For a discussion of British patent law specific to this issue, see Van Dulken, *British Patents of Invention*, 81, 111.

18. Ford Motor's approval of Headen's gasket is noted in "More About Crankcase Dilution," *RN*, May–June 1935, 16. Remarkable invention quote and the price reduction based on lower manufacturing costs are noted in "Remarkable Economies Effected by the Headen Keil Gasket, Announcement of 40 Per Cent. Reduction in Price," *RN*, March–April 1936, 36. Other discussion of Headen's gasket in *RN* includes "The Headen Keil Gasket for Preventing Crankcase Oil Dilution with Internal Combustion Engines," advertising flyer, insert to *RN*, July–August 1935; and "The H. K. Gasket and Crankcase Oil Dilution," *RN*, July–August 1935, 20; Consideration of Headen's gasket for a silver medal is discussed in "III. Cylinder Head Gasket. The Headen Keil Engineering Co., Ltd., Camberley," in "Report on New Implements, Wolverhampton Show, 1937," *Journal of the Royal Agricultural Society of England*, 1937, 482–83.

19. *Finance Act of 1935*, July 10, 1935, Part I, Customs and Excise, Chapter 24, Sections 2, 3, 4, 25, 26, Geo. 5, 2–7, http://www.legislation.gov.uk/ukpga/1935/24/pdfs/ukpga_19350024_en.pdf. For a discussion of the act and its implications, see "The New Duty on Heavy Hydrocarbon Oils, Obligations Upon Users of Heavy Oil Vehicles," *Chemical Age*, July 27, 1935, 83–84. Insuperable difficulties quote from J. A. Duff, "Running on Paraffin (letter)," in "Correspondence," *The Motor*, October 25, 1938, 617.

20. For discussions of Britain's agricultural depression, see Bellerby, "The Distribution of Farm Income in the U.K., 1867–1938," 262–63; Martin, *The Development of Modern Agriculture*, 10–17. For "nadir" quote, see Martin, 11. For founding of the Agricultural Research Council, see DeJager, "Pure Science and Practical Interests," 129–50; and Cooke, *Agricultural Research, 1931–1981*. Martin notes that farmers in Scotland, northern England, and Wales were significantly more resistant to adopting the tractor than their counterparts in southwestern and southeastern England. See Martin, *The Development of Modern Agriculture*, 17.

21. For Roadless's discussion of the gasket's utility for older tractors, see "The H. K. Gasket and Crankcase Oil Dilution," *RN*, July–August 1935, 20.

22. "A Hermes on Heavy Oil," *The Aeroplane*, November 6, 1935, 565.

23. "The H. K. Gasket and Crankcase Oil Dilution," *RN*, July–August 1935, 20; Headen, "Charge Mixing and Heating Device and/or Vaporizer for Use in Cylinders of Internal Combustion Engines," U.S. Patent 2,092,454. In a letter to the National Institute of Agricultural Engineering, Headen noted his difficulty in obtaining "the basis from which this gasket was made" (i.e., copper). See L. A. Headen, letter, November 12, 1942, to National Institute of Agricultural Engineering, Silsoe Research Institute Records, SR SRI AD8/3/2/8, Correspondence with Manufacturing Company-H-1942-1957, MERL.

24. "Exhibits at the Royal Agricultural Show, Wolverhampton," *Engineering: An Illustrated Weekly Journal*, July 23, 1937, 93–94. His device is also described in "IV. Crude Oil Carburettor. The Headen Keil Engineering Co., Ltd., Camberley," in "Report on New Implements, Wolverhampton Show, 1937," *Journal of the Royal Agricultural Society of England*, 1937, 482–83. Patents for the carburetor and improvements are: Headen, "Improvements in Vaporizers or Heaters for Use in Internal Combustion Engines," GB Patent 459,603; Headen, "Improvements in Vaporisers for Internal Combustion Engines," GB Patent 469,826; and Headen, "Perfectionnements aux Appareils de Vaporisation pour Moteurs à Combustion Interne," FR Patent 806,631. Vaporizer types and improvements in bi-fuel carburetors are discussed in Kewley and Gilbert, "Kerosine," 2470–85.

25. Headen's participation in the Oxford Conference is documented in "Discussion on Papers Dealing with Tractor Performance and Row Crop Cultivation, Tuesday, January 5, Afternoon," *Second Conference on Mechanized Farming*, Oxford, England: Oxford University, 1937, 3; and "Effect of Dilution on Tractor Upkeep, Oxford Conference Agrees That Dilution of Lubricant by Fuel Is the Main Cause of Tractor Troubles," *CM*, May 21, 1937, 497. See also "Mechanised Farming, Underloaded Tractors Cause Wastage," *The Mercury*, April 5, 1937, 3, https://trove.nla.gov.au/newspaper/article/25389302/1838866.

26. "New Camberley Industry," *CN*, August 20, 1937, 5. Col. W. Sturmy-Cave, DSO, TD, was a decorated RAF officer who served in World War II as deputy director of the Directorate of Planning of War Production for the Air Ministry, http://deriv.nls.uk/dcn23/9603/96034881.23.pdf.

27. Hideous factories quote from W. Cyprian Bridge, Penthryn, Camberley, letter to the editor, *CN*, April 21, 1944, reprinted in Sparey, *Dear Sir*, 82. Although this letter was published several years after Keil's meeting with the reporter, it reflects a sentiment already common in the town in the 1930s. The growing reluctance of women to enter domestic labor, despite high unemployment, is discussed in Major W. R. J. Ellis, Camberley, "Unemployment, To the Editor, 'Camberley News,'" *CN*, January 8, 1937, 3.

28. The call for deicing devices was led by public figures such as Sir Robert Perkins. Perkins, speaking before Parliament's House of Commons on November 17, 1937, sharply criticized the Air Ministry for its lack of deicing research. See "Civil Aviation," in Parliament, House of Commons, *Parliamentary Debates, House of Commons Official Report, Fifth Series, Volume 329*, London, His Majesty's Stationery Office, 1937, 432–34, https://api.parliament.uk/historic-hansard/commons/1937/nov/17/civil-aviation-1. Not all his criticism was fair. The ministry was, in fact, at work on the issue. In early September 1937, it had reported on deicing methods then being tested, and at the time of Perkins's address, it was issuing a notice that all civil aircraft would be required to carry deicing equipment. See "Air Ministry Notice," *Aircraft Engineering*, November 1937, 303. See also *The Aeroplane*, September 1, 1937, 256–59. For an early description of Goodrich's "boots," see "Overshoes for Plane End Ice Danger," *Popular Mechanics*, February 1931, 28. For good explanations of their function, see Noth and Polte, *The Formation of Ice on Airplanes*, 13; and Bugos, "Lew Rodert, Epistemological Liaison," 32. For a description of the "fine-weave metallic matting" offered to the Air Ministry by inventor Granville Bradshaw in late September 1937, see "De-icing by Bradshaw, Deformable Matting Scheme to Be Tested by Air Ministry," *Flight*, November 4, 1937, 456.

29. Headen received two patents for his ice prevention methods. See Headen, "A New or Improved Apparatus for Preventing Ice Formation on Aircraft Surfaces," GB Patent 486,549; and Headen, "Improvements in or Connected with Means for Preventing Ice Formation on Control Services of Aircraft," GB Patent 505,772.

30. For Theodorsen and Clay's experiments with steam, see Theodorsen and Clay, *Ice Prevention on Aircraft*, 1–24. For the device they patented, see Theodorsen and Clay, "Vapor Heating System," U.S. Patent 2,081,963.

31. For a summary of the problems encountered in early experiments with exhaust gases and heated air, see "Preventing Ice Formation, The Thermal, Mechanical and Chemical Methods of Combating the Danger: A Résumé of the Paper Read by Mr. B. Lockspeiser Before the R.Ae.S," *Flight*, November 14, 1935, 510–12. Clumsy and heavy comment from Theodorsen and Clay, *Ice Prevention on Aircraft*, 15.

32. Headen received two patents for his propeller deicing methods. See Headen, "Improvements in or Connected with Means for De-icing Aircraft Propellers," GB Patent 504,737; and Headen, "Improvements in or Connected with Means for De-icing Aircraft Propellers," GB Patent 506,444.

33. Entry for Luccan [Lucean] A. Headen, Frimley and Camberley U.D., Surrey, England, Registration District and Sub-District: 32/5, Schedule No. 224, Schedule Sub No. 8, FindMyPast.com, *1939 Register for England and Wales*. For discussion of experiments with radio-controlled airplanes at Farnborough, see Cooper, *Farnborough: 100 Years of British Aviation*, 68–69, 72.

34. For a discussion of the development of war industries at St. Mary's Works, see Bennett, *Camberley, A History*, 97–99. Aerolex Ltd. fronted Bridge Road. See entry for Aerolex Ltd. in "Suppliers to the Aircraft Industry," *Grace's Guide, 1939*, https://www.gracesguide.co.uk/1939_Suppliers_to_the_Aircraft_Industry. Close is listed as a director of Aerolex in "Here and There, News of the Latest Developments in the Industry and Elsewhere," *Flight*, November 26, 1936, 574. Harley held at least sixteen patents on aviation components. For information on Aerolex's products, see "Marshland Site Converted to Important Factory," transcribed clipping, *CN*, 1948, in Aerolex business file, SHM. For information on Wilkinson Rubber Linatex, see "'To Save Life . . .': A Short Account of Our War Service," Camberley, England: Wilkinson Rubber Linatex Limited [1946?], in Wilkinson Rubber Linatex Ltd. business file, SHM, Camberley; and "Wilkinson Rubber Linatex, Ltd.," in "Aeronautical Materials," *Flight*, September 9, 1948, 322.

35. For a description of the porous leather anti-icing device developed by B. Lockspeiser and J. E. Ramsbottom of the RAE in Farnborough, and its adoption by the Dunlop Rubber Company, see "Combating Ice Formation, the Dunlop 'Anticer' Demonstrated: A Device Which Prevents the Formation of Ice and Which Does Not Spoil the Shape of the Leading Edge," *Flight*, July 4, 1935, 33. For discussion of early wind tunnel tests and other icing research at Farnborough, see "Preventing Ice Formation, The Thermal, Mechanical and Chemical Methods of Combating the Danger: A Résumé of the Paper Read by Mr. B. Lockspeiser Before the R.Ae.S.," *Flight*, November 14, 1935, 510–12. For the request by the RAE that the National Research Council of Canada take over its deicing work, see Middleton, *Mechanical Engineering at the National Research Council of Canada*, 128. Deicing is not mentioned as a wartime RAE research topic by Cooper in his Farnborough history, suggesting that *all* work on the topic ceased there. The director of scientific research for the British Ministry of Aircraft Production also looked to the Canadians for help, stating that although propeller deicing was his first priority, he was relying on the Canadians to develop a practical method. For discussion of the RAE's early focus on chemical solutions, its lack of attention to thermal deicing during the war, and the lack of direct coordination on this issue between U.S. and British scientists, see Bugos, "Lew Rodert, Epistemological Liaison," 29–58. Ultimately, the RAF would decide not to include deicing equipment on its bombers due to the weight it added. See Jones, *The Wizard War*, 387–89. Thanks to Roger Connor of the National Air and Space Museum for providing the *Flight* article on icing research at Farnborough.

36. Peter Procter, "Life & Work of Sir Alan Cobham," *Aerospace*, March 1975, 24–25; and Marcus Langley, "Setting the Record Straight," *Aerospace*, May 1975, 16–17.

37. For documentation of the NACA's development of exhaust gas and heated-air systems at the Langley Memorial Aeronautical Laboratory and the Ames Aeronautical Laboratory, see Gray, *Frontiers of Flight*, 307–24, and Bugos, "Lew Rodert, Epistemological Liaison," 29–58. For discussion of the NACA's rejection of chemical deicing for propellers and its work to develop a heated-air deicing method for them after World War II, see Gray, *Frontiers of Flight*, 317–18. The claim that Rodert's advances laid the basis for later systems appears in "Military and Commercial Aircraft," MPTD-3, 9/14/04, VWR Draft, chap. 3, http://citeseerx.ist.psu.edu/viewdoc/download?doi=10.1.1.606.7247&rep=rep1&type=pdf.

38. For John King Hardy's role at NACA's Ames Research Center, see Hartman, *Adventures in Research*, 75–76; and Gray, *Frontiers of Flight*, 327–28.

39. "The Offensive on the Farm," *West Sussex County Times*, April 3, 1942, 2.

40. "Paraffin Conversion for Aveling Dumpers," *CM*, December 16, 1939, 25; "Engineering Plans of Aveling-Barford," Collection 2-AB (2d Accession), Aveling-Barford, Lincolnshire Archives, Newlands. For the Air Ministry's 1936 order from Roadless Traction, and the later use of these Roadless-supplied Fordsons in World War II, see "Tractors for Air Ministry," *RN*, March–April 1936, 1–2; and DK Publishing, *Tractor: The Definitive Visual History*, 75, 96–97. For other military uses of Roadless tractors, see "The Bombing of the Scharnhorst, a Fordson Roadless Tractor Assists in the Preparations," *RN*, September–October 1942, 21–22; and Church, *Military Vehicles of World War 2*, 21. For paraffin's use in tanks and planes, see "More Tanks, Planes Change Over to Paraffin," *West Sussex County Times*, April 10, 1942, 2.

41. Stephen Corsi, "Second World War Memories of Stephen Corsi, 1939–1945," Article ID A4056518, in BBC, "WW2 People's War: An Archive of World War Two Memories—Written by the Public, Gathered by the BBC," https://www.bbc.co.uk/history/ww2peoples war/stories/18/a4056518.shtml.

42. For sample advertisements, see "To Fordson Tractor Owners," *Staffordshire Advertiser*, April 12, 1941, 2; "'Headen Keil' Heat Unit," *West Sussex County Times*, July 3, 1942, 2; "Saving; Cut Fuel Consumption with the Headen Keil Heat Unit," *West Sussex County Times*, July 10, 1942, 2; "Headen Heat Units for Fordson Tractors," *Aberdeen Press and Journal*, September 30, 1943, 4; February 5, 1944, 3; and February 10, 1944, 4; "Tractor Accessories," *Dundee Courier*, January 17, 1944, 1; "Tractor Fuel Economy," *Dundee Courier*, February 12, 1944, 1. Headen's report of sales appears in L. A. Headen, letter, November 12, 1942, to National Institute of Agricultural Engineering, Silsoe Research Institute Records, SR SRI AD8/3/2/8, Correspondence with Manufacturing Company-H-1942-1957, MERL. The number of Fordsons in use during the war is from L. Dudley Stamp, "Wartime Changes in British Agriculture," *The Geographical Journal* (The Royal Geographic Society with the Institute of British Geographers) 109 (1/3, January–March 1947): 4.

43. Letter, January 28, 1955, Lucean A. Headen, Frimley, Surrey, England, to the American Embassy, London, England, attachment to Foreign Service Despatch No. 48, March 29, 1955, box 3199, item 741.5621/3-2955, Central Decimal File, 1945–49, RG 59, General Records of the Department of State, NARA, College Park.

44. For a description of Camberley Court Hotel, see Barson, *Camberley & Yorktown Between the Wars*, 59; and Clark, *Around Camberley*, 23. Headen's ownership of both a Ford and a Hudson automobile is noted on his National Registration Identity Card. For residents surrounding Headen, see entry for Luccan [Lucean] A. Headen, at Camberley Court Hotel, Frimley and Camberley U.D., Surrey, England, Registration District and Sub-District: 32/5, Schedule No. 224, Schedule Sub No. 8, FindMyPast.com, *1939 Register for England and Wales*.

45. William N. Jones, "London Y.M.C.A. Refuses Room to Afro Editor," *BAA*, November 11, 1933, 3; J. A. Rogers, "Ruminations, The Color Line in Merrie England," *New York Amsterdam News*, May 19, 1934, 8. Headen was described as "medium light" on his passport. See [Lucean] Arthur Headen, certificate no. 51370, February 16, 1915, *U.S. Passport Applications*. Hattie Hayes Warrington, Lucean and Nannie's cousin, described Nannie's skin tone as "medium brown." In the 1940s, Nannie served as the directress of Hattie's college dormitory at North Carolina College (now North Carolina Central University) in Durham. Warrington, telephone conversation with the author, December 8, 2014. Headen's stays at the Queens and Grand Hotels in 1940 and 1941, respectively, are documented on his National Registration Identity Card.

46. Dr. Alan Keil, Calgary, Canada, email communication with the author, October 5, 2016; "An American Who Settled in Frimley Green Dies," *CN*, September 27, 1957, 6.

47. Smith, *When Jim Crow Met John Bull*, 32.

48. Letter, L. A. Headen, Camberley, Surrey, England, to Robert Abbott, Chicago, Ill., April 1, 1935, Super Series 1, Series 3: Correspondence, box 6, folder 46 (Headen, L. A.), Abbott-Sengstacke Family Papers, Vivian Harsh Collection, CPL.

49. A review of all extant copies of *The Keys: The Official Organ of the League of Coloured Peoples*, London, 1933–1939, finds no mention of Headen.

50. Letter, L. A. Headen, Duke of York Hotel, Camberley, Surrey, England, to Robert Abbott, Editor, in "Congratulations," *CD* (nat. ed.), June 8, 1935, 16.

51. The reflection of things is quoted from Letter, L. A. Headen, Camberley, England, to Robert S. Abbott, Chicago, Ill., June 12, 1934, Super Series 1, Series 3: Correspondence, box 6, folder 46 (Headen, L. A.), Vivian Harsh Collection, CPL. Eslanda (Essie) Robeson quoted in Duberman, *Paul Robeson*, 87. Original quote from Essie Robeson's diary, Moorland-Spingarn Research Center, Howard University, Washington, D.C. For Abbott's exclusion from London hotels, see "R. A. Abbott Refused Hotel Accommodations," *New York Amsterdam News*, September 4, 1929, 1. Jones quote from William N. Jones, "London Y.M.C.A. Refuses Room to Afro Editor," *BAA*, November 11, 1933, 3.

52. See, for example, "Current Comment," *The Keys: The Official Organ of the League of Coloured Peoples*, January–March 1936, 29–30; "The Americanization of London," *PC* (Home Final ed.), September 14, 1929, pt. 1, 12; "London Hotels Bow to American Racial Prejudice, Britain Will Investigate Color Line," *CD* (nat. ed.), September 7, 1929, 4; William Pickens, quoted in "Pickens Speaks on London Hotel Case," *CD* (nat. ed.), September 28, 1929, 2; Robert S. Abbott, "My Trip Abroad, IX—We Arrive in England," *CD* (nat. ed.), January 4, 1930, 1–2.

53. Letter, L. A. Headen, Camberley, Surrey, England, to Robert Abbott, Chicago, Ill., June 12, 1934, Super Series 1, Series 3: Correspondence, box 6, folder 46 (Headen, L. A.), Abbott-Sengstacke Family Papers, Vivian Harsh Collection, CPL.

54. H. A. Wiseman, "News of Colored People in the City and County, First Auto Factory," *WSJ*, March 8, 1926, 10. Headen's son notes that his parents corresponded with Nannie when he was a child, and that after his father's death, his mother continued the correspondence. He also recalls Nannie sending him U.S. Savings Bonds. Lucean Headen Jr., conversation with the author, November 2, 2016, Swansea, Wales.

55. Quote from letter, L. A. Headen, London, England, to Robert Abbott, Chicago, Ill., in "Prepare for War," *CD* (nat. ed.), September 10, 1938, 16; Cross, *Our Homefront*, 57.

56. The bombing in Farnborough is described in Cooper, *Farnborough*, 72; and the bombing of the Staff College in UK War Cabinet, Chiefs of Staff, "Home Security Situation, by Night, 68," in *Weekly Résumé (No. 74) of the Naval, Military and Air Situation from 12 Noon January 23rd, to 12 Noon January 30th, 1941*. W. P. (41) 20, 10, in Records of the Cabinet Office, Cabinet Minutes and Papers, CAB 66-War Cabinet and Cabinet, Memoranda, WP Series, CAB 66/14-WP Series, Reference cab/66/14/42, NA, Kew.

57. "Local Defence Volunteers, on Duty in Camberley," *CN*, May 31, 1940, 3. The training received by local Home Guard platoons is described in Cross, *Our Homefront*, 24. Headen's National Registration Identity Card shows that he stayed at the Greyhound Hotel in Builth Wells in late November 1940.

58. Headen's curfew times are marked on his National Identity Registration Card (in possession of Lucean Headen Jr.). The fining of the Belgian businessman is noted in "Alien Fined, Failure to Report Change," *CN*, May 3, 1940, 1. Headen's purchase of bonds is documented in letters, Post Office Savings Bank, Yorkshire, Harrogate, Yorkshire, to L. A. Headen, October 9, 1942, and October 4, 1943; and letters, N. Tucker, the Chancellor of the Exchequer, Treasury Chambers, London, to L. A. Headen, July 17, 1943, and August 29, 1944 (in possession of Lucean Headen Jr.); and Headen Jr., conversation with the author, November 2, 2016, Swansea, Wales.

59. General Register Office, marriage application no. 5335109-1, Lucean Arthur Headen and Gladys Hollamby, November 3, 1945, Surrey North-Western District, Surrey County, England.

60. Burial record, William Hollamby Sr., "Burial in the Parish of Ash in the Diocese of Guildford and County of Surrey in the Year 1936," 88, Ancestry.com, *Surrey, England, Church of England Burials*; burial record, Mary Hollamby, "Burial in the Parish of Ash in the Diocese of Guildford and County of Surrey in the Year 1941," in Ancestry.com, *Surrey, England, Church of England Burials*. Residences for William Hollamby Sr., Mary Hollamby, Ivy Hollamby, and Winifred Hollamby between 1929 and 1935, and for Mary Hollamby, Ivy Hollamby, and Winifred Hollamby, 1937, 1939, are from Ancestry.com, *Surrey, England, Electoral Registers*.

61. Lucean and Gladys's honeymoon at the Ritz Hotel in London is documented in Hotel Account, L. A. Headen, Esq., Room 222, the Ritz Hotel, London, November 3–5, 1945, in personal collection of his son. Headen Jr. describes his parents' relationship as a loving one, and a 1957 family photo shows the couple clasping hands as they face the camera. Headen Jr., conversation with the author, November 1, 2016, Swansea, Wales.

62. In 1946, as its chairman, Keil oversaw the liquidation of Rowlands Metal Windows. Wilkinson Novatex Ltd., a Wilkinson Rubber Linatex subsidiary located at St. Mary's Works, closed soon afterward. See "Wilkinson Novatex Limited," *London Gazette*, April 23, 1948, 2545. For a description of Keil's new aeronautical business, Ancillary Developments, founded with garage owner Percy White and first located at Blackbushe Aerodrome, see Bennett, *Camberley, A History*, 97–98; and "News in Brief," *Flight*, January 4, 1951, 5.

63. Kewley and Gilbert, "Kerosine," vol. 4, 2484. Developments in diesel and petrol engines are discussed in "Farm Implements and Mechanization, Tractors," *Journal of the Royal Agricultural Society of England* 98 (1937): 201; DK Publishing, *Tractor: The Definitive Visual History*, 120–21; and Peter Small, "From Tanks to Tractors," *Courier & Advertiser*, October 14, 2015.

64. The Red Dragon is described in "Agricultural Machinery Exhibition at Earls Court," *The Engineer*, December 15, 1950, 591.

65. "Headen Novelty Company," *Foreign Commerce Weekly*, April 24, 1948, 35.

66. Despatch No. 520 (with attachment), Barry T. Benson, Second Secretary of Embassy, to U.S. State Department, March 1, 1948, box 5751, folder (untitled), item 840.50 Recovery/3-148, Central Decimal File, 1945–1949, RG 59, General Records of the Department of State, NARA, College Park.

67. "Import Opportunities, England—Headen Novelty Co., Ltd.," *Foreign Commerce Weekly*, April 24, 1948, 35. Headen Novelty occupied 15 Victoria Avenue until May 8, 1951, when it was taken over by J. H. Kerr & Partners Ltd. See *Rate Book for the General Rates,*

1950–1951 (Camberley, Surrey), 244, SHM. Also see letter, K. W. Smith, Clerk, Frimley and Camberley Urban District Council, Camberley, to "Dear Sir," February 26, 1951, in "Businesses—General, 1950s–1990s File," SHM; and H. J. [Illegible]ford, Town Planning Officer, "Factory Premises, 15, Victoria Avenue, Camberley," Frimley and Camberley Urban District Council Memorandum from the Town Planning Officer to the Clerk of the Council, April 5, 1955, in Victoria Avenue File, SHM. For Headen's plowshare tip patent, see Headen, "Improvements Relating to Plough Shares," GB Patent 641,825. Although notices of the dissolution of the company appeared in 1951 and 1952 in the *London Gazette*, these appear to have been generated by the late payment of taxes rather the company's demise. Headen continued to sell the Headen Cap until at least 1954. See Headen Novelty Company Limited, Notices of Dissolution, in *London Gazette*, November 30, 1951, 6257, and April 4, 1952, 1892; "Headen Novelty Company, Ltd.," *Farm Mechanization Directory*, vol. 31, 413. Testing of Headen's cap was carried out in India in 1953. See Indian Agricultural Research Institute, "Test of Plough Share Caps," 106.

    68. Lucean Arthur Headen Jr., certificate of baptism, no. 354, December 26, 1948, Camberley Church, Camberley, Surrey, England, in personal collection of Lucean Headen Jr.

    69. Headen Jr., conversations with the author, November 1–2, 2016, Swansea, Wales. The enthusiasm Graham's revivals stirred in Surrey are described in Team Captain, "Calling All Youth," *CN*, May 21, 1954, 5. According to a history of the Frimley Green Methodist Church, the hearing aid equipment was installed in 1954. See Bailey, *A Short History of Frimley Green Methodist Church*, 15. Confirmation of the Headens' attendance at the church was provided by Lucean Headen Jr. and by churchmember Ann Taylor. Headen Jr., conversation with the author, November 2, 2014, Swansea, Wales. Taylor, conversation with the author, November 9, 2016, Frimley Green, England.

    70. According to its stationery, the Junior Specialty Company occupied the Headen Novelty's earlier quarters on Bedford Lane. However, by 1955 Headen had given up this space. On a letter written that year, he struck out the Bedford Lane address and changed it to his home address of 153 Worsley, Frimley. See letter, February 9, 1955, Lucean A. Headen, Junior Specialty Company, Frimley, Surrey, to the Secretary to the President, the White House, Washington, D.C., attachment, Memorandum, February 24, 1955, Edward L. Beach, Naval Aide to the President, the White House, to the Secretary of State, Washington, D.C., box 3199, item 741.5621/2-2455, Central Decimal File, 1955–1959, RG 59, General Records of the Department of State, NARA, College Park.

    71. Letter, Lucean A. Headen, Frimley, Surrey, to the American Embassy, London, January 28, 1955, attachment to Dwight E. Scarborough, U.S. Embassy, London, England, Foreign Service Despatch 2848, March 29, 1955, to the Department of State, Washington, D.C., box 3199, item 741.5621/3-2955, Central Decimal File, 1955–1959, RG 59, General Records of the Department of State, NARA, College Park.

    72. Letter, Lucean A. Headen, Frimley, Surrey, to the American Embassy, London, January 28, 1955, attachment to Dwight E. Scarborough, U.S. Embassy, London, England, Foreign Service Despatch 2848, March 29, 1955, to the Department of State, Washington, D.C., box 3199, item 741.5621/3-2955, Central Decimal File, 1955–1959, RG 59, General Records of the Department of State, NARA, College Park.

    73. Letter, February 9, 1955, W. J. Schlacks Jr., Commander, U.S. Navy, U.S. Embassy, London, England, to L. A. Headen, Frimley, Surrey, attachment to Dwight E. Scarborough, U.S.

Embassy, London, England, Foreign Service Despatch 2848, March 29, 1955, to the Department of State, Washington, D.C., box 3199, item 741.5621/3-2955, Central Decimal File, 1955–1959, RG 59, General Records of the Department of State, NARA, College Park.

74. Dwight E. Scarborough, U.S. Embassy, London, England, Foreign Service Despatch 2848, March 29, 1955, to the Department of State, Washington, D.C., RG 59, General Records of the Department of State, Central Decimal File, 1955–1959, box 3199, item 741.5621/3-2955. Letter, Lucean A. Headen, Junior Specialty Company, Frimley, Surrey, February 9, 1955, to the Secretary to the President, the White House, Washington, D.C., attachment, Memorandum, February 24, 1955, Edward L. Beach, Naval Aide to the President, the White House, to the Secretary of State, Washington, D.C., box 3199, item 741.5621/2-2455, Central Decimal File, 1955–1959, RG 59, General Records of the Department of State, NARA, College Park; Pathé Gazette, "Eisenhower at Sandhurst," newsreel, available at https://www.youtube.com/watch?v=cHi7LvjVxZg.

75. Headen Jr., conversation with the author, October 25, 2016, London, England; Fred Penhallow and Jack Day, conversation with the author, November 9, 2016, Cedar Lodge Nursing Home, Frimley Green, England. For Headen's cyclist protection method patent application, see Headen, "Improved Means of Protecting a Cyclist from Rain and Other Adverse Weather Conditions," GB Patent 765,784 (patent approved but not sealed due to his death).

76. For discussion of Curtiss-Wright's wartime production numbers, see Hyde, *Arsenal of Democracy*, 71–74.

77. Curtiss-Wright's situation after the war is discussed in Eltscher and Young, *Curtiss Wright, Greatness and Decline*, 130–31. A full analysis of the possibilities of a North Atlantic airline route can be found in J. E. Parkin, Director, Division of Mechanical Engineering, National Research Council, Ottawa, Ontario, "North Atlantic Air Service, London–Montreal," *Engineering Journal*, August 1937, 611–55. Quote is from Curtiss-Wright's 1944 market analysis in "Cold Weather Operation," in McDonald and Drew, *Air Transportation in the Immediate Post-War Period*, 42.

78. Enos, "Deicing Means for Propellers," U.S. Patent 2,619,305.

79. Dean, "Deicing System for Propeller Blades," U.S. Patent 2,449,457; Headen, "Improvements in or Connected with Means for De-icing Aircraft Propellers," GB Patent 506,444; Houston, "Propeller," U.S. Patent 1,899,689. Houston's direct exhausting of the gases increased engine power, lessened the drag created by exterior exhaust pipes, and coated the blades with exhaust, reducing friction. His system used the centrifugal force of the propeller to suck the exhaust gases from the engine into the propeller hub, then exhausted them into the propeller cores and out a hole in the blade tip.

80. For Palmatier's work at Curtiss-Wright during the war, see Palmatier, *Thermal Propeller Anti-Icing Means*. His relevant patents include Palmatier, "Deicing System for Aircraft Surfaces," U.S. Patent 2,440,115; Palmatier, "Deicing System for Aircraft Surfaces," U.S. Patent 2,503,451; and Palmatier, "Deicing System for Aircraft," U.S. Patent 2,507,044.

81. Stuart and Berkley, "Anti-icing of Variable Pitch Propeller Blades," U.S. Patent 2,553,218A; Martin, "Means for Heating Hollow Propeller Blades," U.S. Patent 2,522,955; Thomas, "Air Foil Conditioning Means," U.S. Patent 2,514,105.

82. Sikorsky, "Rotar Blade," U.S. Patent 2,606,728; Mayne, "Airfoil, and Particularly Helicopter Blade," U.S. Patent 2,589,193A; Elliott, "Anti-icing and Intake Means for

258 Notes to Epilogue

Turbine-Propeller Units," U.S. 2,668,596A; Elliott, "Airscrew-Driving Gas Turbine Engine Power Plant with Anti-Icing Means for the Airscrews," U.S. 2,681,191A. For information on Elliott, see A. A. Rubbra, FRAeS, "A. G. Elliott, CBE, FRSA, MIME, FRAeS," *Aerospace*, April 1976, 32–33. For recent citations of Headen related to aircraft anti-icing systems, see Wright, "Anti-icing System for Aircraft," U.S. Patent 9,764,847 B2; Padden, "Strain Isolator Assembly," U.S. Patent 5,390,878; Morishita et al., "Anti-icing System and Aircraft," U.S. Patent Application 2017/0210476 A1.

83. See Bahuguni, Kandasamy, and Wong, "De-Icing of a Wind Turbine Blade," U.S. Patent 10,041,477 B2. According to David Weston, Vestas's system in 2018, already in use for several years, consisted of "projecting hot air from the root of the blade along the blade cavity." The company was also experimenting with electrothermal deicing. See David Weston, "Vestas Launches Electrothermal Anti-Ice System," *Wind Power Monthly*, February 5, 2018, https://www.windpowermonthly.com/article/1456241/vestas-launches-electrothermal-anti-ice-system.

84. Quote from Albert G. Elliott, "Turbine Engine Icing Problems," *The Aeroplane* (British Aircraft Industry Number), September 5, 1947, 309. For citations of Headen's vaporization patents, see Jury and Dehn, "Intake Manifold Regulators for Internal Combustion Engines," U.S. Patent 7,556,019 B2; Konomi, Nurita, and Tanazawa, "Intake Manifold Flow Equalizing Means," U.S. Patent 4,020,805; Konomi, Nurita, and Tanazawa, "Intake Manifold of the Internal Combustion Engine," U.S. Patent 4,038,950; Gospodar, Reichel, Vogelsang, and Thauer, "Induction Pipe for Internal Combustion Engines," U.S. Patent 3,811,416; George, Headley, Wilkes, and Wilkes, "Treating Charge Supplied to an I.C. Engine," GB Patent 2,169,654A; Lipski, "Spark-Ignition Engine," U.S. Patent 5,046,466.

85. "An American Who Settled in Frimley Green Dies," *CN*, September 27, 1957, 6; "Report of the Death of an American Citizen," Lucean Arthur Headen, September 27, 1957, box 953, item 241.113, Central Decimal File, 1955–1959, RG 59, General Records of the Department of State, NARA, College Park; entry for Lucean A. Headen in "Burials in the Parish of Frimley in the County of Surrey in the Year One-Thousand Nine Hundred and Fifty-Seven," in *Register of Burials, in the Parish of Frimley, in the County of Surrey*, London, Shaw & Sons, Ltd., 1952–1963, 52, Anglican Parish Registers, SHC.

Epilogue

1. "Invention Against U-Boats, Chicago Man Would Wrap Chasers in Magic Cloak, Torpedo Wall," *WMS*, May 16, 1917, 5.

2. Washington, "The Atlanta Address," 79.

3. Guy Tyson's affiliation with the Ashley & Bailey Silk Mill, and a sales trip he took on its behalf to the D.C. area (where he stayed with his brother Henry) in 1902, are discussed in "City Paragraphs," *CA*, June 14, 1902, 16. One writer described Jerry Headen by 1925 as "one of the wealthiest farmers" in the Aberdeen area. See H. A. Wiseman, "News of Colored People in the City and County, Mrs. W. A. Jones Returns to City," *WSJ*, July 2, 1925, 11.

4. Alger Jr., *The Erie Train Boy*.

5. Untitled editorial, *NYA*, January 25, 1912, 4; "Change 100-Mile Derby to 100-Miles of Auto Racing," *CD* (city ed.), August 30, 1924, 10; "Race Notes," *California Eagle*, May 19, 1917,

1; Work, *Negro Year Book, 1912,* 208; and Harrison, *Colored Girls' and Boys' Inspiring United States History,* 177.

6. Headen Motor Company brochure, 1922.

7. He rose quote from "The First Aeroplane School," *CD* (Big Weekend ed.), February 25, 1911, 1; dumfounded quote from "Chicagoan Invents Submarine Device," *CD* (Big Weekend ed.), May 12, 1917, 1.

8. Fouché, *Black Inventors in the Age of Segregation,* 8–25.

9. Eugene Marshall, *Royal Messenger,* quoted in "Comments of the Age Editors on Sayings of Other Editors," *NYA,* February 7, 1925, 4; Benjamin F. Thomas, "The Automobile and What It Has Done for the Negro," *New York Amsterdam News,* December 18, 1929, A16.

10. Franz, "'The Open Road,'" 131–54; Franz, *Tinkering,* 2–3; Seiler, *Republic of Drivers,* 111–13.

11. Headen's and his family's story supports Urry's argument that the automobile has been a key factor in the ability of diverse groups to safeguard and expand social capital in an increasingly mobile world. See Urry, "Mobility and Proximity," 264–65.

12. Gill, *Beauty Shop Politics.* Wynn was identified as a state organizer in "Georgia State, Gainesville, Ga.," *CD* (nat. ed.), August 23, 1930, 17. When she visited Gainesville to open a new club there in 1930, she and Headen may have been traveling together. He was noted as in the city as the same time as Wynn. For information on Wynn's activities in Albany, see "Georgia, Albany, Ga.," *CD* (nat. ed.), December 29, 1923, 14. Another beauty culturist who used the automobile to her advantage was Marjorie Stewart Joyner, inventor of the "Permanent Waving Machine" and a "Scalp Protector." Joyner, driving across the country as an agent for Madame C. J. Walker, towed behind her a trailer filled with demonstration products. See Blackwelder, *Styling Jim Crow,* 34–35. For Joyner's patents, see Joyner, "Permanent Waving Machine," U.S. Patent 1,693,515, and "Scalp Protector," U.S. Patent 1,716,173.

13. Coleman's plans to start a salon to fund her school are noted in Rich, *Queen Bess,* 101–5. Poro College, founded in St. Louis, moved to Chicago in 1930. See "Poro College Moves from St. Louis to Chicago," *CD* (nat. ed.), August 9, 1930, 3. The opening of Robinson's school and Malone's role are noted in "Aviation College Is Opened Here by Col. John Robinson," *CD* (city ed.), October 3, 1936, 5; "Students Enroll in Brown Condor's Air College," *CD* (nat. ed.), October 10, 1936, 5. For Robinson's providing rides to Malone's employees, see Associated Negro Press, "Takes to the Air," *California Eagle,* July 16, 1937, 2-A. For a description of Robinson's school and its offerings, see "The Colonel John C. Robinson Aviation Activities, Inc.," advertising flyer, box 171, folder 3, in Claude A. Barnett Papers, CHS; and *Vocational Studies in Chicago, Volume 1, Industrial and Trade Schools,* National Youth Administration of Illinois, June 1937, 43–52, in unnumbered box, RG 119, NYAR, State Publications (Illinois), NARA, Washington.

14. Many children of artisans, including auto manufacturer Fred Patterson, inherited their parents' artisanal outlook. In 1901, Charles Richard Patterson, successful Ohio carriagemaker and Patterson's father, modeled the blending of business and social goals for his son, announcing proudly to the NNBL that his carriage company was providing employment for thirty-five to fifty skilled mechanics, and that in his shop black and white employees worked side by side. See C. R. Patterson, "Carriage Building," In *Report of the Second Annual Convention of the National Negro Business League at Chicago, Illinois, August 21-22-23, 1901,* Chicago, R. S. Abbott Publishing Co., 1901, 64–66 (microfilm reel #1, frames 0218–0220), Records

of the NNBL, Part 1: Annual Conference Proceedings and Organizational Records, 1900–1919, LC.

15. Walker, *The History of Black Business in America*, 67–107; Juliet E. K. Walker, *Free Frank*. John E. McWorter held three aeronautical patents ("Flying-Machine," U.S. Patent 1,114,167, "Aeroplane," U.S. Patent 1,115,710, and "Flying Machine," U.S. Patent 1,438,929). McWorter demonstrated his 1914 aeroplane, a helicopter-like machine, on July 31, 1919, to Lt. Col. Thurman H. Bane of the Army Signal Corps' Engineering Division. His 1922 "Flying Machine" patent was assigned for production to the Autoplane Company of America, St. Louis, Missouri. See "General Race News," *The Half-Century Magazine*, September 1916, 8.

16. Bishir, *Crafting Lives*.

17. See Rich, *Queen Bess*, 101–5; and Snider, "'Great Shadow in the Sky'," 105–46. Coleman's early black entertainment backers included Theater Owners' Booking Association agent D. Ireland Thomas, syndicated columnist and organizer James A. "Billboard" Jackson, and filmmaker Peter Jones, head of the Seminole Film Producing Company in New York. For a full discussion of her relationship (and conflicts) with these three men (all unsuccessful in their attempts to cast her in their own mold), see Snider, "Flying to Freedom," 134–237. Coleman attended Langston University in Oklahoma, which later became a primarily industrial arts school. However, at the time of her attendance in 1911, it offered an equal mix of liberal arts and industrial courses. For her record at Langston, see Langston Colored Agricultural and Normal University catalog, 1910–11.

18. For a discussion of Powell's activities, see Powell, *Story of William J. Powell*; and Snider, "William Jenifer Powell," 458–60.

19. Patent citation statistics for 1928–29 are from Lamoreaux, Sokoloff, and Sutthiphisal, "The Reorganization of Inventive Activity," 250.

20. Scathing critiques of the emergent black middle class have enjoyed a long history in academic publishing, spanning from E. Franklin Franzier's 1957 *Black Bourgeoisie* to Kevin Gaines's 1996 *Uplifting the Race*.

21. Marie Tyson was active in almost every facet of social work within West Philadelphia's black community. Described as "one of the most enthusiastic and faithful members," she chaired the Independent Women's Welfare Council No. 3. See "Social Revue and Society," *PT*, November 14, 1929, 4; untitled item, *PT*, January 23, 1930, 4; and "Philly Honors Social Worker," *PT*, October 5, 1929, 6. In 1932, she headed Lombard Central Presbyterian Church's Emergency Aid Committee, and in 1934 served as corresponding secretary for the Women's Board of Managers of Mercy Hospital. See "Rev. Imes Addresses Favorite Church Club," *PT*, June 2, 1932, 1; and "Board of Managers Elect New Officers," *PT*, May 3, 1934, 7. In 1940, after Central Presbyterian relocated from Lombard Street to Powelton Avenue, across the street from the Tysons' home, Marie participated in the new edifice's dedication. See "Tea Climaxes Dedication at New Central Church," *PT*, May 16, 1940, 9. She was also a steady patron of the Lyceum in Philadelphia and was an early worker for women's suffrage. See "The Lyceum Makes Debut to Philadelphia," *PT*, October 5, 1933, 7; and Sara Neely, "Mrs. Helen Duckett Is a Modern Cinderella," *BAA*, March 4, 1939, 17. She was also elected president of the Berean School Associate Committee of Women for 1930. See "Phillygrams, Berean Activities," *PC*, November 23, 1929, 10. Nan Headen Jones was a leader in civic affairs in Winston-Salem for more than twenty years. For her role in the Phillis Wheatley Branch of the YWCA, founded in 1918, see H. A. Wiseman, "News of Colored People in the City and County,

Y.W.C.A.," *WSJ*, March 29, 1923, 8; and H. A. Wiseman, "News of Colored People, Y.W.C.A. Meeting," *WSJ*, January 25, 1929, 9. Although financially comfortable when her husband died, the stock market crash of 1929 forced Nannie to return to work. By 1930 she was earning income as a skilled dressmaker and was renting rooms in her home to local schoolteachers. See *Fifteenth United States Census: 1930*, Household of Nannie Jones, Winston-Salem, Forsyth Co., N.C., ED 34-49, sheet 7A. In 1938, she began teaching at Philadelphia's Sleighton Farm School for Girls. See Priscilla Penn, "Society at a Glance, Mrs. Guy Tyson Gives a Bridge," *PT*, February 3, 1938, 5. For information on the Sleighton School, see Arnold, Buck, Merriam, and Stockover, "Study of Delinquent Girls at Sleighton Farm," 598. Nannie left Philadelphia in 1939 to become a house directress for North Carolina College in Durham (today North Carolina Central University). Her first presence there is noted in Genevieve Smith, "N.C. College News Items," *Carolina Times*, December 23, 1939, 7. She was still a faculty member in 1948. See "Faculty and Staff," *Maroon and Gray*, vol. 5, 1948, 15.

22. Louise Headen, after graduating from Winston-Salem Teachers College and the Pratt Institute in Brooklyn, New York, began teaching in Greensboro, South Carolina. In 1929, she married Harold B. Chandler, an A&T graduate. After divorcing, she relocated to teach at the Morningside School in Statesville, North Carolina. In 1937, Louise married Fred Ables, an Atlanta native, and moved with him to Richmond, although she continued to teach during the school year in Statesville until she and Fred moved to Pittsburgh in 1942. See "Mrs. Harold B. Chandler," *NYA*, March 16, 1929, 1; "Greensboro, N.C.," *PC*, March 30, 1929, 6; Louise Headen [Chandler] and Frederick Douglass Ables, marriage certificate, June 28, 1937, Aberdeen, N.C., in FamilySearch.com, *North Carolina Marriages, 1759–1979*; "Mostly About State Capital People, Personals," *New Journal and Guide*, April 19, 1941, 18. For discussion of the work of Jane Ables Greenwood see, for example, "Greenwood Encourages Corporate Support for NAACP," *PC*, December 7, 1996, 2; Christian Morrow, "CCAC Celebrates Opening of Food Pantries at All Campuses with Ribbon Cutting," *PC*, April 29, 2018, https://newpittsburghcourieronline.com/2018/04/29/ccac-celebrates-opening-of-food-pantries-at-all-campuses-with-ribbon-cutting/. For a full discussion of the role of the black middle class in creating economic opportunities for subsequent generations, and the example it provides for future progress, see Butler, *Entrepreneurship and Self-Help Among Black Americans*, 335–41. I agree with Butler's emphasis on self-help, entrepreneurship, and social networking for expanding opportunities. However, I am not fully convinced of the assertion that this approach alone provides a clear blueprint for individuals living in core poverty. Butler argues that black Americans after the Civil War built an enduring black middle class "from nothing." Families such as Headen's, however, cannot be accurately described as such. They had distinct advantages. Their more salient legacy, I believe, is their demonstration that a communal, network-based approach must be a key part of building individual and community success.

23. Ashton, *How to Fly a Horse*, 13.

Bibliography

Primary Sources

MANUSCRIPT COLLECTIONS

Camberley, Surrey, England
  Surrey Heath Museum
    Business Files
    Chancellor's Book, 1935–1939
    Tax Rate Books
    Victoria Avenue File
Cambridge, Mass.
  Harvard University
    Minstrel Sheet Music Collection, Harvard Theatre Collection
Carthage, N.C.
  Moore County Public Library
    Moore County Library Historical Collection
      Pamphlet Files
  First Presbyterian Church Office
    Session Book, Carthage Church [later First Presbyterian Church]
Chantilly, Va.
  National Air and Space Museum, Steven F. Udvar-Hazy Research Center
    Biographical Files
      Henry Winter correspondence, draft autobiography (manuscript), n.d.
      Dr. Bessica Faith Raiche
    Curtiss-Wright Papers
    Vin Fiz Special Papers
Chapel Hill, N.C.
Wilson Special Collections Library, University of North Carolina
  North Carolina Collection
    Moore County File
  Map Collection
    H[enry] C. Brown, preparer. *Railroad Map of North Carolina, 1900,* North Carolina Corporation Commission, 1900
Chicago Ill.
  Chicago Historical Society
    Grace Presbyterian Church Records
      Session Minutes, 2 vols., and "Celebrate the Journey" manuscript
  Chicago Public Library
    Records of the Circuit Court of Cook County

264 Bibliography

  Vivian Harsh Collection
   Abbott-Sengstacke Family Papers
 Newberry Library
  McCormick Family Financial Records, 1890–1958
   Cyrus R. McCormick Jr. Ledgers
  Pullman Company Records (Manuscript)
   RG 06, Subgroup 02, Series 06, Discharge and Release Records
   RG 06, Subgroup 03, Series 06, Individual Pensioner Files
  Pullman Company Records (Microfilm)
  Pre-1917 Personnel Cards, Porters & Maids
College Park, Md.
 National Archives and Records Administration, College Park
  RG 59, General Records of the Department of State
   Central Decimal File, 1945–1949
   Central Decimal File, 1955–1959
  RG 62, Records of the Council of National Defense
   General Munitions Board & Munitions Standards Records, *Volume 1, Minutes, General Munitions Board* (April 9, 1917–August 9, 1917)
Colorado Springs, Colo.
 U.S. Air Force Academy Library, Special Collections Branch
  Henry J. Winter Collection
Greenville, N.C.
 J. W. Joyner Library, East Carolina University
  George W. McNeill Papers
Kansas City, Mo.
 National Archives and Records Administration, Kansas City
  RG 241, U.S. Patent and Trademark Office, Patent Case Files
Kew, Richmond, Surrey, England
 National Archives, Kew
  Admiralty Records
   ADM 116/1430, Record Office: Cases, Board of Invention and Research
   ADM 293/10, Board of Invention and Research: Minutes and Reports
   ADM 293/20, Reports of Director of Experiments and Research
  Records of the Cabinet Office, Cabinet Minutes and Papers
   CAB 66-War Cabinet, Memoranda
Lake Forest, Ill.
 Lake Forest College
  Joseph Medill Patterson Papers
London, England
 British Library
  Science, Reference and Information Service, *Register of Stages of Progress*
Madison, Wis.
 State Historical Society of Wisconsin
  McCormick Collection

        Series B (Nettie Fowler McCormick)
        Series C (Cyrus McCormick Jr.)
Morrow, Ga.
    Georgia Archives
        Dougherty County Tax Digests, 1927, 1928, and 1929
        Business Services & Regulation, Corporations Registrations Ledgers, 1906–1941
Newlands, Lincoln, Lincolnshire, England
    Lincolnshire Archives
        Collection 2-AB (2nd Accession), Aveling-Barford
New York, N.Y.
    Museum of the City of New York
        Henry Winter, "Early Aviation U.S.A." (manuscript autobiography, Boston, 1978). Note: An earlier draft is held by NASM UHRC, Chantilly, Va.
    New York Public Library, Schomburg Center for Research in Black Culture
        UNIA Almanac, 1921
Philadelphia, Pa.
    Presbyterian Historical Society
        Minutes, Yadkin Presbytery, vol. 2, 2nd series
        Data Files
            Inez Moore Parker, comp., "Albion Academy, Franklinton," n.d.
        RG 314, First African Presbyterian Church (Philadelphia) Records
            "Register of Members, Baptism, and Deaths, VI. Alphabetical Index to Roll of Communicants, 1904"
        RG 376, Board of Missions for Freedmen Records
            Records of the Presbyterian Committee for Freedmen, vol. 4
        RG 395, African American Synods and Presbyteries Collection
Raleigh, N.C.
    North Carolina State Archives
        Collection PC 1761, Alexander Hamilton McNeill Papers (Addition)
        Governor's Papers
            Governor William W. Holden Correspondence
        Record of Deeds, 1888–1961, Moore Co., N.C. (Microfilm)
        Records of Wills, 1783–1965, Moore Co. Wills, Will Book B (Microfilm)
        Records of Wills, 1946–1949, Moore County Wills, vol. P (Microfilm)
Reading, Berkshire, England
    Museum of English Rural Life
        Silsoe Research Institute Records
St. Louis, Mo.
    Presbyterian Church in America (PCA) Historical Center
        Edward A. Steele Papers
    State Historical Society of Missouri
        Collection S0151, Kinloch Committee Historical Records
            Folder 13, *Kinloch: Yesterday, Today, and Tomorrow*

Washington, D.C.
  Library of Congress Manuscript Division
    Green-Driver Collection
      Name File, 1896–1968
    Hanna-McCormick Family Papers
      Medill McCormick Correspondence Series
    Institute of Aerospace Sciences Archives
      Biographical Files Series
      Oversize Series
      Scrapbook Series
    Josephus Daniels Papers (Microfilm)
      Navy Files, Reel 28
    Mary Church Terrell Papers (Microfilm)
      Untitled Flyer, January 1, 1892
    National Association for the Advancement of Colored People (NCAAP) Papers
      Part I: Branch Files, 1910–1947
    Records of the National Negro Business League (NNBL) (Microfilm)
      Part 1: Annual Conference Proceedings and Organizational Records, 1900–1919
  National Archives and Records Administration, Washington
    RG 80, General Records of the Department of the Navy
      Records of the Office of Inventions, Case Files, 1915–1934
    RG 119, National Youth Administration Records
    Record of Appointment of Postmasters, 1832–Sept. 30, 1971, Microfilm Publ. M841
  National Museum of American History, Archives Center
    Sam DeVincent Collection
Wheaton, Ill.
  Colonel Robert R. McCormick Research Center, Cantigny Foundation
    Robert R. McCormick Papers, Series I-60
Wilmington, N.C.
  New Hanover Public Library
    Bill Reaves Collection
Woking, Surrey, England
  Surrey History Centre
    Anglican Parish Registers
    Camberley: Deeds, 1871–1967 (Ref 6736)
    Map Collection

NEWSPAPERS

Aberdeen Press and Journal (Aberdeen, Scotland)
The Advance (Elizabeth City, N.C.)
Africo-American Presbyterian (Wilmington and Charlotte, N.C.)
Albany Herald (Albany, Ga.)
Amsterdam News (New York)
The Anglo-Saxon (Rockingham, N.C.)
Asheboro Courier (Asheboro, N.C.)
Asheville Citizen-Times (Asheville, N.C.)
Atlanta Constitution (Atlanta)
Augusta Chronicle (Augusta, Ga.)
Baltimore Afro-American (Baltimore)
Belfast Telegraph (Belfast, Ireland)

Border Cities Star (Windsor, Ontario, Canada)
Boston Evening Transcript (Boston)
Broad Ax (Chicago)
Brooklyn Daily Eagle (Brooklyn, N.Y.)
Brunswick News (Brunswick, Ga.)
Carolina Times (Durham, N.C.)
California Eagle (Los Angeles)
Carthage Blade (Carthage, N.C.)
The Carthaginian (Carthage, N.C.)
Charlotte Daily Observer (Charlotte, N.C.)
Charlotte News (Charlotte, N.C.)
Charlotte Observer (Charlotte, N.C.)
Chatham Record (Pittsboro, N.C.)
Chicago Daily News (Chicago)
Chicago Defender (Chicago)
Chicago Examiner (Chicago)
Chicago Tribune (Chicago)
Cleveland Gazette (Cleveland)
Colorado Statesman (Denver)
Colored American (Washington, D.C.)
Columbus Daily Inquirer (Columbus, Ga.)
Courier & Advertiser (Perth, Australia)
Dallas Express (Dallas)
Day Book (Chicago)
Derby Daily Telegraph (Derby, Derbyshire, England)
Derby Evening Telegraph (Derby, Derbyshire, England)
Detroit Free Press (Detroit)
Dundee Courier (Dundee, Scotland)
Dundee Evening Telegraph (Dundee, Scotland)
Durham Sun (Durham, N.C.)
The Economist (Chicago)
El Paso Herald (El Paso, Tex.)
Evening Star (Washington, D.C.)
Evening Telegram (New York)
Fayetteville Observer (Fayetteville, N.C.)
Fayetteville Weekly Observer (Fayetteville, N.C.)
Florida Sentinel (Orlando, Fla.)
Franklin Times (Louisburg, N.C.)
Freeport Journal-Standard (Freeport, Ill.)
The Freeman (Indianapolis)

The Gazette (Raleigh, N.C.)
Globe-Democrat (St. Louis, Mo.)
Greensboro Patriot (Greensboro, N.C.)
Houston Informer (Houston, Tex.)
Indianapolis Star (Indianapolis)
Inter-Ocean (Chicago)
Iowa State Bystander (Des Moines, Iowa)
Jonesboro Leader (Jonesboro, N.C.)
Kansas City Sun (Kansas City, Mo.)
Lincoln Courier (Lincolnton, N.C.)
London Gazette (London, England)
Macon Telegraph (Macon, Ga.)
Marietta Journal (Marietta, Ga.)
The Mercury (Hobart, Tasmania, Australia)
Miami Herald (Miami)
Moberly Evening Democrat (Moberly, Mo.)
Moore County News (Carthage, N.C.)
Moore Gazette (Carthage, N.C.)
Moore Index (Carthage, N.C.)
Morning News (Wilmington, Del.)
Morning Post (Raleigh, N.C.)
Nashville Globe (Nashville, Tenn.)
Negro World (New York)
Newport Daily News (Newport, R.I.)
News & Observer (Raleigh, N.C.)
New York Age (New York)
Norfolk Journal & Guide (Norfolk, Va.)
North Carolinian (Raleigh, N.C.)
Nottingham Evening Post (Nottingham, Nottinghamshire, England)
Oakland Sunshine (Oakland, Calif.)
Omaha Daily Bee (Omaha, Neb.)
Omaha World Herald (Omaha, Neb.)
Palladium and Sun-Telegram (Richmond, Ind.)
People's Advocate (Washington, D.C.)
Philadelphia Tribune (Philadelphia)
The Pilot (Southern Pines, N.C.)
Pinehurst Outlook (Pinehurst, N.C.)
Pittsburgh Courier (Pittsburgh)
Pittsburgh Gazette Times (Pittsburgh)
Post-Dispatch (St. Louis, Mo.)
Progressive Farmer (Winston-Salem, N.C.)
Raleigh Daily Times (Raleigh, N.C.)
Raleigh Times (Raleigh, N.C.)

Reno Evening Gazette (Reno, Nev.)
Richmond Planet (Richmond, Va.)
Richmond Times-Dispatch (Richmond, Va.)
Roanoke Beacon (Plymouth, N.C.)
Roxboro Courier (Roxboro, N.C.)
Sanford Express (Sanford, N.C.)
Savannah Tribune (Savannah, Ga.)
Southern Cross (Savannah, Ga.)
Southern Indicator (Columbia, S.C.)
Southern Protectionist (Carthage, N.C.)
Staffordshire Advertiser (Stafford, Staffordshire, England)
Star of Zion (Petersburg, Va.)
State Chronicle (Raleigh, N.C.)
Statesville Daily Record (Statesville, N.C.)
Statesville Record & Landmark (Statesville, N.C.)
Sunday Worker (Pittsburgh)
Sussex Agricultural Express (Lewes, Sussex, England)
Sydney Morning Herald (Sydney, Australia)
Tallahassee Daily Democrat (Tallahassee, Fla.)
Tampa Morning Tribune (Tampa, Fla.)
Thomasville Times Enterprise (Thomasville, Ga.)
The Times (Richmond, Va.)
Times-Visitor (Raleigh, N.C.)
Twin City Daily Sentinel (Winston-Salem, N.C.)
Virginian-Pilot and Norfolk Landmark (Norfolk, Va.)
Washington Bee (Washington, D.C.)
Washington Post (Washington, D.C.)
Washington Progress (Washington, N.C.)
Weekly Star (Plymouth, Pa.)
West Sussex County Times (Horsham, West Sussex, England)
Western Sentinel (Winston-Salem, N.C.)
Wilmington Messenger (Wilmington, N.C.)
Wilmington Morning Star (Wilmington, N.C.)
Wilmington Post (Wilmington, N.C.)
Wilmington Star (Wilmington, N.C.)
Winston-Salem Journal (Winston-Salem, N.C.)
Yorkshire Evening Post (Leeds, West Yorkshire, England)

TRADE, PROFESSIONAL, CHURCH, CLUB, AND POPULAR JOURNALS

Aerial Age (Chicago)
Aero, America's Aviation Weekly (Chicago: Aero Club of Illinois)
Aeronautics: The American Magazine of Aerial Locomotion (New York)
The Aeroplane (London)
Aircraft Engineering and Aerospace Technology: An International Journal (London)
Air-Scout: Official Organ of the United States Aeronautical Reserve (New York)
Aerospace (London: Royal Aeronautical Society)
American Contractor (Chicago)
American Garage and Auto Dealer (Chicago)
American Mercury (New York)
The Argonaut (San Francisco)
Assembly Herald, the Magazine of the Presbyterian Church, U.S.A. (Pittsburgh)
The Automobile (New York)
Automotive Industries (Philadelphia)
The Bladesman (Caldwell, N.J.)
Chemical Age (London)
Church at Home and Abroad (Philadelphia)
Club Journal (London: Royal Automobile Club)
Commercial Motor (London)

Country Life in America (Garden City, N.Y.)
The Crisis: A Record of the Darker Races (New York: NAACP)
Cycle and Automobile Trade Journal (Philadelphia)
The Dragon (Fafnir Ball Bearing Co., New Britain, Conn.)
The Educator (Fayetteville, N.C.)
Engineering: An Illustrated Weekly Journal (London)
Engineering Journal (Montreal, Canada)
Erie Railroad Employes' Magazine (New York)
Flight: The Aircraft Engineer and Airships (London)
Fly (Philadelphia)
Flying (New York)
Foreign Commerce Weekly (London)
Freemason and Masonic Illustrated: A Weekly Record of Progress in Freemasonry (London)
Gas Engine (New York)
Gas Power (St. Joseph, Mich.)
The Hub (New York)
Home Mission Monthly (Pittsburgh)
Iron Age (New York)
Journal of the Aeronautical Sciences (Easton, Pa.: Institute of Aeronautical Sciences)
Journal of the National Medical Association (Silver Spring, Md.)
Journal of the Royal Agricultural Society of England (London)
Journal of the Society of Automotive Engineers (New York)
The Keys: The Official Organ of the League of Coloured Peoples (London)
Lincoln University Herald (Lincoln University, Pa.)
Manufacturers Record (Atlanta)
The Motor (London)
Motor Age (New York)
Motor Transport (London)
Oil and Gas Journal (Tulsa)
Pearson's Magazine (New York)
Presbyterian Monthly Record (Philadelphia)
Roadless News (Hounslow, Middlesex, England)
S.A.L.magundi (Portsmouth, Va.)
Sportsman Pilot: The Magazine of Private Aviation (New York)
The South, an Immigration Journal (Weldon, N.C.)
Southern Workman (Hampton, Va.)
The Wood-Worker, a Journal for Machine Wood Workers (Indianapolis)
World's Carriers and Carrying Trades' Review (London)
WWI Aero: The Journal of the Early Aeroplane (Poughkeepsie, N.Y.)

PATENTS CITED

Many of the surviving records for these patents are available in Google Patents and other international databases. However, these databases often contain only preliminary specification documents, rather than sealed patents. Confirmation of the sealing is from the British Library's Science, Reference and Information Service's *Register of Stages of Progress*.

Prior to 1977, the term "sealed" (rather than the more recently adopted "granted") was the official British term for an awarded patent; see Stephen Van Dulken, *British Patents of Invention, 1617–1977: A Guide for Researchers* (London: The British Library, 1999), 33. Thus, the term "sealed" is used here for all British patents. The term "granted," historically used by the U.S. Patent Office, however, is used for U.S. patents.

Patent records for all patents cited in this book are available at Google Patents (https://patents.google.com/).

PATENTS HELD BY HEADEN (BY TYPE, FILING DATE)

Ignition Device

Headen, Lucean A., and Henry A. Petit. "Ignition Device." US Patent 1,780,076 (assigned to National Oil Manifolds, Inc., and Albert S. Bacon), filed August 1, 1929, and granted October 28, 1930.

Vaporizing Manifold

Headen, Lucean A. "Vaporizer." US Patent 2,017,497, filed May 16, 1930, and granted October 15, 1935.

———. "Improvements in or Relating to Vaporizers for Internal Combustion Engines." GB Patent 381,588, filed July 8, 1931, and sealed January 4, 1933. Sealing date from *Register of Stages of Progress*, vol. 357,001–382,000.

Pre-ignition Device

Headen, Lucean A. "Improvements in or Relating to the Formation of Charges Supplied to Internal Combustion Engines." GB Patent 396,834, filed February 23, 1932, and sealed November 8, 1933. Sealing date from *Register of Stages of Progress*, vol. 382,001–407,000.

Antidilution Gasket

Keil, James Richard McLean (Assignee) [Lucean Arthur Headen, Inventor]. "Improvements in or Relating to Charge Mixing and Heating Devices and/or Vaporisers for Use in the Cylinders of Internal Combustion Engines." GB Patent No. 437,020, filed January 23, 1934, and sealed January 22, 1936. Sealing date from *Register of Stages of Progress*, vol. 432,001–457,000. Note: British patent law allowed an assignee to apply for a patent in their name. The corollary U.S. Patent (2,092,454), however, was granted directly to Headen, because U.S. patent law required all patents bear the inventor's name. See Van Dulken, *British Patents of Invention*, 81, 111. The Canadian patent (CA 362,088) was also issued in Headen's name.

Headen, Lucean A. "Charge Mixing and Heating Device and/or Vaporizer for Use in Cylinders of Internal Combustion Engines." US Patent 2,092,454 (assigned to George P. Koelliker), filed January 23, 1935, and granted September 7, 1937. (See Keil, GB Patent 437,020.)

———. "Engine Charge Device/Dispositif a Cylindrees de Moteur." CA 362,088 (assigned to George P. Koelliker), filing date unknown, granted November 11, 1936. (See corollary Keil, GB Patent 437,020.)

Oil-Burning Carburetor
Headen, Lucean A. "Improvements in Vaporizers or Heaters for Use in Internal Combustion Engines." GB Patent 459,603, filed July 12, 1935, and sealed April 28, 1937. Sealing date from *Register of Stages of Progress*, vol. 457,001–480,000.
———. "Improvements in Vaporisers for Internal Combustion Engines." GB Patent 469,826, filed February 3, 1936, and sealed November 3, 1937. Sealing date from *Register of Stages of Progress*, vol. 457,001–480,000.
———. "Perfectionnements aux Appareils de Vaporisation pour Moteurs à Combustion Interne." FR Patent 806,631, filed May 20, 1936, and granted December 21, 1936.

Methods for Ice Prevention on Aircraft Control Surfaces
Headen, Lucean A. "A New or Improved Apparatus for Preventing Ice Formation on Aircraft Surfaces." GB Patent 486,549, filed December 7, 1936, and sealed September 7, 1938. Sealing date from *Register of Stages of Progress*, vol. 480,001–500,000.
———. "Improvements in or Connected with Means for Preventing Ice Formation on Control Services of Aircraft." GB Patent 505,772, filed November 16, 1937, and sealed August 16, 1939. Sealing date from *Register of Stages of Progress*, vol. 500,001–520,000.
———. " Ice Formation Preventing Apparatus for Aircraft/Appareil Empêchant la Formation de la Glace sur Avion." CA Patent 376,999, filing date unknown, granted October 11, 1938.
———. "Dispositif pour Empêcher la Formation de Givre sur les Surfaces des Aéronefs." FR Patent 825,715, filing date unknown, granted November 3, 1938.

Methods for Deicing Propellers
Headen, Lucean A. "Dispositif pour Déglacer les Hélices d'avions." FR Patent 837,466, filing date unknown, granted February 10, 1939.
———. "Improvements in or Connected with Means for De-icing Aircraft Propellers." GB Patent 504,737, filed October 29, 1937, and sealed July 26, 1939. Sealing date from *Register of Stages of Progress*, vol. 500,001–520,000.
———. "Improvements in or Connected with Means for De-icing Aircraft Propellers." GB Patent 506,444, filed February 8, 1938, and sealed August 30, 1939. Sealing date from *Register of Stages of Progress*, vol. 500,001–520,000.

Plough Share Tip
Headen, Lucean A. "Improvements Relating to Plough Shares." GB Patent 641,825, filed January 2, 1948, and sealed August 23, 1950. Sealing date from *Register of Stages of Progress*, vol. 640,001–660,000.

Cyclist Protection
Headen, Lucean A. "Improved Means of Protecting a Cyclist from Rain and Other Adverse Weather Conditions." GB No. 765,784, filed June 29, 1953, advertisement of complete acceptance November 21, 1956, patent not sealed before Headen's death.

OTHER PATENTS CITED

Bahuguni, Anand, Ravi Kandasamy, and Voon Hon Wong. "De-Icing of a Wind Turbine Blade." US Patent 10,041,477 B2 (assigned to Vestas Wind Systems A/S), filed December 14, 2010, and granted August 7, 2018.

Bensing, LeRue P. "Electrolytic Rectifier." US Patent 1,628,785 (assigned to George P. Koelliker), filed January 18, 1926, and granted May 17, 1927.

Cole, Eugene Macon. "Seed-Planter." US Patent 439,773, filed August 8, 1899, and granted November 4, 1890.

Dean, George A. "Deicing System for Propeller Blades." US Patent 2,449,457 (assigned to Curtiss-Wright Corporation), filed May 25, 1946, and granted September 14, 1948.

Downer, George F. "Storage Battery." CA Patent 259,854 (assigned to George P. Koelliker and John W. Fraser), filed ca. 1922–1925, and granted April 13, 1926.

Elliott, Albert George. "Airscrew-Driving Gas Turbine Engine Power Plant with Anti-Icing Means for the Airscrews." US Patent 2,681,191 (assigned to ROTOL, Ltd.), filed July 30, 1948, and granted June 15, 1954.

———. "Anti-icing and Intake Means for Turbine-Propeller Units." US Patent 2,668,596 (assigned to ROTOL, Ltd.), filed June 29, 1948, and granted February 9, 1954.

Enos, Louis H. "Deicing Means for Propellers." US Patent 2,619,305 (assigned to Curtiss-Wright Corporation), filed December 9, 1939, and granted November 25, 1952.

George, Ronald, Alphonso Headley, John Wilkes, and Stephen John Wilkes. "Treating Charge Supplied to an I.C. Engine." GB Patent 2,169,654A (assigned to Genie Economy Components), filed January 12, 1985, and granted May 4, 1989.

Gospodar, Reinhold, Kurt Reichel, Gustav Vogelsang, and Peter Thauer. "Induction Pipe for Internal Combustion Engines." US Patent 3,811,416 (assigned to Volkswagenwerk A/G), filed December 8, 1970, and granted May 21, 1974.

Houston, George. "Propeller." US Patent 1,899,689 (assigned to Bendix Research Corporation), filed August 4, 1930, and granted February 28, 1933.

Joyner, Marjorie S[tewart]. "Permanent Waving Machine." US Patent 1,693,515 (assigned to Madame C. J. Walker Manufacturing Company), filed May 16, 1928, and granted November 27, 1928.

———. "Scalp Protector." US Patent 1,716,173 (assigned to Madame C. J. Walker Manufacturing Company), filed May 16, 1928, and granted June 4, 1929.

Jury, Brett, and James J. Dehn. "Intake Manifold Regulators for Internal Combustion Engines." US Patent 7,556,019 B2 (assigned to Briggs and Stratton Corporation), filed December 15, 2006, and granted July 7, 2009.

Konomi, Toshiaki, Joji Nurita, and Yasushi Tanazawa. "Intake Manifold Flow Equalizing Means." US Patent 4,020,805 (assigned to Toyota Jidosha Kogyo Kabushiki Kaisha), filed December 11, 1975, and granted May 3, 1977.

———. "Intake Manifold of the Internal Combustion Engine." US Patent 4,038,950 (assigned to Toyota Jidosha Kogyo Kabushiki Kaisha), filed December 11, 1975, and granted August 2, 1977.

Lewis, James Keeler. "Electrolytic Rectifier." US Patent 1,775,417 (assigned to George P. Koelliker), filed May 23, 1925, and granted September 9, 1930.

Lipski, Frank F. "Spark-Ignition Engine." US Patent 5,046,466 (assigned to Fazer Environmental Technologies Corporation), filed September 20, 1990, and granted September 10, 1991.

Martin, Erle. "Means for Heating Hollow Propeller Blades." US Patent 2,522,955 (assigned to United Technologies Corporation), filed September 14, 1944, and granted September 19, 1950.

Mayne, Robert. "Airfoil, and Particularly Helicopter Blade." US Patent 2,589,193 (assigned to Goodyear Aircraft Corporation), filed November 29, 1946, and granted March 11, 1952.

McWorter, John E. "Aeroplane." US Patent No. 1,115,710, filed June 26, 1911, and granted November 3, 1914.

———. "Flying-Machine." US Patent No. 1,114,167, filed May 9, 1913, and granted October 20, 1914.

———. "Flying Machine." US Patent No. 1,438,929 (assigned to Autoplane Company of America), filed July 18, 1921, and granted December 12, 1922.

Morishita, Masatoshi, Masanori Tsujita, Satoshi Watanabe, Yoichi Uefuji, Kazuhiro Kawai, Toshiyuki Ishida, Gento Ichikawa, and Go Fujita. "Anti-icing System and Aircraft." US Patent Application 2017/0210476 A1 (assigned to Mitsubishi Aircraft Corporation), filed December 27, 2017, and patent pending.

Padden, Vincent T. "Strain Isolator Assembly." US Patent 5,390,878 (assigned to Grumman Aerospace Corporation, Vought Aircraft Industries), filed February 9, 1993, and granted February 21, 1995.

Palmatier, Everett P. "Deicing System for Aircraft Surfaces." US Patent 2,440,115 (assigned to Curtiss-Wright Corporation), filed January 11, 1944, and granted April 20, 1948.

———. "Deicing System for Aircraft Surfaces." US Patent 2,503,451 (assigned to Curtiss-Wright Corporation), filed January 11 1944, and granted April 11, 1950.

———. "Deicing System for Aircraft." US Patent 2,507,044 (assigned to Curtiss-Wright Corporation), filed September 20, 1943, and granted May 9, 1950.

Sikorsky, Igor. "Rotar Blade." US Patent 2,606,728 (assigned to United Technologies Corporation), filed December 4, 1945, and granted August 12, 1952.

Stuart, Joseph, III, and Warren D. Berkley. "Anti-icing of Variable Pitch Propeller Blades." US Patent 2,553,218 (assigned to General Motors Corporation), filed May 1, 1944, and granted May 15, 1951.

Theodorsen, Theodore, and William C. Clay. "Vapor Heating System." US Patent 2,081,963, filed September 26, 1935, and granted June 1, 1937.

Thomas, Wilfred. "Air Foil Conditioning Means." US Patent 2, 514,105, filed September 26, 1935, and granted June 1, 1937.

Wright, Robert Steven. "Anti-icing System for Aircraft." US Patent 9,764,847 B2 (assigned to The Boeing Company), filed January 16, 2014, and granted September 19, 2017.

GOVERNMENT SOURCES

Agricultural and Manufacturing Census Records of Fifteen Southern States for the Years 1850, 1860, 1870, and 1880. Original data, U.S. Bureau of the Census, *North Carolina Manufacturing Census*, Microfilm Publ. M1805, *Nonpopulation Census Schedules for North Carolina, 1850–1880: Mortality and Manufacturing*, Roll 9: 1880, Manufacturing: Gaston-Yancey Counties, and *Nonpopulation Schedules for North Carolina, 1850–1880: Agriculture: North Carolina*, Washington, D.C.: National Archives.

City of Baltimore. *One Hundred and Twenty-Fifth Annual Report of the Department of Health, 1939.* Baltimore: Department of Health, 1939.

Gibson, Campbell, and Kay Jung. *Historical Census Statistics on Population Totals by Race, 1790 to 1990, and by Hispanic Origin, 1970 to 1990, for Large Cities and Other Urban Places in the United States*. Population Division Working Paper No. 76. Washington, D.C.: U.S. Census Bureau, 2005.

Harris, Robert. "Report of the Principal of the State Colored Normal School, for the School Year 1878-'79." In *North Carolina Executive and Legislative Documents, Session 1881*. Document 5, 34–42. Raleigh: *News & Observer*, State Printers & Binders, 1881.

Illinois Office of Secretary of State. "Corporations for Profit." In *Biennial Report of the Secretary of State of the State of Illinois, Fiscal Years Beginning October 1, 1914, and Ending September 30, 1916*. Springfield: Illinois State Journal, State Printers, 1916.

Indian Agricultural Research Institute. "Test of Plough Share Caps." *Annual Scientific Report, 1949*. In *Scientific Reports of the Indian Agricultural Research Studies, New Delhi*. New Delhi: Indian Agricultural Research Institute, 1953.

Ministry of Agriculture and Fisheries, Agricultural Machinery Testing Committee, Certificates and Reports No. 68. "Headen Keil Anti-Dilution Cylinder-Head Gasket, Tested by the Institute for Research in Agricultural Engineering, University of Oxford." London: His Majesty's Stationery Office, 1938.

New Jersey Department of State, Census Bureau. *1905 State Census of New Jersey*. Trenton: State of New Jersey, 1905, Microfilm, 49 Reels. New York: New York Public Library.

New Jersey Secretary of State. *Corporations of New Jersey, List of Certificates Filed in the Department of State from 1895 to 1899, Inclusive*. Trenton: Murphy Publishing Co., 1900.

North Carolina Department of Labor and Printing. *Annual Report of the Bureau of Labor Statistics of the State of North Carolina for the Year 1899*. Raleigh: Edwards & Broughton, and E. M. Uzzell, State Printers, 1900.

North Carolina Department of Public Instruction. *Annual Report of the Superintendent of Public Instruction for the Fiscal Year Ending September 1st, 1880*. Raleigh: P. M. Hale & Edwards, Broughton & Co., State Printers and Binders, 1881.

———. *Biennial Report and Recommendations of the Superintendent of Public Instruction of North Carolina to Governor Charles B. Aycock*. Raleigh: E. M. Uzzell, State Printers and Binders, 1904.

———. *Biennial Report of the Superintendent of Public Instruction of North Carolina for the Scholastic Years, 1881–'82*. Raleigh: Ashe & Gatling, State Printers and Binders, 1883.

———. *Biennial Report of the Superintendent of Public Instruction for North Carolina for the Scholastic Years 1889 and 1890*. Raleigh: Josephus Daniels, State Printer and Binder, 1890.

———. *Biennial Report of the Superintendent of Public Instruction of North Carolina for the Scholastic Years 1900–1901 and 1901–1902*. Raleigh: Edwards & Broughton, State Printers, 1902.

———. *Biennial Report of the Superintendent of Public Instruction of North Carolina, 1904–1906, Recommendations and Statistical Summary*. Raleigh: Office State Superintendent Public Instruction, 1907.

North Carolina General Assembly. "An Act to Incorporate the Africo-American Presbyterian Publishing Company." In *Laws and Resolutions of the State of North Carolina Passed by the General Assembly at the Session of 1889, Begun and Held in the City* of Raleigh, on Wednesday, the Ninth Day of January, A.D. 1889, chap. 230, 936–37. Raleigh: Josephus Daniels, State Printer and Binder, 1889.

———. "An Act to Incorporate the Carthage Railroad." In *Laws and Resolutions of the State of North Carolina, Passed by the General Assembly at Its Session of 1885, Begun and Held in the City of Raleigh on Wednesday, the Seventh Day of January, A.D. 1885*, chap. 215, 398. Raleigh: P. M. Hale, State Printer and Binder, 1885.

———. "An Act to Promote the Comfort of Travellers on Railroad Trains, and for Other Purposes." In *Public Laws and Resolutions of the State of North Carolina, Passed by the General Assembly at its Session of 1899, Begun and Held in the City of Raleigh on Wednesday, the Fourth Day of January, A.D. 1899*, chap. 384, 539–40. Raleigh: Edwards & Broughton, and E. M. Uzzell, State Printers and Binders, 1899.

———. "An Act to Provide for the Holding of Elections in North Carolina." In *Public Laws and Resolutions of the State of North Carolina Passed by the General Assembly at the Session of 1901, Begun and Held in the City of Raleigh, Wednesday, the Ninth Day of January, A.D. 1901*, chap. 89, sec. 12, 246. Raleigh: Edwards & Broughton and E. M. Uzzell, State Printers and Binders, 1901.

———. "Suffrage and Eligibility to Office," chap. 2, art. VI, sec. 4, North Carolina Constitution. In *Laws and Resolutions of the State of North Carolina Passed by the General Assembly at the Adjourning Session 1900 Begun and Held in the City of Raleigh, Tuesday the Twelfth of June, Nineteen Hundred*, 55. Raleigh: Edwards & Broughton and E. M. Uzzell, 1900.

Rossiter, William S. *Increase of Population in the United States, 1910–1920: A Study of Changes in the Population of Divisions, States, Counties, and Rural and Urban Areas and in Sex, Color, and Nativity, at the Fourteenth Census*. Census Monographs 1. Washington, D.C.: Government Printing Office, 1922.

State of Florida, Office of the Secretary of State. "Domestic Corporations." In *Biennial Report of the Secretary of State, of the State of Florida, for the Period Beginning January 1, 1921, and Ending December 31, 1922, Part 2, Corporations and Drainage Districts Trademarks*. Tallahassee: T. J. Appleyard, Printer, 1922.

State of Ohio. *The Official Roster of Ohio Soldiers, Sailors and Marines in the World War, 1917–18*. Vol. 7. Columbus: F. J. Heer Printing Co., 1926.

U.S. Bureau of the Census. *Thirteenth Census of the United States Taken in the Year 1910, Volume IV, Population, 1910, Occupation Statistics*. Washington, D.C.: Government Printing Office, 1914.

U.S. Bureau of the Census. *Fourteenth Census of the United States Taken in the Year 1920, Volume III, Population, 1920, Composition and Characteristics of the Population by States*, sec. 3, Georgia. Washington, D.C.: Government Printing Office, 1922.

———. *Negroes in the United States, 1920–1932*. 2nd ed. Washington, D.C.: Government Printing Office, 1935.

———. *Statistics of the Population of the United States at the Tenth Census (June 1, 1880)*. Department of the Interior, Census Office [predecessor of the U.S. Census Bureau]. Washington, D.C.: Government Printing Office, 1883.

U.S. Civil Service Commission. *Official Register of the United States, Containing a List of Officers and Employe[e]s in the Civil, Military and Naval Service, on the First of July, 1883*. Vol. 2, *The Post Office Department and the Postal Service*. Washington, D.C.: Government Printing Office, 1884.

U.S. Congress. *Biographical Dictionary of the United States Congress, 1774–2005.* Washington, D.C.: Government Printing Office, 2005.

U.S. Congress, House of Representatives. *Legislative, Executive, and Judicial Appropriation Bill, 1922: Hearing Before Subcommittee of House Committee on Appropriations,* 66th Cong., 3rd Sess. Washington, D.C.: Government Printing Office, 1920.

U.S. Congress, Joint Select Committee on the Condition of Affairs in the Late Insurrectionary States. *Testimony Taken by the Joint Select Committee to Inquire into the Condition of Affairs in the Late Insurrectionary States, Vol. 2, North Carolina.* Washington, D.C.: Government Printing Office, 1872.

U.S. Post Office Department. *Record of Appointment of U.S. Postmasters, 1832–Sept. 30, 1971.* Microfilm Publ. M-841. Washington, D.C.: National Archives.

U.S. Superintendent of Documents, *Investigation of Improper Activities in the Labor or Management Field, Hearings Before the Select Committee on Improper Activities in the Labor or Management Field, Eighty-Fifth Congress, Second Session, Pursuant to Senate Resolutions 74 and 221, 85th Congress, March 21, July 8, 9, 10, and 11, 1958,* Part 33. Washington, D.C.: Government Printing Office, 1958.

Williams, W. T. B. "The Negro Exodus from the South." In *Negro Migration in 1916–17,* with an introduction by J. H. [James Hardy] Dillard, 93–111. U.S. Department of Labor, Division of Negro Economics. Washington, D.C.: U.S. Government Printing Office, 1919.

BUSINESS, CITY, AND SOCIAL DIRECTORIES

United States

Simms, James N., comp. and publ. *Simms' Blue Book and National Negro Business and Professional Directory.* Chicago: James N. Simms, 1923.

Florida

Tampa

Polk, R. L., and J. Wiggins. *Polk's Tampa City Directory, 1924.* Jacksonville: R. L. Polk & Co., 1924.

Scholes, A. E. *Scholes' Directory of the City of Tampa, 1899.* Savannah, Ga.: Morning News Print, 1899.

Georgia

Albany

Miller's Albany, Georgia, City Directory, Vol. III, 1928–1929. Asheville, N.C.: Piedmont Directory Co., 1929.

Miller's Albany, Georgia, City Directory, Vol. IV, 1930–1931. Asheville, N.C.: Piedmont Directory Co., 1930.

Polk's Albany City Directory, 1922. Atlanta: R. L. Polk & Co., Publishers, 1922.

Polk's Albany City Directory, 1925. Detroit: R. L. Polk & Co., Publishers, 1925.

Atlanta

Norwood Connelly & Co. *The Directory of Atlanta, Georgia.* Atlanta: Constitution Printing Co., 1887.

Saunders, H. G. *Atlanta City Directory for 1893.* Atlanta: Constitution Publishing Co., 1893.

Weatherbe, Charles F. *Weatherbe's Atlanta, Ga., Duplex City Directory,* Atlanta: Dunlop & Cohen Printers, 1886.

Savannah
Savannah 1916 Directory. Savannah: Savannah Directory Publishing Co., 1916.
Savannah City Directory, 1920. Savannah: Savannah Directory Publishing Co., 1920.

Illinois
Chicago
Black, Ford S., comp. *Black's Blue Book: Directory of Chicago's Active Colored People and Guide to Their Activities*. Chicago: Ford S. Black, 1917.
———. *Black's Blue Book, Business and Professional Directory, 1918*. Chicago: Ford S. Black, 1918.
———. *Colored People's Guide Book for Chicago, 1915–1916*. Chicago: White, 1915.
The Chicago Blue Book of Selected Names of Chicago and Suburban Towns Containing the Names and Addresses of Prominent Residents, Arranged Alphabetically and Numerically by Streets, Membership List of the Leading Clubs, and Other Valuable Information, for the Year Ending 1913. Chicago: Chicago Directory Co., 1912.
Chicago Blue Book of Selected Names of Chicago and Suburban Towns Containing the Names and Addresses of Prominent Residents, Arranged Alphabetically and Numerically by Streets, Membership List of the Leading Clubs, and Other Valuable Information, for the Year Ending 1914. Chicago: Chicago Directory, 1913.
Donnelley, Reuben H., comp. *The Lakeside Annual Directory of the City of Chicago*. Chicago: The Chicago Directory Co., 1913.
———. *The Lakeside Annual Directory of the City of Chicago*. Chicago: The Chicago Directory Co., 1914.
———. *The Lakeside Annual Directory of the City of Chicago*. Chicago: The Chicago Directory Co., 1916.
———. *The Lakeside Annual Directory of the City of Chicago*. Chicago: The Chicago Directory Co., 1916.
———. *The Lakeside Annual Directory of the City of Chicago*. Chicago: The Chicago Directory Co., 1917.
Lakeside Classified Directory, Chicago, Ill., 1914.

Maryland
Baltimore
Polk's Baltimore City Directory, 1923. Baltimore: R. L. Polk & Co., 1923.

Massachusetts
Lowell
The Lowell Directory, 1898, No. 47. Boston: Sampson, Murdock, & Co., 1898.

New Jersey
Jersey City
Boyd's Jersey City and Hoboken Directory, 1906–1907. Jersey City: Howell & Co., Publishers, 1906.

North Carolina
Branson, Levi, ed. *Branson's North Carolina Business Directory, 1890*. Vol. 7. Raleigh: Levi Branson, 1889.

News & Observer. *The North Carolina Year Book and Business Directory, 1906.* Raleigh: Allied Printing, 1906.

Moore County

Branson, Levi, ed. *Branson's Moore County Business Directory, 1898.* Raleigh: Levi Branson, 1898.

Wilmington

J. L. Hill Printing Co.'s Directory of Wilmington, N.C., 1897. Richmond: J. L. Hill Printing Co., 1897.

J. L. Hill Printing Co.'s Directory of Wilmington, N.C., 1900. Richmond: J. L. Hill Printing Co., 1899.

Ohio

Cleveland

The Cleveland Directory Co.'s Cleveland (Ohio) City Directory, 1929. Cleveland: Cleveland Directory, 1929.

The Cleveland Directory Co.'s Cleveland (Ohio) City Directory, 1930. Cleveland: Cleveland Directory, 1930.

The Cleveland Directory Co.'s Cleveland (Ohio) City Directory, 1931. Cleveland: Cleveland Directory, 1931.

Pennsylvania

Philadelphia

Boyd's Philadelphia City Directory, Published Annually, 1916. Philadelphia: C. E. Howe & Co., 1916.

Gopsill's Philadelphia City Directory. Philadelphia: James Gopsill's Sons, 1905.

Rhode Island

Newport

The Newport Directory, Containing the City Record, a General Directory of the Citizens, and a Complete Business Directory and Register for the Year Commencing July 1, 1879. Newport: J. A. & R. A. Reid, 1879.

The Newport Directory, 1897. Boston: Sampson, Murdock, & Co., 1897.

The Newport Directory, 1898. Boston: Sampson, Murdock, & Co., 1898.

The Newport Directory, 1899. Boston: Sampson, Murdock, & Co., 1899.

The Newport Directory, 1901. Boston: Sampson, Murdock, & Co., 1901.

The Newport Directory, 1902. Boston: Sampson, Murdock, & Co., 1902.

The Newport Directory, 1903. Boston: Sampson, Murdock, & Co., 1903.

Virginia

Alexandria

Emerson, Charles, comp. *Chataigne's Alexandria City Directory, 1881–'82.* Alexandria: J. H. Chataigne, Publ., 1881.

United Kingdom

London

Post Office, London Post Office Directory. London: Kelly's Directories, 1934.

Post Office, London Post Office Directory. London: Kelly's Directories, 1936.

SCHOOL PUBLICATIONS

Albion Academy. *Catalogue of Albion Academy, Normal and Industrial School, Franklinton, Franklin County, N.C., for the Academic Year 1901–02.* Raleigh: Edwards & Broughton, 1902.

———. *Sixth Annual Catalogue of Albion Academy and State Colored Normal School at Franklinton, Franklin County, North Carolina, 1884–'85.* Raleigh: P. M. Hale, State Printer and Binder, Presses of E. M. Uzzell, 1885.

Biddle University. *General Catalogue of Biddle University, Thirty-Fifth Annual Session of Biddle University. Charlotte, N.C., 1903–1904.* Charlotte: Observer Printing House, 1904.

———. *General Catalogue of Biddle University, Forty-Second Annual Session of Biddle University, Charlotte, N.C., 1909–1910.* Charlotte: Biddle University, 1910.

Claflin University. *Catalogue of Claflin University College of Agriculture and Mechanics' Institute, Orangeburg, S.C., 1889–1890.* Charleston: Walker, Evans, & Cogswell, Co., Printers, 1890.

———. *Catalogue of Claflin University College of Agriculture and Mechanics' Institute, Orangeburg, S.C., 1890–1891.* New York: Hunt & Eaton, 1891.

Fayetteville State Colored Normal School (earlier the Howard School). *Catalogue of the North Carolina State Colored Normal School, Fayetteville, N.C., for the Year 1881–82.* Fayetteville: J. E. Garrett, Book and Job Printer, 1882.

———. *Thirty-Second Annual Catalogue of the North Carolina State Normal School for 1908–'09, Fayetteville, N.C.* Fayetteville: Judge Printing Co., Book and Job Printers, 1909.

Fisk University. *Catalogue of the Officers and Students of Fisk University, Nashville, Tennessee, 1906–1907.* Nashville: Press of Folk-Keelin Printing Co, 1907.

———. *Catalogue of the Officers and Students of Fisk University, Nashville, Tennessee, 1907–1908.* Nashville: Press of Marshall & Bruce Co., 1908.

Greensboro A&M College (today North Carolina A&T State University). *Second Annual Catalogue of the Agricultural and Mechanical College for the Colored Race, Greensboro, North Carolina, 1895–'96.* Greensboro: Reece & Elam, 1896.

———. *Ninth Annual Catalogue of the Agricultural & Mechanical College for the Colored Race, Greensboro, N.C., 1903–1904.* Greensboro: J. M. Reece & Co., 1903.

Harvard University. *Report of the President of Harvard College and Reports of Departments.* Cambridge, Mass.: Harvard University, 1908.

Howard University. *Catalogue Howard University, 1910–11.* Vol. 5, No. 2. Washington, D.C.: Howard University, March 1911.

———. *Catalogue Howard University, 1914–1915.* Vol. 9, No. 3. Washington, D.C.: Howard University, May 1915.

Langston University. *Annual Catalogue of the Colored Agricultural and Normal University, 1910–1911.* Langston, Okla.: Colored Agricultural and Normal University, 1911.

Lincoln University. *Catalogue of Lincoln University, Chester County, Pennsylvania, for the Academical Year 1882–83.* Oxford, Pa.: Press Print, 1883.

———. *Lincoln University: College and Theological Seminary, Biographical Catalogue, 1918.* Lancaster, Pa.: Press of the New Era Printing Co., 1918.

———. *The Alumni Directory of Lincoln University, Centennial Edition*, edited by H. Alfred Farrell. Chester, Pa.: Lincoln University, 1954.

North Carolina College (today North Carolina Central University). *The Eagle.* Durham: North Carolina College, 1940.

———. *The Maroon and Gray.* Vol. 4. Durham: North Carolina College, 1946.

Scotia Seminary. *Twelfth Annual Catalogue of the Officers and Students of Scotia Seminary, Concord, N.C., 1881–82.* Pittsburgh: Presbyterian Committee of Missions for Freedmen, 1882.

———. *Twenty-Fifth Annual Catalogue of the Officers and Students of Scotia Seminary, Concord, N.C., 1894–95.* Pittsburgh: Presbyterian Board of Missions for Freedmen, 1895.

———. *Twenty-Sixth Annual Catalogue of the Officers and Students of Scotia Seminary, Concord, N.C., 1895–96.* Pittsburgh: Presbyterian Board of Missions for Freedmen, 1896.

———. *Twenty-Seventh Annual Catalogue of the Officers and Students of Scotia Seminary, Concord, N.C., 1896–97.* Pittsburgh: James McMillan Printing Co., 1897.

———. *Twenty-Eighth Annual Catalogue of the Officers and Students of Scotia Seminary, Concord, N.C., 1897–98.* Pittsburgh: Presbyterian Board of Missions for Freedmen, 1898.

———. *Twenty-Ninth Annual Catalogue of the Officers and Students of Scotia Seminary, Concord, N.C., 1898–99.* Pittsburgh: Presbyterian Board of Missions for Freedmen, 1899.

PRESBYTERIAN CHURCH RECORDS

Board of Missions for Freedmen. *Twenty-Fourth Annual Report of the Board of Missions for Freedmen of the Presbyterian Church in the United States of America. To the General Assembly of the Presbyterian Church, from March 31st, 1888, to April 1st, 1889.* Pittsburgh: Office of the Board, 1889.

———. *Twenty-Fifth Annual Report of the Board of Missions for Freedmen of the Presbyterian Church in the United States of America to the General Assembly of the Presbyterian Church, from March 31st, 1889 to April 1st, 1890.* Philadelphia: Board of Education of the Presbyterian Church in the United States of America, 1890.

———. *Twenty-Eighth Annual Report of the Board of Missions for Freedmen of the Presbyterian Church in the U.S.A., Presented to the General Assembly, May, 1893.* Pittsburgh: James McMillan, 1893.

———. *Thirty-Eighth Annual Report of the Board of Missions for Freedmen of the Presbyterian Church in the United States of America, Presented to the General Assembly, May 1903.* Pittsburgh: Office of the Board, May 1903.

Minutes of the General Assembly of the Presbyterian Church in the United States of America (GAMPCUSA).

PCUSA. *Reports of the Missionary and Benevolent Boards and Committees to the General Assembly of the Presbyterian Church in the United States of America, 1893.*

GENEALOGICAL DATABASES

Ancestry.com. *British Phone Books, 1880–1984.* Directory, *Norwich / Cambridge / Essex / East Suffolk / East Hertfordshire / South Midland / Guildford / Brighton / Tunbridge Wells / Canterbury / Southampton / Portsmouth / Bournemouth / Bristol / Exeter / Plymouth / South Wales / Gloucester,* 1929, 1932, 1933, 1934. Original data, Board of Trade (BT) Archives, London, England.

———. *British Phone Books, 1880–1984. London Surnames A–K,* February 1933. Original data from *British Phone Books, 1880–1984,* BT Archives, London, England.

———. *Cook County, Illinois, Marriage Index, 1871–1920.* Original data, Cook County Clerk, comp. *Cook County Clerk Genealogy Records.* Cook County Clerk's Office, Chicago, 2008.

———. *Georgia Marriage Records, from Select Counties, 1828–1978*. Original data, *County Marriage Records, 1828–1978*. Morrow: Georgia Archives.

———. *Illinois, Deaths and Stillbirths Index, 1916–1947*. Original data Cook County Clerk Genealogy Records, Cook County Clerk's Office, Chicago, 2008.

———. *New York, New York, Extracted Marriage Index, 1866–1937*. Original data, *Index to New York City Marriages, 1866–1937*. New York: New York City Department of Records, Municipal Archives.

———. *New York, Passenger and Crew Lists (including Castle Garden and Ellis Island), 1820–1957*. Original data, *Passenger Lists of Vessels Arriving at New York, New York, 1820–1897*. Microfilm Publ. M237. Washington, D.C.: National Archives.

———. *North Carolina Deaths, 1906–1930*. Original data, *North Carolina, Deaths, 1906–1930*. Salt Lake City: FamilySearch, 2013.

———. *North Carolina, Death Certificates, 1909–1976*. Original data, North Carolina State Board of Health, Bureau of Vital Statistics, *North Carolina Death Certificates*. Raleigh, N.C.: North Carolina State Archives.

———. *Reports of Deaths of American Citizens Abroad, 1835–1974*. Original data, *Reports of the Deaths of American Citizens* (Publication A1 5166. NAI: 613857), and *Death Reports of U.S. Citizens Abroad, 1920–1962* (Publication A1 205), RG 59, General Records of the Department of State. College Park, Md.: National Archives.

———. *North Carolina, Marriage Records, 1741–2011*. Original data, North Carolina County Registers of Deeds. RG 048 (Microfilm). Raleigh, N.C.: North Carolina State Archives.

———. *Surrey, England, Electoral Registers, 1832–1962*. Original data Surrey Electoral Registers. Woking, U.K.: Surrey History Centre.

———. *Surrey, England, Church of England Burials, 1813–1987*. Original data, Anglican Parish Registers. Woking, U.K.: Surrey History Centre.

———. *UK, Incoming Passenger Lists, 1878–1960*. Original data, *Board of Trade: Commercial and Statistical Department and Successors: Inwards Passenger Lists*. Kew, U.K.: National Archives.

———. *UK, Outward Passenger Lists, 1890–1960*. Original data, *Board of Trade: Commercial and Statistical Department and Successors: Outwards Passenger Lists*. BT27. Records of the Commercial, Companies, Labour, Railways and Statistics Departments. Records of the Board of Trade and of successor and related bodies. Kew, U.K.: National Archives.

———. *U.S. City Directories, 1822–1995*. Original data, sources vary according to directory. Includes directories for Atlanta and Albany, Ga.

———. *U.S. Federal Census Collection*. Population Schedules. *Seventh Census of the United States: 1850 through Sixteenth Census of the United States: 1940*. Original data, Microfilm Publs. M432 (1850), M653 (1860), M593 (1870), T9 (1880), T623 (1900), T624 (1910), T625 (1920), T626 (1930), and T-627 (1940). Washington, D.C.: National Archives.

———. *U.S. Passport Applications, 1795–1925*. Original data, Microfilm Publ. M1490, *Passport Applications, January 2, 1906–March 31, 1925*. Washington, D.C.: National Archives.

———. *U.S. Presbyterian Church Records, 1701–1970*. Original data, Presbyterian Historical Society, Philadelphia.

———. *U.S. Social Security Applications and Claims Index, 1936–2007*. Original data, *Social Security Applications and Claims, 1936–2007* (Microfilm). Washington, D.C.: Social Security Administration (copies of applications require FOIA request).

282 Bibliography

———. *U.S. World War I Draft Registration Cards, 1917–1918.* Original data, *World War I Draft Registration Cards*, Microfilm Publ. M150. Washington, D.C.: National Archives.
———. *U.S. World War II Draft Registration Cards, 1942.* Original data, *U.S. Selective Service System, Selective Service Registration Cards, World War II*, RG 147. Washington, D.C.: National Archives.
FamilySearch.com. *Florida, Deaths, 1877–1939.* Original data, Family History Library.
———. *Florida, Marriages, 1837–1974, Index.* Original data, Family History Library.
———. *Indiana, Marriages, 1810–2001.* Original data, Family History Library.
———. *New York, New York City Municipal Deaths, 1795–1949.* Original data, Family History Library.
———. *North Carolina County Marriages, 1762–1979.* Original data, Family History Library.
———. *North Carolina, Marriages, 1759–1979.* Original data, Family History Library.
FindMyPast.com. *British Royal Air Force, Officers' Service Records, 1912–1920.* Original data, AIR 79, National Archives, Kew.
———. *1939 Register for England and Wales.* Original data, National Archives, Kew.
Fold3.com. *Naturalization Petition and Record Books for the U.S. District Court for the Northern District of Ohio, Eastern Division, Cleveland, 1907–1946.* Original data, Microfilm Publ. M1995. Washington, D.C.: National Archives.

FILMS

Pathé Gazette. "Eisenhower at Sandhurst." Newsreel, 1944. Accessed August 20, 2019, at youtube, https://m.youtube.com/watch?v=cHi7LviVxZg.
Powell, William J. "Unemployment, the Negro, and Aviation." Los Angeles, 1935. Excerpts accessed November 25, 2018, at Oxford African American Studies Center, http://www.oxfordaasc.com/public/features/archive/1213/essay.jsp.

Published Primary Sources

Alger, Horatio, Jr. *The Erie Train Boy.* New York: United States Book Co., 1891.
Armstrong, Louis. *Louis Armstrong, in His Own Words: Selected Writings.* Edited by Thomas Brothers. New York: Oxford University Press, 1999.
Arpee, Edward. *Lake Forest, Illinois: History and Reminiscences, 1861–1961.* Lake Forest: Rotary Club of Lake Forest, 1963.
Chicago Tribune. *The W.G.N. Handbook of Newspaper Administration.* Chicago: Tribune, 1922.
Cromwell, John W. *History of the Bethel Literary and Historical Association, Being a Paper Read Before the Association by Mr. John W. Cromwell (of the Washington Public Schools) on Founder's Day, February 14, 1896.* Washington, D.C.: Press of M. L. Pendleton, 1896.
Du Bois, W. E. B. *The Negro Artisan, Report of a Social Study Made Under the Direction of Atlanta University, Together with the Proceedings of the Seventh Conference for the Study of Negro Problems, Held at Atlanta University, on May 27th, 1902.* Atlanta: Atlanta University Press, 1902.
Goode, Corp. W. T. *The Eighth Illinois.* Chicago: The Blakely Printing Co., 1899.

Hall, Rev. John. *History of the Presbyterian Church in Trenton, N.J.: From the First Settlement of the Town*. 2nd ed. Trenton, N.J.: MacCrellish & Quigley, 1912.

Harrison, William Henry Jr. *Colored Girls' and Boys' Inspiring United States History; And a Heart to Heart Talk About White Folks*. Allentown, Pa.: Searle & Dressler Co. 1921.

Holley, Joseph W. *You Can't Build a Chimney from the Top*. Edited by Russell Wilcox, with an introduction by Roberta S. Ramsey. Lanham, Md.: University Press of America, 1992, reprint, originally published 1948.

Ireland, E. A., comp. *The Nation's Peril: Twelve Years' Experience in the South, the Ku Klux Klan, a Complete Exposition of the Order, Its Purpose, Plans, Operations, Social and Political Significance: The Nation's Salvation*. New York: Friends of the Compiler, 1872.

MacMillan, Allister, comp. *The Red Book of West Africa: Historical and Descriptive, Commercial and Industrial, Facts, Figures, & Resources*. London: Frank Cass, 1968, reprint of 1920 edition.

McCormick, Robert R. *With the Russian Army*. New York: MacMillan, 1915.

Muirheid, Walter G[regory], ed. *Jersey City of To-day: Its History, People, Trades, Commerce, Institutions and Industries*. Jersey City, NJ: Review Special, 1910.

Noble, Dudley, ed. *The Jubilee Book of the Royal Automobile Club, 1897–1947, the Record of a Historic 50 Years During Which the R.A.C. Has Fostered the Development and Progress of Automobilism in All Its Many and Varied Aspects*. London: Royal Automobile Club, 1947.

Oxford University. *Second Conference on Mechanized Farming, Rhodes House, Oxford, January 5–8, 1937, Report of Discussions*. Oxford, England: University of Oxford, 1937.

Powell, William J. *Black Wings*. Los Angeles: Ivan Deach, 1934.

———. *The Story of William J. Powell, a New Edition of William J. Powell's 1934 Black Wings*, with an introduction by Von Hardesty. Washington, D.C.: Smithsonian Institution Press, 1994.

Randolph Guide. The Bicentennial Report, 1776–1976. Asheboro, N.C.: Randolph Guide, 1976.

Richings, G[eorge]. F. *An Album of Negro Educators*. [Philadelphia?]: Author, 1900.

———. *Evidences of Progress Among Colored People*. 8th ed. Philadelphia: Geo. S. Ferguson, 1902.

Robb, Frederick H. H., ed. and comp. *The Negro in Chicago, 1779–1929*. Vol. 1, *1927 Intercollegian Wonderbook*. Chicago: Washington Intercollegiate Club of Chicago, 1927.

Rose, Theodore C., and James F. Burke, stenogs. *Proceedings of the Tenth Republican National Convention Held in the City of Minneapolis, Minn., June 7, 8, 9 and 10, 1892*. Minneapolis: Harrison and Smith, Printers, 1892.

Siloam Presbyterian Church. *Siloam Presbyterian Church, 160 Prince Street, Near Willoughby Street, Brooklyn, N.Y., Semi-Centennial, May 21st to July 25th, 1899*. Brooklyn: Nolan Bros., Steam Book and Job Printers, 1899.

Sixth Grace Presbyterian Church. *Sixth Grace Presbyterian Church, U.S.A., the 200th Anniversary of the Presbyterian Church (U.S.A.) and the 100th Anniversary of the Founding of the Grace Presbyterian Church*. Chicago: Sixth Grace Presbyterian Church, 1988.

Smith, Charles Lee. *The History of Education in North Carolina*, Bureau of Education Circular of Information No. 2, 1888. Washington, D.C.: Government Printing Office, 1888.

Sparey, June. *Dear Sir: Readers' Letters Published in the Camberley News, 1939–1945*. Camberley, U.K.: Kall-Kwik Printing, 1992.

Taitt, John, comp. *Souvenir of Negro Progress: Chicago, 1779–1925*. Chicago: De Saible Association, 1925.

284 Bibliography

Tandy, Edward T. *An Epitome of the Work of the Aeronautic Society from July, 1908, to December, 1909.* Bulletin No. 1. New York: Aeronautic Society, 1910.
Thorne, Jack [pen name of David B. Fulton]. *Recollections of a Sleeping Car Porter.* Jersey City, N.J.: Doan & Pilson, Book and Job Printers, 1892.
Tyson, Mrs. L. P. "Tyson and Jones Buggies Kept Rolling On and On." *Moore County News* (Centennial ed.), February 19, 1975, reprinted in Emma Phillips Paschal and Marshall R. Old, *The Methodists of Carthage, 1837–1987.* Charlotte, N.C.: Herb Eaton Historical Publications, 1987.
Washington, Booker T. "The Atlanta Address." Delivered at the Atlanta Cotton States and International Exposition, September 18, 1895. In Washington, *Up From Slavery: An Autobiography*, 218–25. Gretna, La.: Pelican, 2010, reprint of 1900 edition.
Wise, John. *Through the Air: A Narrative of Forty Years' Experience as an Aeronaut.* New York: Arno Press, 1972, reprint of 1873 edition.
Work, Monroe N. *Negro Year Book and Annual Encyclopedia of the Negro, 1912.* Tuskegee, Ala.: Negro Year Book Co., Tuskegee Institute, 1913.
———. *The Negro Year Book, An Encyclopedia of the Negro, 1918–1919.* Tuskegee, Ala.: Negro Year Book Publishing Co., 1919.

Secondary Sources

Adjutant General (Massachusetts), comp. *Massachusetts Soldiers, Sailors, and Marines in the Civil War.* Vol. 4. Norwood, Mass.: Norwood Press, 1932.
Arnold, Charlotte, Edith Buck, Katharine Merriam, and Julia Stockover. "Study of Delinquent Girls at Sleighton Farm." *Journal of the American Institute of Criminal Law and Criminology* 15, no. 4 (1925): 598–619.
Ascoli, Peter M. *Julius Rosenwald: The Man Who Built Sears, Roebuck and Advanced the Cause of Black Education in the American South.* Bloomington: Indiana University Press, 2006.
Ashe, Bertram D. *From Within the Frame: Storytelling in African-American Fiction.* New York: Routledge, 2002.
Ashton, Kevin. *How to Fly a Horse: The Secret History of Creation, Invention, and Discovery.* First Anchor Books ed. New York: Penguin, 2015.
Avery, Elroy McKendree. *A History of Cleveland and Its Environs: The Heart of New Connecticut.* Vol. 2, *Biography, Illustrated.* Chicago: Lewis Publishing, 1918.
Avery, Sheldon. *Up from Washington: William Pickens and the Negro Struggle for Equality, 1900–1954.* Newark: University of Delaware Press, 1989.
Bacon, Mary Ellen. *Albany on the Flint, Indians to Industry, 1836–1936.* Albany, Ga.: Albany Town Committee of the Colonial Dames of America in the State of Georgia [1970].
Bailey, Irene. *A Short History of Frimley Green Methodist Church.* Frimley Green, U.K.: Author, 1989.
Baker, Henry E. *The Colored Inventor, A Record of Fifty Years.* New York: Crisis Publishing Company, 1913.
Baldassaro, Lawrence, and Richard A. Johnson, eds. *The American Game: Baseball and Ethnicity.* Carbondale: Southern Illinois University Press, 2002.

Baldwin, Davarian L. *Chicago's New Negroes: Modernity, the Great Migration, and Black Urban Life*. Chapel Hill: University of North Carolina Press, 2007.
Barbour, George Edward. "Early Black Flyers of Western Pennsylvania, 1906–1945." *Western Pennsylvania Historical Magazine* 69 (April 1986): 95–97.
Barson, Graham. *Camberley & Yorktown Between the Wars*. Stroud, U.K.: Sutton, 2007.
Bellerby, J. R. "The Distribution of Farm Income in the U.K., 1867–1938." In *Essays in Agrarian History*. Vol. 2. Reprints edited for the British Agricultural History Society. Edited by W. E. Minchinton, 261–79. New York: Augustus M. Kelley, 1968.
Bennett, Mary Ann. *Camberley, A History*. Chichester, U.K.: Phillimore, 2009.
Bishir, Catherine W. *Crafting Lives: African American Artisans in New Bern, North Carolina, 1770–1900*. Chapel Hill: University of North Carolina Press, 2013.
Blackwelder, Julia Kirk. *Styling Jim Crow: African American Beauty Training During Segregation*. College Station: Texas A&M University Press, 2003.
Bolden, Tonya. *Searching for Sarah Rector: The Richest Black Girl in America*. New York: Abrams, 2014.
Boris, Joseph J., ed. *Who's Who in Colored America: A Biographical Dictionary of Notable Living Persons of African Descent in America, 1930-1931-1932*. New York: Who's Who in Colored America, 1932.
Borton, [Thomas E.], and [Fred S.] Borton. *Borton's Pocket Manual of Cleveland Securities*. 10th ed. Cleveland: Press of the Lezius Printing Co., 1923.
Bradley, Mark. *Bluecoats and Tar Heels: Soldiers and Civilians in Reconstruction North Carolina*. Lexington: University of Kentucky Press, 2009.
Brooks, F. Erik, and Glenn L. Starks, eds. *Historically Black Colleges and Universities: An Encyclopedia*. Santa Barbara, Calif.: ABC-CLIO, 2011.
Brown, Allan E., ed. *History of America's Speedways, Past & Present*. 2nd ed. Comstock Park, Mich.: America's Speedways, 1994.
Brown, Canter, Jr. *African Americans on the Tampa Bay Frontier*. Tampa Bay History Center Reference Library Series, No. 3. Tampa: Tampa Bay History Center, 1997.
Bruce, Janet. *The Kansas City Monarchs: Champions of Black Baseball*. Lawrence: University Press of Kansas, 1986.
Bugos, Glenn E. "Lew Rodert, Epistemological Liaison, and Thermal De-Icing at Ames." In *From Engineering Science to Big Science: The NACA and NASA Collier Trophy Project Winners*. NASA SP-4219. Edited by Pamela E. Meek, 29–58. Washington, D.C.: National Aeronautics and Space Administration, 1998. https://history.nasa.gov/SP-4219/Chapter2.html.
Bundles, A'Lelia Perry. *On Her Own Ground: The Life and Times of Madam C. J. Walker*. New York: Scribner's, 2001.
Burgess, Charles O. *Nettie Fowler McCormick: Profile of an American Philanthropist*. Madison: State Historical Society of Wisconsin, 1962.
Butler, John Sibley. *Entrepreneurship and Self-Help Among Black Americans: A Reconsideration of Race and Economics*. Rev. ed. SUNY Series in Ethnicity and Race in American Life. New York: State University of New York Press, 2005.
Caldwell, Arthur Bunyan, ed. *History of the American Negro*. Vol. 4. North Carolina ed. Atlanta: A. B. Caldwell, 1921.
Carriker, S. David. *Railroading in the Carolina Sandhills, Volume 1: The 19th Century (1825–1900)*. Matthews, N.C.: Heritage, 1985.

Cassanello, Robert. "Avoiding 'Jim Crow': Negotiating Separate and Equal on Florida's Railroads and Streetcars and the Progressive Era of the Modern Civil Rights Movement." *Journal of Urban History* 34, no. 3 (March 2008): 435–57.

Cecelski, David S., and Timothy B. Tyson, eds. *Democracy Betrayed: The Wilmington Race Riot of 1898 and Its Legacy*. Chapel Hill: University of North Carolina Press, 1998.

Chambliss, Julian C. "A Question of Progress and Welfare: The Jitney Phenomenon in Atlanta, 1915–1925." Rollins College Faculty Publications (Winter 2008). https://scholarship.rollins.edu/cgi/viewcontent.cgi?article=1095&context=as_facpub.

Chandler, John, Bancroft Davis, Henry Putzel, Henry C. Lind, and Frank D. Wagner, eds. *United States Reports: Cases Adjudged in the Supreme Court, October Term, 1917*. Vol. 246. New York: Banks & Bros., Law Publishers, 1921.

Chicago Commission on Race Relations. *The Negro in Chicago: A Study of Race Relations and a Race Riot*. Chicago: University of Chicago Press, 1922. https://archive.org/details/negroinchicagostoochic/.

Church, John. *Military Vehicles of World War 2*. New York: Crescent Books, 1985.

Clark, Ken. *Around Camberley*. Stroud, U.K.: Nonsuch, 1995.

Coleman, Alan. *Railroads of North Carolina*. Charleston, S.C.: Arcadia, 2008.

Connor, R. D. W., comp. and ed. *The North Carolina Manual, Issued by the North Carolina Historical Commission, for the Use of Members of the General Assembly, Session 1913*. Raleigh, N.C.: E. M. Uzzell & Co., State Printers, 1913.

Cooke, George William, ed. *Agricultural Research, 1931–1981: The Origins of the Agricultural Research Council and a Review of Developments in Agricultural Science During the Last Fifty Years*. London: Agricultural Research Council, Great Britain, 1981.

Cooper, Peter J. *Farnborough: 100 Years of British Aviation*. Hinckley, U.K.: Midland, 2006.

Coulter, Charles E. *Take Up the Black Man's Burden: Kansas City's African American Communities, 1865–1939*. Columbia: University of Missouri Press, 2006.

Craig, Lee A. *Josephus Daniels: His Life and Times*. Chapel Hill: University of North Carolina Press, 2013.

Cross, Sharon, ed. *Our Homefront: Memories of Life in Surrey Heath During World War II*. Camberley, U.K.: Surrey Heath Borough Council, 1995.

Crouch, Tom D. *The Bishop's Boys: A Life of Wilbur and Orville Wright*. New York: Norton, 2003.

Dade, George C., and Frank Strnad, *Picture History of Aviation on Long Island, 1908–1938*. Mineola, Minn.: Dover, 1989.

Dailey, Maceo Crenshaw, Jr. "The African Union Company of the 1920s and Its Black Business Activities in Africa and the United States." In *Black Business and Economic Power*. Rochester Studies in African History and the Disaspora, edited by Alusine Jalloh and Toyin Falola, 528–29. Rochester, N.Y.: University of Rochester Press, 2002.

DeJager, Timothy. "Pure Science and Practical Interests: The Origins of the Agricultural Research Council, 1930–1937." *Minerva* 31, no. 2 (1993): 129–50.

Dickerson, Dennis Clark. "George E. Cannon: Black Churchman, Physician, and Republican Politician." *Journal of Presbyterian History* 51, no. 4 (Black Presbyterians in Ministry Issue) (Winter 1973): 411–32.

———. "George Epps Cannon." In *African-American National Biography*, vol. 2, 2nd ed., edited by Henry Louis Gates Jr. and Evelyn Brooks Higginbotham, 514–16. New York: Oxford University Press, 2013.
DK Publishing. *Tractor: The Definitive Visual History*. New York: Penguin Random House, 2015.
Dressman, Frances. "Yes, We Have No Jitneys!" In *Black Dixie: Afro-Texan History and Culture in Houston*, edited by Howard Beeth and Carrie D. Wintz, 116–24. College Station: Texas A&M University Press, 1992.
Duberman, Martin B. *Paul Robeson*. New York: Knopf, 1988.
Elm, Mostafa. *Oil, Power, and Principle: Iran's Oil Nationalization and Its Aftermath*. Syracuse, N.Y.: Syracuse University Press, 1994.
Eltscher, Louis R., and Edward M. Young. *Curtiss-Wright, Greatness and Decline*. New York: Twayne, 1998.
Formwalt, Lee W. "Albany." *New Georgia Encyclopedia*. Online resource. Georgia Humanities Council and University of Georgia Press, 2014. http://www.georgiaencyclopedia.org/articles/counties-cities-neighborhoods/albany.
Fouché, Rayvon. *Black Inventors in the Age of Segregation: Granville T. Woods, Lewis H. Latimer, & Shelby J. Davidson*. Baltimore: Johns Hopkins University Press, 2003.
Franz, Kathleen. "'The Open Road': Automobility and Racial Uplift in the Interwar Years." In *Technology and the African-American Experience: Needs and Opportunities*. Published in cooperation with the Lemelson Center for the Study of Invention and Innovation at the Smithsonian Institution, edited by Bruce Sinclair, 131–54. Cambridge, Mass.: MIT Press, 2004.
———. *Tinkering: Consumers Reinvent the Early Automobile*. Philadelphia: University of Pennsylvania Press, 2005.
Frazier, E[dward] Franklin. *Black Bourgeoisie*. Glencoe, Ill.: Free Press, 1957.
Gaines, Kevin K. *Uplifting the Race: Black Leadership, Politics, and Culture in the Twentieth Century*. Chapel Hill: University of North Carolina Press, 1996.
Gibbs, Warmoth T. *History of the North Carolina Agricultural and Technical College*. Dubuque, Iowa: Wm. C. Brown, 1966.
Gill, Tiffany M. *Beauty Shop Politics: African American Women's Activism in the Beauty Industry*. Women in American History Series. Urbana: University of Illinois Press, 2010.
Gilmore, Glenda Elizabeth. *Gender and Jim Crow: Women and the Politics of White Supremacy in North Carolina, 1896–1920*. Chapel Hill: University of North Carolina Press, 1996.
Goodspeed, Thomas Wakefield. *A History of the University of Chicago, Founded by John D. Rockefeller, the First Quarter-Century*. Chicago: University of Chicago Press, June 1916.
Gould, Todd. *For Gold and Glory: Charlie Wiggins and the African-American Racing Car Circuit*. Bloomington: Indiana University Press, 2002.
Grant, Donald G. *The Way It Was in the South: The Black Experience in Georgia*, edited and introduction by Jonathan Grant. New York: Birch Lane, 1993.
Gray, Carroll F. "Cicero Flying Field; Origins, Operations, Obscurity and Legacy, 1891–1916, Part 1 of 3." *WW1 Aero: The Journal of the Early Aeroplane* 186 (November 2004): 22–41.
———. "Cicero Flying Field: Origin, Operation, Obscurity and Legacy, 1891 to 1916, Part 2 of 3." *WW1 Aero: The Journal of the Early Aeroplane* 187 (February 2005): 12–30.
Gray, George W[illiam]. *Frontiers of Flight*. New York: Knopf, 1948.

Haley, John H. *Charles N. Hunter and Race Relations in North Carolina.* Vol. 60, James Sprunt Studies in History and Political Science, edited by George B. Tindall, Michael R. McVaugh, William S. Powell, James W. Prothro, and Richard J. Richardson. Chapel Hill: University of North Carolina, 1987.

Hamilton, Joseph Grégoire de Roulhac, William K. Boyd, and R. D. W. Connor, *History of North Carolina, North Carolina Biography.* Chicago: Lewis Publishing Co., 1919.

Harold, Claudrena N. *The Rise and Fall of the Garvey Movement in the Urban South, 1918–1942.* New York: Routledge, 2007.

Hardesty, Von. "Introduction. " In *Black Aviator: The Story of William J. Powell* (a new edition of William J. Powell's *Black Wings*) by William J. Powell. Washington, D.C.: Smithsonian Institution Press, 1994.

Harris, Theodore H. H. "Kelly, Adam David." In *The Encyclopedia of Northern Kentucky*, edited by Paul A. Tenkotte and James C. Claypool, 501. Lexington: University Press of Kentucky, 2015.

Hartman, Edwin P[helps]. *Adventures in Research: A History of Ames Research Center, 1940–1965.* NASA Center History Series, NASA SP-4302. Washington, D.C.: National Aeronautics and Space Administration, 1970.

Hawkins, Carrie Savage. "A Brief History of Albion Academy." 1966, 3, cited in National Register of Historic Places Inventory—Nomination Form, Dr. J. A. Savage House, Albion Academy, Franklinton, N.C., 1980.

Hawkins, Walter L. *Black American Military Leaders: A Biographical Dictionary.* Jefferson, N.C.: McFarland, 2007.

Heckman, Oliver S. "The Presbyterian Church in the United States of America in Southern Reconstruction, 1860–1880." *North Carolina Historical Review* 20, no. 3 (July 1943): 219–37.

Hidden, William Earl. "Addendum to the Minerals and Mineral Localities of North Carolina." *Journal of the Elisha Mitchell Scientific Society.* Chapel Hill, N.C.: Elisha Mitchell Scientific Society 6, no. 2 (July–December 1889): 45–79.

Hill, Robert, ed. *The Marcus Garvey and Universal Negro Improvement Association Papers, Vol. II: 27 August 1919–31 August 1920.* Vol. 2. Berkeley: University of California Press, 1983.

Hill, Robert Milton. *Little Known Story of a Land Called Clearing.* Chicago: Author, 1983.

Hintz, Eric S. "Portable Power Inventor Samuel Ruben and the Birth of Duracell." *Technology and Culture* 50, no. 1 (January 2009): 24–57.

———. "The Post-Heroic Generation: American Independent Inventors, 1900–1950." *Enterprise & Society* 12, no. 4 (December 2011): 732–48.

Holden, Henry M., with Captain Lori Griffith. *Ladybirds: The Untold Story of Women Pilots in America.* Freedom, N.J.: Black Hawk, 1991.

Hughes, Thomas P. *American Genesis: A Century of Invention and Technological Enthusiasm, 1870–1970.* New York: Viking, 1989.

Hyde, Charles K. *Arsenal of Democracy: The American Automobile Industry in World War II.* Detroit: Wayne State University Press, 2013.

Ingham, John N. *Biographical Dictionary of American Business Leaders.* Vol. 1, A–G. Westport, Conn.: Greenwood, 1983.

Jackson, David H. Jr. *Booker T. Washington and the Struggle Against White Supremacy: The Southern Educational Tour, 1908–1912*. New York: Palgrave MacMillan, 2008.

Johnson, Curt, with R. Craig Sautter. *The Wicked City: Chicago from Kenna to Capone*. Chicago: Da Capo, 1998.

Johnson, Robert Wayne. *Through the Heart of the South: The Seaboard Air Line Railroad Story*. Erin, Ontario: Boston Mills, 1995.

Jones, R[eginald] V[ictor]. *The Wizard War: British Scientific Intelligence, 1939–1945*. New York: Coward, McCann & Geoghegan, 1978.

Jordan, Weymouth T., comp., and Louis H. Manarin, unit histories. *North Carolina Troops, 1861–1865: A Roster*. Vol. 7, *Infantry, 22nd–26th Regiments*. Raleigh: North Carolina Division of Archives and History, 1979.

Justesen, Benjamin R. "Black Tip, White Iceberg: Black Postmasters and the Rise of White Supremacy in North Carolina, 1897–1901." *North Carolina Historical Review* 82, no. 2 (April 2005): 193–227.

———, comp. and ed. *In His Own Words: The Writings, Speeches, and Letters of George Henry White*. Lincoln, Neb.: iUniverse, 2004.

———. *George H. White: An Even Chance in the Race of Life*. Baton Rouge: Louisiana State University Press, 2001.

Kewley, J., and C. L. Gilbert. "Kerosine." In *The Science of Petroleum: A Comprehensive Treatise of the Principles and Practice of the Production, Refining, Transport, and Distribution of Mineral Oil*. Vol. 4. Edited by A. E. Dunstan, A. W. Nash, Benjamin T. Brooks, and Sir Henry Tizard, 2470–85. London: Oxford University Press, 1938.

Koster, Lawrence. *The Post Offices of Moore County, North Carolina, A List of More than 150 Post Offices, with Location Information and Postmaster Names*. 2nd ed. Hudsonville, Mich.: Author, 2013.

———. *The Story of the Tyson & Jones Buggy Company, Carthage, NC, 1850–1929, from the Building of a Few Wagons and Buggies to Becoming the Largest Carriage Factory in the South*. Whispering Pines, N.C.: Author, 2010.

Krist, Gary. *City of Scoundrels: The 12 Days of Disaster that Gave Birth to Modern Chicago*. New York: Crown, 2012.

Lamoreaux, Naomi R., and Kenneth L. Sokoloff. "Inventors, Firms, and the Market for Technology in the Late Nineteenth and Early Twentieth Centuries." In *Learning by Doing in Markets, Firms, and Countries*. A National Bureau of Economic Research Conference Report, edited by Naomi R. Lamoreaux, Daniel M. G. Raff, and Peter Temin, 19–60. Chicago: University of Chicago Press, 1999.

———. "The Rise and Decline of the Independent Inventor, A Schumpeterian Story?" In *The Challenge of Remaining Innovative, Insights from Twentieth-Century American Business*, edited by Sally H. Clarke, Naomi R. Lamoreaux, and Steven W. Usselman, 43–78. Stanford, Calif.: Stanford University Press, 2009.

Lamoreaux, Naomi, Kenneth Lee Sokoloff, Dhanoos Sutthiphisal, and National Bureau of Economic Research. "The Reorganization of Inventive Activity in the United States During the Early Twentieth Century." In *Understanding Long-Run Economic Growth: Geography, Institutions, and the Knowledge Economy*, edited by Dora L. Costa and Naomi R. Lamoreaux, 235–74. Chicago: University of Chicago Press, 2011.

Lanctot, Neil. *Fair Dealing and Clean Playing: The Hilldale Club and the Development of Black Professional Baseball, 1910–1932.* Syracuse, N.Y.: Syracuse University Press, 1994.

LeBow, Eileen F. *Cal Rodgers and the Vin Fiz: The First Transcontinental Flight.* Washington, D.C.: Smithsonian Institution Press, 1989.

Lester, Larry. *Rube Foster in His Time: On the Field and in the Papers with Black Baseball's Greatest Visionary.* Jefferson, N.C.: McFarland, 2012.

Lewis, Harold O. "A General View of the Negro in Europe." In *Negro Year Book 1947: A Review of Events Affecting Negro Life, 1941–1946, Part III.* 10th ed., edited by Jessie Parkhurst Guzman, 577–91. Tuskegee, Ala.: Tuskegee Institute, 1947.

Lombardo, Robert M. "The Black Mafia: African-American Organized Crime in Chicago, 1890–1960." *Crime, Law, and Social Change* 38, no. 1 (July 2002): 33–65.

———. *Organized Crime in Chicago: Beyond the Mafia.* Urbana: University of Illinois Press, 2013.

Longworth, Alice Roosevelt. *Crowded Hours: The Reminiscences of Alice Roosevelt Longworth.* New York: Scribner's, 1933.

Longyard, William H. *Who's Who in Aviation: 500 Biographies.* Navato, Calif.: Presidio, 1994.

Mabry, William Alexander. "'White Supremacy' and the North Carolina Suffrage Amendment." *North Carolina Historical Review* 13, no. 1 (January 1936): 1–24.

MacLeod, Roy M., and E. Kay Andrews. "Scientific Advice in the War at Sea, 1915–1917: The Board of Invention and Research." *Journal of Contemporary History* 6, no. 2 (1971): 3–40.

Magnaghi, Russell M. *Prohibition in the Upper Peninsula: Booze & Bootleggers on the Border.* Charleston, S.C.: American Palate, 2017.

Marszalek, John F. *A Black Congressman in the Age of Jim Crow: South Carolina's George Washington Murray.* Gainesville: University Press of Florida, 2006.

Martin, John. *The Development of Modern Agriculture, British Farming Since 1931.* New York: St. Martin's, 2000.

Mather, Frank Lincoln, ed. *Who's Who of the Colored Race, a General Biographical Dictionary of Men and Women of African Descent.* Vol. 1, memento ed., *Half-Century Anniversary of Negro Freedom in U.S.* Chicago, 1915.

May, Henry A. *First Black Autos: The Charles Richard "C. R." Patterson & Sons Company, African-American Automobile Manufacturer of Patterson-Greenfield Motor Cars, Buses and Trucks.* Mount Vernon, N.Y.: Stalwart, 2010.

McBeth, B[rian] S. *British Oil Policy, 1919–1939.* London: Frank Cass, 1985.

McBride, William M. "The 'Greatest Patron of Science?' The Navy-Academic Alliance and U.S. Naval Research, 1896–1923." *Journal of Military History* 56, no. 1 (January 1992): 7–33.

McCray, R. Y., ed. *Representative Clevelanders: A Biographical Directory of Leading Men and Women in Present-Day Cleveland Community, 1927.* Cleveland: Cleveland Topics Co., 1926.

McDonald, B[ernard] A., and J[ohn] L. Drew. *Air Transportation in the Immediate Post-War Period.* Report No. BR-69. Buffalo, N.Y.: Curtiss-Wright Corporation, 1944.

McElrath, Joseph R., Jr., and Robert C. Leitz III, eds. *"To Be an Author": Letters of Charles W. Chesnutt, 1889–1905.* Princeton, N.J.: Princeton University Press, 1997.

McLaurin, Melton A. "The Nineteenth-Century North Carolina State Fair as a Social Institution." *North Carolina Historical Review* 59, no. 3 (July 1982): 213–29.

Michaeli, Ethan. *The Defender: How the Legendary Black Newspaper Changed America.* Boston: Houghton Mifflin Harcourt, 2016.

Michie, Thomas J., ed. *Railroad Reports (Vol. 30 American and English Railroad Cases, New Series), a Collection of All the Cases Affecting Railroads of Every Kind, Decided by the Courts of Last Resort in the United States.* Vol. 7. Charlottesville, Va.: Michie Co., 1903.

Middleton, W[illiam] E[dgar] Knowles. *Mechanical Engineering at the National Research Council of Canada, 1929–1951.* Waterloo, Ontario: Wilfred Laurier University Press, 1984.

Mordecai, Samuel Fox. "Chapter III, Constitutional Law." In *Law Lectures, A Treatise, from a North Carolina Standpoint, on Those Portions of the First and Second Books of the Commentaries of Sir William Blackstone Which Have Not Become Obsolete in the United States.* 2nd ed. Raleigh: Commercial Printing Co., 1916.

Morgan, Gwen, and Arthur Veysey. *Poor Little Rich Boy: The Life and Times of Colonel Robert R. McCormick.* Carpentersville, Ill.: Crossroads Communications, 1985.

Murray, Andrew E. *Presbyterians and the Negro—A History.* Philadelphia: Presbyterian Historical Society, 1966.

Nelson, Christopher L. *The C. R. Patterson and Sons Company: Black Pioneers in the Vehicle Building Industry, 1865–1939.* Hurricane, W.Va.: Hurricane, 2010.

Nicholas, Tom. "The Role of Independent Invention in U.S. Technological Development, 1880–1930." *Journal of Economic History* 70, no. 1 (March 2010): 57–82.

———. "Spatial Diversity in Invention: Evidence from the Early R&D Labs." *Journal of Economic Geography* 9 (January 2009): 1–31.

Noble, David F. *America by Design: Science, Technology, and the Rise of Corporate Capitalism.* Oxford: Oxford University Press, 1977.

Noth, H., and W. Polte. *The Formation of Ice on Airplanes.* Technical Memorandum No. 786. Washington, D.C.: National Advisory Committee for Aeronautics, 1935.

Pacyga, Dominic. *Chicago, a Biography.* Chicago: University of Chicago Press, 2009.

Palmatier, Everett P. *Thermal Propeller Anti-Icing Means. Analysis of the Heat Loss from a Hollow Steel Blade Through Which Hot Air Is Directed.* E.W.O. D-516-Project No. 1, Progress Report No. 3, Curtiss-Wright Corporation, Curtiss Propeller Division, October 31, 1942.

Parker, Inez Moore. *The Rise and Decline of the Program of Education for Black Presbyterians of the United Presbyterian Church U.S.A., 1865–1970.* San Antonio, Tex.: Trinity University Press, 1977.

Paschal, Emma Phillips, and Marshall R. Old. *The Methodists of Carthage, 1837–1987.* Charlotte, N.C.: Herb Eaton Historical Publications, 1987.

Patterson, Homer L., comp. and ed. *Patterson's American Educational Directory.* Vol. 18. Chicago: American Educational Company, 1921.

Paxson, Frederic L. "The American War Government, 1917–1918." *American Historical Review* 26, no. 1 (October 1920): 54–76.

Perman, Michael. *Struggle for Mastery: Disfranchisement in the South, 1888–1908.* Chapel Hill: University of North Carolina Press, 2001.

Phillips, Lou. *Cars, 1895–1965.* Bloomington, Ind.: Xlibris, 2011.

Pointer, Sonya. "Reinventing the Jitney in St. Louis." M.A. thesis, Ball State University, 2013.

Pope, Stephen, and Elizabeth-Anne Wheal. *Dictionary of the First World War.* Barnsley, U.K.: Pen & Sword, 2003.

Prather, H. Leon, Sr. "The Red Shirt Movement in North Carolina, 1898–1900." *Journal of Negro History* 62, no. 2 (April 1977): 174–84.

———. *We Have Taken a City: Wilmington Racial Massacre and Coup of 1898*. Rutherford, N.J.: Fairleigh Dickinson University Press, 1984.

Randolph County Historical Society and Randolph Arts Guild. *Randolph County—1779–1979*. Winston-Salem, N.C.: Hunter, 1980.

Reaves, William M. *"Strength through Struggle": The Chronological and Historical Record of the African-American Community in Wilmington, North Carolina, 1865–1950*. Wilmington, N.C.: New Hanover, 1998.

Reed, Christopher Robert. *Knock at the Door of Opportunity: Black Migration to Chicago, 1900–1919*. Carbondale: Southern Illinois University Press, 2014.

Reilly, John G. "Tyson & Jones Buggy Company: The History of a Southern Carriage Works." *North Carolina Historical Review* 46, no. 3 (Summer 1969): 201–13.

Restuccia, B[ernard] S., with E. Edward Gibson and Geraldlyn Sanders. *An Extraordinary Man, Homer B. Roberts, 1885–1952*. Ann Arbor, Mich.: Rustic Enterprise, 2001.

Reynolds, Kelly. *Henry Plant, Pioneer Empire Builder*. Cocoa: Florida Historical Society Press, 2003.

Rich, Doris L. *Queen Bess, Daredevil Aviator*. Washington, D.C.: Smithsonian Institution Press, 1993.

Richardson, Clement, ed. *The National Cyclopedia of the Colored Race*. Vol. 1. Montgomery, Ala.: National Publishing, 1919.

Ritchie, Andrew. *Major Taylor: The Extraordinary Career of a Champion Bicycle Racer*. San Francisco: Bicycle Books, 1988.

Robie, Bill. *For the Greatest Achievement: A History of the Aero Club of America and the National Aeronautic Association*. Washington, D.C.: Smithsonian Institution Press, 1993.

Rolinson, Mary G. *Grassroots Garveyism: The Universal Negro Improvement Association in the Rural South, 1920–1927*. Chapel Hill: University of North Carolina Press, 2007.

Rosenberg, Charles. "George Washington Murray." In *African-American National Biography*, vol. 2, 2nd ed., edited by Henry Louis Gates Jr. and Evelyn Brooks Higginbotham, 388–90. New York: Oxford University Press, 2013.

Scamehorn, Howard L. *Balloons to Jets: A Century of Aeronautics in Illinois, 1855–1955*. Chicago: Henry Regnery, 1957.

Schneider, Mark Robert. *"We Return Fighting": The Civil Rights Movement in the Jazz Age*. Boston: Northeastern University Press, 2002.

Scott, Emmett J. *Scott's Official History of the American Negro in the World War*. Chicago: Homewood, 1919.

Scott, Lloyd N. *The Naval Consulting Board of the United States*. Washington, D.C.: Government Printing Office, 1920.

Seawell, Meade. *Edgehill Entry, Tale of a Tarheel Town*. Raleigh, N.C.: Broughton, 1970.

Seiler, Cotten. *Republic of Drivers: A Cultural History of Automobility in America*. Chicago: University of Chicago Press, 2009.

Smith, Graham. *When Jim Crow Met John Bull: Black American Soldiers in World War II Britain*. New York: St. Martin's, 1987.

Smith, Jessie Carney. "Overton, Anthony (1865–1946)." In *Encyclopedia of African American Business*, vol. 2, K–Z, 2nd ed., edited by Jessie Carney Smith, 671–73. Santa Barbara, Calif.: ABC-CLIO, 2017.

Smith, Richard Norton. *The Colonel: The Life and Legend of Robert R. McCormick, 1880–1955*. Evanston, Ill.: Northwestern University Press, 2003.

Snider, Jill D. "Flying to Freedom: African American Visions of Aviation: 1910–1927." Ph.D. dissertation, University of North Carolina at Chapel Hill, 1995.

———. "'Great Shadow in the Sky': The Airplane in the Tulsa Race Riot of 1921 and the Development of Black Visions of Aviation, 1921–1926." In *The Airplane in American Culture*, edited by Dominick A. Pisano, 105–46. Ann Arbor: University of Michigan Press, 2004.

———. "William Jenifer Powell." In *Encyclopedia of African American Business History*, edited by Juliet E. K. Walker, 458–60. Westport, Conn.: Greenwood, 1999.

Sollors, Werner, Caldwell Titcomb, and Thomas A. Underwood, eds. *Blacks at Harvard: A Documentary History of African-American Experience at Harvard and Radcliffe*. New York: New York University Press, 1993.

Stevenson, Andrew. *Chicago: Pre-eminently a Presbyterian City*. Chicago: Winona Publishing, 1907.

Stolz, Claudia Matherly. "Chicago (Ill.) Riot of 1919." In *Encyclopedia of American Race Riots*, vol. 1, A–M, Greenwood Milestones in African American History Series, edited by Walter Rucker and James Nathaniel Upton, 100–106. Westport, Conn.: Greenwood, 2007.

Suggs, Jon-Christian. "Romanticism, Labor, and the Suppression of African-American Citizenship." In *Race and the Production of Modern American Nationalism*, Wellesley Studies in Critical Theory, Literary History, and Culture, vol. 18, edited by Reynolds J. Scott-Childress, 67–95. London: Routledge, Taylor & Francis, 2013.

Takaki, Ronald T. *A Pro-Slavery Crusade: The Agitation to Reopen the African Slave-Trade*. New York: Free Press, 1971.

Tata, Robert. *How Detroit Became the "Automotive Capitol of the World": The Story Behind the Founding of the U.S. Auto Industry*. Bloomington, Ind.: AuthorHouse, 2013.

Taylor, Elizabeth Dowling. *The Original Black Elite: Daniel Murray and the Story of a Forgotten Era*. New York: Amistad, 2017.

Taylor, Major. *The Fastest Bicycle Rider in the World: The Story of a Colored Boy's Indomitable Courage and Success Against Great Odds, an Autobiography by Marshall W. "Major" Taylor*. Worcester, Mass.: Wormley, 1928.

Thackray, Brian. *The AEC Story: From the Regent to the Monarch*. Stroud, U.K.: Amberley, 2012.

Theodorsen, Theodore, and William C. Clay. *Ice Prevention on Aircraft by Means of Engine Exhaust Heat and a Technical Study of Heat Transmission from a Clark Y Airfoil*. Report No. 403, Langley Memorial Aeronautical Laboratory. Washington, D.C.: National Advisory Committee for Aeronautics, 1931.

Thompson, Ernest Trice. "Black Presbyterians, Education and Evangelism After the Civil War." *Journal of Presbyterian History* 76, no. 1 (Spring 1998): 55–70.

Travis, Dempsey J. "Bronzeville." In *The Electronic Encyclopedia of Chicago*. Chicago: Chicago Historical Society, 2005. http://www.encyclopedia.chicagohistory.org/pages/171.html.

Trohan, Walter. "My Life with the Colonel." *Journal of the Illinois State Historical Association* 52, no. 4 (Winter 1959): 477–502.

Tuttle, William M., Jr. *Race Riot: Chicago in the Red Summer of 1919*. Urbana: University of Illinois Press, 1970.

Tye, Larry. *Rising from the Rails: Pullman Porters and the Making of the Black Middle Class*. New York: Holt, 2004.

Tygiel, Jules. "Unresolved Strivings: Baseball in Jim Crow America." In *The American Game: Baseball and Ethnicity*, edited by Lawrence Baldassaro and Richard A. Johnson, 68–91. Carbondale: Southern Illinois University Press, 2002.

Urry, John. "Mobility and Proximity." *Sociology* 36, no. 2 (May 2002): 255–74.

Van Dulken, Stephen. *British Patents of Invention, 1617–1977: A Guide for Researchers*. London: British Library, 1999.

Van Ells, Mark D. *America and World War I: A Traveler's Guide*. Northampton, Mass.: Interlink, 2015.

Van Tassel, David D., and John J. Grabowski. *The Encyclopedia of Cleveland History*. Bloomington: Indiana University Press, 1987.

Vincent, Theodore G. *Black Power and the Garvey Movement*. Rev. ed. San Francisco: Ramparts, 1972.

Voogd, Jan. "Washington (D.C.) Riot of 1919." In *Encyclopedia of American Race Riots*, vol. 2, N–Z, Greenwood Milestones in African American History Series, edited by Walter Rucker and James Nathaniel Upton, 681–83. Westport, Conn.: Greenwood, 2007.

Walker, Juliet E. K., ed. *Encyclopedia of African American Business History*. Westport, Conn.: Greenwood, 1999.

———. *Free Frank: A Black Pioneer on the Antebellum Frontier*. Lexington: University of Kentucky Press, 1983.

———. *The History of Black Business in America: Capitalism, Race, Entrepreneurship, Vol. I to 1865*. 2nd ed. Chapel Hill: University of North Carolina Press, 2009.

Weir, Gary E. "Surviving the Peace—The Advent of American Naval Oceanography, 1914–1924." *Naval War College Review* 50, no. 4 (Autumn 1997): 85–103.

Wellman, Manly Wade. *The Story of Moore County: Two Centuries of a North Carolina Region*. Southern Pines, N.C.: Moore County Historical Society, 1974.

Whitehouse, Jack. *Fire Island: Heroes & Villains on Long Island's Wild Shore*. Charleston, S.C.: History Press, 2011.

Wiggins, David K. "'Black Athletes in White Men's Games': Race, Sport and American National Pastimes." *International Journal of the History of Sport* 31, nos. 1–2 (March 2014): 181–202.

Wilkerson, J. L. *Story of Pride, Power, and Uplift: Annie T. Malone*. Kansas City, Mo.: Acorn, 2003.

Williams, Michael. *Farm Tractors: A Complete and Illustrated History*. Irvine, Calif.: i-5 Press, 2016.

Wilmington Race Riot Commission. *1898 Wilmington Race Riot Report*. Raleigh: Office of Archives and History, North Carolina Department of Natural and Cultural Resources, 2006.

Wood, A[lbert] B[eaumont]. "From Board of Invention and Research to the Royal Naval Scientific Service. *Journal of the Royal Naval Scientific Service, Albert Beaumont Wood, O.B.E., D.Sc., Memorial Issue* 20, no. 4 (July 1965): 16–97.

Yenser, Thomas, ed. and publ. *Who's Who in Colored America: A Dictionary of Notable Living Persons of African Descent in America.* 3rd ed. Brooklyn, N.Y.: Who's Who in Colored America, 1933.

Yergin, David. *The Prize: The Epic Quest for Oil, Money & Power.* New York: Free Press, 2008.

WEBSITES

Energy Institute

"UK Petrol Prices (1902–2008) and Diesel Prices (1989–2008)." https://knowledge.energyinst.org/search/record?id=58969

Measuring Worth, measuringworth.com

"Computing 'Real Value' Over Time with a Conversion between U.K. Pounds and U.S. Dollars, 1774 to Present." https://measuringworth.com/calculators/exchange/.

Index

AAAA, or Four As (Afro-American Automobile Association), 91–92, 95–96, 98–101, 106. *See also* NCAA

Abbott, Robert S., 76, 105; Coleman and, 93, 167; friendship of with Headen, 66, 73–74, 87, 106, 108, 128, 146–48, 163; Headen Motor Co. and, 83; nature of heroes he created, 56, 164. *See also Chicago Defender*

Aberdeen, N.C., 7, 28, 35, 115, 162, 179n4

Ables, Fred D., 170

Ables, Louise Headen, 35, 115, 170

Academy Heights School, 42

Adams, Amy Irwin. *See* McCormick, Amy Irwin Adams

Admiralty, UK (British Admiralty), 71–73, 89, 155. *See also* BIR; DER

Aerial Age, 53–54, 58

Aero Club of America, 52

Aero Club of Illinois, 53–54

Aero Club of New York, 37, 49

Aerolex Ltd., 141, 150

Aeronautic School of Engineers, 46, 56

Aeronautical Society of New York, 37, 40, 45, 49–51, 70, 111

African Americans. *See* black artisans; black auto racers; black aviators; black beauty culturists; black educators; black inventors; black migrants; blacks in the military

Africo-American Presbyterian, 14, 18, 22

Afro-American Automobile Association. *See* AAAA

Agricultural Research Council, 136

agriculture in Australia, Headen's engine products and, 138

agriculture in Europe: Headen Cap and, 153; Headen's engine products and, 138

agriculture in India, Headen Cap and, 153

agriculture in the UK: Agricultural Research Council and, 136; bi-fuel Fordson tractors and, 129, 135; Finance Act of 1935 and, 136–38; Headen Cap and, 153; Headen's engine products and, 133, 135, 138, 144; Headen's furtherance of, 136, 169; mechanization of, 143; "nadir of arable farming" in, 136; National Institute of Agricultural Engineering and, 144; Oxford Conference on Mechanized Farming (1937) and, 138; Royal Agricultural Society of England and, 129, 135, 138. *See also* bi-fuel engines; trade and agricultural shows in Britain

Air Ministry (UK), 137, 139, 142–43

Albany, Ga., 102–5, 110–13, 115–17, 124–27. *See also* racial violence; Tift Silica Brick Co.

Albany Herald, 18, 117; coverage of Headen's activities by, 103–4, 109, 119, 123

Albany-South Georgia Fair Grounds, 115

Albion Academy (Franklinton Colored State Normal and Industrial School), 25, 31–35, 39, 42, 59, 60–61, 145, 162

Alger, Horatio, 162

Allimono, Leontina, 126

Allimono, Walter D., 66–67, 87–88, 107, 126

Alverstone Hotel, 144

American Community Advertising Association, 118

American Woodmen of the World, 85, 87

Anderson, Walter B., 66–67

Anglo-Persian Oil Co., 129

anti-icing (deicing and ice prevention) technologies: Air Ministry's support for, 139, 142; alcohol spray methods for, 139–41; Curtiss-Wright research on, 142, 156–57; electrothermal methods and, 141, 157; Goodrich ice removal "overshoes"

anti-icing (deicing and ice prevention) technologies (cont.)
and, 139; Headen's pressure jet system for control surfaces and, 139–40, 157–58; Headen's propeller deicing method and, 140–42, 142; heated-air methods for, 139–42, 156–58; influence of Headen's patents on industrial anti-icing R&D, 141–42, 156–59; metallic matting ice removal method and, 139; NACA and, 140, 142–43; National Research Council of Canada and, 141, 157; problems of using exhaust gases for, 142, 144; RAE and, 141, 143; Sir Alan Cobham and, 141–42; wind turbine and gas engine turbine blades and, 142, 158. *See also full list of Headen's patents and their citations in the bibliography*

Armstrong, Louis, 97, 107
Armwood, Idella. *See* Street, Idella Armwood
Armwood, Levin Sr., 114
Armwood, Walter, 118
Ashley & Bailey Silk Mill, 28, 162, 196n9, 258n3
Associated Business Club, 106
Atlantic Coast Line Railroad, 29, 111
Atwood, Harry, 38
Auto & Aero Mechanical School, 92
automobile racing (dirt track): alcohol use and, 107; black dirt track races, 96–104; black manhood and, 109; black speedway associations and, 76, 95–98, 100–104; black women drivers and, 100, 107; black-white cooperation and, 96, 101, 103, 106; bootlegging and gambling as sources of capital for, 98, 106–7; criticisms of, 106–7; deaths in, 97, 100; professionalism and, 98
automobiles and the black middle class: black auto clubs, 45; black auto manufacturers (besides Headen), 80–81; black automobility, 111–15, 165–66; black beauty culturists and the automobile, 112–13, 165–66; black visions for the automobile, 89–94; black women and safety on the road, 86, 91, 109; black-owned auto schools and garages, 45, 76–78, 80, 92–93; challenges on the road, 91; Jim Crow and the automobile, 91–92, 114–15, 163–64

Aveling-Barford Ltd., 143
aviation in Britain: Air Ministry and, 137, 139; Finance Act of 1935 and, 137. *See also* anti-icing (deicing and ice prevention) technologies
aviation in the United States: black beauty culturists and, 165–66; black-owned aviation businesses and, 46, 56, 92, 166, 168; color line in, 49, 54, 56, 89, 163; professionalism and, 53; racial stereotypes in, 57; search for aeronautical stabilizer and, 41; spectators and, 54, 57; U.S. Army Signal Corps and, 49, 166. *See also* anti-icing (deicing and ice prevention) technologies; black aviators
Aycock, Charles, 27, 33

Bacon, Albert S., 126
Baker, Henry, 100
Baker, Henry E., 24, 42
Baker, James E., 85, 87
Baker, Vera L., 34
Baldwin Thomas, 38, 49–50, 52
Barrett, Harold W., 45, 86, 88, 99, 109
Beatty, Blanche Armwood, 88–89, 118
Benchke, David, 167
Bennett Seminary, 11
Berean Manual and Training School, 170
Berkley, Warren (General Motors), 157
Berry, Lizzie Palmer, 45, 89, 108
Bessie Coleman Aero Club, 94, 168
Bethel Literary and Historical Association, 23, 44, 88
bi-fuel engines: advantages of, 122; diesel engine versus, 121, 137, 152; distributors of Headen's products for, 133–135; employment of in tractors, 120, 122, 129, 133, 135, 138, 143–44; Finance Act of 1935 and, 136–37; fuels for (*see* heavy oils); Headen antidilution gasket for, 135–38, 143; Headen converter kit (Headen Heat Unit)

for, 133, 143–44; Headen design to combat pre-ignition in, 132–34; Headen manifold for, 123–26, 129–31, 133, 134; Headen oil-burning carburetor for, 137–38; Headen-Petit "spark ignition" device for, 122–23; investors in, 124–26, 134, 137; Royal Agricultural Society of England and, 129; Royal Automobile Club and, 129–30; vaporizers in, 123; versus gasoline engines, 122–23; viability of in road vehicles, 120, 122. *See also* World War II

Bindbeutel, George, 53

BIR (Board of Invention and Research), 71–73. *See also* DER

Bishir, Catherine, 166

black artisans: American success myth and, 162; as architects, 46–47, 92, 118; blacksmiths, 10, 15–16, 27–28, 32, 63; brick masons, 11, 14, 46; builders and carpenters, 31–32, 74, 112, 118; enthusiasm of for transportation technologies, 112, 166–67; painters, 28, 46; paper hangers, 46; as slaves, 3, 10; social status of, 10–11; stonemasons, 67; tailors, 33, 36, 127; tinners, 46; wheelwrights, 2, 9, 63, 76, 80–81; white artisans' objections to, 28. *See also* Networks

black auto racers, 96–98, 100–4, 106–7

black aviators, 5, 50–59, 92–94, 108–10, 166

black beauty culturists, 74, 92, 111–13, 165–66

black business: ambivalence toward vice as source of capital for, 107; slave entrepreneurship and, 166–67; white investors in, 68, 71–72, 81–82, 124–26, 130–32, 134; women as owners of, 88, 111–13. *See also* black beauty culturists; "coalition economics"; NNBL

black educators: in Georgia, 103, 109, 119; in North Carolina, 13–14, 23, 31–36, 42, 44, 115; in Pennsylvania, 170

blackface minstrelsy, 57, 102, 170

black inventors, artisanal origins of, 46, 166; in Bethel Literary and Historical Society, 23–24; black inventor myth and, 164; challenges faced by, 3–4, 25, 43, 46,

75, 167; financial strategies of, 47, 66, 167; as heroes in black press, 38

Blackman, William "Bill," 101, 104

black middle class: contributions of, 169–70; growth of, 77–78, 82; historians' attacks on, 169. *See also* Automobiles and the black middle class

black migrants: intraregional movements of, 35, 61, 67, 74, 86; regional movements of, 22–23, 35–36, 105, 110, 112, 116–18, 126

black press: distribution of by railroad porters, 46; locality columns in, 113–14; pressures faced by, 87; views of automobile in, 91, 113–14; views of England in, 71, 147; views of France in, 71

blacks in the military: 8th Illinois (370th) Infantry and, 66–67, 78; 54th Massachusetts Infantry and, 20; 365th Infantry and, 93; peacetime U.S. Navy and, 20

Blue, Daniel, 7

Blue's Crossing, N.C. *See* Aberdeen, N.C.

Board of Invention and Research. *See* BIR

Board of Missions for Freedmen (PCUSA), 13–14, 20–21

bootlegging, 76–77, 98, 106–7

Bordentown Manual Training School, New Jersey, 115

Bottoms, Lesta, 107

Bottoms, William, 98, 103, 106–7

Bradford, Fred L., 55, 93

Brewer, Chester, 85

Briggs, William, 159

Britain: oil supplies in, 129, 144; petrol prices in, 121; race relations in, 73, 145–48. *See also* Admiralty, UK; agriculture in the UK; aviation in Britain; British Ministry of Shipping; trade and agricultural shows in Britain

British Ministry of Shipping, 73, 89, 120

Brotherhood of Railroad Trainmen, 38

Brown, Nathan, 15

Bruen, Joe, 102, 104

Bryant, Sarah Drye, 34

Buckner, Thomas W., 28

Buick Racing Team, 45

Burgess, James, 100
Burnham Beauty College, 92

Camberley, England: Camberley and Frimley Urban Council and, 134; hotels in, 132, 144–45; industrial development of, 132, 134, 138, 141; Laurel Works in, 132; opposition to industry in, 138–39; postwar education in, 153–54; servant shortage in, 138; St. Mary's Works in, 132, 134, 141, 150, 152. *See also* Headen Hamilton Engineering Co. Ltd.; Headen Keil Engineering Co. Ltd.; Headen Novelty Co. Ltd.; World War II
Camden, N.C., 88
Canfield Oil Co., 124
Cannon, Clorena, 44
Cannon, Genevieve, 44, 88
Cannon, George E., 39, 44–45, 88, 114
Cannon, Mary. *See* Spraggins, Mary Cannon
Cannon, Sultana, 114
Cannon, Vivian, 114
Cape Fear Presbytery (PCUSA), 34
Carden-Ford "Flying Flea," 137
Carey, Archibald J., 69
Carson, William, 97, 100
Carthage, N.C.: 2–3; black businesses in, 11, 15–16, 18–19, 27–28, 162; enthusiasm for invention in, 17; forest fire outside of, 18; industrial and economic development of, 8–9; racial climate of, 6–7, 26–30; remarks by Bishop John Walker Hood in, 26. See also *Carthage Blade*; Carthage Presbyterian Church; Carthage Railroad; *Carthage Vindicator*; John Hall Chapel; racial violence; Tyson & Jones Buggy Co.
Carthage Blade, 8, 10–11, 16–18, 26
Carthage Presbyterian Church, 12, 27, 36
Carthage Railroad, 8, 18, 27, 29, 36
Carthage Vindicator, 21, 191n45
Catus, Constance. *See* Gantt, Constance "Connie" Catus
Cave, W. Sturmy, 138

Central Industrial Insurance Co., 88
Chappelle, Charles Ward, 46–47, 66, 92, 166
chauffeurs: 46, 112; black-owned schools for, 45, 92; duties of, 63; relationship with employers of, 60–65, 126
Cheatham, Henry P., 23
Cheek, Matilda, 7
Chesnutt, Charles, 23, 42
Chestnut Street Presbyterian Church, 33–35
Chicago, Ill.: black auto businesses in, 76, 78, 80, 82–94; black auto racing in, 96–98; black middle class in, 77–78; corruption in, 106–7; Headen's early coalition in, 60–61, 65–74. *See also Chicago Defender*; *Chicago Tribune*; Grace Presbyterian Church; Headen Motor Co.; Headen Spring-in-a-Tube Co., McCormick family (Chicago); racial violence
Chicago Colored Auto Racing Association: founding of, 96; rivalry with Indianapolis of, 98, 100, 104; vice syndicate and, 98, 106. *See also* Dreamland Derby
Chicago Defender, 46, 77, 96–98; coverage of Headen, 61, 65–66, 69, 74, 81, 163–64; coverage of Tena, 66, 108, 127; creation of militant heroes in, 56, 127, 164, 167; Headen on, 146–48; Lake Forest column in, 63; portrayal of European capitals in, 71; role of in Election Day Race, 99–100; role of in Negro National League, 83–84; support of Headen Motor Co. by, 83; Sylvester Russell as writer for, 55, 66
Chicago Tribune, 61–62, 65, 67, 161
Cicero Field, 53, 62
Cicero-Aurora Aviation Meet, 53
City Federation of Colored Women's Clubs, 112, 165
Clay, William, 140, 142
Clegg, Tom, 29
Cleveland, Ohio, 59, 124–26, 129, 132
Close, Edwyn T., 134, 141
"coalition economics": adoption of by black aviation pioneers, 167–68;

automobility and, 165; Headen's use of, 3, 68, 75–76, 81, 95–96, 108, 111, 119; limits of, 91, 95, 104–5, 108–9, 119, 132, 169; research needed on, 168; Wood as model for, 3, 20–21, 60

Cobham, Sir Alan, 141–42

Coffin, Howard, 69

Coleman, Bessie, 92–94, 165, 167–68

Colored Industrial Fair (Raleigh, N.C.), 23

Colored Speedway Racing Association (Indianapolis), 96, 98, 101, 103. *See also* NCAA

Combined Christian Churches, 86

Combined John Robinson and Franklin Brothers Circus, 18

Commercial Motor Transport Exhibition (Olympia, England), 134

Cook, Charles, 71

Cosmopolitan Auto School, 45, 92

Cotton States and International Exposition, 10, 16–17, 119, 162

County Garage Co., 144

Crabb, Edward, 38–39

Craftsmen of Black Wings, 168

Crawford, John P., 87

Curtiss-Wright Corporation of New York, 142, 156–57

Cuthbert & Son, Dundee, Scotland, 133

Daniels, Josephus, 68–71, 144, 164

Davison, Louis, 39, 74

Day, Jack, 156

Dayton, Margaret, 21

Dayton Academy, 13–16, 21–22, 24–25, 28, 30–31, 35, 42, 145; photo of, 16

Dayton Industrial and Normal School. *See* Dayton Academy

Democratic Party: in Chicago, 82; in Franklin Co., N.C., 33; in Moore Co., N.C., 6–7, 22, 28, 30; in Wilmington, N.C., 25–26

DER (Director of Experiments and Research), 72–73. *See also* BIR

Detroit House of Correction, 77

Dickinson School, 42

diesel engines, 121, 136–37, 152

diesel oil. *See* heavy oils

Director of Experiments and Research. *See* DER

dirt-track racing. *See* automobile racing (dirt track)

disfranchisement. *See* voter suppression and disfranchisement in North Carolina

Dixie Highway, 77, 110

Douglass, Charles, 29

Dozier, Oscar, 79

Dreamland Derby, 96–98, 100–101, 106–7

Drye, Amelia Hill, 34

Drye, Edward, 34

Drye, George, 35–36, 74

Drye, James David, 33–34

Drye, James Festus, 34, 36

Drye, Jenny Scull, 34

Drye, Oliver (Ollie), 34, 101

Drye, Sarah. *See* Stanley, Sarah Drye

Drye, Tena Elizabeth. *See* Meares, Tena Elizabeth Drye Headen

Drye, William, 34

Duke of York Hotel, 132, 144–45

Dunnington, Harry, 96, 98

Dwyer, Patrick J., 81–83, 107

Earl, Harry, 96, 106

Eastern Automobile Association, 101

Edison, Thomas A., 17, 37, 38, 43, 46, 75, 171

Elliott, Albert G. (Rolls-Royce Co.), 158

Emancipation Celebration (St. Louis, Mo., 1912), 55–58, 71

emigrants (black American) to England, 146–48

Enos, Louis (Curtiss-Wright), 156–57

Erie Railroad, 38–41, 43, 46, 48–50, 99, 162

Evans, Victor, 130

Evershed, H. R., 133

fairs, expositions. *See* trade and agricultural shows, fairs, and expositions in the United States; trade and agricultural shows in Britain

Fayetteville State Normal and Industrial School, 11, 23, 196n9
Federated Women's Clubs of New Jersey, 45
Fédération Aéronautique Internationale, 52, 93
Felton, William McDonald, 92
Finance Act of 1935 (UK), 136–37
First International Aviation Show (New York), 46
First Presbyterian Church (Trenton), 20–21
Flight Refuelling Ltd., 141–42
Flynn, N.C., post office in, 22, 28
Ford Motor Co.: 75, 80–81, 83, 90, 98, 122, 131, 137, 141, 152, 164; Fordson tractor of, 129, 133, 135, 138, 143–44; Model T of, 45, 65, 83, 112, 120; warranty approval of Headen's anti-dilution gasket by, 135–36
Fouché, Rayvon, 23, 164
Foushee, Charles, 22, 42
Française Americaine Aeroplane Cie (Francia Aviation Co.), 50
France, 73, 78; Coleman learns to fly in, 93; as market for Headen, 138–39, 152; as symbol for black Americans, 56–57, 89–90, 147; Wood tours, 20
Franklinton Colored State Normal and Industrial School. *See* Albion Academy
Franz, Kathleen, 165
Freeman, 55, 86, 98
Frimley, England, 154, 156, 159
Frimley Green, England, 145, 150, 153–156, 159
Fuller, Henry, 31–32
Fusion politics in North Carolina, 22, 25, 33, 35

Gannaway, John, 92
Gantt, Constance "Connie" Catus, 34, 108
Garvey, 105–6, 147. *See also* UNIA
gasoline: price of in Britain versus United States, 120–21; properties of, 122; as smallest product of crude oil distillation process, 120; use of in bi-fuel engines, 122
gasoline engines: improvements to, 152; mechanics of, 122–23
gasoline-kerosene engines. *See* bi-fuel engines

Georgia: 29, 50; auto racing in, 101–3; black car ownership in, 113; exodus of blacks from, 116–17; protests against gas prices in, 120–21; UNIA in, 105, 116. *See also* racial violence
Georgia Normal and Agricultural College, 103, 109, 126
Georgia State Negro Fair, 50, 54
Gibbs, Joseph, 74
Gladden, S. H., 41
Goins, King, 29
Goins' Tonsorial Parlor (Chicago), 93
Gold and Glory Sweepstakes, 96, 98, 100, 106–7
Good Roads Movement, 110
Good Samaritan Hospital, 42
Grace Presbyterian Church (Chicago), 66, 68, 79, 86, 108–9, 128
Graham, Billy (Greater London Crusade, 1954), 153
Grand Hotel, 145
Gray, Carroll, 62
Great Cold Wave of 1912, 51
Great Lakes Naval Training Station, 70
Green, John Benjamin, 86
Greensboro, N.C., 11, 23, 78, 99, 114, 126, 165, 170
Greenwood, Jane Ables, 170
Gunnell, Joshua, 43

Hamilton, George D., 125–26, 129–32, 134
Handlan Park (St. Louis), 57
Hanson Automobile Co., 80
Hardy, John King, 143
Harris, Edward E., 112, 115, 118
Harrisburg, Pa., 34, 92
Harrison, Benjamin, 163
Harvard University: Booker T. Washington visit to, 42; French Tyson at, 42
Hawkins, Anna, 72
Hawkins, Wilmot Comfort, 60, 65, 68, 71–72
Hawthorne Race Track, 54, 98
Hayes, Forrest, 43
Headen, Allis, 7
Headen, Cherryl Thomas, 160
Headen, Delia, 7

Headen, Gladys Hollamby, 150–51, *151*, 153, 159–60
Headen, Jerry M., 6–8, 11, 13, 18–19, 26–28, 35, 115, 162
Headen, Laura A. Tyson, 6–7, 11, 19
Headen, Louise. *See* Ables, Louise Headen
Headen, Lucean Arthur Jr., 153–55, 159–60
Headen, Lucean Arthur Sr.: American citizenship and, 69, 148, 153; as auto manufacturer, 1, 3, 76, 81–90, 93, 96–102, 107–9, 111–12, 118–19, 123, 127, 145, 163, 165, 167 (*see also* Headen Motor Car Co.; Headen Motor Co.); as auto racer/promoter, 96–108 (*see also* AAAA; NCAA); on the automobile, 89–92, 95, 99, 164; as aviator, 5, 50–59; birth and early life of, 6–9; as bootlegger, 76–77; as chauffeur, 61–65; descriptions of/comments on, 5, 39–40, 52, 59, 61, 65, 74, 102, 120, 124, 128, 153, 162–64, 169; disfranchisement of, 27–28, 32–33; divorce of, 126–28; early influences on, 13–14, 16, 18–24; emigration to England by, 130, 149, 158; as Erie Railroad waiter, 40–41, 43, 49; fatherhood and, 153, 155, 160; financial strategy of (*see* "coalition economics"); friendship with Robert Abbott of, 66, 73–74, 89, 106, 108, 128, 146–48, 163; as hero/role model, 56–57, 92, 99–100, 163–64, 170; as independent inventor, 3, 38, 43, 47, 75, 125, 142–43, 158, 167; influence of on anti-icing researchers, 141, 156–59; influence of on black aviation pioneers, 92–94, 167–68; influence of on engine designers, 158; Jim Crow and, 26, 29, 32, 38–39, 90; marriage of (first), 33; marriage of (second), 150; as member of Home Guard, 149; patents of (*see full list of patents and their citations in bibliography*); photos of, 64, 72, 131, 149; as Pullman porter, 29–30, 39–40; as racial advocate, 147–48; religion and, 12, 14, 31, 39–42, 66, 153, 161–62; as student, 13–14, 25, 31–33, 35, 39, 59. *See also* Headen Novelty Co. Ltd.; Headen Spring-in-a-Tube Co.; Junior Specialty Co.
Headen, Nannie Kathleen. *See* Jones, Nannie Kathleen Headen
Headen, Nettie B. Jackson, 28
Headen, Tena Elizabeth Drye. *See* Meares, Tena Elizabeth Drye Headen
Headen anti-dilution gasket, 135–38, 143, 150
Headen Cap, 152–55
Headen Hamilton Engineering Co. Ltd., 130–32, 151; converter kit of, 133–34
Headen Keil Engineering Co. Ltd., 134, 138; products of (*see* bi-fuel engines); unmarketed designs of (*see* anti-icing (deicing and ice prevention) technologies)
Headen Motor Car Co. (Albany, Ga.), 3, 111–12, 118–20, 123, 127, 165
Headen Motor Co. (Chicago), 3, 76, 81–90, 93, 97–102, 107–9, 127, 163, 167; advertising brochure (photo of cover), 84
Headen Novelty Co. Ltd., 152–53
Headen oil-burning carburetor. *See* bi-fuel engines
Headen Repair Shop, 76, 78, 82, 93
Headen & Shaw Machine Shop, 80, 82
Headen Spring-in-a-Tube Co., 66–68, 83
Headen & Tyson Saw and Shingle Mill, 18–19, 22, 27–28, 162
heavy-oil engines. *See* bi-fuel engines
heavy oils (kerosene, paraffin, diesel oil, vaporizing oil [TVO], waste oil): distillation improvements for, 152; duties on, 136–38; grades of created in crude oil distillation process, 120; use of in bi-fuel engines, 120, 122, 129, 135–38, 143–44, 152. *See also* gasoline
Hintz, Eric, 125
Ho-Ho-Kus Race Track, 99–101, 105, 126
Hollamby, Gladys. *See* Headen, Gladys Hollamby
Hollamby, Mary, 150
Hollamby, William Jr., 150
Hollamby, William Sr., 150
Holley, Joseph W., 103, 109, 111, 118–19, 126
Home Guard. *See* World War II

Hood, Bishop James Walker, 26
Hotel Maceo, 45
Howard University, 42
Hughitt, Martin, 60
Hunter, Mattie, 100, 107, 109
Hunter, R. W., 80

IBPOEW (Improved Benevolent and Protective Order of Elks of the World), 111–12
Improved Benevolent and Protective Order of Elks of the World. *See* IBPOEW
independent inventors: competition of with industrial scientists, 3; delay in age of productivity of, 43; Eric Hintz on, 125; finance options of, 125, 167; influence of on industrial scientists, 158, 168; racial cooperation among, 111, 120–25; racial restrictions and, 3, 38, 47, 75, 142–43
Independent Order of Good Templars, 12
Independent Women's Welfare Council (Philadelphia), 170
Indianapolis 500, 81, 86, 95
Institutional Methodist Church of Chicago, 69
International Brotherhood of Sleeping Car Porters, 43
International Harvester, 61

Jack Johnson Gala Day, 54–55
Jackson, Nathaniel, 42
Jackson, Sandy A., 28
Jacksonville, Tampa, & Key West Railway Co., 19
Jefferies, William (Wild Bill), 98, 106–7
Jerry, A., 88
Jersey City, N.J., 36–39, 46, 49, 52, 60–61, 74, 86, 108, 127; Erie Railroad trainmen in, 39–41, 43, 46; Pullman porters in, 36, 39–40. *See also* Lafayette Presbyterian Church
Jim Crow. *See* segregation
John C. Robinson Air College and Automotive Engineering School, 166

John Hall Chapel (Carthage Church), 12–15, 20–21, 27, 30, 35–36, 42, 145
Johnson, Alberta, 74
Johnson, Jack, 54–56, 96
Johnson, William, 86
Jones, John W., 35, 42, 111
Jones, Nannie Kathleen Headen, 3, 7, 11–12, 14–15, 20, 26, 31, 33, 35, 78–79, 87, 145, 148, 159–60, 170; automobility and, 114–15; photo of, 159
Jones, Phil, 81, 84
Jones, Walter D., 76
Jones, William A., 3, 35, 42, 59, 65, 78, 111
Jones, William N., 145, 147
Jones, William T., 6, 8, 21
Jones Drug Store, 35, 42, 78
Jordan, James R., 87
Jordan, Joseph, 66, 68, 70, 109
Junior Specialty Co., 154

Kansas City Monarchs, 84
Keil, Alan, 145
Keil, James Richard McLean, 132, 134, 138, 145, 151
Kelly, Adam David, 42
Kelly, Alexander, 10
Kelly, Charles, 42
Kelly, Edinboro, 10, 12, 15, 28
Kelly, George B., 12
Kelly, Kade, 10–11, 14, 42
kerosene. *See* heavy oils
Knights of Pythias, 87, 111, 115
Koelliker, George P., 124–26, 129, 137
Ku Klux Klan (KKK). *See* racial violence

Lafayette Presbyterian Church, 39, 42–44, 50, 66–67, 86, 108
Lake Forest, Ill., 62–63
Lamoreaux, Naomi, 43
Larramore, D. A., 88
Latimer, Lewis, 38, 46, 75
Laurel Works, 132
League of Coloured Peoples (London), 146
Lemon, Harvey Brace, 68, 70
Lewis, Cary B., 83–84, 109

Liberty Life Insurance Co., 68
Liebrandt, George F., 68–70
Lincoln State Bank, 68
Lincoln University, 12, 20, 31
Lloyd Presbyterian Church, 35
Lombard Presbyterian Church, 170
Long Island, N.Y., 1, 5, 37–38, 48–51, 74, 100
Lyceum (Philadelphia), 170
Lyndhurst Preparatory School, 154, 159

Macon, Ga., 50, 54, 102, 109
Macon Telegraph, 102, 104, 118, 120, 124
Madden, Martin B., 69
Malone, Annie, 112–13, 166
M.A.P. Trading and Transport Co. of London, 130–31
Marshall, John Randolph, 66
Martin, Erle (General Motors), 157
Mayne, Robert (Goodyear Aircraft), 158
McAlpin Hotel (Chicago), 128
McBryan, Mrs. William, 114
McCormick, Amy Irwin Adams, 62–64
McCormick, Cyrus Hall Jr., 60–61
McCormick, Cyrus Hall Sr., 60
McCormick, Edith Rockefeller, 61
McCormick, Harold Fowler, 61–62
McCormick, Medill, 69
McCormick, Nettie Fowler, 60–61, 69
McCormick, Robert R., 60–67, 69
McCormick family (Chicago), 60–61; support of Headen by, 69–70, 171
McCoy, Elijah, 38
McFarland, Clarence R., 106
McGilvary, Elizabeth Tyson, 10
McIntosh, Hugh, 110, 117
McIver, James D., 7, 20, 27
McKinney, Nina Mae, 146
McNeill, Alexander H., 17, 20–21, 30
McNeill, George W., 30
McRae, Duncan J., 11–14, 27, 42
McRae, James Garland, 102
McRae, Susan "Susie" Nichols, 13, 15, 26, 30, 35, 45
McWorter, Frank, 166
McWorter, John E., 166

Meares, Lucy, 127
Meares, Norfleet, 127–28, 165
Meares, Tena Elizabeth Drye Headen, 2–3, 127; auto trips with Headen and, 74, 85–86, 109; birth and early life of, 33–35; caricature of by *Chicago Defender*, 108; church and civic activities of, 34, 39, 44, 66, 108; divorce of, 126–28; friends of, 34, 49, 74, 89, 108, 126, 128; marriage of (first), 33; marriage of (second), 128; Scotia Seminary and, 33–35, 44; social status of in Chicago, 66, 127; support of Headen's career and, 2, 44–45, 65–66, 76, 88–89, 107–9, 171; as teacher, 33; train travel and, 34, 52, 85, 108
Meares, William J., 126–27, 165
Mercy Hospital (Philadelphia), 170
Meteoric Aeroplane Co., 46
Metropolitan Mutual Benefit Association, 45, 86
Mills Aviators, 55, 57
Mitchell, Edith Tyson, 15, 28
Moffett, William A., 70
Monroe, Mich., 76–77
Monsen, Adolph, 81
Moore, Fred, 45, 50
Moore Co., N.C., 7, 19; black public schools in, 13, 21; courthouse in, 6, 8, 17, 23, 27; diphtheria outbreak of 1875 in, 11–12; gold mines in, 17–18; Post-Reconstruction Democratic Party in, 6, 22, 28, 30; Post-Reconstruction Republican Party in, 6, 12, 22. *See also* racial violence; "Redemption" movement
Morningside School, 42
Motor Accessments Ltd., 134
Motor Transport, 131, 133
Murray, George Washington, 88, 166

NAACP (National Association for the Advancement of Colored People), 44, 100, 147; in Albany, Ga., 112
National Association for the Advancement of Colored People. *See* NAACP
National Auto Show (Chicago, 1930), 126

National Colored Automobile Association. See NCAA
National Defense Council, Advisory Committee to, 69
National Federation of State Women's Clubs, 89
National Institute of Agricultural Engineering (Silsoe Institute), 144
National Medical Association Pharmaceutical Section, 65
National Negro Business League. See NNBL
National Oil Manifolds, 125
National Research Council of Canada, 141–42, 157
National Urban League (Tampa), 88, 91
Naval Consulting Board, 68–73, 154
NCAA (National Colored Automobile Association), 95; bars Headen, 102–4; merger of AAAA and Colored Speedway Racing Association (Indianapolis) to form and mission of, 101; races sponsored by, 103–4. See also AAAA; Colored Speedway Racing Association
Neal, Louis B., 31
Negro Men's Racing Association, 101
Negro National League, 83–84
Negro World. See UNIA
Nelson, James S., 66–67
networks: church, school, fraternal, political, professional, and women's club networks and Headen's success, 3, 6, 18–19, 31, 44–45, 60–61, 65–67, 86, 111–12, 118, 164; role of automobile in maintaining and expanding artisanal networks, 4, 114; social capital and, 165
New South, 21, 119
New York Age, 38, 42, 45–46, 71; coverage of Headen's activities by, 5, 50–52, 55, 58–59, 99–101, 163; coverage of Tena's activities by, 108
New York International Auto Show, 38
Nichols, Tena, 26, 45
NNBL (National Negro Business League), 47, 168; Madame C. J. Walker attendance at 1912 convention of, 112; in New York,

N.Y., 45; in Richmond, Va., 76; Will Jones address to in 1908, 42
North Carolina College, 159, 170
North Carolina State Fair, 16, 18
North Jersey Medical Association Automobile Club, 45

Olive Street Terrace Realty Co., 58
Osborn, Chase, 117
overseers, black, 10
Oxford Conference on Mechanized Farming, 138

Padden, Vincent T. (Grumman Aerospace), 158
Paget, Sir Richard, 73
Palmatier, Everett P. (Curtiss-Wright, Carrier Corp.), 156–57
Palmer, Lizzie. See Berry, Lizzie Palmer
Palmer & Singer (P&S) Garage, 45, 48
paraffin. See heavy oils
patent process: advantages of, 43; in Britain (assignee may apply), 249n17; color blindness of, 18; complexity of, 19, 24, 60; description of, 67; Headen's access to, 24, 60; infringement and, 125; intent to manufacture and, 131; patent agents/lawyers in, 18, 71–72, 130; patent citations and, 168; patent examination in, 124; speculators in, 124
Patterson, Fred D., 80–81
Patterson Motor Co., 81
Pau, France, 73, 89
Payne, Felix, 84–85
PCUSA (Presbyterian Church in the United States of America) (Presbyterian Church North), 13–14, 20–22, 26, 31–34, 60–61
Peace, Calvin, 28
Person, A. Thomas, 28
Person, Benjamin A., 31
Petit, Henry Aloysius, 111, 120–25
petrol. See gasoline
petrol-paraffin engines. See bi-fuel engines
Pickens, William H., 100, 147
Pinckney, Thomas H., 88

Pioneer Club, 106
Pioneer Garage, 106
Pittsburgh, Pa., 46, 108, 170
Plummer, Henry Vinton Jr., 105–6, 112, 116
Poindexter, Henry J., 80
Polite, William, 18, 161
Pollard, Lee Anderson, 45–46, 92
Poro College of Beauty, 112, 166
Porter, George M., 65, 67, 81
porters (railroad), 46; duties and community standing of, 29–30. *See also* Pullman Company
Powell, Louis and Lula Jenifer, 93
Powell, William Jenifer, 93–94, 167–68
Pratt, J., 81
Presbyterian Church in the United States of America. *See* PCUSA
Pullman Company: Headen and, 29–30, 39–40; Norfleet Meares and, 128; Samuel Stanley and, 39; *Vin Fiz Special* and, 48; working conditions at, 30, 40. *See also* Railroad Porters' and Waiters' Voluntary Subscription Fund

Queens Hotel, 145
Quinn, Julia, 45
Quinn, Walter Jr., 66–67
Quinn, Walter Sr., 45, 67

RAC (Royal Automobile Club), 129–30
"race man," 163
race riots. *See* racial violence
racial violence: in Chicago, 78–80 (gang attacks, bombings, Chicago Race Riot of 1919); in Colquitt and Dougherty Cos., Ga., 116–17 (KKK attacks); in Moore Co., N.C., 7, 26 (murders, KKK attacks); in Springfield, Ill., 55 (Springfield Race Riot of 1908); in Tulsa, Okla., 93 (Tulsa Race Riot of 1921); in Washington, D.C., 78 (Washington, D.C., Riot of 1919); in Wilmington, N.C., 25–28, 35 (Wilmington Race Riot of 1898 and coup of city government); in Winston-Salem, N.C., 78 (Winston-Salem Race Riot of 1919)

RAE (Royal Aircraft Establishment), 141, 143, 148
RAF, 74, 132, 143
Raiche, Bessica, 38, 49–54
Raiche, François (Frank C. Wright), 38, 49–54
Railroad Porters' and Waiters' Voluntary Subscription Fund, 43–44
Raleigh & Augusta Air Line Railroad, 8, 29
Rankin & White Drugstore, 67
Rector, Rosa, 85
Rector, Sarah, 85
Red Shirts, 25, 27
"Redemption" movement, 25, 28, 33, 68. *See also* racial violence; segregation; voter suppression and disfranchisement in North Carolina
Reginald Tildesley Ltd., 144
Republican Party: in Chicago (1920s), 69, 82, 106; in Franklin Co., N.C. (1890s–1905), 33; in New Jersey (1900s–1910s), 88–89; in Washington, D.C. (1880s–1920s), 23, 88; in Wilmington, N.C. (1890s), 35. *See also* Fusion politics in North Carolina; Moore Co., N.C.
ReVere automobile, 81, 83
Ritter, George, 26–27
Ritter, Thomas, 7, 20
Ritz Hotel (London), 151
Roadless News, 129, 135–36
Roadless Traction Ltd., 135–37, 143
Robert, J. Albert, 45
Roberts, Homer, 83, 85
Roberts Company Motor Mart, 83
Robertson, Will, 29
Robeson, Eslanda, 147
Robeson, Paul, 146–47
Robinson, Bill (Bojangles), 100
Robinson, Cornelius, 40, 45
Robinson, John C., 166
robotic mechanisms, 138, 141
Rodert, Lewis, 142–43
Rodgers, Calbraith, 48–49
Rogers, Joel A., 145
Rogers, Leslie, 84

Rosenwald, Julius, 69–70
Rough Riders, 25
Rowlands Metal Windows, 132, 138, 151
Royal Agricultural Society of England, 129, 135, 138
Royal Air Force. *See* RAF
Royal Aircraft Establishment. *See* RAE
Royal Automobile Club. *See* RAC
Royal Gardens, 106
Rucker, William, 96, 103–4
Russell, George, 49–50
Russell, Sylvester, 55, 66, 86
Rutherford, Sir Ernest, 71

Sanders of the River, 146
Sandhurst Royal Military College, 131–32, 148, 155
Sanford, N.C., 15, 17
Sassafras Springs, 12, 15
Savage, John, 31, 33
Savannah, Ga., 1, 93, 96, 101–3, 105, 111, 113
Sawyer, S. W. [possibly Searetta], 87–88
Schilling, Oscar, 96, 106
Scotia Seminary, 11, 15, 26, 31, 33–35, 44, 63, 108, 127
Scott, Ulysses Grant, 45–47, 49, 56, 66, 92, 164
Seaboard Air Line Railway, 29
Seawell, Isaac, 10
segregation: in Albany, Ga., housing, 111; on American roadways, 91; black businesses and, 82; in Carthage, N.C., churches, 12; of Chicago beaches, 79; in public transportation, 26, 65, 114; use of airplane to combat, 94; use of automobile to combat, 90–92, 114–15
Seiler, Cotten, 165
Shaw, Edward G., 80
Shaw, Fred, 97
Shaw University, 31, 35
Sikorsky, Igor, 158
Silsoe Institute. *See* National Institute of Agricultural Engineering
Simpkins, Guyrene Tyson, 28, 99, 115
Sleighton Farm School, 170
Sloan, Clifford, 63

Sloan, Mollie, 63
Small, Ida Irwin, 64
Smith, Alvin, 103
Smith, Art, 57
Smith, Frank, 70–71
Smith, Howard, 84–85
Smith, William Strother, 70
social networks. *See* networks
Sokoloff, Kenneth, 43
South Kinloch Park, 58
Spraggins, Mary Cannon, 44–45
Spraggins, Traverse, 44–45
Spruill, Frank, 27, 33
St. Augustine AMEZ Church, 20
St. James Presbyterian Church, 74
St. Mary's Works, 132, 134, 141, 150, 152
St. Peter's Churchyard, 159
Standard Aviation School, 51–53
Stanley, Samuel J., 36, 39, 74
Stanley, Sarah Drye, 34, 36, 39, 74
Statesville, N.C., 42, 115, 170
Stevens, Ernest and Henryene, 107
Stevenson, Joseph, 49–50
Stovall, Annie, 100, 107, 109
Strand Palace Hotel, 130, 145
Strauss, Joseph B., 71–72
Strauss Yielding Barrier Co., 71–72
Street, Idella Armwood, 3, 88, 91, 114, 118
Street, James Lillie, 3; birth and early life of, 19; business and civic activities of, 88, 91; death of, 99; marriage of, 88; photo of, 89
Street, Lillie Ann, 19
Street, Mariah, 7
Stretch, Charles, 81–83
Stuart, Joseph III (General Motors), 157
Stuart, William J., 20
submarine warfare. *See* World War I
Supreme Circle of Benevolence, 111–12, 116

Tampa, Fla., 19, 29, 82, 88–89, 91, 114, 118
Taylor, Robert, 42
Taylor Manufacturing Co. of Maryland, 8
technology and society: black Americans and mechanical ingenuity, 2, 5, 19, 31, 40, 57–58, 68, 161; black automobility, 111–15,

165; black women and transportation technologies, 34, 52, 81, 85–86, 88, 90–94, 100, 107–9, 111–13, 118, 163, 165–66, 168–69; new technologies and social openness, 49, 111; technology and manhood, 18, 90; transformative versus practical technologies, 158–59, 168–69
Terrell, Mary Church, 23, 44
Terrell, Robert H., 23, 44
Thomas, Benjamin Franklin, 45–46, 164, 166
Thomas, James A., 32–33
Thomas, Wilfred (Grumman Aerospace), 157–58
Thomasville, Ga., 103, 112, 124
Tift Silica Brick Co., 126
Todd, E. Lillian, 49–50
tractor vaporizing oil (TVO). *See* heavy oils
trade and agricultural shows, fairs, and expositions in the United States: Chicago Auto Show (1922), 82; [Colored Agricultural and Industrial Fair] (Albany, Ga. 1925), 115–17; Colored Industrial Fair (North Carolina Colored Industrial Association Fair, Raleigh, N.C., 1879), 23; Cotton States International Exposition (Atlanta, 1895), 10, 16–17, 119, 162; First International Aviation Show (New York), 46; Georgia State Negro Fair (Macon, 1910), 50, 54; National Auto Show (Chicago, 1930), 126; North Carolina State Fair (Raleigh), 16, 18; St. Louis County Fair (Hibbing, Minn.), 101
trade and agricultural shows in Britain: Commercial Motor Transport Exhibition (Olympia, 1933), 134; Royal Agricultural Show (Wolverhampton, 1937), 138
Traveler's Aid Society, 91
Trenton, N.J., 20–21, 118
Triple City Aviation Meet, 53
Tri-State Exposition Grounds, 102
Tucker, Charles E., 31
Tulsa Race Riot of 1921, 93
Tyson, Adam Guy Jr. (Guy), 3, 11, 15, 18–22, 26–28, 35–36, 44, 69, 74, 99, 114, 125, 148, 162, 170

Tyson, Adam Guy Sr. (Adam), 2, 4, 6, 9–12, 15, 15–18, 25, 27, 29, 166
Tyson, Alice, 11
Tyson, Ann Person, 6, 11–12, 15, 23
Tyson, Edith. *See* Mitchell, Edith Tyson
Tyson, Edwin French (French), 42, 114
Tyson, Elizabeth (daughter Adam Tyson Sr.), 11
Tyson, Elizabeth (daughter Thomas Tyson I). *See* McGilvary, Elizabeth Tyson
Tyson, Guyrene. *See* Simkins, Guyrene Tyson
Tyson, Henry C., 11, 13, 19, 22–24, 42, 69–70, 79
Tyson, James A., 11
Tyson, Jane, 13, 35, 44, 79
Tyson, Jenny, 9, 15
Tyson, John (planter), 9–10
Tyson, John (son Adam Tyson Sr.), 11–12, 15
Tyson, Joseph, 9–10, 15–16, 23, 25–26, 32, 162
Tyson, Laura A. *See* Headen, Laura A. Tyson
Tyson, Lucean, 11–12
Tyson, Lucien Person, 30
Tyson, Marie Walker, 13–16, 28, 35–36, 51, 74, 99, 114, 125, 148, 170
Tyson, Morris, 28, 183n14
Tyson, Roland, 28, 99, 114
Tyson, Thomas Bethune, 8–12, 21, 30
Tyson, Thomas Bethune II, 30
Tyson, Wilbur, 28
Tyson, William Thomas, 11–12
Tyson & Jones Buggy Co. (Tyson & Kelly), 8–10, 12, 15, 27–30, 36

UNIA (Universal Negro Improvement Association), 116, 168; Headen's alliance with, 105–6; *Negro World* coverage of Headen, 105. *See also* Garvey, Marcus; Plummer, Henry Vinton Jr.
Union Presbyterian Church, 12
Union Transportation Co., 91
United Charities Association, 34–35
Universal Negro Improvement Association. *See* UNIA

Urry, John, 165
U.S. Army Signal Corps, 49, 166
U.S. Embassy (London), 144, 152–55, 161

Vanderbilt, William, 37, 46
Vestas Wind Systems of Denmark, 142, 158
Vivian Loyd & Co. Ltd., 141, 152
voter suppression and disfranchisement in North Carolina: 1900 amendment and, 27; 1901 election law and, 32–33; in Moore County, N.C., in 1876 election, 6; white artisans and, 28; in Wilmington, N.C., in state elections of 1898, 25–26

Walden, Henry, 38, 49–50
Walker, Madame C. J., 74, 112–13
Walls, Fred, 80
Ward, James, 48
Washington, Booker T., 42, 119, 162, 168. *See also* NNBL
waste oil. *See* heavy oils
White, George H., 26, 35, 44
White, John F. (Jack), 66–67, 83, 85, 87, 106
Wiggins, Charlie, 107
Wiggins, Roberta, 107
Wiley, Norbert, 97
Wilkinson Rubber Linatex Co., 141
Williams, Eddie, 81
Williams, Eugene, 79
Williams, Virgil L., 106
Wilmington, N.C., 18, 161; black civic organizations in, 34; Chestnut Presbyterian Church in, 33–35; Drye family of, 2–3, 33–36, 39–40, 45, 52, 61, 65–66, 68, 74, 76, 78–79, 85–86, 88–89, 101, 107–9, 114, 126–28, 150, 165, 171; Meares family of, 127–28, 165. See also *Africo-American Presbyterian*; racial violence
Wilson, Alphonso, 83–85, 88
Winston, N.C. *See* Winston-Salem, N.C.
Winston-Salem, N.C.: auto travel and, 115; coverage of Headen by *Winston-Salem Journal*, 59, 148; Jones Brothers in, 42, 87; Knights of Pythias in, 87; Louise attending school in, 115; Nannie moves to, 35; Phillis Wheatley YWCA in, 170; visit of Booker T. Washington to, 42. *See also* Ables, Louise Headen; Jones, John W.; Jones, Nannie Kathleen Headen; Jones, William A.; racial violence
Winter, Henry J., 45, 49–50
Wizard Automobile Co., 80
Wood, Albert B., 73
Wood, Anna M. Riter, 13, 15–16, 35
Wood, Henry Davis, 3, 13–14, 16, 19–22, 28, 31, 33, 59–61, 68, 71, 75, 95, 119, 139, 163, 167, 171, 190n41
Woods, Granville T., 38
Work, Monroe, 59, 163
World War I: 365th Infantry and, 93; 370th Infantry and, 78; the BIR, 71–72; Chicago supporters of Headen's optical cloaking device for submarine chasers in, 67–70; the DER and, 72–73; Headen's cloaking device and the Naval Consulting Board, 69–70; Headen's work for the British Shipping Ministry, 73, 89, 120
World War II: bombing of Camberley area in, 141, 148; Camberley war industries and, 140–41; Headen's inventions and the war effort, 136, 140–44, 148–50, 169; Home Guard (Camberley Regt., Surrey 1st Bn.) and, 149
Wright, Frank A. *See* Raiche, François
Wright Brothers, 5, 37, 41, 43, 52, 62, 90
Wynn, Emma V., 111–13, 118, 165
Wynn, William, 111–12, 118

Yadkin Presbytery (PCUSA), 20–22
YMCA (Young Men's Christian Association), 51, 91
Young Men's Christian Association. *See* YMCA
Young Men's Investment League, 76
Young Women's Christian Association. *See* YWCA
YWCA (Young Women's Christian Association), 167, 170